Jessica Berg

Rāmāyaṇa and Mahābhārata in Stone

Jessica Berg

Rāmāyaṇa and Mahābhārata in Stone

The Narrative Friezes of the Kṛṣṇa Temple at Pāṭan, Nepal

ERGON VERLAG

Supported by the Gerda Henkel Stiftung
as part of the Funding Initiative „Patrimonies“

Dissertation submittet to the Department for South Asian Studies, Humboldt-Universität zu Berlin.
First reviewer: Prof. Dr. Michael Mann. Second reviewer: Prof. Dr. Adalbert J. Gail.

Cover illustration:
The Kṛṣṇa Temple at Pāṭan, October 2015.

Illustrations:
Ashesh Rajbansh took the excellent photos from both the narrative friezes,
Rāmāyaṇa and Mahābhārata, on the Kṛṣṇa Temple at Pāṭan (pp. 43–143).
All Hadal-Nārāyanpur pictures by Manojit Pal (Pls. 19, 20 & 25a).
Picture from Angkor Wat by Adalbert J. Gail (p. 195).
All other photos taken by the author.

The Deutsche Nationalbibliothek lists this publication in the
Deutsche Nationalbibliografie; detailed bibliographic data
are available on the Internet at http://dnb.d-nb.de.

Overall responsibility for manufacturing (printing and production) lies with
Nomos Verlagsgesellschaft mbH & Co. KG.
Printed on age-resistant paper.
Cover Design: Jan von Hugo

www.ergon-verlag.de

ISBN 978-3-95650-931-5 (Print)
ISBN 978-3-95650-932-2 (ePDF)

Table of Contents

Acknowledgements

First and foremost, I would like to thank my doctorate supervisors, Adalbert Gail and Michael Mann. Thank you for guiding me over the years, for inspiration, support and lots of good advice.

Actually, it was long before I even thought of writing a doctoral thesis that Adalbert Gail first drew my interest to the friezes of the Kṛṣṇa Temple in a lecture. It was immediately clear to me that I would like to deal with this topic again at some point. When I read his second volume of "Tempel in Nepal", in which some of the Rāmāyaṇa scenes are already illustrated, this idea became more concrete. I am very glad that I actually got the opportunity to write this thesis. It is indeed a small miracle after the abolishment of the subject of Art History of South Asia at the Freie Universität Berlin. At this point, I would like to expressly thank Michael Mann, who, although the topic does not really fit his research focus, immediately gave his consent to supervise the PhD project at the Department for South Asian Studies at the Humboldt-Universität zu Berlin. I am glad and grateful for the new insights that I gained through this collaboration and very happy that further considerations enrich the work.

I would like to go back a little further, to my time as a master student and also heartily thank Monika Zin. You were always a great inspiration to me, conveying learning content with so much enthusiasm that I just couldn't help but also be enthusiastic throughout.

Furthermore, I would like to express my thanks to the Gerda Henkel Stiftung, for supporting my project as part of the Funding Initiative "Patrimonies". I was delighted already when I learned that the foundation supports the restoration of the Kṛṣṇa Temple, that was necessary after the earthquake in 2015. How wonderful that my project fit in so well!

I am extremely grateful also to Niels Gutschow and the team of the Kathmandu Valley Preservation Trust for their immeasurable help in situ. Many thanks to Nutan Sharma for reading the inscriptions with me. It was a unique experience to climb the scaffolding to read even the inaccessible inscriptions of the Mahābhārata frieze and I am happy that you were with me, always with so much delight. Likewise, I am extremely grateful for the excellent photographs of both the friezes provided by Ashesh Rajbansh. This book simply wouldn't be what it is without your pictures. Many thanks also to Suresh Man Lakhe, Museum Officer at Pāṭan Museum, for being always positive and ready to help.

My thanks further go to my family and friends. Thanks to Timo Berthold for being the greatest motivator of all times. Thanks to my wonderful travel companions: to my husband Adrian Zeunert for collecting the first impressions of the Mahābhārata frieze together with me in 2015, to my brother Maurits Berg for keeping company with me in 2017, always ready for another cappuccino, and to Axel Metzler for accompanying me in 2018, visiting 40 places across India in two weeks only. What a trip!

All this would not have been possible without my parents, Gabriela and Joachim Berg. You were there whenever I needed you, devoting all your free time to the kids and thus allowing me to free up the time I needed for my studies. Likewise, I would like to thank my grandmother, Hedwig Weidenauer, for supporting me in all situations. You are with me today like you have always been.

The biggest thanks, however, go to the four suns around which my world revolves: Jonah, Levin, Tristan and Merlin. Thank you for the love that you give every day, for the joy that you bring to my life and for making every single moment so incredibly precious. I love you more than I can tell. This book is dedicated to you.

1. Introduction

Epigraphical sources as well as early sculptures testify to the existence of Viṣṇuism in the Kathmandu Valley in the early centuries of the Christian Era, at least since the 2nd century CE. The Licchavi king Haridatta Varman is said to have introduced Viṣṇuism as royal cult in the 4th century CE. The early Licchavis might have been influenced in propagating Viṣṇuism by the Indian Guptas, to whom they were also related by marriage. During the following centuries many viṣṇuite temples were erected. The best known one is certainly the hilltop temple of Caṅgu Nārāyaṇa, north of Bhaktapur City. Mānadeva's pillar inscription, dating from 464 CE, reveals that a Viṣṇu shrine was located here even before Mānadeva's reign (464-505 CE). This place is therefore the one with the longest traceable tradition of Viṣṇu worship in Nepal.[1]
Viṣṇuism increasingly gained in importance, certainly because it is a cult that matches perfectly with the idea of universal authority and thus with the concept of kingship. Viṣṇu acts to the welfare of gods, nature and mankind alike. His attributes symbolise happiness and riches (the conch, sa. *śaṅkha*) as well as power and far-reaching authority (the discus, sa. *cakra*). It is believed that the king identifying with Viṣṇu acquires far-reaching ever-expanding power, too.[2] Nevertheless, that such an important temple as Caṅgu Nārāyaṇa fell into disrepair indicates that Viṣṇuism somehow declined, presumably from the 14th until the early 16th century CE. The temple was restored in 1585 CE, at the time when Viṣṇuism in Nepal received revivalistic impulses from Northeast India. Escaping the Islamic conquests, Viṣṇuites immigrated from Bihar and Bengal but also from Rajasthan and the western foothills of the Himālaya.[3] These immigrants influenced the spiritual life as well as the arts of the valley and thus, the 16th and, to an even greater extent, the 17th century CE mark a great revival of the Viṣṇu cult in Nepal. Many viṣṇuite temples were built at the Malla kingdoms' palace squares as well as at more distant places.

Within this period falls also the consolidation of the Kṛṣṇa cult in Nepal. Kṛṣṇa is of particular importance for the Kathmandu Valley. According to Hindu tradition, the demon king Mahendrada-mana once dammed up the Bāgmatī and the Valley became a hill-ringed lake inhabited by *nāgas*. Due to a boon granted by Brahmā, Mahendradamana could not be slain by the gods and it was thus up to Kṛṣṇa's son, Pradyumna, to kill him. Afterwards, Kṛṣṇa cut a gorge into the rocks with his disk (sa. *cakra*) to free the holy river whereby he drained off the water from the lake. The myth is narrated in Nepalese *purāṇas*[4] and also subject of several dramas from the late Malla period.[5] Interestingly, not only the viṣṇuite Nepālamāhātmyas focus on this legend, it also makes up more than half of the śivaite Paśupatipurāṇa. The buddhist Svayambhūpurāṇa tells a similar story. According to this text, the Bodhisattva Mañjuśrī cleft the hill with his sword and drained away the waters in order to make the place habitable and more accessible to pilgrims.[6] These legends seem to mythologise an actual geological event. According to Boesch, there is no doubt that a standing water body did at one time emerge in the valley, though it was for the most part likely rather an amphibian marshland than a deep, clear mountain lake.[7]

The legend about the draining of the Kathmandu Valley leaves no doubt that Kṛṣṇa was well known in Nepal at a very early stage. Nevertheless, Kṛṣṇaism in Nepal gained in importance only in the beginning of the 17th century CE. Like Viṣṇuism, Kṛṣṇaism was transmitted to the Nepal Valley's population by those fleeing north to escape the Islamic conquest. It is important to note that the Kṛṣṇa glorified later in deeply felt devotion (sa. *bhakti*) was quite different from the heroic god of the Mahābhārata, whom the Licchavis already knew.[8] The re-awakening of Kṛṣṇaism originated in India, in Bihar and Bengal, from the 11th century CE onwards. It had additionally been on the increase in Garwhal and the Punjab since the 16th century CE. Kṛṣṇaite themes gained in importance in sculpture and painting in the Kathmandu Valley from the 15th century CE onwards.[9] Siddhinarasiṃhamalla, the donor of the Kṛṣṇa Temple, played the most decisive role in the consolidation and spread of

1 Lienhard (1991) discusses the early rise of Viṣṇuism in Nepal.
2 Lienhard 1995, pp. 17-20: Viṣṇuism and Kingship.
3 ibid., p. 24.
4 Brinkhaus 1987, pp. 29ff.
5 ibid., pp. 112ff.
6 Smith and Bajracharya 1978, p. 11.
7 Boesch 1974, p. 23.
8 Lienhard 1995, pp. 22f.
9 ibid., p. 24.

Kṛṣṇaism in Nepal. Until today, Kṛṣṇa is most celebrated in Pāṭan and the Kṛṣṇa Temple at the Pāṭan Palace Square is the god's principal shrine in the valley. Since it houses an image of Bālagopāla, Kṛṣṇa's form as the youthful cowherd, the Kṛṣṇa Temple is also known as Bālagopāla Temple. The Pāṭan Palace Square with its many impor-tant monuments was declared a world heritage site by UNESCO in 1979. At the same time six other Monument Zones of the Kathmandu Valley have been inscribed on the World Heritage List, too. These are the Palace Squares of Kathmandu and Bhaktapur, the Buddhist Sva-yambhūnāth and Bauddhanāth, the śivaite Paśupatināth Temple of Deopatan and the viṣṇuite Cāṅgunārāyaṇa Temple in Bhaktapur District.[10] These groups together illustrate very well the cultural heritage of the Kathman-du Valley.

The Kṛṣṇa Temple is architecturally remarkable for the structure combines Indian and Nepalese elements. This is quite evident and generally well known. Another peculiarity, to which too little attention has been paid up to now, are the extensive narrative friezes that wrap the structure. They give the story of the two great Indian epics, the Rāmāyaṇa and the Mahābhārata at length. The Rāmāyaṇa is depicted in 99 scenes, the longer Mahābhārata in as many as 165 scenes. The individual scenes are identified by inscriptions. Gail has worked on the Rāmāyaṇa frieze and published part of it in 1988.[11] The Mahābhārata frieze is by contrast entirely unpublished so far. This is undoubtedly due to its unfavourable location. It is not possible to look at it in its entirety from the ground and even from the balconies one can only follow the visual narrative with difficulty. It was only in course of the restoration work, that was necessary after the devastating 2015 earthquake, that this project became possible. With the help of Niels Gutschow and under the auspices of the Kathmandu Valley Preservation Trust, I had the opportunity to climb the scaffolding. The grave earthquakes that hit Nepal at intervals make it very clear how important it is to preserve the endangered heritage in every possible way. Documentation also constitutes a good basis for any future reconstruction.

Hinduism always was of central importance for the valley's population. Until the abolition of the monarchy in 2008, Nepal was even the only Hindu kingdom in the world. One should therefore assume that both the epics are of particular importance for the local population. However, comparable Nepalese representations simply don't exist. The narrative representations of the Rāmāyaṇa and the Mahābhārata on the Kṛṣṇa Temple at Pāṭan are the only ones of their kind throughout Nepal. Moreover, they are earlier testimonia of Nepalese epic tradition than their literary counterparts. The Kṛṣṇa Temple was built in 1637 CE but Nepalese adaptions of the two epics only date from the 19th and 20th centuries CE. Therefore, relations between the Nepalese representations and Indian literary traditions are to be clarified. For want of comparable Nepalese representations material predominantly from India must also be referenced. Representations of the epics on temple walls are found especially in Karnataka and Tamil Nadu. The comparison with possible Indian literary sources as well as with comparable representations, especially from South India, is interesting to the extent that this can shed some light on the character of early Nepalese epic tradition.

In concrete terms the treatment of the subject prompts the following questions:

1. What is depicted?
2. Which important deviations or maybe common features can be identified when comparing the content with literary and pictorial traditions from India?
3. What conclusions can be drawn from the comparisons made? Or more specifically: in what way do the representations of both friezes reveal an impact of region-specific charecteristics of Hindu beliefs?

The thesis contributes to the preservation and popularisation of Nepal's cultural heritage through the publication of the entire friezes. Furthermore, new insights in the fields of Nepalese art and cultural history will hopefully be gained.

---

10 http://whc.unesco.org/en/list/121/
11 Gail 1988, pp. 31ff.

2. The Significance of the Kṛṣṇa Temple

Before describing and analysing both the friezes in detail, the significance of the Kṛṣṇa Temple will be discussed - historically and present day, architecturally as well as culturally.

2.1. Historical Background

The Kṛṣṇa Temple at Pāṭan was built slightly more than a century before Malla rule was brought to an end. The following sections give the history until this turning point, first in brief for the Kathmandu Valley at large and thereafter again in more detail for Pāṭan only. A description of the Pāṭan Palace Square will give an idea about the temple's immediate vicinity and the central position that the Kṛṣṇa Temple occupies. A statement about the effects of the 2015 earthquake will finally attest to the importance of the documentation and preservation of the endangered cultural heritage in the Kathmandu Valley.

2.1.1. The Kathmandu Valley

Present day Nepal is physiographically divided into three east-west directed main regions. The southernmost ecological belt is called *terāī* (ne. *wettish land*) and refers to the fertile lowlands. The central belt marks the hilly region with the outer footlands of the Himālaya and the northern belt is defined by the Himālayan highlands. The Kathmandu Valley is an extraordinary land formation, located within the central belt. It covers an area of approximately 650 square kilometres at a level of some 1,300 metres and is surrounded by mountains reaching heights between 2,000 and 2,500 metres.[12] Though geographically isolated, the mountain valley is of great importance for the nation's history. The flat ground and fertile soil of the formerly lake basin has, in combination with the favourable climate, always facilitated human habitation. The Kathmandu Valley is located on one of the major routes between India and Tibet/China and was long a renowned centre of trade. It is therefore not surprising that, as noted by Slusser, the Kathmandu Valley is and has always been the politically, economically and culturally dominant part of the country.[13]

For a long time *Nepal* simply meant the geographically isolated mountain valley.[14] Other traditional names for this region were *Nepāladeśa* and *Nepālamaṇḍala*.[15] Only from 1769 CE onwards, surrounding tribes and principalities were united with the valley to form the greater nation, and the valley is thenceforth called the *Kathmandu Valley*, after the nation's capital city.

The Licchavis are the first historically attested dynasty in Nepal. According to local chronicles (sa. *vaṃśāvalīs*), dynasties like the Kirātas and Gopālas ruled the Kathmandu Valley before but since the chronicles were written down only from the 14th century CE, the authenticity of the given information is very uncertain. The word *kirāṭa* (sa. *kira*-edge and *aṭ*-to roam) appears often in Indian epic literature where it is applied to any aboriginal people of the Himālayas. Nevertheless, it can be assumed that *kirāṭa* once meant a specific Himālayan tribe and that the term was only later expanded to embrace any hill tribe.[16] The reign of the Licchavis began no later than 300 CE, most likely even before. The first tangible historical document is a pillar inscription of Mānadeva I at Cāṅgunārāyaṇa, corresponding to 464 CE, but several preceeding Licchavi rulers are mentioned in both, chronicles and inscriptions.[17] During Licchavi reign, the official language was Sanskrit and the script used was that of Gupta India. The Licchavis were engaged in agriculture and animal husbandry and already trade was fundamental to the economy. Buddhism and Hinduism existed harmoniously side by side and no matter whether Buddhist, Vaiṣṇava or Śaiva in name, each ruler gratified the other gods as well.[18] Several other groups dwelt in the Kathmandu Valley during the Licchavi period, among them the Ābhīra Guptas. It is unlikely that they were related to the Guptas of India. More likely, the Ābhīra Guptas were descendants of the Gopālas mentioned before. From 506 to 641 CE the Ābhīra Guptas intermittently shared the rule with the Licchavis in name and in some instances, it appears that they even ruled surpreme.[19]

It is difficult to say when the reign of the Licchavis came to an end. The last record that refers specifically to a Licchavi king is an inscription of Jayadeva II, issued in

12 Gutschow 2011 I, p. 35.
13 Slusser 1982, p. 7.
14 ibid.
15 Regmi 1965, pp. 512ff.

16 Slusser 1982, pp. 9ff.
17 ibid., pp. 22f.
18 ibid., pp. 37ff.
19 ibid., pp. 27ff.

733 CE at Paśupatināth. He was possibly the last Licchavi ruler of political importance. Since there is no evidence for a dramatic extinction of the Licchavi dynasty, the Licchavi dynasty most likely declined slowly.[20] A new era began in 879 CE with the introduction of the lunar calender Nepāl Samvat.[21]

There are only very few documents to reveal the history of the Kathmandu Valley from Licchavi decline until the second half of the 14th century CE. Often, these centuries' rulers are known by name only. The earlier ones have been designated as Ṭhakurī, a term derived from the Sanskrit word *ṭhakkura* (man of rank). As Slusser points out, this was no name actually borne by the kings. The title was applied to them centuries later to denote superior rank and has no dynastic connotation.[22]

From Licchavi decline until the 14th century CE, the throne apparently did not pass from father to son but alternated between parallel royal families. Several separate kingdoms or city-states emerged. Often, it is not clear whether certain kings ruled at the same time or sequentially. In 1147 CE, Ānandadeva built the palace Tripura at Bhaktapur. Bhaktapur remained the nations capital until 1482 CE although the general political situation remained turbulent and unstable until the second half of the 14th century CE.[23] Weak kings wore the crown whereas the nobles ruled. Moreover, there were devastating foreign raids, that the politically fragmented country was powerless to prevent. At the end of the 13th and the beginning of the 14th centuries CE, the Maithilīs from the nearby southern plains and the Khasa, who controlled the basin of the Karṇālī River in western Nepal and parts of Tibet, raided the Valley in turns. Additionally, the Muslims made one devastating sweep across the Valley in 1349 CE.[24] During this period, Hinduism and Buddhism, as in all times, comfortably coexisted. Most surviving documents of this period were written in Sanskrit but the style of writing changed. Various ornate scripts were introduced and Newari began to appear in written form, too. The earliest surviving inscription in Newari dates from 1173 CE.[25]

The period between 1200 and 1769 CE is referred to as the Malla Period. In terms of the history of the Kathmandu Valley, the Sanskrit term *malla* (wrestler, victor) does not denote a new dynasty, but was only employed as a title of honour. However, unlike *ṭhakurī*, the title *malla* was chosen and borne by the kings themselves. They added it as a suffix to their names, in the same way that kings already previously added the suffix *deva* to their names. The first king who assumed the title *malla* was Arimalla I, who ruled from 1200 to 1216 CE. Afterwards, some kings also added the suffix *malla* to their names, while others again chose the suffix *deva*. It was only in 1382 CE that *malla* became a regular part of the kings names.[26]

The year 1382 CE marks a turning point in Nepalese history. From that time on there are many documents to reveal the history. It is the date of the accession of Sthitirājamalla. In the following century the state began to achieve unity under strong rulers. Sthitirājamalla (also Sthitimalla or Jayasthiti), was possibly a Maithilī who was selected in 1354 CE as husband for the then eight-year-old orphaned Bhaktapur princess Rājalladevī. Sthitirājamalla's ascendancy began in 1370 CE, long before his accession, so while Arjunadeva still wore the crown, Sthitirājamalla wielded the real power. He became co-ruler in 1372 CE and after the demise of the king, Sthitirājamalla assumed the throne himself in 1382 CE. Sthitirājamalla curbed the powers of the nobles and gave the kingdom a stability and internal strength that defied foreign raids. After his death, instead of again splitting the kingdom, his three sons all ruled together. The kingdom broke apart as Yakṣamalla followed suit and after his death in 1482 CE bequeathed the kingdom to his six sons and the son of his daughter. They, too, were expected to rule jointly but soon, they began to devide the kingdom into segments over which one or the other then ruled supreme.[27]

Again, the kingdom broke apart into multiple ministates. Not quite three years after Yakṣamalla's death, Kathmandu became an independent state under the reign of his son Ratnamalla. He also tried to seize Pāṭan but was not able to subdue the long entrenched nobles. His eldest brother, Rāyamalla, ruled supreme but collegially with the others over Bhaktapur until after his death, only his descendants were to reign. Banepa became independent under Yakṣamalla's son Raṇamalla but was reincorporated into the Bhaktapur kingdom about a century later. In

20 Slusser 1982, p. 23.
21 See Regmi 1965, pp. 51ff: The Nepal Era of 879 A.D. and the Event it Commemorates.
22 Slusser 1982, p. 42.
23 ibid., pp. 44f.
24 ibid., pp. 56ff.
25 ibid., pp. 43ff.
26 ibid., pp. 52ff.
27 ibid., pp. 58ff.

1597 CE, Śivasiṃha, a descendant of Ratnamalla and king of Kathmandu, seized Pāṭan under unknown circumstances and annexed it to the Kathmandu city. After his death about 1619 CE, Kathmandu was given to one grandson and Pāṭan to the other one. That way, three separate Malla-ruled city-states emerged, namely Bhaktapur, Kathmandu and Pāṭan. Each one consisted of it's capital city and the surrounding territory.[28]

The relations of the three kingdoms' rulers were antagonistic and characterised by continuous insults and quarrels. These quarrels soon spread beyond the Valley. The Malla kings took sides in the disputes of the surrounding hill states and even more often asked these outsiders to participate in their own conflicts. The most important of the surrounding kingdoms was Gorkhā, in the west of the Valley. From 1744 CE onwards the Gorkhālis conquered the surrounding hill states until finally, the Valley was completely encircled by Gorkhāli holdings. In 1768 CE, the Gorkhāli king Pṛthvī Nārāyaṇ Śāh first seized Kathmandu, then Pāṭan and in 1769 CE Bhaktapur. His military campaigns caused the end of Malla rule. The seat of power was shifted to Kathmandu while the Pāṭan Palace was abandoned by royalty.[29] Pṛthvī Nārāyaṇ Śāh is today honoured as the founder of unified Nepal.

2.1.2. Pāṭan

Pāṭan is attached to the city of Kathmandu. It is located south of the capital city, just across the Bāgmatī River. At present, Pāṭan is the third largest city of Nepal after Kathmandu and Pokharā – according to the census of 2011 with a population of 226,728 inhabitants.[30] The city of Pāṭan was known historically by various other names. Its probably eldest name is Yāla (also Yahraṃ or Ñala). Long ago, this term referred to a settlement at the spot where the Pāṭan Palace Square is situated today. The Licchavi name for their community (sa. *grāma*) at the exact same spot was Yūpagrāma, the Sanskrit term *yūpa* being a (probably erroneously imposed) translation of the Newari name Yāla. Both words denote a sacrificial post but according to tradition, the Newari name is a derivation of Yalambara or Yellung, a legendary Kirāṭa king. The name Yūpagrāma was used only during the Licchavi period whereas the older name Yāla is popular down to the present day. By the 10th century CE, Yāla was additionally known as the city Lalita (sa., lovely, pleasing). Many words for *city* were added as a suffix, in consequence of what Yāla was then also known as Lalitakramā, Lalitabrumā, Lalitapura, Lalitanagara and Lalitapattana/Lalitapaṭṭana. As the name Lalitapura steadily gained popularity, yet another name was applied to the city, Māṇigvala (with many variations). Lalitapura or Lalitpur is until today an alternate name for Pāṭan. The name Māṇigvala survives only in a corrupt form and refers to the shopping area of the Pāṭan Palace Square, the Maṅgal Bazār. Lastly, the name Pāṭan itself is the Nepali simplification of Lalitapaṭṭana and does not appear before the 17th century CE.[31]

The site of Pāṭan was one of the earliest settled sites in the Valley. Legend and custom suggests that the city originated as a Buddhist community well before the beginning of the Christian Era. However, the first written records are those of Mānadeva I. Whether or not the site served as a capital for the Licchavis is debatable, but the Pāṭan communities were certainly among their principal settlements. Their most important community in the Pāṭan area was the above mentioned Yūpagrāma (Yāla) at the site of the Pāṭan Palace Square. Gradually, the settlement grew into a town by absorbing other villages.[32] It is likely that, after the decline of Licchavi rule, the site of Pāṭan became some sort of Buddhist university town, perhaps in emulation of the great Indian centres.[33] The Muslim conquest in North India at the end of the 12th century CE resulted in many Indian refugees, moving into Nepal and surely contributed to a growing Buddhist population in Pāṭan. The Buddhist character of the city remains today, as there are numerous Buddhist monasteries (sa. *vihāras*) as well as mounds (sa. *stūpas*), shrines (sa. *caityas*) and sacred Buddhist images. Along with other cities of the Valley, Pāṭan was affected by the Maithilī raids at the end of the 13th and beginning of the 14th century CE. In the final raid of 1311 CE many buildings in the city centre were destroyed.[34]

28 Slusser 1982, pp. 61ff.
29 ibid., pp. 63ff.
30 http://cbs.gov.np/image/data/Publication/Statistical Pocket Book 2014.pdf, p. 27.
31 Slusser 1982, pp. 97f.
32 ibid., pp. 96f.
33 ibid., p. 48.
34 ibid., p. 56.

In a land transfer dated 1283 CE, the Pāṭan *pātras* (sa., councellor, representative of the king) are mentioned for the first time.[35] They were the principal nobles who controlled the city and they built their mansions where today the Palace Square is situated. They had the control over the city until the late 16th century CE. From 1382 CE onwards, the state in general began to achieve unity under strong rulers but still Pāṭan remained an almost independent principality under *mahāpātra*-rule. During Sthitirājamalla's time (1382 to 1395 CE), Pāṭan was controlled by three feudatories of seven noble families (sa. *saptakuṭumbajas*). Officially, they accepted Sthitirājamalla as their leader, but they were still the ones who exercised the real authority. During the following century the noble families ruled jointly. Ratnamalla, after his father's death in 1482 CE, failed to seize the city and the *mahāpātras* essentially ignored Yakṣamalla's rightful successors for a long time. They no longer pretended to be the vassals of the Malla kings. In 1530 CE, Viṣṇusiṃha, one of the three feudatories of Pāṭan, ousted the other two and became sole ruler.[36] As the leader of a fully independent state, Viṣṇusiṃha was now dealing on equal terms with the Malla kings of Kathmandu and Bhaktapur. While retaining the old title *mahāpātra*, Viṣṇusiṃha also coined a new one, *māṇiglādhipati* (Lord of Māṇig(va)la). This title was later adopted by subsequent kings of the city, too.[37]

It was mentioned before that in 1597 CE, Śivasiṃhamalla in unclear circumstances annexed Pāṭan to the Kathmandu kingdom and that, after his death about 1619 CE, Kathmandu was given to one of his grandsons and Pāṭan to the other one. The name of the first was Lakṣmīnarasiṃhamalla, the second one was Siddhinarasiṃhamalla, the donor of the Kṛṣṇa Temple. It was thus under his rule, from 1619 to 1661 CE, that Pāṭan again became independent. The site from which the city had been governed under *mahāpātra* rule remained as the Malla seat.[38]

After the Gorkhali conquest all attention was concentrated on Kathmandu. Pāṭan did not noticeably develop any further until the mid-20th century CE when gradually here, too, nontraditional houses were built.[39] Consequently, among the three royal cities, the Pāṭan Palace Square has best preserved the 17th and 18th century milieu of the late Malla kings.

2.1.3. The Pāṭan Palace Square

The Pāṭan Palace Square is located in the centre of the city. It is one of the most beautiful structural ensembles of the valley and one of the seven Monument Zones which were accorded the status of a World Heritage Site by the UNESCO in 1979. Figure 1 shows the Pāṭan Palace Square with all its important monuments.

On the east side, the Palace Complex is situated. The royal palaces were called *lāykū* (new.), *rājakula prāsāda* (sa.) or *darbār* (fa.)[40] and until today, the Anglo-Persian name Darbār Square is used alternately with reference to the Palace Square. Three tiered temples are built atop the courtyard palaces. Behind the Palace Complex lies the Bhaṇḍārakhāla, a garden area with a sculptured tank, the Lohanhiṭī. On the west side, the main Temple Complex is situated. It comprises a bunch of magnificent temples built on stepped plinths, including the Kṛṣṇa Temple. The entire complex, as it survives today, was built within only two centuries.

The following rulers are connected with the construction process:

Purandarasiṃha	1560 – 1597
Śivasiṃhamalla	1597 – 1619
Siddhinarasiṃhamalla	1619 – 1661
Śrīnivāsamalla	1661 – 1684
Yognarendramalla	1684 – 1705
and his daughter Yogamatī	
Viṣṇumalla	1729 – 1745

Most of the impressive monuments of the Pāṭan Palace Square were constructed during the 17th century CE. The relations between the kingdoms' rulers were antagonistic and their rivalry showed up not only in political affairs but also in artistic competitions. In Kathmandu, Lakṣmīnarasiṃha had left the affairs of state in the hands of his son, Pratāpamalla,[41] and in Pāṭan Siddhinarasiṃha possessed the throne. Bhaktapur entered the artistic combat a few years later with Jagatprakāśa's enthronement in 1644 CE.[42]

35 Slusser 1982, p. 60.
36 Regmi 1966 II, pp. 258ff.
37 Slusser 1982, p. 62.

38 ibid., p. 199.
39 ibid., pp. 98f.
40 ibid., p. 188.

41 Regmi 1966 II, pp. 57ff.
42 ibid., pp. 220ff.

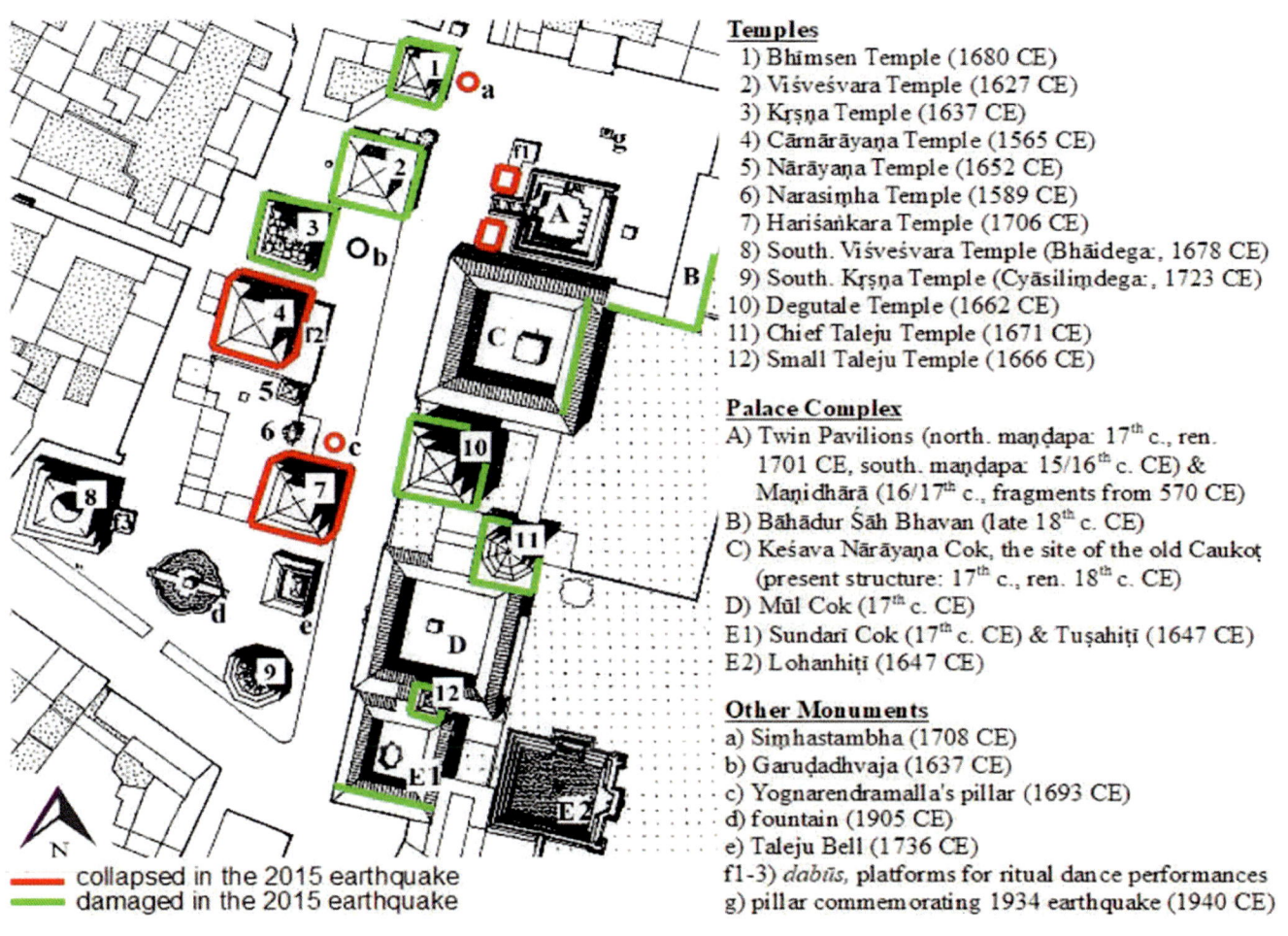

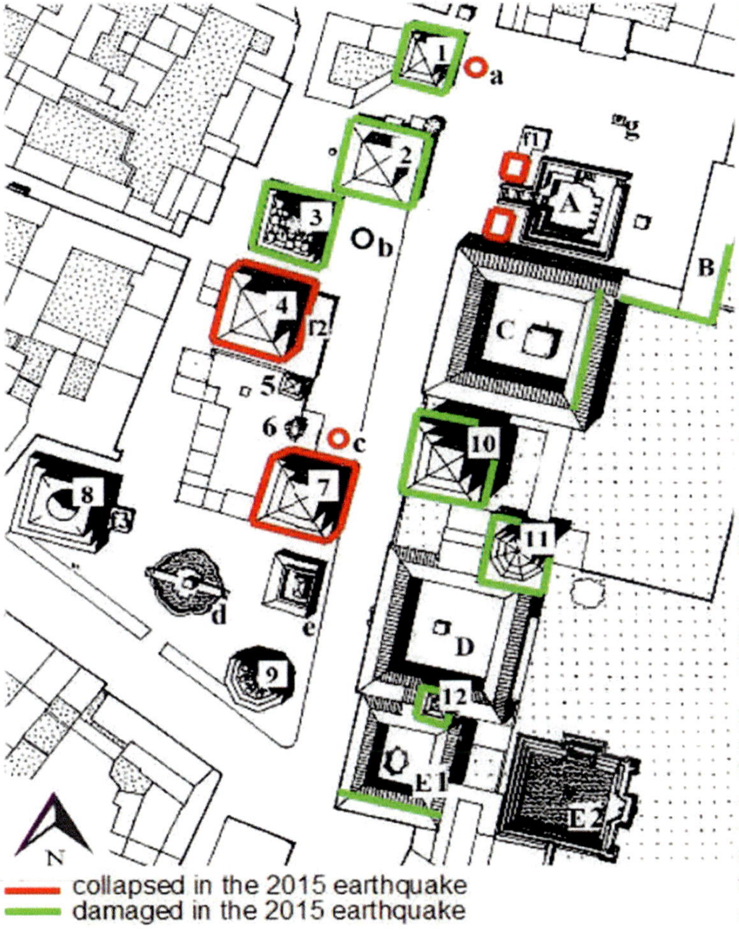

Temples

1) Bhīmsen Temple (1680 CE)
2) Viśveśvara Temple (1627 CE)
3) Kṛṣṇa Temple (1637 CE)
4) Cārnārāyaṇa Temple (1565 CE)
5) Nārāyaṇa Temple (1652 CE)
6) Narasiṃha Temple (1589 CE)
7) Hariśaṅkara Temple (1706 CE)
8) South. Viśveśvara Temple (Bhāidega:, 1678 CE)
9) South. Kṛṣṇa Temple (Cyāsiliṃdega:, 1723 CE)
10) Degutale Temple (1662 CE)
11) Chief Taleju Temple (1671 CE)
12) Small Taleju Temple (1666 CE)

Palace Complex

A) Twin Pavilions (north. maṇḍapa: 17th c., ren. 1701 CE, south. maṇḍapa: 15/16th c. CE) & Maṇidhārā (16/17th c., fragments from 570 CE)
B) Bāhādur Śāh Bhavan (late 18th c. CE)
C) Keśava Nārāyaṇa Cok, the site of the old Caukoṭ (present structure: 17th c., ren. 18th c. CE)
D) Mūl Cok (17th c. CE)
E1) Sundarī Cok (17th c. CE) & Tuṣahiṭī (1647 CE)
E2) Lohanhiṭī (1647 CE)

Other Monuments

a) Siṃhastambha (1708 CE)
b) Garuḍadhvaja (1637 CE)
c) Yognarendramalla's pillar (1693 CE)
d) fountain (1905 CE)
e) Taleju Bell (1736 CE)
f1-3) *dabūs*, platforms for ritual dance performances
g) pillar commemorating 1934 earthquake (1940 CE)

fig. 1: The Pāṭan Palace Square. Source of the original map: Pruscha 1975, P-MZ 1

Only a little is known about the appearance of the city by the time that Siddhinarasiṃhamalla assumed the throne. Some of the popular monuments were already standing. The oldest architectural fragments date back to the Licchavi Period and form part of the deep fountain at the northern end of the royal palace. According to an inscription, the fountain was built in 570 CE by one Bhāravi and named Maṇidhārā (sa., jewel fountain).[43] The stepwell's present shape probably dates to the 16th or early 17th century CE. It is alternately called Maṅga(l)hiṭī, referring to Māṇigvala, the old name for the city of Pāṭan.

The oldest surviving temples of the Pāṭan Palace Square were built under *mahāpātra* rule. In 1565 CE Purandarasiṃha built the Cārnārāyaṇa Temple and in 1589 CE additionally the Narasiṃha Temple. The first was built in memory of his father, Viṣṇusiṃha,[44] the latter one in memory of his brother who also bore the name Narasiṃha.[45] A palace building, the Caukoṭ or Caukvatha (sa./new., Four-Cornered Fort), also existed by the time of Siddhinarasiṃhamalla and even before the 17th century CE. The Caukoṭ was long eponymic for the Palace Square, then commonly referred to as Caukoṭ Darbar. The palace building was renovated many times and is today referred to as Māni Keśava Nārāyaṇa, after a fragmentary Keśava (Viṣṇu) Temple in the courtyard.

43 Gutschow 2011 II, p. 307.
44 Regmi 1966 II, p. 266, n. 10.
45 Slusser 1982, p. 199.

After the annexation of Pāṭan to Kathmandu in 1597 CE Śivasiṃhamalla built a Degutale Temple, a temple (new. *degaḥ/-la, degū*) to the goddess Taleju, at the Palace Square.[46]

The first temple which Siddhinarasiṃhamalla built is the Viśveśvara Temple. According to its inscription, the temple was consecrated on 12 January 1627 CE.[47] Ten years later, consecrated on 23 February 1637,[48] he built the Kṛṣṇa Temple, together with its Garuḍadhvaja. In 1641 CE Siddhinarasiṃhamalla refurbished the Degutale Temple that was built by Śivasiṃhamalla and six years later, he additionally gilded one of the temple's roofs, by that time five in total. The Degutale Temple is not preserved in this condition. It was destroyed by fire during the reign of Siddhinarasiṃhamalla's son, Śrīnivāsamalla.[49] In 1661 CE Śrīnivāsamalla rebuilt the temple with only three roofs, as it exists today, though the present one is a recontruction. It was destroyed again in the 1934 earthquake and built anew in 1940 CE.[50]

46 ibid., p. 319.
47 Gail 1988, p. 30, n. 9.
48 ibid., p. 30.
49 Slusser 1982, pp. 200f
50 Gutschow 2011 II, p. 306.

The three quadrangles, the Keśava Nārāyaṇa Cok, Mūl Cok (ne., Main Courtyard) and Sundarī Cok (ne., Beautiful Courtyard) were, according to a number of sources, constructed by Siddhinarasiṃhamalla and his son Śrīnivāsamalla. It is believed that a decisive part was built by Siddhinarasiṃhamalla on the occasion of his son's birth in 1627 CE. Whether or not he incorporated earlier foundations for the layout of Mūl Cok and Sundarī Cok remains open to speculation. At the entrance to Sundarī Cok, Siddhinarasiṃhamalla placed three stone images, one portraying Hanūmān, one Narasiṃha and the third a five-faced Gaṇeśa. In 1647 CE he built the royal bath, the Tuṣahiṭī (new., cold fountain), as well as the adjacent tank in the Bhaṇḍārakhāla, the Lohanhiṭī (new., stone fountain).[51] The latter he built in honour of Taleju, the tutelary deity of the Mallas, and he is said to have gathered lotuses from this tank as his daily offering to her.[52] Śrīnivāsamalla later again entirely renovated the palace complex.

51 ibid., p. 307.
52 Regmi 1966 II, pp. 272, 276

Śrīnivāsamalla continued the ambitious construction process begun by his father. After his accession to the throne in 1661 CE, he entirely renovated the palace complex, where he inter alia rebuilt the entire palace front. He rebuilt the Degutale Temple and in 1652 CE he built the small Nārāyaṇa Temple. In 1666 CE Śrīnivāsamalla additionally enlarged the Mūl Cok and he built a small Taleju Temple into its south wing. A while later (1671 CE), he constructed the chief Taleju Temple which apparently replaced an earlier one, and in 1679 CE he built an *āgamachem̩* (new., a house for private/family gods) in the northwest corner of the Mūl Cok. The shrine collapsed in the 1934 earthquake and was not rebuilt afterwards. In 1680 CE Śrīnivāsamalla restored the northern extension of the palace proper, the old Chaukoṭ, but the following year, an earthquake hit the palace severely as a result of which its southern part collapsed in 1693 CE.

During the 1730s the palace was rebuilt by Viṣṇumalla and it was additionally extensively renovated in the 19th and 20th century CE, especially after the 1934 earthquake again hit the palace complex. It caused the eastern wing of the Keśava Nārāyaṇa Cok to collapse, as well as the north-western corner of Mūl Cok and the upper storeys of the eastern and northern wings of Sundarī Cok.[53]

53 Gutschow 2011 II, pp. 307f.

In 1680 CE Śrīnivāsamalla also constructed the Bhīmsen Temple. The construction of the southern Viśveśvara Temple in 1678 CE is attributed to Śrīnivāsamalla's chief minister, the *cautārā* Bhagiratha Bhaiyā (Bhāgaju). After the donor, the temple is popularly known as Bhāidega:. It was originally a three-tiered temple but after the 1934 earthquake it was restored with a dome.[54]

In 1693 CE Yognarendramalla's pillar was erected[55] and in 1701 CE Yognarendramalla renovated the northern of the two free standing open pavilions, a council hall (sa. *sabhāmaṇḍapa*) thenceforth known as Maṇimaṇḍapa.[56] The original construction dates of the twin pavilions cannot be confirmed. However, the structure of the northern one likely dates to the early 17th century CE and that of the southern one to the 16th or even 15th century CE.[57] The pavilions flank the access stairs to the Maṇidhārā. The northern pavilion served as a council hall and it was also the place where priests and astrologers assembled to decide the moment for initiating local festivals. Additionally, the kings of Pāṭan were occasionally crowned here. The southern *maṇḍapa* used to be the town weighing station and a centre for market price exchange.[58]

54 Slusser 1982, pp. 201ff.
55 Gutschow 2011 II, p. 317.
56 Slusser 1982, p. 203.
57 KVPT Report 2016, p. 12.
58 Slusser and Vajrācārya 1974, pp. 174f.

In 1705 CE Yognarendramalla died and the following year the Hariśaṅkara Temple was built in his memory. The donor was most likely his daughter Yogamatī, who acted as regent after the king's death.[59] The Lion Pillar (sa. *siṃhastambha*) in front of the Bhīmsen Temple was built in 1708 CE in the reign of Indramalla[60] and the southern Kṛṣṇa Temple, popularly known as Cyāsiliṃdega: (new., Octagonal Temple), was again built by Yogamatī in 1723 CE.[61]

In 1734 CE Viṣṇumalla rebuilt the old Chaukoṭ and in 1736 CE, he and his queen Chandra Lakṣmīdeva replaced a smaller bell by the ponderous bronze bell in the southern part of the Palace Square.[62] Initially, the bell was used for special proclamations by the Malla Kings. Now it is rung in honour of the goddess Taleju during Vijayadaśamī in September/October. The festival celebrates the triumph over the forces of evil through the worship of the deity. The northern wing of the palace complex was probably built by Bāhādur Śāh in the late 18th century CE and is therefore known as Bāhādur Śāh Bhavan.[63]

59 Gail 1984 I, p. 44 + n. 5 ref. Regmi 1966 II, pp. 340f.
60 KVPT Report 2016, p. 419.
61 Slusser 1982, p. 203.
62 Pruscha 1975 II, p. 162.
63 Gutschow 2011 II, pp. 317f.

2.1.4. Effects of the 2015 Earthquake

As the section above suggests, Pāṭan is located in a seismically active region. Beside countless minor tremors, several destructive earthquakes occured over the centuries. These include the severe earthquakes of 1833 and 1934. The last serious earthquake struck Nepal on 25 April 2015. The epicentre of the 7.6 magnitude earthquake was in the city of Gorkhā, about 50mi/80km northwest of Kathmandu. Tremors were also reported in Tibet, North- and Northeast India, China, Pakistan and Bangladesh. 37 aftershocks followed the same day, and hundreds later, including the severe aftershocks in the district of Dolakhā, east of Kathmandu, on 26 April 2015 as well as on 12 May 2015 with magnitudes up to 6.9.[64]

The Gorkhā Earthquake was not only a humanitarian catastrophe but also a cultural-historical disaster. The tremors caused damage to numerous significant historic structures and some buildings were even brought down completely. The monuments of the Pāṭan Palace Square have not been spared (see fig. 1). In the Core Zone Area of the Pāṭan Palace Square, the Cārnārāyaṇa and the Hariśaṅkara Temple collapsed completely above the plinth, as did also the twin pavilions (sa. *maṇḍapas*) north of the palace complex. The Kṛṣṇa Temple and the Viśveśvara Temple were severely damaged and the Bhīmsen and Degutale Temple suffered damage, too. The pillar of Yognarendramalla and the Lion Pillar of Bhīmsen Temple collapsed and broke into several pieces. The East wing of Sundarī Cok collapsed, the chief Taleju Temple suffered extensive damage at the upper levels and the small Taleju Temple suffered damage at the uppermost level, too. Of the Bāhādur Śāh Bhavan particularly the northeastern and eastern parts were damaged, of the Keśava Nārāyaṇa Cok the northern part. Beyond that, in close proximity of the Palace Square, the Rādhā Kṛṣṇa Temple in Swatha district collapsed and several other monuments suffered severe damage.The restoration of the monuments within the Core Zone Area was begun immediately after the earthquake, mainly leaded by the Kathmandu Valley Preservation Trust (hereafter KVPT), in close collaboration with the Government of Nepal, Department of Archaeology, as well as local and international specialists. The KVPT is a charity dedicated to architectural conservation, preservation and restoration of significant historic structures in the Kathmandu Valley and since its foundation in 1991 CE present in situ. The trust's projects are financed by local and international donations.

The restoration of the Kṛṣṇa Temple was financed by the Gerda Henkel Foundation with € 85,000 and the Embassy of Japan in Nepal with approximately € 9,000.[65] The Kṛṣṇa Temple fortunately did not collapse but it was severely damaged especially at the second floor. Due to the earthquake, some columns had moved out of plumb while others were damaged. Window frames and key stones had become dislodged and especially those stones at the corners of the innermost sanctum (sa. *garbhagṛha*) were severely damaged, too. Old repairs also came out.[66] The important Rāmāyaṇa and Mahābhārata friezes have fortunately survived the earthquake almost free of damage. However, some cracks are found (Pl. 1a-c). Rāma's head was still in place in scene 80 in Oktober 2015 (Pl. 1a) but it was lost in 2017 (Pl. 1b).

The building of the scaffolding around the temple (Pl. 1d) was completed in August 2016. Some of the damaged stones were repaired with mortar in situ, while others were removed, repaired and afterwards reinstalled in place. Severely damaged stones were replaced with new ones, whereby stone carvers carefully replicated the carving details on the new stones. The out of plumb columns were realigned and carved stones were cleaned with a soft brush and an acetone-based fluid.[67] The conservation work of the Kṛṣṇa Temple was completed in late 2018.[68]

64 http://www.seismonepal.gov.np/

65 KVPT Report 2017, p. 20.

66 KVPT Report 2016, p. 346.

67 KVPT Report 2017, pp. 3ff.

68 DoA Report 2019, p. 23.

Effects of the Earthquake

a

b

c

d: scaffolded Kṛṣṇa Temple and destroyed Cārnārāyaṇa Temple

Plate 01

a: Garuḍa facing the Kṛṣṇa Temple

b

c

d

e

Plate 02

2.2. Architecture and Design

Two different kinds of temples are prevalent in the Kathmandu Valley. These are firstly, the typical Nepalese multi-tiered temples, culminating in a pyramidal top, and secondly, temples with a curvilinear superstructure, referred to as *śikhara* temples. Literally the Sanskrit word *śikhara*, applied to the curvilinear superstructure, means *peak* or *top of a mountain*. Typically built of stone, these temples not only stand in clear contrast in form to the Nepali-style temples of brick and timber. It is thus beyond doubt that Indian precedents served as a model for the Nepalese *śikhara* temples. After providing some more information about this, the structure of the Kṛṣṇa Temple itself will be described, concerning architecture, artistic design and sculptural programme.

2.2.1. Śikhara Temples in India and Nepal

śikhara temples are frequently found in northern and central India. The *śikhara* visually emphasises the sanctum. Earlier Gupta superstructures already served the same purpose. Built in the shape of a stepped truncated pyramid, consisting of recessed horizontal tiers, the Gupta superstructures are intermediate in form between flat-roofed shrines and temples with fully evolved *śikharas*.[69] The brick temple at Bhītargaon (5th c. CE) and the Viṣṇu Temple at Deogaṛh (early 6th c. CE) have also a superstructure consisting of stepped horizontal tiers. As Vats states, their superstructures do not suggest a curvilinear spire.[70] However, it has to be noted that they already have triple facets, just like later *śikhara* temples.

69 Chandra 1970, p. 126.
70 Vats 1999 (1952), pp. 10f.

The earliest examples with a fully evolved *śikhara* date back to the late 7th and early 8th centuries CE. Among the earliest are some of the Early Cāḷukyan temples at Mahākūṭa[71] and Aihoḷe.[72] The temples at Paṭṭadakal are slightly later. According to Michell, the Early Cāḷukyas imported the style from Āndhra, where they sought refuge after the Pallavas occupied Badāmi in 642 CE.[73]

The earliest *śikhara* temple in Nepal with a dated inscription is the Narasiṃha Temple at the Pāṭan Palace Square (1589 CE). As Gail points out, *śikhara* temples were in all likelyhood built already earlier in Nepal, for the Narasiṃha's inscription by no means stresses the construction as a novelty.[74] From the 17th century CE onwards, numerous *śikhara* temples were found in Nepal. The Kṛṣṇa Temple is one of the most ancient extant *śikhara* temples at Pāṭan and probably also the most important *śikhara* temple in the whole valley. It is a hybrid of Indian and Nepalese architectural designs as it combines the north Indian *śikhara* with the stepped arcaded substructure of the Nepali-style temples. One-storeyed *śikhara* temples in the valley, like the 19th century Rādhā Kṛṣṇa Temple at Teku, south of the Kathmandu city core,[75] occasionally also have a typical Nepalese roofing beneath the *śikhara*. The Kṛṣṇa Temple by contrast displays a Mughal influence with its many domed pavilions (sa. *chattris*).

71 Michell 2014, pp. 83ff. (Saṅgameśvara and Virūpākṣeśvara Temples).
72 ibid. pp. 109ff. (Durga, Sūryanārāyaṇa, Chakragudi, Tarappa, Hucchappayyagudi and Hucchimalligudi Temples).
73 ibid., p. 22.
74 Gail 1988, p. 28.
75 Pruscha 1975 II, p. 91 (K 260).

As a fact, Nepalese art always drew on influences from Indian culture. The unique intermingling of styles that was implemented with the construction of the Kṛṣṇa Temple, is also reminiscent of a stylistic intermingling that was ongoing in North India at that time. Afghan and Central Asian invaders had caused widespread devastation in North India from the 12th century CE onwards. Religious monuments were destroyed and temple building activity was interrupted for a conside-rable time. As constructions were resumed in the late 15th century CE, past building forms were imitated but also elements derived from different traditions were combined, including elements from non-indigenous building traditions. Since Nepal was spared from the Islamic conquests, the conquests propelled many Indian refugees here, among them religious men and artists as well. They found new engagements at the Malla courts and they influenced spiritual life as well as Nepalese art and architecture.

The Kṛṣṇa Temple is the valley's finest stone wrought monument and at the same time the most important one for, as Gutschow notes, its innovative design had a significant impact on many temples built subsequently. This is evident in the design of the southern Kṛṣṇa Temple (1723 CE) at the same palace square, commonly referred to as the Cyāsiliṃdega:.[76]

76 Gutschow 2011 II, pp. 530f.

2.2.2. The Kṛṣṇa Temple

The Kṛṣṇa Temple is situated in the Core Zone Area of the Pāṭan Palace Square. Its main entrance is located on the eastern side, facing the main entrance of the royal palace. This alignment already gives a hint to Siddhinarasiṃhamalla's attachment to the worshipped deity. The temple has a second entrance located on the south side but this one is made use of only on Kṛṣṇajanmāṣṭamī, the annual festival in honour of Kṛṣṇa's birth.

In front of the temple's main entrance Siddhinarasiṃhamalla placed a Garuḍadhvaja, a Garuḍa-crowned pillar. It is common practice to place an image of Garuḍa, Viṣṇu's companion and mount (sa. *vāhana*), in front of a Viṣṇu temple. Garuḍa honouring Kṛṣṇa thus stresses Kṛṣṇa's identification with Viṣṇu. The statue is made of gilt copper. Garuḍa faces the temple in a half-kneeling pose (Pl. 2a). He has his hands joined in reverential gesture (sa. *añjalimudrā*). With the exception of his wings he his entirely represented in human form. This is true for the most Garuḍa images in Nepal, from the Licchavi period up to the end of the Malla period. Only from the 18th century CE onwards, Garuḍa is represented in Nepal also in the bird form.[77]

The three-storeyed Kṛṣṇa Temple raises on a wide low platform and a twofold square plinth (Pl. 2b). The whole structure is almost 21 metres high. The plinth is decorated with a latticed band and flowery designs. The entire temple is guarded by numerous lions and griffins. The lions protect it on the ground while the griffins protect it further up. Likewise, the principal access from the east is guarded by a pair of lions on the lower level and a pair of griffins on the upper level (Pl. 2c). The ground floor's base additionally bears lion blocks all around. Lion protomes are lowering out of small shrines, some fierceful looking, others rather playful. They are differently designed but all have a protruding tongue and strikingly, a moustache (Pl. 2d,e).

77 Slusser 1982, pp. 250f.

Ground Floor

The ground floor is an arcaded square room with nothing inside but stairs leading up to the first floor. More interesting than the interior, is the design of the outer walls and the arcade. Each of the four facades is visually divided by colonnettes into five sections (Pl. 3a). These sections are designed as blind double-leafed doors set in trefoil or quintuple foil arches, with the exception of the two sections actually providing access to the interior and the section containing the consecration inscription. Apart from the blind door leaves, the entire facade is embellished with beautiful floral designs. The false doors might be topped by a face of glory (sa. *kīrthimukha*) de-vouring the cloud foliage, complete with hands and fangs (Pl. 3b), as it first appears on the 1487 built Yakṣeśvara Temple at Bhaktapur.[78] The arches above the two real doors are beautifully designed, too, but the one on the east side is worn out so much that the figures are only scarcely traceable now. The arch above the western entrance (Pl. 3c) reveals what was once to be seen above the eastern one, too. The lower ends are occupied by a pair of *makaras* while in the centre, a projecting Garuḍa attracts the attention, grasping a pair of *nāgas* with his claws. This corresponds to a standardised programme that was developed already hundreds of years before.[79]

78 Gutschow 2011 II, p. 385.

Round the central room runs an arcade aisle with seven intercolumniations on each side. On the lintels, the Rāmāyana frieze runs clockwise around the whole temple (Pl. 3d). It will be discussed at length later. The capitals supporting the lintels of the ground floor all have a Garuḍa in the centre, in a reverential pose. To both sides either birds are depicted or deer taking flight from big cats (Pl. 3e,f).

First Floor: The Vi ṣṇu Temple Level

The central shrine (sa. *garbhagṛha*) was raised to the first floor, according to Gutschow in order to provide stability to the structure.[80] On a reduced area, the shrine houses an image of Bālagopāla, that is Kṛṣṇa in his form as the *youthful cowherd*. Since he is represented playing the flute, he is also described as Kṛṣṇa Veṇudhara (sa., *holding the flute*). Such images were especially popular during the late Malla Period.[81] Kṛṣṇa is accompanied by his consorts Rukmiṇī and Satyabhāmā.

The cella is again encircled by an arcade aisle. On the first floor, open and sheltered areas alternate due to eight pavilions (sa. *chattris*), visually three on each side, projecting from the arcade. The parapet has on each side eight gods of the Hindu pantheon, among them the Lokapālas, the guardians of the directions (Pl. 4) and the Navagrahas, nine personified heavenly bodies (Pl. 5).

79 ibid., p. 388.
80 ibid., p. 530.
81 Slusser 1982, p. 250.

a

b

c

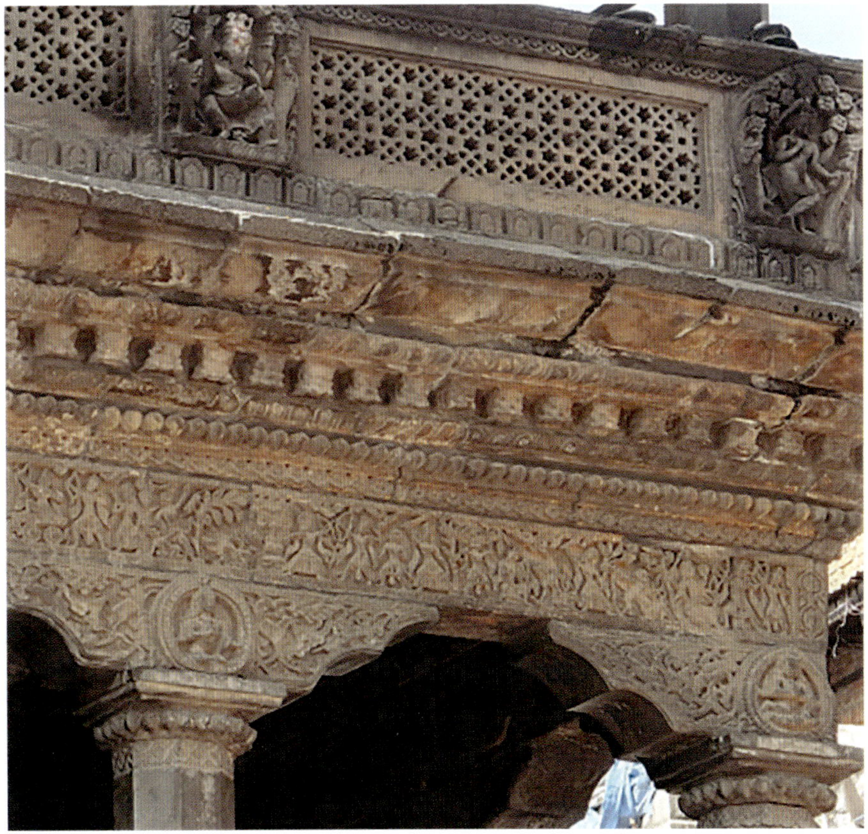
d

e

f

Plate 03

Lokapālas

Indra (O)

Agni (SO)

Yama (S)

Nairṛtya (SW)

Plate 04 Varuṇa (W)

Vāyu (NW)

Kubera (N)

Īśāna (NO)

Navagrahas

Sūrya

Candra

Maṅgala

Budha

Bṛhaspati

Śukra

Śani

Rāhu

Ketu

Plate 05

Plate 06

The Mahābhārata frieze runs clockwise around the whole temple, on the lintels meandering around arcade and pavilions. Like the Rāmāyana frieze, it will be discussed at length later. The capitals supporting the lintels of the first floor (Pl. 6a-c) all have an image of Kṛṣṇa in the centre. Details like his attributes vary but he is in all cases depicted with a cow, playing the flute. To both sides fierce fabulous creatures are depicted, some of which are being ridden.

The pavilions' roofings have different shapes. Each one is crowned with a golden finial and on top of the corner pavilions three griffins protect the structure (Pl. 6d-f). On the east and the west side, a bust of Kṛṣṇa is attached to the central pavilion's roof, set inside a niche framed by colonnettes supporting an arch with a pair of *makaras* and a face of glory (sa. *kīrthimukha*), grasping and devouring the cloud foliage. Additionally, two snakes wind around these roofs.

An entrance at the rear side provides access to the second floor, past an image of Rāma and Sītā. The outer walls of the shrine additionally have eight niches, two on each side, with further incarnations (sa. *āvatāras*) of Viṣṇu.

By manifesting in different shapes, Viṣṇu is believed to defend against evil forces, or more precisely against powerful demons who trouble the worlds. Different texts contain series of Viṣṇu's manifestations varying widely in number and list. Today, the series as given in Kṣemendra's Daśāvatāracarita (11th c. CE) serves as standard list. Specified therein are Viṣṇu's manifestations as Matsya (Fish), Kūrma (Tortoise), Varāha (Boar), Narasiṃha (Man-Lion), Vāmana (Dwarf), Paraśu-rāma (Rāma with the Axe), Rāma, Kṛṣṇa, Buddha and Karki/Kalkin, the *avatāra* yet to come.[82]

In Nepal, early sculptural representations are available only of Trivikrama/Vikrānta (associated with the Vāmanāvatāra), Varāha, Kṛṣṇa and Narasiṃha. Well known are the Viṣṇu Vikrānta image of Caṅgu Nārāyaṇa, commissioned by Mānadeva I in 467 CE,[83] the Varāha image of Dhumvārāhī (Kathmandu), assignable to the 7th century CE,[84] and the contemporaneous image of Kṛṣṇa subjugating Kāliya (Kāliyadamana) at Hanumān Dhoka.[85]

The earliest extant depiction of Narasiṃha in Nepal is again found at Caṅgu Nārāyaṇa. Bangdel dates the Narasiṃha stele to the 14th century CE.[86] Though comparatively late, this is also a dynamic representation with narrative emphasis that contrasts with the late Malla images – typically single iconic figures with less dynamic tension and drama. The early worship of Narasiṃha in Nepal is also attested in a 7th century inscription of Aṃśuvarman.[87] It was only at the time of the late Mallas that the remaining manifestations of Viṣṇu were represented, too. Consequently, the Kṛṣṇa Temple's *daśāvatāra* series is among the earliest in the valley. Of the Kṛṣṇa Temple's images only Balarāma and Kalkin have been published so far.[88]

Figure 2 shows a cross section of the Kṛṣṇa Temple's central room (sa. *garbhagṛha*) with the location of the ten *avatāras*.

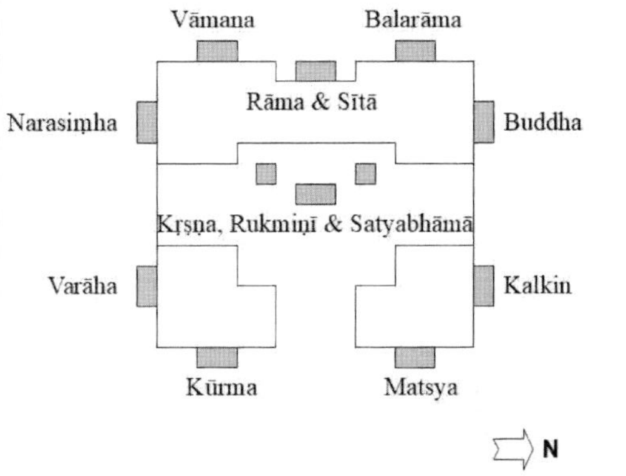

fig. 2: Location of the *daśāvatāras* at Kṛṣṇa Temple

The cult image of Kṛṣṇa mentioned before, forms part of this *daśāvatāra* series. Since the Kṛṣṇa Temple is dedicated to him, he occupies a central position. Unfortunately, I had no chance to see the image and it is thus not possible to give further details. Rāma is granted a special position, too, in a niche of the rear entrance. This is certainly because, being the main character of the Rāmāyaṇa represented here at great length, he deserves particular worship as well.

82 Chakraborty 1991, pp. 215ff.
83 Bangdel 1995, pp. 53f., illustration: p. 365.
84 ibid., p. 54, illustration: p. 107.
85 ibid., p. 54f., illustration: p. 121.
86 ibid., p. 55, illustration: p. 367.
87 ibid.
88 Deva 1984, Pls. 34b,35a.

The rear entrance is framed by colonnettes supporting a trefoil arc (Pl. 7a). In the lower margin it has a pair of half-human, half-bird creatures playing the flute (sa. *Kinnaras*). In the upper margin, Garuḍa grasps a pair of snakes (sa. *Nāgas*), flanked by a pair of celestial musicians (sa. *gandharvas*).

Rāma is accompanied by Sītā (Pl. 7b). He is represented four-armed, pointing out his divine nature. With his lower hands he holds bow and arrow, with his upper ones the conch (sa. *śaṅkha*) and presumably one of the other attributes connected with Viṣṇu, either discus (sa. *cakra*), mace (sa. *gadā*) or lotus (sa. *padma*). Rāma and Sītā are both wearing jewellery and elegant clothes. Rāma additionally wears a crown, while Sītā has her hair pinned up in a top knot.

The remaining eight *avatāras* are located on the outer walls of the shrine. All of them are depicted on a lotus pedestal, framed by colonnettes supporting a trefoil arc with a pair of *makaras* and a face of glory (sa. *kīrtimukha*). The motive was developed further, for the *kīrtimukha* no longer grasps and devours the cloud foliage but instead a pair of snakes (sa. *nāgas*).

Matsya (Pl. 7c) and Kūrma (Pl. 7d) are represented on the east side. They both have an animal head but the body is represented in human form. Matsya has all four attributes of Viṣṇu: conch, discus, mace and lotus. Kūrma supports with his upper left hand the mountain he bore on his back in the course of the churning of the ocean of milk.

On the south side of the temple, Varāha (Pl. 7e) and Narasiṃha (Pl. 7f) are represented. On his snout, Varāha carries the earth goddess Bhūdevī whom he rescued from the depths of the ocean. Narasiṃha is depicted ripping open the demon Hiraṇyakaśipu.

On the west side of the temple, Vāmana and Balarāma are represented. Vāmana (Pl. 7g) is depicted as a dwarf mendicant carrying an umbrella and a small vessel for alms. Next to him appears the demon king Mahābalī. He is crowned and richly bejewelled. With his upper hands he holds bow and arrow, with his lower right hand a single pennant standard and with his lower left hand, he shows the boon-granting gesture (sa. *varadamudrā*). This refers to him affirming that he would grant Vāmana as much land as he could cover in three steps. Represented is thus the moment before Vāmana turns into Trivikrama and measures the whole universe in three strides. Next, Balarāma, Kṛṣṇa's elder brother, is represented (Pl. 7h). He is frequently incorporated into the *daśāvatāra* series. Some refuse to accept Buddha as an *avatāra* of Viṣṇu and include Balarāma instead. Others equate Kṛṣṇa with Viṣṇu himself so that he becomes the source of all (*avatāras*), and list Balarāma in place of Kṛṣṇa. Here however, Balarāma takes the place of Paraśurāma. He is represented four-armed, holding the plough (sa. *hala*) and the pestle (sa. *musala*) in his upper hands, a flask of wine (sa. *surāmbudhi*) in his lower left hand and a staff (sa. *daṇḍa*) in his lower right hand.

On the north side of the temple the last two manifestations of the series, Buddha and Kalkin, are to be seen. Buddha (Pl. 7i) is represented wearing a robe, the one end of which he holds with his left hand. With his right hand he shows the gesture of granting wishes (sa. *varadamudrā*). Kalkin (Pl. 7j) sits atop his horse, the sword (sa. *khaḍga*) raised in his upper right hand. His other attributes are shield (sa. *kavaca*), discus (sa. *cakra*) and conch (sa. *śaṅkha*). Incised on his lotus-pedestal is the *mantra 'Om namo magavate Vāsudevāya'* (read: *bhagavate*). This links Kalkin with Kṛṣṇa, Vasudeva's son, and thereby also equates Kṛṣṇa with Viṣṇu as superior to all. Another *mantra*, the *'Hari om tatsat'*, proclaims that Viṣṇu is the divine truth of all. It is incised on Varāha's pedestal.

Plate 07

a b c d e

Plate 08

Second Floor: The Śiva Temple Level

The programme of the second floor contrasts with the otherwise Viṣṇu-centric programme of the temple. On a further reduced area, a second shrine is located. It houses a *liṅga*, the abstract (sa. *niṣkala*) form of Śiva (Pl. 8a). It is a simple shaft of carved stone, set in a water-carrier (sa. *jalahārī*), interpreted as female counterpart. Unfortunately, it was damaged in the 2015 earthquake. Maybe the *liṅga* was exchanged at some point, for Regmi describes the *liṅga* inside the Kṛṣṇa Temple is a *caturmukhaliṅga* with four life size images of different aspects of Śiva.[89]

The shrine of the second floor is again encircled by an arcade with eight projecting pavilions (sa. *chattris*) and the pavilions are again adorned with different roofings, golden finials and, the corner ones each with three griffins. The brackets have representations of Śiva, varying in detail (Pl. 8b-d). The god is accompanied by his bull, Nandī, and flanked by representations of birds, winding in flowery foliage. On the second floor only the lintels of the pavilions' front sides are embellished with a frieze. This one is not a narrative frieze but has 108 tiny *liṅga*-depictions.

Gutschow has already worked on these depictions and published his result in 2011.[90] According to him, 99 of these *liṅgas* are named and 96 refer to *liṅgas* located within the sacred landscape of Benāras (also Vārāṇasī or Kāśī) in Uttar Pradesh. The number 108 also links the representations to the sacred landscape of Benāras. Gutschow explains that, in combination with the encircling quality of the frieze, the number recalls the Pañcakrośīyātrā, the pilgrimage that visits 108 places and temples along a path defining Kāśīkṣetra, the sacred realm of the Gaṅgā. The 108 *liṅga*-representations forming the frieze, do however, as Gutschow also states, not refer to those along the Pañcakrośīyātrā per se. Nine of the *liṅgas* depicted are not identified by inscription. That way, one can include other *liṅgas* within or outside of Kāśīkṣetra, according to personal preferences. Gutschow conclusively remarks that the whole construction is a symbolic one in which the king and his deity occupy the centre, and that the symbolic construction of Kāśī on the temple both translocates and recreates Kāśī in Pāṭan. It is believed that those who die within Kāśīkṣetra attain liberation (sa. *mokṣa*) and Siddhinarasiṃhamalla might have translocated Kāśī for these liberating qualities. Siddhinarasiṃhamalla also repeatedly renounced the throne and went on pilgrimages to Kāśī and other sacred places in North India.[91]

Third Floor and Superstructure

The temple's uppermost level has an empty sanctum, accessible from the west. Although no worship takes place here, this level has an important function, as it supports the towering curvilinear superstructure (sa. *śikhara*).

The *śikhara* tower raises above the cella (Pl. 8e). It has seven plain bands on each face. At either side a columned pavilion (sa. *chattri*) is engaged against its base, of which the western one provides the entrance to the above mentioned empty sanctum. The engaged pavilions replace the characteristic prominent frontal projections of the early Indian precedents, conceived as enlarged mouldings, literally shaped like a cow's eye (sa. *gavākṣa*). Typically, such mouldings on the *śikhara's* base contain carved figures and one would expect the engaged pavilions to house images, too, yet they remain empty. The four pavilions have a consistent roofing and each one is crowned by another golden pot-like finial. Instead of a sculptured lintel with brackets, the columns of these pavilions support a trefoil arch with a pair of *makaras* and a central face of glory (sa. *kīrtimukha*), grasping and devouring a pair of snakes (sa. *nāgas*). In the corners between the pavilions four lions carrying guardians protrude from the shaft. The lions are shown in a belligerent position and the riders have their weapons raised for battle.

The *śikhara* closes with a multilayered string course. The pinnacle above consists of a bell-shaped base (sa. *ghaṇṭākār*), a circular element with stylised myrobalan fruits (sa. *āmalaka*) and one last golden finial. Representations of Viṣṇu on Garuḍa are attached to the pinnacle in the four cardinal directions. In between, guardians riding on fierce lions appear again. A standard is attached to the pinnacle, with a metal flag and a discus (sa. *cakra*), indicating the presence of Viṣṇu.

89 Regmi 1966 II, p. 272.
90 Gutschow 2011 II, pp. 528f.
91 V. infra, pp. 32f.

2.3. The Kṛṣṇa Temple Then and Now

The Kṛṣṇa Temple is, and has always been, of great importance for the valley's population. After first giving the essence of the consecration inscription, Siddhinarasiṃhamalla's role in the popularisation of Kṛṣṇaism will be discussed. This section deals with the cultural importance of the Kṛṣṇa Temple – from back then at the time of its construction, until today.

2.3.1. The Consecration Inscription

The consecration inscription is incised on a stele fixed to the ground-floor walls of the temple. More precisely, the stele is placed in the leftmost arch alcove of the east face. The round-top part of the stele has a representation of Kṛṣṇa, to whom the temple is dedicated. He is depicted playing the flute, flanked by his consorts Rukmiṇī and Satyabhāmā.

The inscription comprises 56 lines in total. The language is first Sanskrit and in the last portion Newari. The script is Nepālākṣara throughout, the common alphabet for classical Newari texts.[92] A transcription was first published in 1880 by Indraji and Bühler in *The Indian Antiquary*, together with a brief summary.[93] In 2004 Bledsoe published a thorough English translation[94] to which Gutschow in 2011 added a rubbing of the inscription.[95] The complete translation is given in Appendix I.

92 Lienhard 1988, p. xviii.
93 Indraji and Bühler 1880, pp. 184ff.
94 Bledsoe 2004, pp. 129ff.
95 Gutschow 2011 II, p. 543.

The Sanskrit portion of the inscription comprises 45 lines, consisting of 35 couplets. It opens with an invocation to Gopāla, that is Kṛṣṇa in his form as a youthful cowherd. He is worshipped as Trimūrti, embodying the cosmic functions of creation, preservation and destruction/ transformation (v. 1). The deity's worship is limited to this first verse only. As Bledsoe points out, instead the mortals are considered central and all-pervasive in the following part.[96]

Verses 2 to 14 give the royal genealogy of the temple's donor, king Siddhinarasiṃhamalla. The lineage begins with Harisiṃhadeva (v. 2) who ruled over the Nepal valley in the beginning of the 14th century CE. The next king listet is Mahendramalla (vs. 3f.) who ruled more than 200 years later, from 1560 CE, over Kathmandu as a separate kingdom. The lineage continues with Mahendramalla's son, Śivasiṃhadeva (vs. 5f.), and grandson, Hariharasiṃha (vs. 7f.). Hariharasiṃha was married to Lālamatī (v. 9), of royal descent, too, and their common son was Siddhinarasiṃhamalla (vs. 10-14). All the kings mentioned are said to have been great warriors and donors, bestowing on their people all sorts of things just like the wish-fulfilling tree of Indra's celestial abode. The eulogy (sa. *praśasti*) ends with stating that Siddhinarasiṃhamalla is the greatest of all, in every respect. The remaining verses deal with the consecration (sa. *pratiṣṭhā*) of the Kṛṣṇa Temple, referred to as a *maṭha to Bālagopāla*.

96 Bledsoe 2004, p. 130.

The date of consecration is given in verse 17 as well as at the beginning of the Newari part: the 10th of bright Phālguṇa in the Nepali year 757, a Thursday, corresponding to 23 February 1637 CE.[97] The temple was decora-ted with 21 golden finials, corresponding to the golden spires adorning the 16 pavilions, the 4 niches adjecent to the *śikhara* and the 1 on top of the *śikhara* itself. According to the inscription (v. 16) these golden finials make the temple look like a mountain of gold if seen from the perspective of the gods, that is from above. According to the inscription, the consecration ceremony was disturbed when suddenly the *crooked king* besieged the city (v. 18). It is well known that the *crooked king* was Siddhinarasiṃhamalla's nephew Pratāpamalla of Kathmandu.[98] According to Bledsoe, the duel is described in the chronicles as a legendary one of tantric powers, since Pratāpamalla appears in the form of a black snake, attempting to destroy the sacrifice.[99] Bledsoe points out that every sacrifice to celebrate the birth of a king (sa. *rājasūyayajña*) requires a military triumph to be successful, for this triumph contributes considerably to the transformation of the agent.[100] Next, the inscription records Siddhinarasiṃhamalla's victory. We are informed that an extended sacrificial session was held, after the king drove off the enemies with ease (vs. 22ff.).

97 Gail 1988, p. 30.
98 Regmi 1966 II, p. 72.
99 Bledsoe 2004, p. 129.
100 ibid., p. 135.

Due to his generosity, Siddhinarasiṃhamalla is repeatedly compared with Karṇa (vs. 25,31), one of the Mahābhārata's central characters. It is striking that, after the short invocation at the beginning, neither Kṛṣṇa nor Viṣṇu himself figures prominently in the text. Bledsoe assumes that maybe, the chief priest mentioned in verses 20 and 21, Viśvanātha Upādhyāya, wished to figure as master of the sacrificial session without being put in the rear by some deity appearing on scene.[101] Anyway, a more elaborate worship would have easily been possible without offending his honour.

The second part in Newari consists of 11 lines written in prose. The date of consecration here is given with additional astrological details about the lunar mansion (sa. *nakṣatra*) and the planetary combination (sa. *yoga*). Thereafter, the granted benefits of agricultural land made to the Kṛṣṇa Temple are listed. The revenues from these lands were to cover the necessary expenditure for festivities and other forms of worship. The first set of assignments concerns the daily worship (sa. *pūjā*) and the lighting of lamps on special occasions. The second set of assignments concerns the annual festivals and special worship of the deity's image like swinging or bathing. The third and last set concerns solely the lighting of lamps during Kārttika, the most important month for Kṛṣṇaites, and an additional grant to cover supplementary costs.

The intention of giving lands and determining the use of their income was certainly to retain a vibrant worship of the deity in this particular image. As there is no association (new. *guṭhi*) mentioned to manage the income and the performances prescribed, Bledsoe concludes that the temple's own liturgists were entrusted with this task.[102] She further states that down to the present day, Viśvanātha's descendants number among the temple's officiants.[103]

2.3.2. Siddhinarasiṃhamalla, Donor of the Kṛṣṇa Temple

Siddhinarasiṃhamalla ruled Pāṭan from 1619 to 1661 CE. He was one of Pāṭans most outstanding kings. After the city had been dependent on Kathmandu in the beginning of the 17th century CE, it became independent again under the rule of Siddhinarasiṃhamalla in 1619 CE. The various sources, architectural, artistically and literary, all testify to the impact that this monarch had on the development not only of Pāṭan but on the Nepal Valley as a whole.

Siddhinarasiṃhamalla was born in 1606 CE. He was Śivasiṃhamalla's grandson, son of Hariharasiṃha and his wife Lālamatī. In 1620 CE he obtained the throne as a youth. His father most likely had already died before his birth and thus his grandfather, Śivasiṃhamalla, after his death split the kingdom handing over the control over Pāṭan to Siddhinarasiṃhamalla and the control over Kathmandu to his half-brother Lakṣmīnarasiṃhamalla.[104]

Siddhinarasiṃhamalla was married to Bhānumatī. Apart from the name nothing is known about her. They had at least two sons, Śrīnivāsamalla and Jyotinarasiṃhamalla, and one daughter named Bhīmalakṣmī.[105]

Like many other Indian and Nepalese kings, Siddhinarasiṃhamalla regarded himself as an outward manifestation of Viṣṇu. A strong affiliation to Viṣṇu is indicated already by the name that his parents gave him, for Narasiṃha is one of Viṣṇu's main incarnations. What Siddhinarasiṃhamalla left for posterity reveals that he was devoted, more precisely, to Kṛṣṇa. Siddhinarasiṃhamalla most likely, played the most decisive part in the consolidation and spread of Kṛṣṇaism in Nepal and his temple to Bālagopāla is until today the most important Kṛṣṇa Temple in the whole valley.

Like already the Licchavi rulers, later Nepalese kings engaged in more than one faith, too. This applies also to Siddhinarasiṃhamalla. Apart from Viṣṇuism he payed particular attention to Śivaism and Buddhism. Śivaism always occupied a prominent position at the Nepalese royal court. Nepal's rulers reigned by the grace of Śiva Paśupati and additionally, Taleju, an outward manifestation of Durgā, was their tutelary deity. It is thus not surprising that the first temple Siddhinarasiṃhamalla built was dedicated to Śiva Viśveśvara, and it is neither strange that he worshiped Taleju daily. What concerns the patronage of Buddhism, Siddhinarasiṃhamalla is said to have reorganised monasteries (sa. *vihāras*) and introduced sound administration of their funds and charities. Additionally, he is said to have defined the monks' rights and their relations with the laity.[106] There is evidence even that Siddhinarasiṃhamalla himself also revered

101 Bledsoe 2004, pp. 136f.

102 ibid., p. 138.

103 ibid., p. 137, n. 59.

104 Regmi 1966 II, pp. 268ff.

105 ibid., p. 278.

106 ibid., p. 269.

Buddhist divinities.[107] In the area of non-religious affairs, the king undertook settlement-promoting measures which revived the city's appearance, he attracted merchants from outside and intensified trade with Tibet.[108]

It was already mentioned that Siddhinarasiṃhamalla added considerably to the appearance of the Pāṭan Palace Square through the construction of architectural masterpieces. Siddhinarasiṃhamalla however not only patronised architectural undertakings, he was also keen on poetry and drama. Of utmost interest in this context is a Kṛṣṇalīlā Painting that was thoroughly studied by Lienhard.[109] It was painted during the reign of Siddhinarasiṃhamalla and is kept safe in the Pāṭan Museum. The Kṛṣṇalīlā Painting represents an early example of Nepalese miniature painting. It comprises 31 scenes arranged in five rows, mainly illustrating the games the young Kṛṣṇa plays with the herdswomen (sa. *gopīs*). The white band topping these scenes has just as many songs or poems, dealing with the same subject. The language of these songs is classical Newari, written in Nepālākṣara script. The central scene dominates the painting. Depicted is Kṛṣṇa Veṇudhara, the flute-playing god, flanked by two *gopīs*. Siddhinarasiṃhamalla himself is depicted twice in this painting. In scene 1 he worships Śiva Paśupati and in scene 2 he is represented with his queen Bhānumatī on a visit to Kṛṣṇa. The king is depicted with blue colour, indicating his strong affiliation with Viṣṇu. Interestingly, the content of scene 1 at the same time hints to the above mentioned prominent position Śivaism occupied at the royal court. Most important, however, is that Siddhinarasiṃhamalla himself is believed to be the author of the songs in the Kṛṣṇalīlā Painting. Except for song 1, which is devoted to Śiva, all others close with a stanza in which Kṛṣṇa alias Gopīnātha (sa., Lord of the *gopīs*) is worshipped as the *Lord of Siddhinarasiṃha.* This is particularly well expressed in song 17: "While coming, while sitting, while sleeping and dreaming, my mind is (always) intent upon beholding (the Lord). (King) Siddhinarasiṃha's Lord, Gopīnātha, keeps my life (pulsing).".[110] Until today Siddhinarasiṃhamalla's songs are popular and performed regularly.

Siddhinarasiṃhamalla is said to have inaugurated the Kārttik-nāc, too, a dance drama with a mainly viṣṇuite-kṛṣṇaite content, that is until today performed every year.[111] He is also said to have composed religious lyrical poetry in Maithili and Bengali. The play Hariścandranṛtyaṃ for example dates from his time.[112] It was composed 1651 CE and deals with the life of Hariścandra, a celebrated mythological Indian king. The language is a mixture of Bengali and Maithili with Sanskrit verses interpersed here and there. There are two dramas centered on Viṣṇu, either ascribed to Siddhinarasiṃha[113] or to his son Śrīnivāsa,[114] the Ekādaśīnāṭaka and the Daśāvatāranāṭaka. The first one deals with Viṣṇu's sleep (sa. *hariśayana*) from the 11th day (sa. *ekādaśī*) of bright Āṣāḍha until the 11th day of bright Kārttika when he reawakes (sa. *haribodhinīekādaśī*). The second drama deals with Viṣṇu's ten incarnations (sa. *daśāvatāras*).

Siddhinarasiṃhamalla spent much time on meditation. He practised great charity but was himself leading a modest life. On this point, it is said that he collected as few taxes as possible.[115] Legend says, he considered it a sin to acquire anything more than what he basically needed to live and that he forbade his wife and daughters to wear jewellery.[116] He is reputed to have reduced his intake of rice to a minimum and to have slept on a stone bed. Due to his pious disposition he was called *the royal saint* (sa. *rājaṛṣi*) and *the great saint on the lion throne*.[117] It is said that Siddhinarasiṃhamalla thrice renounced wordliness and entered hermitage. During his absence his son, Śrīnivāsamalla, already was entrusted with governmental powers.[118] In 1652 CE king Siddhinarasiṃhamalla relinquished the throne and went on a pilgrimage to Banāras (Vārāṇasī) and other sacred places in North India. When he returned about two years later his second son Jyotinarasiṃhamalla had died. For some time, Siddhinarasiṃhamalla might have ruled in joint capacity with Śrīnivāsamalla but, in 1661 CE the latter became sole ruler.[119] As the chronicles report, Siddhinarasimhamalla personally placed the crown on his son's head and renounced the throne forever in order to emigrate to India.[120] The date of Siddhinarasiṃhamalla's death is un-

107 Regmi 1966 II, p. 273.
108 Lienhard 1995, p. 25.
109 ibid., pp. 35ff.

110 ibid., p. 139.
111 V. infra, pp. 33f.
112 Lienhard 1995, p. 34.
113 Bledsoe 2004, p. 136.
114 Lienhard 1995, p. 34.

115 ibid., p. 26.
116 Regmi 1966 II, pp. 275f.
117 Lienhard 1995, pp. 25f.
118 Regmi 1966 II, p. 272.
119 ibid., pp. 275ff.
120 ibid., p. 282.

known. According to a journal (new. *ṭhyāsaphu*) he lived to the age of 104, dying in 1710 CE. Legend even has it that he still lives. Accordingly, when death finally occurs the guardian stone elephants of his Viśveśvara Temple will announce it by descending to drink in the opposite Maṇidhārā.[121] Linked with this idea is also the fact that, until approximately 1980 CE, Siddhinarasiṃhamalla's bed was made every day and his water-pipe prepared with fresh tobacco in expectation of his return from his last pilgrimage.[122]

2.3.3. Ceremonies and Festivals Today

Like all cultural sites of the Kathmandu Valley, the Pāṭan Palace Square is not just remains of a past civilisation but living heritage down to the present day. While the many temples are not open to public, devotees are allowed to enter and worship their deities. Visually outstanding and a centre of vibrant worship, the Kṛṣṇa Temple is the valley's best known temple, domestic and abroad. Kṛṣṇa is worshiped twice every day. In course of the morning *pūjā*, the cult images of Kṛṣṇa and his consorts are washed, dressed and decorated. In the evening, devotional songs are sung and candles are lit. In between the morning and the evening *pūjā* the temple is closed but if they are lucky worshipers are let inside after knocking at the door.

What concerns annual festivals, the consecration of the Kṛṣṇa Temple is celebrated, of course, on the tenth day of bright Phālguna (February/March). Among the other festivals in connection with the Kṛṣṇa Temple, Kṛṣṇajanmāṣṭamī and Kārttik-nāc are of peculiar interest.

121 Slusser 1982, p. 201.
122 Lienhard 1995, p. 26.

Kṛṣṇajanmāṣṭamī

Kṛṣṇajanmāṣṭamī is the most popular term that is used for the great annual festival in honour of Kṛṣṇas birth (sa. *janma*). The festival is known under various other names, such as Kṛṣṇāṣṭamī, Kṛṣṇajayanti or Gokulāṣṭamī. The birth of Kṛṣṇa is celebrated on the eighth day (sa. *aṣṭamī*) of dark Bhādra (August/September).
That the Kṛṣṇa Temple of Pāṭan is the most important Kṛṣṇa Temple in the Valley is evident since every year, thousands of people come together here to celebrate Kṛṣṇajanmāṣṭamī. Kṛṣṇa's birth is commemorated on the stroke of midnight. Throughout the day the people fast. They decorate the temple with flowers and thousands of flickering oil lamps are lit. People make their way through the many sitting, praying and chanting devotees to the interior of the temple in order to worship Kṛṣṇa. They offer food (sa. *prasāda*), flowers and money and in return receive consecrated food or flowers from the temple priests. The people keep vigil all night and sing holy songs. The following day, a procession takes place that includes the bearing of an image of Kṛṣṇa.[123] Until the monarchy was abolished even the king attended the festivities.[124]

Kṛṣṇajanmāṣṭamī is popular not only in Nepal but all over India, too, and in every other country where Hinduism is practised. The customs for this festival vary significantly. The best known ones are concerned with aspects of Kṛṣṇas youthful days. In cities of the north Indian state of Uttar Pradesh like Mathurā and Vṛndāvan, the *rās(a)-līlā* is staged, a play (sa./hi. *līlā*) dealing with the games and dancing (hi. *rās/-a*) of the young Kṛṣṇas with the herdswomen (sa. *gopīs*). In Mahārāṣṭra the custom of *dahī haṇḍī* is popular. The *haṇḍī* (hi.) is a small earthen pot that is traditionally filled with curd (hi. *dahī*) but nowadays mostly with money and sweets. The pot is hung high up above the streets and male youths build a human pyramid in order to break it or bring it down. The event recalls Kṛṣṇa's occasional stealing of butter or curd as a child. Neither *rās(a)līlā* nor *dahī haṇḍī* are connected in the Nepal Valley with Kṛṣṇa's birth but both aspects might be performed in course of another festival, that is the Kārttik-nāc inaugurated by Siddhinarasiṃhamalla.

123 Bangdel 1987, p. 39.
124 Gail 1988 (II), p. 30.

Kārttik-nāc

The Kārttik-nāc (new. Kāttī-pyākhaṃ) is a dance festival (ne. *nāc*, new. *pyākhaṃ*) performed in the month of Kārttika (October/November). From the time of Yoganarendramalla until 1949 CE the festivities were extended to a whole lunar month. From 1949 to 1979 CE, the play was reduced to two days only, until in 1980 CE the Kārttik Dance Management Committee was created.[125] At present the duration of the festival again corresponds to its original duration of one or two weeks. I had the chance to attend the play in 2017 when it was staged over twelve consecutive evenings. Lienhard describes a cele-

125 Toffin 2012, p. 130.

bration for ten days,[126] while Toffin gives a length of only eight consecutive evenings.[127] Since it was founded by Siddhinarasiṃhamalla, the dance festival is closely connected with the Kṛṣṇa Temple. This connection is also apparent from the place of event. The various episodes, mainly viṣṇuite-kṛṣṇaite ones, are performed after sunset on the platform (new. *dabū*) next to the temple. Slight changes are made from one year to the next, concerning not only the duration of the play but also the episodes staged. Figure 3 gives the programme of 2017, when I had the chance to attend the festivities, compared with the programme Lienhard published in 1995 (possibly staged earlier) and the programme of 2008, published by Toffin.

day	programme 1995 (?)	programme 2008	programme 2017
			Sudāmā Tales
			Bāḥthaḥ Tales (humorous sketches)
	Kṛṣṇalīlā	Bāḥthaḥ Tales (humorous sketches)	Uṣāharaṇalīlā 1: Blessing of Bāṇāsura
	Sudāmā Tales	Bāḥthaḥ Tales (humorous sketches)	Uṣāharaṇalīlā 2: Uṣā and Aniruddha
	Bāḥthaḥ Tales (humorous sketches)	Bāḥthaḥ Tales (humorous sketches)	Uṣāharaṇalīlā 3: Dance of the Devīs
	Bāḥthaḥ Tales (humorous sketches)	The Art of War: Kṛṣṇa versus Śiva	Uṣāharaṇalīlā 4: The Art of War
	Dance of the Devis: Kumārī, Lakṣmī	Dance of the Devis: Kumārī, Lakṣmī	Uṣāharaṇalīlā 5: Defeat of Bāṇāsura
ekādaśī	Samudramanthana: Churning of the Ocean	Jalaśayana: Defeat of Madhu and Kaiṭabha	Jalaśayana: Defeat of Madhu and Kaiṭabha
	Varāha: Defeat ofHiraṇyākṣa	Varāha: Defeat of Hiraṇyākṣa	Varāha: Defeat of Hiraṇyākṣa
	Narasiṃha: Defeat of Hiraṇyakaśipu	Narasiṃha: Defeat of Hiraṇyakaśipu	Narasiṃha: Defeat of Hiraṇyakaśipu
	Vastraharaṇalīlā: Kṛṣṇa Stealing the Clothes		Vastraharaṇalīlā: Kṛṣṇa Stealing the Clothes
	Dadhilīlā: Kṛṣṇa Breaking the Jar of Curd		Dadhilīlā: Kṛṣṇa Breaking the Jar of Curd

fig. 3: Episodes staged at Kārttik-nāc

Devotional Songs

During the month of Kārttika not only the dance festival takes place. Additionally, every evening one of the songs contained in the Kṛṣṇalīlā Painting ascribed to Siddhinarasiṃhamalla is sung inside the Kṛṣṇa Temple. The songs are further sung all day long next to the Kṛṣṇa Temple, during Jyeṣṭhapūrṇimā, the full moon day of the month Jyeṣṭha (May/June).[128] According to Lienhard, on this day also Siddhinarasiṃhamalla's throne is shown and the Kṛṣṇalīlā painting displayed.[129] The songs of the Kṛṣṇalīlā Painting are occasionally sung at other settings, too.[130]

All things considered, the Kṛṣṇa Temple at Pāṭan is an imposing structure of an outstanding monarch that has remained the centre of Kṛṣṇaism in Nepal ever since its consecration down to the present day.

The following chapters will bring to light the likewise outstanding narrative representations on the Kṛṣṇa Temple of the great Indian epics, the Rāmāyaṇa and the Mahābhārata.

126 Lienhard 1995, pp. 32f.
127 Toffin 2012, pp. 132ff.
128 Lienhard 1995, p. 43.
129 ibid., p. 29.
130 ibid., pp. 33,43.

3. The Narrative Friezes of the Kṛṣṇa Temple

After some introductory remarks, the impressive narrative friezes of the Rāmāyaṇa and the Mahābhārata on the Kṛṣṇa Temple will be discussed in detail. In the course of this, relations of the representations to different literary traditions will be pointed out where possible.

3.1. General Remarks

These remarks concern the literary transmission of both the epics and their artistic realisation on the Kṛṣṇa Temple.

3.1.1. Rāmāyaṇa and Mahābhārata Tradition in India and Nepal

The Rāmāyaṇa is traditionally ascribed to Vālmīki. In its present form, however, it was evolved over centuries. The story is divided into seven sections (sa. *kāṇḍas*), the first and the last book being later additions to the core story. According to Goldman,[131] the oldest parts of the surviving text might have been composed between the beginning of the 7th century BCE and the mid-6th century BCE. The story has survived in numerous partial and complete manuscripts and in two major recensions, a northern and a southern one. During 1951 to 1975, scholars, attempting to recover the original form of the poem, prepared a Critical Edition of the Rāmāyaṇa at the Oriental Institute, Baroda.

The considered author of the Mahābhārata is Vyāsa but again, the text as it stands today is the product of multiple authors. Debroy gives a span from 800 BCE to 400 CE for the composition of the original text.[132] Again, there are two major recensions, a northern and a southern one. The Critical Edition of the Mahābhārata was commenced in 1919 at the Bhandakar Oriental Research Institute (BORI), Pune. The whole work was completed in 1966. With nearly 74,000 couplets (sa. *ślokas*) in 18 books (sa. *parvas*), the Mahābhārata is almost four times the size of the Rāmāyaṇa.

Various regional Indian versions exist of both the epics. Sanskrit adaptions of the Rāmāyaṇa include the Yogavasiṣtha Rāmāyaṇa (12th c. CE), the Adhyātma Rāmāyaṇa (12th -14th c. CE), the Adbhuta Rāmāyaṇa (composed after the Adhyātma Rāmāyaṇa), the Bhuśuṇḍi Rāmāyaṇa (14th c. CE), the Ānanda Rāmāyaṇa (15th c. CE) and the Tattvasaṃgraha Rāmāyaṇa (~17th c. CE).[133] Important recensions in South Indian languages include Kambar's Tamil Irāmāvatāram (12th c. CE), the Telugu Rāmāyaṇas of Bhāskara (12th c. CE) and Raṅganātha (13th c. CE)[134] and, in Kannada, the Jain Pampa Rāmāyaṇa of Nāgacandra (~12th c. CE) as well as Kumāra Vālmīki's Torave Rāmāyaṇa (~1500 CE)[135]. Important recensions in North Indian languages include the Bengali Kṛttivāsi Rāmāyaṇa (15th c. CE[136]), Durgāvarā's Assamese Gīti Rāmāyaṇa (1514-1540[137]), Tulsīdās' Rāmacaritamānasa in Avadhi (1570s CE[138]) and Eknāth's Marathi Bhāvārtha Rāmāyaṇa (1590s CE[139]).

Nepali versions of the Rāmāyaṇa are of the 19th and 20th century CE only but the Rāmāyaṇa was well known in Nepal long before. Apart from a 6th century manuscript recently discovered in Kolkata,[140] the oldest surviving Rāmāyaṇa manuscript known is a palm-leaf manuscript from Nepal, dated 1020 CE. This and a second Nepali manuscript, dated 1675 CE, were used in the Critical Edition of the Vālmīki Rāmāyaṇa. Both manuscript cover all seven section (sa. *kāṇḍas*), though in case of the first one some folios are missing.[141] As Bhatt states, the Nepali versions agree with the Maithili and Bengali versions of the Vālmīki Rāmāyaṇa.[142] Rao lists some of the recent versions and remarks that most of them are based on the Adhyātma Rāmāyaṇa rather than on the Vālmīki Rāmāyaṇa.[143] The popularity of the Adhyātma Rāmāyaṇa in Nepal can also be deduced from Lienhard's work, in which he lists two incomplete but extensive Nepalese manuscripts of this version, with 528 and 135 surviving folios respectively.[144] While the first manuscript covers the entire story, the second one is preserved only up to the 4th chapter of the Sundarakāṇḍa.

131 Goldman 1984: I, pp. 14ff.

132 Debroy 2015 (2010): I, pp. xxi, xxix.

133 Bose 2010, pp. 21ff.

134 Rao 1984, p. 36.

135 ibid., pp. 43f.

136 Nagar and Nagar 1997, p. xv.

137 Rao 1984, p. 25.

138 Nagar 2014 II, p. 1104.

139 Abbott 1983 (1927), p. xxvi.

140 The Times of India, Dec. 18, 2015.

141 Bhatt 1960, pp. xv, xvi.

142 ibid., p. i.

143 Rao 1984, pp. 29f.

144 Lienhard 1988, pp. 53ff.

Familiarity with the Rāmāyaṇa is also evident in the Gopālarājavaṃśāvalī, the oldest preserved Nepalese chronicle (sa. *vaṃśāvalī*). The Gopālarājavaṃśāvalī is a palm-leaf manuscript consisting of two loosely related texts: *vaṃśāvalī I* (folios 17 to 30) and *vaṃśāvalī II* (folios 31 to 63, plus an extra folio numbered 50). As the first 16 folios are missing, the manuscript is incomplete. The *vaṃśāvalī* contains dated entries from 1057 to 1389 CE. The compilation of the chronicle was most probably completed during the reign of Sthitirājamalla (1382-1395 CE).[145] References to the Rāmāyaṇa occur in several places. Folios 18 and 19 give a genealogy of Rāma as the descendant of Brahmā, who emerged from the lotus-shaped navel of Viṣṇu.[146] Folio 21 mentions for the first time a performance of the Rāmāyaṇa, staged in four acts (sa. *caturaṅka*), on the occasion of the consecration of a shrine (sa. *caitya*) by king Campādeva in the 6th century CE.[147] In the 14th century CE the Caturaṅka Rāmāyaṇa was again staged, on the occasion of the expected birth of Sthitirājamalla's son, Dharmamalladeva (folios 29 and 54). As ten years later Dharmamalladeva's initiation (sa. *vaṭūkaraṇa*) was completed, a second play was staged, the Bālarāmāyaṇa (folios 29 and 57).[148] One last reference to the Rāmāyaṇa occurs on folio 30 where Sthitirājamalla, after having been equated with Buddha and the Lokapālas on folio 29, is also compared to Rāma. The text reads as follows: "Gentle in dealing with his people, enjoying the full cooperation of his good courtiers, he (Sthitirājamalla) is like an incarnation of the virtuous Rāma. He was enthroned as king by the noble king (Jayārjunadeva) himself, just as in the past Rāmachandra put his (Rāvaṇa's) own brother Vibhīṣaṇa on the throne by destroying the great enemy (Rāvaṇa) [...].".[149]
Among the heroes of the Rāmāyaṇa, apart from Rāma himself, Hanumān is especially worshipped in Nepal. He is thought of as a protector as he guards the gate to the old palace at Kathmandu, popularly known as Hanumāndhoka.

The possibly most important South Indian recension of the Mahābhārata is Pampa's Kannada Jain adaption, known as Pampabhārata or Vikramārjuna Vijaya (mid-10th c. CE[150]). Others are Villiputtūr Āḻvār's Tamil Bhārata (~1400 CE[151]) or Kumāra Vyāsa's Bhārata, again in Kannada (15th c. CE[152]). Important North Indian recensions include the Bengali Mahābhāratas of Sañjaya (~15th c. CE)[153] and Kāśīrām Dās (17th c. CE), Sāralā Dās' Oriya Mahābhārata (15th c. CE)[154] and Rāma Sarasvatī's Assamese Mahābhārata (mid-16th c. CE). In the early 17th century CE Mukteśvar (1574-1645 CE), Eknāth's grandson, additionally composed the Ādi, Sabhā, Vana and Virāṭaparvas of the Mahābhārata in Marathi.[155]

The Mahābhārata was translated in Nepali at least in the 15th or 16th century CE. The five Nepali manuscripts collated for the Critical Edition, as a group, are older than any other manuscripts used in the Critical Edition. They are closely related to the Maithili, Bengali and Devanagari manuscripts and in this regard, it is interesting to note that three of the five Maithili manuscripts were collated in Nepal, too. Nepali manuscripts were found only for four of the eighteen *parvas*, namely the Ādi, Sabhā, Sauptika and Strīparva.[156]
References to the Mahābhārata are also found in the Gopālarājavaṃśāvalī. It is stated in the first preserved folio of the manuscript (no 17) that Yudhiṣṭhira's feet were decorated with a garland of crowns of all kings.[157] Also of importance are some of the names the Nepal Valley's rulers bore. Already one of the obscure Gopāla kings may have been named Bhīmagupta.[158] Among the Licchavi kings the charecteristic names of Bhīmadeva, Bhīmārjunadeva and Balārjunadeva occur.[159] The early Mallas bore among others the names of Jayabhīmadeva (13th c. CE) and Jayārjunadeva (14th c. CE).[160]
Among the heroes of the Mahābhārata, apart from Kṛṣṇa, Bhīma is especially worshipped in Nepal. Several temples are dedicated to him. Like also the cult of Hanumān, it is a form of hero-worship and Bhīma is usually portrayed as a warrior.

145 Vajrācārya and Malla 1985, pp. i,ii.
146 ibid., p. 122.
147 ibid., p. 124.
148 ibid., pp. 132, 157, 159.
149 ibid., p. 133, ll. 24ff.
150 Loizeau 2017, p. 28.
151 ibid., p. 27.
152 ibid., p. 28.
153 Paniker 1997, pp. 727ff.
154 ibid., pp. 397ff.
155 ibid., p. 362.
156 Dunham 2007 (1991), pp. 6f.
157 Vajrācārya and Malla 1985, p. 121.
158 ibid.
159 ibid., p. 231 or folios 21, 22 and 23.
160 ibid., p. 233 as well as folios 26 (text 1) and 36f. (text 2) for Jayabhīmadeva and folios 28 (text 1), 50, 54f. and 60 (text 2) for Jayārjunadeva.

3.1.2. The Artists

The cities of Kathmandu, Pāṭan and Bhaktapur owe their artistically beauty to the Newars. They are the chief artisans in the Kathmandu Valley from time immemorial and well trained in painting and working with wood, stone and metal. The extensive reliefs of the Rāmāyaṇa and the Mahābhārata at the Kṛṣṇa Temple attest very well to their artistic skill.

The word Newar (*nevār*) is in all likelihood a variant form of the word *Nepal* and is the prevalent term to designate the indigenous people of the Nepal Valley (Kathmandu Valley), at least since the 17th century CE.[161] According to the 2011 census, 20% of the people in the central hill region which includes the Kathmandu Valley are nowadays Newars.[162] The Newars speak Newari (*nevārī*), a language of the Tibeto-Burman family. Their upper social class seems to have constantly mingled with immigrants, especially from India and Tibet. These immigrants have influenced Newar culture and of course the art of the Newars, too. The Newar society is divided into a Buddhist and a Hindu community, though this distinction is neither clearly defined nor seems to be of too great an importance.[163] The artisan communities, however, belong almost exclusively to the Buddhist section. Among the communies, the expertise is passed down from generation to generation and kept within the family. Frequently, and especially with larger works like the friezes under discussion, a master makes the design and then instructs others what to work on while he himself does his part.

3.1.3. Composition

The reliefs on the lintels have a height of only 14 to 15 cm. Both the narrative friezes, the Rāmāyaṇa and the Mahābhārata, begin on the east side of the temple, slightly offset above its main entrance. They run clockwise around the whole structure until finally the last scene again adjoins to the first one. The reading direction of the story is thus from right to left. The width of the individual scenes varies widely and is above all dependent on the number of the figures represented. Scene 33 of the Rāmāyaṇa frieze, for example, shows only one figure and is accordingly short, whereas scene 165 of the Mahābhārata, with 18 figures, extends across the entire front face of the eastern central pavilion.

Almost always, the individual scenes of both the friezes are clearly separated from one another. For the most part tall trees or other high-growing plants serve as scene dividers. They have a variety of different designs. They might be palm trees with prominent leaf scars (R.sc. 8 et al.) or multi-steemed trees (R.sc. 71/72, Mbh.sc. 78/79 et al.). Frequently, branches or arabesques extend into the image to fill up the otherwise empty space and many are embellished with flowers and fruits. In case of the Mahābhārata frieze, the side walls of a building might also serve as scene dividers. Only in some instances of the Mahābhārata frieze individual scenes are not clearly separated visually, that is where immediately consecutive events are depicted in duplicated chambers under a continuous roofing (Mbh.scs. 93-98, 118/119 et al.). In case of the Rāmāyaṇa frieze, rock formations and side walls can be considered as additional scene dividers where they occur, but the tree is pretty much never missing (R.scs. 6, 50 et al.). Only in one instance a rock formation replaces the tree (R.sc. 61/62) and in one instance a *dharmastambha*, a pillar with a superimposed wheel of the law (R.sc. 25/26). Likewise, in one instance of the Mahābhārata frieze a battle standard serves as scene divider (Mbh.sc. 121). It must be recognised that both, the *dharmastambha* as well as the battle standard, have a symbolic meaning related to the context.

Occasionally, the characters from one scene might visually bear upon the characters of the previous one (R.sc. 19 et al.) but in general, the alignment of the figures additionally helps to divide the scenes. However, where this device is the only one used to separate two courses of action, I have chosen to count the section as one scene only, with two partial image areas (R.scs. 7, 32 et al.). This seemed more logical for in other instances a character might be represented only once for two consecutive acts (R.scs. 12, 71 et al.). According to this counting method, the Rāmāyaṇa frieze consists of 99 scenes, the Mahābhārata frieze of 165.

The figures are predominantly shown in ¾ view. If a character is depicted in upright position, walking or standing, the upper body might be turned towards the viewer to such an extent that it appears to be frontal (Mbh.sc. 17 et al.). Still the way of representation contrasts with *real* frontal depictions (R.sc. 22 et al.) due to a twist of the feet or, in other instances, a lateral viewing

161 Slusser 1982, p. 9.
162 http://unstats.un.org/unsd/demographic/sources/census/2010_phc/Nepal/Nepal-Census-2011-Vol1.pdf, p. 154.
163 Fürer-Haimendorf 1956, pp. 17f.

direction and the position of the hands. Apart from a few exceptional cases, the figures are placed next to each other throughout. Even if they form part of a group the figures generally do not overlap. Exceptions occur where the individuals of a group are not identified by inscription (R.sc. 92, Mbh.scs. 106, 137 et al.). Subsidiary figures, such as charioteers or courtly attendants, might be represented smaller and in some instances the artists thereby create depth (R.scs. 55, 86 et al.). To a certain degree, an action might even take place in the background. That is Kaikeyī supporting Daśaratha's head from behind (R.sc. 18), Hanumān destroying Indrajit's sacrifice (R.sc. 91) and Arjuna taking the bow, partially obscured by a pillar (Mbh.sc. 31). Figures are also depicted smaller if they are located way up in the sky (R.scs. 10, 85). That neither gods nor colossal demons are represented any taller is certainly due to the limited height of the frieze, already completely occupied by the mortals.

The way the characters are dressed is consistent with the dress form that was in favour at the Moghul court in India and also in Nepal, in the 17th and 18th century CE. Male figures wear long, often pleated tail-coats with cummerbund and sash, as well as long, waving cloths around the neck. Kings and princes, as well as other members of the royal family, have crowns of varying shapes and designs. The monkeys have harnesses and platelegs. Other battle heroes wear chestplates, whether engaged in fighting or not. The long cloth around the neck, unsuitable for fighting purposes, is never missing. In case of the Mahābhārata frieze distinctive attributes help to identify the Pāṇḍava brothers (Mbh.scs. 17ff.). The clothing might also help to identify the figures. Most notably, Bhīma's appearance differs from that of his brothers. Strikingly, he is dressed exactly as Duryodhana, Duḥśāsana and other evil-doers of the story as for example Jarāsandha, Śiśupāla or Kīcaka. Moreover, the appearance of the demons (sa. *rākṣasas*) from the Rāmāyaṇa frieze corresponds to Bhīma's appearance. Gitomer focuses attention on Bhīma's "*rākṣasa* nature" which is revealed in acts like the violent murders of Kīcaka and especially of Duḥśāsana and his unfair killing of Duryodhana.[164] Bhīma repeatedly tears his opponents in two. He additionally weds a demoness, Hiḍimbā, and has a *rākṣasa* son, Ghaṭotkaca. As Gitomer points out, on account of adharmic aspects, the murders conducted by Bhīma indeed "look like the work of a rākṣasa" and "place Bhīma in the center of the opposition between brahmans and rākṣasas".[165] The extreme violence in Bhīma's murder of Duḥśāsana is highlighted in later versions of the story. Already in Bhaṭṭa Nārāyaṇa's Sanskrit Veṇīsaṁhāra (~700 CE) he uses Duḥśāsana's blood to dress Draupadī's hair. In Kannada versions the violence is carried to extremes.[166] As pointed out by Loizeau, already in Cōḷa sculpture Bhīma's appearance differs from that of his brothers and in Hoysaḷa sculpture, Bhīma's appearance corresponds to those of the *rākṣasas* from the Rāmāyaṇa[167] – exactly as in case of the Kṛṣṇa Temple's representations. In Nepal, Bhīma's wrathful nature is further emphasised for he is worshipped as Bhairava, Śiva's wrathful form.[168] Numerous representations of Bhīma ripping open Duḥśāsana's chest and pulling out his intestines are found isolated from the narrative context.

The appearance of the figures might change from one scene to the next. Their clothing is not always accurate to the situation but instead provides some information about the character's nature. Rāma is still pictured with crown and armour after being exiled (R.scs. 20ff.) and Arjuna even retains his crown and armour at the *svayaṃvara* contest (Mbh.sc. 28), where he is according to the text, dressed as a Brahmin. Likewise, Sītā and Draupadī might be depicted wearing elegant clothes and jewellery after having entered the woods (R.scs. 20ff., Mbh.sc. 88). Courtly attendants wear elegant clothing too, occasionally even with a turban (R.scs. 71, 99 et al.). The robes of the sages do not necesarily differ from the others but they wear no jewellery. They have their matted hair tied up, hold the sacred scriptures and sometimes also a rosary of *rudrākṣa* seeds (sa. *akṣamālā*), a waterpot (sa. *kamaṇḍalu*) or a staff (sa. *daṇḍa*).

Additional elements indicate the setting. The action takes place either in the open, that is mostly in the woods, or inside a building, usually a palace or an assembly hall. If the first is the case, frequently foliage is placed at the upper margin to fill up the empty space. In some instances curly cloudscapes replace the foliage (R.scs. 75,90f. et al.). Animals enliven the scenery. Birds, monkeys and nature spirits (sa. *yakṣas*) are represented on trees, frequently feeding upon fruits (Mbh.scs. 19, 108,

164 Gitomer 2007 (1991), pp. 296ff.
165 ibid., p. 296.
166 V. infra, p. 188.
167 Loizeau 2017, pp. 437ff.
168 Bühnemann 2013.

151 et al.). Fish and sea monsters (sa. *makaras*) are depicted in the waters (R.scs. 21, 63 et al.). Mountainscapes and rock formations are represented only if the plot so requires (Mbh.sc. 77 et al.).
If an action takes place inside, there need not necessarily be represented any building structures. Sometimes only canopy-like cloths, indicative of a roofing, give this information (Mbh.sc. 49 et al.). These cloths are often tasselled and decorated with blossoms. In one instance only, an event which takes place inside seems to be depicted outside for not even the canopy-like cloths are there (Mbh.sc. 110). By contrast, these cloths might also be depicted outside, mostly to display a royal atmosphere. Whether inside or outside, they are hung over deities too (Mbh.scs. 1, 165 et al.), and might as well be employed to screen a sacred act like for exemple a sacrificial one, a wedding, a coronation or the conveyance of sacred knowledge (R.sc. 8).
Buildings are most of the time reduced to the essential. Frequently they seem to consist of only one room, bounded by two pillars. The roofing might be indicated by the canopy-like cloths already mentioned, but actual roofs appear, too. These roofs are tapered, sometimes multi-tiered and enriched with small superstructures (R.scs. 72, 82, 84, Mbh.scs. 12, 17 et al.). They represent the typical Nepalese architecture. The floor might be raised and covered with a layer (Mbh.scs. 13, 52 et al.). A back-wall is depicted only in one instance (Mbh.sc. 112). Seating furnitures appear continually for they serve a purpose, whereas additional furnishings are never depicted. Likewise, items not necessarily needed occur only rarely. Exceptions are the vessels depicted where sacrifices are performed (R.sc. 4, Mbh.sc. 145 et al.) and those stored underneath a bed (Mbh.scs. 99, 112). Especially in the Mahābhārata frieze, a variable number of additional chambers can be attached to the central compartment. This is done by just lengthening the roof and adding another pillar (Mbh.sc. 51 et al.). As already mentioned, rarely even consecutive events can be joint in this manner. Doors and windows are beautifully designed with air-permeable, latticed patterns (sa. *jāli*). They appear where no view inside the building is given (R.scs. 72, 84 et al.) and rarely might indicate annexed chambers (R.scs. 18, 71).

3.1.4. Master and Student

It is certain that the reliefs forming the narrative friezes were carved into stone not by one person but by a number of artists. Upon closer inspection of the Rāmā-yaṇa and the Mahābhārata friezes, slight differences in the way of representation can be noted. For example, in scenes 73 and 74 of the Rāmāyaṇa frieze mandorlas are drawn around the heads of Rāma and Lakṣmaṇa. These mandorlas appear nowhere else. For no explanation can be found why the mandorla is depicted exclusively here, it is quite certain that these two successive scenes were carved into stone by one and the same person. Another peculiarity of these scenes is that the monkeys depicted have small hairs on the legs. These hairs appear in only a handfull other images on the legs, arms and tails of the monkeys. Specifically, these are the images depicting Sugrīva's coronation (R.sc. 55), the battle between Rāma and Rāvaṇa (R.sc. 92) and finally Rāma's coronation (R.sc. 99). Strikingly, three of these images (R.scs. 55, 74 and 92) also form part of the few examples where an attempt was undertaken to create some sort of perspective. The motivation to try something different indicates that more skilled artisans were at work here, who must have felt attracted to illustrate these important events.

Less good realised on the other hand, are the scenes dealing with Hanumān forming the friendship between Rāma and Sugrīva (R.sc. 51) and Vidyujjihva bringing Rāma's false head (R.sc. 83). In both cases, the figures depicted loose height from left to right. Especially in the first case this seems awkward for it means in effect that Lakṣmaṇa, who only stands on the side, is taller than the other ones actually acting. The undersized figures on the right side are in both cases dominated by branches extending into the image. The same applies to a scene from the Mahābhārata frieze, where Sahadeva is consequently taller than all others (Mbh.sc. 142). Again, we might conclude that these scenes were carved in stone by one and the same person, someone maybe with a less practised hand.

3.1.5. Inscriptions

Inscriptions below the reliefs identify the figures and provide some information about the course of action. The script is Nepālākṣara, the language is classical Newari with strong influences of Sanskrit. Obly the first inscription of the Rāmāyaṇa frieze, with an invocation to Gaṇeśa, is given in pure Sanskrit. An inscription never refers to several scenes at the same time but explains always just the one scene represented above. The width of the text is invariably in accordance with the width of the image. Hence, the inscriptions also serve as additio-nal scene dividers. In a few instances, where the space below the image is not sufficent, the inscription additionally occupies the space above the image (R.scs. 12, 85 et al.).

Almost invariably, every notation applied opens with the symbol १ and closes with a double *daṇḍa*. According to Sircar, it is an auspicious symbol of varying shape that replaces the word *siddham*, found at the beginning of numerous early records. He further states that the symbol might be followed by the auspicious word *svasti*, too, which, in some cases, also stands singly at the beginning of epigraphic records.[169] This is interesting in so far as the first portion of the Kṛṣṇa Temple's consecration inscription, that is the Sanskrit part, opens with the auspicious symbol, whereas the second part in Newari opens with the word *svasti*. Both the auspicious words, *siddham* and *svasti*, might therefore be used to pronounce the auspicious symbol.

Almost all the figures depicted are identified by inscription. Sometimes only the names are given, with an additional one-word description of the scene like *conversation* (R.scs. 2, 3 et al.) or *fight* (R.sc. 34 et al.). In only a few instances, individuals are not identified by inscription and there is thus room for interpretation (Mbh.scs. 137, 148 et al.). The text is in general rather brief and clearly subordinate to the visual narrative.

169 Sircar 1996 (1965), pp. 92ff.

3.2. The Rāmāyaṇa Frieze

The Rāmāyaṇa frieze of the Kṛṣṇa Temple at Pāṭan begins slightly offset above the temple's main entrance and runs clockwise around the whole structure until the last scene again adjoins to the first one. The frieze consists of 99 scenes, covering sections 1 to 6 from the Rāmāyaṇa with a preference for the events from the Araṇya and Yuddhakāṇḍa, as apparent from the adjacent table. The Uttarakāṇḍa is omitted in the pictorial representation.

Section	Number of Scenes
(introductive invocation)	1
1: Bālakāṇḍa	15 (2-16)
2: Ayodhyākāṇḍa	13 (17-29)
3: Araṇyakāṇḍa	20 (30-49)
4: Kiṣkindhākāṇḍa	13 (50-62)
5: Sundarakāṇḍa	11 (63-73)
6: Yuddhakāṇḍa	26 (74-99)
7: Uttarakāṇḍa	0

In the following, every scene will be discussed separately. First of all, the related inscription will be given in Nepālākṣara script along with a transcription and a translation into English. In general, the inscriptions are preserved in a good condition. Some parts are however covered by a grey cement-like material which was used for repairs at some earlier date and in other places syllables, words or rarely even the entire inscription is worn out too much to be legible. The missing parts of the inscription are given in brackets. For the most part, it was no problem to fill these brackets by conclusion. In other instances, I rely on the records of Nutan Sharma from 1993 which were kindly provided by him. It is interesting to note that in some parts the inscription was obviously still in a better condition only 25 years ago. This is most noticeable where at present the figures depicted are worshipped with red powder, flowers, grains of rice and the like (Mbh.sc. 124b et al.).

Although the Nepālākṣara alphabet is related to the Devanāgarī alphabet, they deviate considerably from each other, in the formation of several akṣaras, ligatures and combinations with the vowels e, ai, o and au. Additionally, among others *v* and *b*, *va* and *o*, *l* and *r*, *ṣ* and *kh* as well as *ṣ/ś* and *s* are freely interchangeable in Newari and consonants are doubled after *r* throughout. This has the result that firstly, varying spellings of one and the same word appear, sometimes even immediately after each other (e.g. *mākara/mākala*, R.sc. 75), and secondly, loanwords appear in unfamiliar spellings, like *parbbata* instead of *parvata* or *asavāra* instead of *aśvavāla*. As for the transcription, variant names and variant forms of spelling are maintained where they occur.

For the translation I have used Jørgensen's dictionary and grammar of the classical Newari. Where other sources were needed, this will be referred to in a footnote. For a better understanding, the suffixes that occur are briefly given here. What concerns case endings, the following are used: the instrumental in *-na*, the sociative in *-va*, the genitive in *-yā* (sg.), the dative in *-yāta* (sg.) and the locative in *-yāke* (sg.) for living beings or *-sa* for other nouns. The instrumental takes also the place of the agential. *-yātana* is a rarely used variant of the dative suffix *-yāta* and occurs only in one place (Mbh.sc. 46). If a plural is indicated, almost exclusively the ending *-pani* is used. The plural ending *-to*, which is usually added to Newari words, appears only once (R.sc. 75).

Subsequent to the translation, the related events are given as according to the Critical Edition of the Vālmīki Rāmāyaṇa. I therefore draw upon the English translation of the Baroda edition, published by Goldman from 1984 to 2017. In a further step, each particular image is described. Where divergences from the Critical Edition occur, other possible literary sources are considered. This will hopefully allow to make qualified statements on region-specific influences in the conclusion part.

The Rāmāyaṇa cycle opens with an invocation to Gaṇeśa.

1. १श्री गणपतय नमः॥

śrī Gaṇapataye namaḥ.

Hail to the illustrious lord of the *gaṇas* (Gaṇeśa).

VR: This is an introductive invocation with no direct connection to the text.

Image: Gaṇeśa is represented eight-armed, dancing on two rats. With both his lowest hands he shows the boon-granting gesture (sa. *varadamudrā*) while his uppermost left hand is depicted beneath his trunk. The bowl with sweets (sa. *modakapātra*) which he usually holds is not depicted. With his remaining hands he holds a drum (sa. *ḍamarū*), an elephant goad (sa. *aṅkuśa*), a rosary of *rudrākṣa* seeds (sa. *akṣamālā*), an axe to smash obstacles (sa. *paraśu*) and, if compared to scene 1 of the Mahābhārata frieze, probably a noose (sa. *pāśa*). Gaṇeśa is accompanied by two smaller dancing figures, a male one with crown and trident (sa. *triśūla*) and a female one with her hands raised above her head. They might refer to Śiva and Pārvatī or simply to the semi-divine *gaṇas* who form part of Śiva's retinue and of whom Gaṇeśa was appointed the leader.

Other sources: The elephant-headed god is worshipped as remover of obstacles (sa. *vināyaka*). Hence, he is also giver of success and good luck. An introductive deference to Gaṇeśa is common at all sorts of beginnings, be it the beginning of a religious ceremony, an individual new start or the beginning of a narrative. Tulsīdās' Rāmacaritamānasa for example opens with "I bow in reverence to lord Gaṇeśa [...]."[170] and it is not surprising that pictorial renderings of popular narratives are begun in the same way. A representation of Gaṇeśa also preceeds the Mahābhārata cycle on the first floor and the Kṛṣṇa panel at Nugaḥ in Pāṭan, dated 1700 CE,[171] begins with an invocation to Gaṇeśa, too.

170 Nagar 2014 I, p. 1.

171 Gutschow 2011 II, pp. 650ff.

Bālakāṇḍa: 'Section of the Childhood'

2. १वाल्मिकिमृषिव् नानदव् संवाद॥

Vālmikirṣiva Nāradava saṃbāda.

Conversation of Sage Vālmīki and Nārada.

The first scene actually belonging to the Rāmāyaṇa shows Vālmīki and Nārada in conversation. Nārada is an itinerant Sage who imparts information otherwise only known to the gods. By telling his stories he spreads enlightening wisdom.

VR: At the beginning of the Bālakāṇḍa (ch. 1) Vālmīki asks Nārada if there is a man who is truly virtuous. Nārada then relates an abridged version of Rāma's life story.

Image: Vālmīki and Nārada are depicted sitting on low stools covered with blankets. Both of them have the matted hair tied up in a knot. They have pointed beards and wear simple robes with long cloths cast around neck and shoulders. Vālmīki additionally has a *rudrākṣa* chain, Nārada a sacred thread (sa. *yajñopavīta*). Both of them hold the sacred scriptures in their left hand, while their gesturing right hand indicates the conversational situation.

3. १नानदव् दशनथनाजाव् संवाद॥

Nāradava Daśaratharājāva saṃbāda.

Conversation of Nārada and king Daśaratha.

VR: There is no such event related in the Vālmīki Rāmāyaṇa. According to the text, Nārada, after giving an account of Rāma's life story to Vālmiki, takes his leave and departs for the world of the gods (ch. 2).

Image: Nārada and Daśaratha are sitting on a stone platform with seat cushions. The king, in contrast to the Sage, wears a crown (sa. *mukuṭa*) and earrings. Daśaratha has his palms joined in reverence (sa. *añjalimudrā*). On either side a fly-whisk carrier is depicted. Daśaratha's attendant represents the courtly ambience. He wears a small crown and heavy earrings. Nārada's attendant has a small top knot and no jewellery.

Other sources: It appears that Nārada informs Daśaratha about the plans of the gods. According to the Raṅganātha Rāmāyaṇa, Nārada in likewise manner appears in a later instance to remind Rāma of his divine form.[172]

172 Sarma 1973, p. 107.

/ 4 / 3 / 2 / 1 /

4. १वशिष्ठ॥ १ऋष्यशृङ्गऋषिन चरु साधन याक॥ १दशरथराजा॥ १कौशल्या॥ १कैकयी॥
Vaśiṣṭha. Ṛṣyaśṛṅgarṣina caru sādhana yāka. Daśaratharājā. Kauśalyā. Kaikeyī.
Vaśiṣṭha. Sage Ṛṣyaśṛṅga prepares the *caru*. King Daśaratha. Kauśalyā. Kaikeyī.

VR: The story takes place in Ayodhyā, the capital of the ancient kingdom of Kośala, north of the sacred river Gaṅgā. Ṛṣyaśṛṅga performs a special sacrifice for Daśaratha to perpetuate his family's lineage. According to the text, the king suffers for the lack of a son but his chief minister, Sumantra, relates a tradition that a son will be born through the help of Sage Ṛṣyaśṛṅga (ch. 8). Ṛṣyaśṛṅga is brought to the court where he performs the *putrakāmeṣṭi*, a son-producing sacrifice (ch. 14). At the same time the gods approach Brahmā for the demon king Rāvaṇa perpetually troubles the worlds. In consequence of a boon, Rāvaṇa can be killed only by a human being and Viṣṇu decides to incarnate as the four sons of Daśaratha. From Daśaratha's sacrificial fire then arises a great being of limitless splendour with a golden vessel in his hands (ch. 15). The king accepts the celestial porridge (sa. *pāyasa*) and distributes it among his three wives.

Image: Ṛṣyaśṛṅga is about to perform the sacrifice. According to the inscription a special oblation of grain boiled in milk or butter (sa. *caru*) is prepared. The *caru* is cooked in a pot hung over the sacrificial fire. The liquid continuously pours out from a small hole at the bottom. With a big wooden ladle (sa. *agnihotrahavanī*) the Sage pours the oblation into the fire. He additionally holds a piece of *khadira* wood shaped like a sword (sa. *sphya*) which is used in sacrifices for various purposes. Various vessels are depicted nearby. Vaśiṣṭha, the family priest of the race of Ikṣvāku, represents the many Sages attending the sacrifice. On the right side, Daśaratha is depicted, accompanied by two attendants and two of his wives, Kauśalyā and Kaikeyī. Daśaratha's third wife, Sumitrā, is missing in the representation.

5. १सुमित्रान् चरु नेवो नव १कैकयीन् चरु नव॥ १कौशल्यान् चरु नव १दशरथन् चरु लहिक
Sumitrāna caru nevo nava. Kaikeyīna caru nava. Kauśalyāna caru nava. Daśarathana caru lahika.

a) Daśaratha cares (for his wives) by giving the *caru*. b) Kauśalyā eats the oblation. c) Kaikeyī eats the oblation. d) Sumitrā eats two parts of the oblation.

VR: According to the text Daśaratha gives half the porridge to Kauśalyā. Then he gives a quarter to Sumitrā, an eighth to Kaikeyī and finally, the remaining eighth again to Sumitrā (ch. 15).
Image: Daśaratha is sitting on a cushioned seat. His wives are facing him. In accordance with the text, Kauśalyā and Kaikeyī each have one portion of the porridge on their plates, while Sumitrā has two portions on hers. Still, the distribution of the porridge as represented here, differs from the version told in the Vālmīki Rāmāyaṇa for there is a bird depicted in front of Sumitrā.
Other sources: The bird refers to Eknāth's rendering of the story.[173] In his Bhāvārtha Rāmāyaṇa a bird snatches away the share of the heavenly dish which was intended for Daśaratha's third wife (p. 16f.). In consequence of this, the other queens both hand off a portion of their own share (p. 19f.). The bird is actually the cursed damsel (sa. *apsara*) Suvarcasā who is freed at the touch of the heavenly dish (p. 15f.). Though the depiction of the bird clearly traces back to this story, the version from the Bhāvārtha Rāmāyaṇa also differs from the content of the image. According to Eknāth, the heavenly dish is dispensed by Vaśiṣṭha who gives the first share to Kauśalyā, the second share to Sumitrā and the last share to Kaikeyī (p.15). In consequence, the bird snatches away Kaikeyī's share from her hand (p. 16f.), Kauśalyā and Sumitrā both hand over a part of their share (p. 19f.) and it is ultimately Kaikeyī who eats two portions and gives birth to twins (p. 39), namely Bharata and Śatrughna.

173 Sathe and Vaishampayana 2016, pp. 15ff. Birth of Kaikeyī's twins: ibid, p. 39.

6. १सुमित्राया लक्ष्मणव शत्रुघ्नव बोव॥ १कैकयीया भरत बोव॥ १कौशल्याया रामचन्द्र बोव॥
Sumitrāyā Lakṣmaṇava Śatrughnava bova. Kaikeyīyā Bharata bova. Kauśalyāyā Rāmacandra bova.

a) Rāma is born of Kauśalyā. b) Bharata is born of Kaikeyī.
c) Lakṣmaṇa and Śatrughna are born of Sumitrā.

VR: Kauśalyā gives birth to Rāma who is formed from one half of the incarnate Viṣṇu (ch. 17). Then Bharata, formed from one quarter of Viṣṇu, is born of Kaikeyī. Sumitrā gives birth to the twins Lakṣmaṇa and Śatrughna, who partake of the last quarter of Viṣṇu's glory. Lakṣmaṇa, the elder one, is from the beginning closer to Rāma, while Śatrughna is dearer to Bharata.
Image: The representation is divided in three compartments. The newly born princes are represented in the arms of their mothers. The women are sitting on low pieces of furniture. The outer ones are covered with blankets while the central one resembles a lotus. The scene is framed by two pillars with summons, indicating the royal palace.

7. १विश्वामित्रन् राम लक्ष्मण फोंङाव यंङ॥ १विश्वामित्रन् दशरथयाके राम लक्ष्मण [फो]न॥
Viśvāmitrana Rāma Lakṣmaṇa phoṅāva yaṃṅa. Viśvāmitrana Daśarathayāke Rāma Lakṣmaṇa phona.

a) Viśvāmitra asks Rāma and Lakṣmaṇa of Daśaratha.
b) Viśvāmitra, after asking, leads Rāma and Lakṣmaṇa away.

VR: As the education of the brothers is completed, Viśvāmitra arrives at court (ch. 17). He tells of the demons Mārīca and Subāhu who perpetually obstruct the completion of his sacrifice and he asks Daśaratha to entrust Rāma on him, for only he would be able to overcome them (ch. 18). Rāma is only fifteen years old at that time and Daśaratha at first refuses to give his approval (ch. 19). On the advice of Vaśiṣṭha, however, he finally gives Rāma and Lakṣmaṇa into the keeping of the Sage (chs. 20f.).
Image: The image comprises two acts. On the right side, the conversation between Viśvāmitra and Daśaratha is represented. On the left side, Viśvāmitra, Rāma and Lakṣmaṇa are leaving the court. The princes are wearing crowns and armours, long

/ 8 / 7 / 6 / 5 /

robes with sashes and cloths around their shoulders. Both of them hold bow and arrow. Viśvāmitra has his matted hair tied up, wears simple garments, holds the scriptures and a bundle of *kuśa* grass.

8. १रामचन्द्रयात् विश्वामित्रन् बलातिबला अम्त्र बिव॥ १लक्ष्मण॥
Rāmacandrayāta Viśvāmitrana balātibalā amtra (read: astra) biva. Lakṣmaṇa.
Viśvāmitra gives Rāma the *balātibalā* weapon. Lakṣmaṇa.

VR: The *balātibalā* weapon is actually a pair of sacred formulas (sa. *mantras*), namely *balā* and *atibalā* (ch. 21). Viśvāmitra bestows them on Rāma on the bank of the river Sarayū. Through their recitation he states, Rāma will achieve supernatural powers and become unequaled on earth.
Image: Viśvāmitra is handing over an arrow to Rāma, who holds his hand ready to receive it. It appears that celestial weapons were nothing tangible but rather knowledge of *mantras* which could be invoked on any object. For example, in the Aiṣīkaparva of the Mahābhārata's Sauptikaparva, Aśvatthāmā invokes the celestial Brahmā Weapon on a reed (Mbh. 10.13).[174] In likewise manner, celestial weapons are described in the Rāmāyaṇa as personified master spells that can take on any form at will (R. 1.26.20). Therefore, the arrow in the image probably does not represent the celestial weapon itself but only an object on which Viśvāmitra explains its use. There are to possible reasons why the artist might have chosen an arrow for this object. Firstly, bow and arrow are the weapons most associated with Rāma and secondly, *balā* also means arrow in Newari, especially if used with the classifier *ti*.[175]

detail of scene 5

174 Debroy 2015 (2013): VIII, p. 53.

175 Kölver und Shresthacarya 1994, pp. 135,230.

9. १गाठकानाज़सी वध॥ १नामवद्र॥ १लक्ष्मण॥

Tāḍakārākṣasī vadha. Rāmacandra. Lakṣmaṇa.

Death of the demoness Tāṭakā. Rāma. Lakṣmaṇa.

VR: The demoness Tāṭakā, the mother of Mārīca and Subāhu, is killed by Rāma (ch. 25). Rāma shoots her with an arrow as she is about to hurl herself upon him. Tāṭakā immediately falls to the ground and dies. Fully satisfied, Viśvāmitra thereupon imparts to Rāma many more divine weapons (ch. 26).
Image: Tāṭakā is depicted lying on the ground, with a shaft piercing her chest. Rāma and Lakṣmaṇa still hold their bows bent. Usually, quivers are not depicted. They are to be imagined on the back of the figures. Here, however, a quiver is attached to Rāma's belt.

10. १नामवद्धन सूवाह् वध याक् मानीव् वायथास्त्रन् रुसन पूयकाव छाक॥

and above the image: १लक्ष्मण॥

Rāmacandrana Subāhu vadha yāka Mārīca vāyavyāstrana phasana puyakāva choka.

Rāma kills Subāhu, Mārīca is blown off with the Northwest Weapon, through wind.

above: Lakṣmaṇa.

VR: Having reached the 'Hermitage of the Perfected Being' (sa. *siddhāśrama*) where Vāmana once attained perfection, Viśvāmitra enters a state of consecration (ch. 28). Rāma and Lakṣmaṇa keep vigil over the ascetics' forest and over the sacrifice. On the sixth day, Mārīca and Subāhu show up with their escort (ch. 29). Rāma wounds Mārīca with the Mānava Weapon, according to a previous passage (ch. 26) a jewel of a sword and the favourite weapon of the celestial musicians (sa. *gandharvas*). Mārīca is hurled into the ocean a hundred leagues away. Thereafter, Subāhu is killed with the Agni Weapon while the remaining demons are all slain with the Vāyu Weapon.
Image: Rāma kills Subāhu while Mārīca, depicted in the upper left corner, flings through the air. In contrast to their mother Tāṭakā, Mārīca and Subāhu are depicted with crown and armour. According to the inscription, Mārīca is blown off with the Northwest Weapon which is the Vāyu Weapon, whereas according to the text, the Mānava Weapon is hurled upon Mārīca and the Vāyu Weapon upon the others.

Southern face of the temple (scenes 11 to 34):

11. १विश्वामित्रन [ङो]व् आश्रमस् यज्ञ याक॥

Viśvāmitrana [ṅo]va āśramasa yajña yāka.

Protected, Viśvāmitra performs the sacrifice at the hermitage.

VR: After Rāma has slain the demons (sa. *rākṣasas*) obstructing the sacrifice, Viśvāmitra completes the sacrifice at the sacred hermitage (ch. 29).
Image: The sacrifice is represented in the same way as the *putrakāmeṣṭi* before (sc. 4). The liquid flow is interrupted as Viśvāmitra collects the offering with his ladle to distribute it out over the fire. Viśvāmitra is in the company of another Sage, representing the many Sages of the hermitage (sa. *āśrama*).

12. १नाम् लक्ष्मण् विश्वामित्र् मिथिलानगन वं॥

and above the image: १नामवद्धया गागन थियाव् नाहा ज़ूयाव चाट् आहल्या् माञ ज़ूव॥

a) Rāma Lakṣmaṇa Viśvāmitra Mithilānagara vaṃ.

Rāma, Lakṣmaṇa and Viśvāmitra go to the city Mithilā.

above: b) Rāmacandrayā totena thiyāva rohā juyāva coṅa Āhalyā mokṣa juva.

After coming into contact with Rāma's leg, Ahalyā, who was in the form of stone, is released.

VR: Having accomplished their purpose, Rāma and Lakṣmaṇa set out with Viśvāmitra for Mithilā, in order to attend the sacrifice of king Janaka (ch. 30). On their way they behold a deserted hermitage (ch. 47). Viśvāmitra relates that once Sage Gautama and his consort Ahalyā engaged in austerities there until one day, when the Sage was absent, Indra took on Gautama's appearance and united with Ahalyā. When Gautama found out about this, he cursed Indra to lose his testicles and he cursed Ahalyā to live there for thousands of years, invisible to all beings, until Rāma would set foot in the hermitage. Gautama then abandoned the hermitage. As Rāma enters now, Ahalyā is released from the curse (ch. 48). She is reunited with Gautama. Afterwards Rāma, Lakṣmaṇa and Viśvāmitra proceed to Mithilā.
Image: The image comprises two events. On the right side, Rāma, Lakṣmaṇa and Viśvāmitra set out for Mithilā, the capital of Videha. The same figures are also as-

/ 13 / 12 / 11 / 10 / 9 /

signable to the second event represented here. Rāma has placed his foot on a stone platform from which Ahalyā arises. She makes a reverential gesture (sa. *añjali-mudrā*).

Other sources: It is not stated in the Vālmīki Rāmāyaṇa that Ahalyā turns into stone but she does so in several other renderings. Already the Kamba Rāmāyaṇa mentions Ahalyā's transformation into stone but here, she changes into a stone image of herself.[176] The transformation of Ahalyā into a boulder is a more popular alteration. This version is found in southern Rāmāyaṇa renditions, too, as for example in Telugu versions like Raṅganātha Rāmāyaṇa,[177] Bhāskara Rāmāyaṇa[178] and Mollā Rāmāyaṇa,[179] and in the Kannada Aṣṭottara and Bhāgavata Rāmāyaṇa.[180] The episode is likewise included in medieval northern Rāmāyaṇa renditions like the Kṛttivāsi Rāmāyaṇa,[181] the Rāmacaritamānasa[182] and the Bhāvārtha Rāmāyaṇa.[183] In all these versions Ahalyā becomes either a boulder or a stone platform and is released from the curse as Rāma places his foot on her.

176 Nagar 2008 I, p. 60.
177 Sarma 1973, p. 75.
178 ibid., p. 123.
179 Rao 1984, pp. 59f.
180 ibid.
181 Nagar and Nagar 1997 I, p. 82.
182 Nagar 2014 I, pp. 343f.
183 Sathe and Vaishampayana 2016, p. 107.

detail of scene 13

13. [१नामवद्र]न धनूर्भ्ङ याक॥ १लक्ष्मण॥ १[विश्वामित्र॥]
Rāmacandra dhanurbhaṅga yāka. Lakṣmaṇa. Viśvāmitra.
Rāma breaks the bow. Lakṣmaṇa. Viśvāmitra.

VR: At Mithilā, Viśvāmitra introduces Rāma and Lakṣmaṇa to king Janaka (ch. 49), who tells the story of Sītā (ch. 65). Once, while Janaka was plowing the field she sprang from the earth and he decided to raise her as his daughter. Now, Janaka has resolved to give Sītā in marriage to the one who succeeds in stringing a divine bow of exceeding power, which Śiva had left long ago as a trust in the hands of Janaka's forebear. No-one has yet been able to even lift it. Rāma however strings the bow with ease and by his immeasurable strength, the bow breaks in two (ch. 66).

Image: Rāma is about to draw back his arrow as the bow breaks in two. Lakṣmaṇa and Viśvāmitra are represented out of the thousands who had assembled.

/ 19 / 18 / 17---

14. १सगानीकमृषि॥ १लक्ष्मण॥ १नामवंद्रया[के]् सी[गा...]॥ १[...]
Satānīkarṣi. Lakṣmaṇa. Rāmacandrayāke Sītā [...]. [...]
Sage Satānīka. Lakṣmaṇa. Sītā [is given in marriage] to Rāma. [Vaśiṣṭha.]

VR: Janaka gives Sītā in marriage to Rāma saying: "This daughter of mine, Sītā, shall be your lawful companion in life's duties. Accept her, bless you. Take her hand in yours." (ch. 72.17). Immediately afterwards, Lakṣmaṇa is married to Sītā's sister, Ūrmilā, and Bharata and Śatrughna are married to Janaka's nieces, Māṇḍavī and Śrutakīrtī. The next day, Viśvāmitra takes his leave (ch. 73).
Image: Unfortunately the key part of the inscription is illegible, yet the plot is clear. Rāma and Sītā are facing each other. Lakṣmaṇa and Janaka's family priest, Śatānīka (Śatānanda), are depicted behind Rāma. Another Sage places Sītā's hands in Rāma's. This has to be Vaśiṣṭha, Daśaratha's family priest, for according to the text (VR 2.69. 15ff.) it is he who, with the permission of Viśvāmitra, recites Daśaratha's lineage.

15. १शत्रुघ्न॥ १तनग॥ १दशनथव् नामव् नाप नाक॥ १सीगा॥ १लक्ष्मण॥
Śatrughna. Bharata. Daśarathava Rāmava nāpa rāka. Sītā. Lakṣmaṇa.
Śatrughna. Bharata. Daśaratha and Rāma meet. Sītā. Lakṣmaṇa.

VR: This scene shows Daśaratha's reunion with Rāma. According to the text, they meet prior to the marriage ceremonies, immediately after Daśaratha has arrived at Janaka's court (ch. 68). Perhaps the two scenes have been consciously switched to bring the act of breaking the bow visually closer to the consequential nuptials.
Image: Daśaratha, Bharata and Śatrughna are shown on one side, Rāma, Sītā and Lakṣmaṇa on the other one. Daśaratha is sitting on a low stool covered with a blanket. The royal canopy is indicated by a tasselled cloth, hung above his head. The king shows the gesture of fearlessness (sa. *abhayamudrā*), while all others have their hands joined in reverence (sa. *añjalimudrā*). For some reason, Rāma and Lakṣmaṇa are not wearing an armour in this scene but Lakṣmaṇa retains his bow and quiver.

16. १पनशुनामव् नामवन्द्रव् युद्ध॥ सीगा॥ १लक्ष्मण॥ १दशनथ॥ १तनग॥ १शत्रुघ्न॥
Paraśurāmava Rāmacandrava yuddha. Sītā Lakṣmaṇa Daśaratha Bharata Śatrughna
Fight between Paraśurāma and Rāma. Sītā Lakṣmaṇa Daśaratha Bharata Śatrughna

VR: Together, they all return to Āyodhya (ch. 73). On the way, they behold terrible omens and amidst of an appalling darkness, Paraśurāma appears. He challanges Rāma to manifest his strength by bending another divine bow, which Paraśurāma's grandfather once received from Viṣṇu (ch. 74). Rāma stretches the bow and looses

--------------------------17 / 16 / 15 / 14 /

an arrow but spares Paraśurāma's life because of his brahminhood (ch. 75). Deprived of his power, Paraśurāma withdraws to his retreat on the Mahendra Mountains and the others proceed towards Āyodhya.

Image: Rāma and Paraśurāma are both depicted bending the bow, pointing their arrow towards the sky. Though actually a brahmin, Paraśurāma is wearing a crown.

Ayodhyākāṇḍa: 'Section of Ayodhyā'

17. १वशिष्ठ॥ १शत्रुघ्न॥ १भरत॥ १सुमित्रा॥ १कैकयी॥ १कौशल्या॥ १दशरथन् राजा सारे धक् रामचंद्र् हात॥ सीता॥ १लक्ष्मण॥

Vaśiṣṭha. Śatrughna. Bharata. Sumitrā. Kaikeyī. Kauśalyā. Daśarathana rājā sāre dhaka Rāmacandra hāta. Sītā. Lakṣmaṇa.

Vaśiṣṭha. Śatrughna. Bharata. Sumitrā. Kaikeyī. Kauśalyā. Daśaratha tells Rāma, he would proclaim (him) king. Sītā. Lakṣmaṇa.

VR: On account of Rāma's virtue, and because he himself has grown old, Daśaratha decides to install Rāma as prince regent (ch. 1). The summoned nobles agree and Daśaratha orders the preparations for the installation to be made (chs. 2f.). It is said later that at this stage, Rāma is 25 years old while Sītā has just turned 18 (VR 3.45.10).

Image: Daśaratha sits opposite Rāma. He shows the gesture of fearlessness (sa. *abhayamudrā*). The figures placed behind him almost all repeat this gesture. Rāma, Sītā and Lakṣmaṇa by contrast make a reverential gesture (sa. *añjalimudrā*). The manifold designs of the seating furniture are worth paying attention to. Canopy-like tasselled cloths cover almost the entire length of the image. Bharata and Śatrughna are depicted, too, although according to the text, they had priorly departed to live with Bharata's maternal uncle (ch. 1).

18. १रामचन्द्रन् वनवास् वनेयात दशरथराजायाके आज्ञा फोङ॥ १भरत॥ १शत्रुघ्न॥ १वशिष्ठ॥ १दशरथ दु म [... त]व॥ १कैकयीव् मन्थराव् ख समधान॥

Rāmacandrana vanavāsa vaneyāta Daśaratharājāyāke ājñā phoṅa. Bharata Śatrughna Vaśiṣṭha. Daśaratha du ma [... ta]va. Kaikeyīva Mantharāva kha samadhāra.

a) Kaikeyī and Mantharā's consultation. b) Daśaratha, not being inside [...].
c) Rāma asks king Daśaratha to agree to his exile. Bharata. Śatrughna. Vaśiṣṭha.

VR: Mantharā, Kaikeyī's family servant, convinces her that with Rāma's coronation her own and Bharata's situation would deteriorate (chs. 7ff.). Earlier, Daśaratha had bestowed two boons on Kaikeyī which she calls in now (ch. 10). She demands of Daśaratha firstly, Bharata's consecration and secondly, the banishment of Rāma for fourteen years. Not being able to give his consent, Daśaratha looses consciousness.

Kaikeyī consequently has to inform Rāma herself and he accepts without perturbation (ch. 16).
Image: On the right side of the image, Kaikeyī and Mantharā are conversing. They are depicted inside a building with tapered roof and latticed window. Daśaratha is standing outside, uninvolved in the talk. On the left side, Rāma is bidding farewell to his unconscious father. As described in the text, Rāma pays obeisance to his feet while Daśaratha, overcome with despair, lays insensible on the couch (ch. 16). Kauśalyā and Sumitrā are clearly suffering on account of Rāma's departure, too. They are depicted with inclined heads and with their hands placed on their chests. Right behind, Bharata, Śatrughna and Vaśiṣṭha say farewell. It is surprising that Kaikeyī who is responsible for the king's discomfiture, is apparently upholding him in the image. This might, however, illustrate her eager pressure on Daśaratha to pull himself up and to be true to his word (ch. 12).

19. (previous page) १लक्ष्मणनं सीतानं् आज्ञा फोङ॥
Lakṣmaṇanaṃ Sītānaṃ ājñā phoṅa.
Lakṣmaṇa and Sītā ask leave.

VR: Rāma informs Sītā about his imminent exile (ch. 23). Not willing to be separated from Rāma, Sītā asks permission to accompany him (ch. 24). After a lengthy discussion, Rāma finally acquiesces in her going (ch. 27). Lakṣmaṇa states that he will supply all their needs during exile and obtains permission to encompany Rāma, too (ch. 28).
Image: This scene is visually connected with the previous one for the figures of Sītā and Lakṣmaṇa apply to the kneeling Rāma in scene 18. Both of them are beseeching Rāma with joined palms (sa. *añjalimudrā*).

20. १गुहव् रामचन्द्रव् नाप राक॥ १सीता॥ १लक्ष्मण॥
Guhava Rāmacandrava nāpa rāka. Sītā. Lakṣmaṇa.
Guha and Rāma meet. Sītā. Lakṣmaṇa.

VR: Rāma, Sītā and Lakṣmaṇa put on robes of bark and leave for the woods (chs. 33ff.). Having crossed the boundaries of the kingdom Kośala, they rest on the bank of the Gaṅgā (ch. 44). Guha, the king of that region, offers Rāma hospitality, food, comfortable beds and provender for the horses. Rāma, however, states his duty would oblige him to dwell in the forest as an ascetic, subsisting only on fruit and roots and therefore refuses all the offers, with the only exception of a little forage for the horses (ch. 44).
Image: Rāma, Sītā and Lakṣmaṇa approach from one side, Guha from the other one. The sovereign of the Niṣādas wears a crown and large earrings. He welcomes Rāma with a reverential gesture (sa. *añjalimudrā*). The quiver on his back links him with the Niṣādas, for they are said to practise fishing and hunting as their chief occupation (ch. 78). Interestingly, Tulsīdās even explicitly states that Guha carries his quiver over the back at his encounter with Rāma.[184] It is by contrast surprising that Rāma and Lakṣmaṇa are further on depicted wearing an armour, crown and jewellery but, as already mentioned, the clothing of the figures is often only meant to provide some information about the character's nature in general.

21. १राम् सीता् लक्ष्मण् गंगा पार याक॥
Rāma Sītā Lakṣmaṇa Gaṅgā pāra yāka.
Rāma, Sītā and Lakṣmaṇa cross the Gaṅgā.

VR: Rāma, Sītā and Lakṣmaṇa cross the Gaṅgā with a boat and rowers provided by Guha (ch. 46). Before they embark, Sumantra is sent back to Ayodhyā and Rāma mats his own and Lakṣmaṇa's hair with the sap of the banyan tree.
Image: The river is beautifully pictured, wavy and alive with fish. On its' bank a bird is feeding upon fruits. By this means, the artist illustrates the atmosphere, sights and sounds of the surrounding nature. Only the key persons are depicted inside the boat. Again, the artist chose not to replace the princely crowns with matted hairs.

184 Nagar 2014 II, p. 713.

/ 24 / 23 / 22 / 21 / 20 /

22. १नाम् सीगा् लक्ष्मण् चित्रकूटपर्ब्बगस वंढ॥
Rāma Sītā Lakṣmaṇa Citrakūṭaparbbatasa vaṃṅa.
Rāma, Sītā (and) Lakṣmaṇa having gone up Mount Citrakūṭa.

VR: On the advice of Sage Bharadvāja, Rāma, Sītā and Lakṣmaṇa decide to spend the time of exile at the mountain Citrakūṭa (ch. 49). Citrakūṭa is described as a sacred place of ravishing beauty, abundant with waters and rich in honey, roots and fruit. Rāma, Sītā and Lakṣmaṇa cross the Yamunā and, having reached the slopes of Citrakūṭa, Lakṣmaṇa builds a leaf-thatched hut for the three of them (ch. 50).
Image: Rāma, Sītā and Lakṣmaṇa are depicted on the outskirts of Citrakūṭa. The mountain is represented by means of geometric patterns. Trees, visually dividing the image into three compartments, indicate the glorious landscape.

23. १दशनथनाजा [मृ]त्यु् जुव॥ १कैकयी॥ १कौशल्या॥ १सुमित्रा॥
Daśaratharājā mṛtyu juva. Kaikeyī. Kauśalyā. Sumitrā.
King Daśaratha's death occurs. Kaikeyī. Kauśalyā. Sumitrā.

VR: Sumantra returns to Ayodhyā and reports to the king (ch. 51). Daśaratha dies in consequence of the grief for his son (ch. 58).

Image: Daśaratha lies dead on his couch. A large flowery tasseled cloth is hung above him. Kaikeyī is represented close by, tenderly holding his head. Kauśalyā and Sumitrā are sitting behind her, sunk in deep mourning. Whereas in scene 18 it was possible to suggest an explanation for Kaikeyī's apparently loving care, this time there is no textual basis for this in the Vālmīki Rāmāyaṇa. Quite the contrary, she is held co-responsible for Daśaratha's death as she is denounced by the people and accused by Kauśalyā to have destroyed the house of the Rāghavas (ch. 60). Only Bharadvāja states that Kaikeyī is not at all to blame, having realised that the banishment of Rāma was for a greater good (ch. 86).[185]
Other sources: What Bharadvāja remarks is developed further in Sanskrit retellings like the Adhyātma, Bhuśuṇḍi and Ānanda Rāmāyaṇa.[186] Here, Kaikeyī acts on behalf of the gods. According to the Adhyātma Rāmāyaṇa, Sarasvatī, commanded by Brahmā, instigates Kaikeyī and Mantharā's plot to ensure Rāvaṇa's fall. In the Ānanda Rāmāyaṇa,[187] Kaikeyī approaches Rāma grief-stricken, seized with remorse, and she begs his forgiveness. Rāma comforts her by explaining that it was at his (Viṣṇu's) own instance that Sarasvatī had influenced her mind through Mantharā. The image likewise seems to portrait a Kaikeyī who is not to blame, maybe remorseful and hence taking special care of Daśaratha.

185 Goldman 1986: II, pp. 55ff.
186 Bose 2010, pp. 21ff.
187 Nagar 2006 I, p. 71.

24. (previous page) [...]लि गने धक वंङ॥
[...] li gane dhaka vaṃṅa.
[Bharata, Śatrughna and Vaśiṣṭha] depart in order to call back[188] [Rāma].

VR: Massengers are sent to Rājagṛha, the home of Bharata's grandfather, in order to bring back Bharata and Śatrughna (ch. 62). Bharata deplores his mother's deeds and refuses the throne (chs. 67f.). He decides to bring back Rāma and to repair to the woods himself. Having performed the funeral rites for his father, Bharata sets out with his forces (ch. 77).
Image: Though the inscription is badly damaged, the plot is clear. Bharata sets out in order to seek out Rāma. He is accompanied by Śatrughna and Sage Vaśiṣṭha. They all show the gesture of fearlessness (sa. *abhayamudrā*) indicating that they are leaving with good intent. There might be a reference here to the fear which Lakṣmaṇa expresses as he spots Bharata's army from atop a tree. His first thought is that Bharata has come to slay them (ch. 90).

25. १वशिष्ठ॥ १शत्रुघ्न॥ १भरतन् रामचन्द्र गंङा॥ १सी[ता॥ १लक्ष्मण॥]
Vaśiṣṭha. Śatrughna. Bharatana Rāmacandra gaṃṅā. Sītā. Lakṣmaṇa.
Vaśiṣṭha. Śatrughna. Bharata has stopped Rāma. Sītā. Lakṣmaṇa.

VR: Rāma pacifies Lakṣmaṇa and the brothers meet (chs. 91ff.). Bharata informs Rāma about Daśaratha's death (ch. 95). He asks Rāma to return to Ayodhyā and to receive the royal anointment but Rāma refuses to do so, in deference to the orders both his father and Kaikeyī had given him (ch. 97).
Image: Bharata, Śatrughna and Vaśiṣṭha again show the gesture of fearlessness (sa. *abhayamudrā*). According to the text, Bharata is dressed as an ascetic, too (VR 2.96.27), but he is likewise depicted wearing a crown and large earrings.

188 Kölver und Shresthacarya 1994, p. 289: li-gane, i.a. to call back.

26. १भरतन् रामचन्द्रयाके कुशपादुका काव॥
Bharatana Rāmacandrayāke kuśapādukā kāva.
Bharata takes the *kuśa*-shoes from Rāma.

VR: Bharata considers himself incapable of ruling and protecting the kingdom all by himself (ch. 104). He presents gold-timmed slippers to Rāma. Rāma puts them on, takes them off again and hands them back to Bharata. Thereafter, Bharata places the slippers upon his head and leaves (ch. 105).
Image: Rāma is depicted handing over the sandals to Bharata. According to the text, these slippers are gold-timmed and ornamented, whereas the inscription labels them as *kuśa-shoes*. Rāma is sitting in some sort of building, indicated by an exterior wall with bracket and pedestal. A gecko enlivens the scenery. The scene dividing tree is missing but a pillar with a superimposed wheel of the law (sa. *dharmastambha*) is depicted in front of the exterior wall of the building. This non-recurrent feature most likely points to the righteousness (sa. *dharma*) of the two brothers' deeds. The text explicitly refers to this, too, in the praises sung by the assembled seers: "Fortunate the man who has such sons as these, sons who know and follow the way of righteousness. How envious we are after hearing their conversation." (VR 2.104.3).

27. १भरत् नंदिग्रामस च्वंङ॥
Bharata Nandigrāmasa coṅa.
Bharata stays in Nandigrāma.

VR: Bharata decides that during Rāma's absence, he himself will live outside the city, too (ch. 107). While awaiting Rāma's return he offers the ruling of the kingdom to his sandals. Bharata retires to Nandigrāma where he lives in the guise of an ascetic, with matted hair, dressed in robes of bark.
Image: Bharata is sitting on a low stool. His head rests on the back of his hand. Quiescent-lookink and deep in thought he awaits Rāma's return. He retains his crown but the chain of *rudrākṣa* seeds (sa. *akṣamālā*) around his neck points to the ascetic life he leads henceforth.

/ 29 / 28 / 27 / 26 / 25 /

28. १कुशपादुका राजा सारावृ तव॥ १कैकयी॥ १कौशल्या॥ १सुमित्रा॥

kuśapādukā rājā sārāva tava. Kaikeyī. Kauśalyā. Sumitrā.

The *kuśa*-shoes have been enthroned. Kaikeyī. Kauśalyā. Sumitrā.

VR: Bharata consecrates the slippers (ch. 107). He states that before giving any order, he would always apprise the slippers first. He further states that he would guard them during Rāma's absence and that he would restore kingship to Rāma after his exile by placing the slippers back on his feet.

Image: In accordance with the inscription, the sandals are depicted as *pādukās*, an ancient Indian footwear, a sole with post and stub between the big and second toe. They have cylindrical heels at the front and the back. The sandals are placed on the royal dais and a large canopy is hung above them. An attendant waves a fly-whisk over them while Bharata sits aside. Kaikeyī, Kauśalyā and Sumitrā are sitting inside the royal palace. According to the text, the women remained in Ayodhyā as Bharata set forth for Nandigrāma (ch. 107). They are represented in the same quiescent-looking position in which Bharata was depicted before. Kaikeyī is depicted in an isolated compartment, while Kauśalyā and Sumitrā are sitting together.

29. १अत्रिऋषि॥ १अनुसूयान् सीतायात् अंगराग विव॥ १रामचंद्र॥ १लक्ष्मण॥

Atriṛṣi. Anusūyāna Sītāyāta aṅgarāga biva. Rāmacandra. Lakṣmaṇa.

Sage Atri. Anusūyā offers Sītā scented cosmetics. Rāma. Lakṣmaṇa.

VR: As demons (sa. *rākṣasas*) start to oppress the Sages who took refuge with Rāma, most of them leave the hermitage on Citrakūṭa (ch. 108). Together with Sītā and Lakṣmaṇa, Rāma then leaves, too (ch. 109). They reach the hermitage of Sage Atri his wife Anusūyā. Anusūyā, an illustrious ascetic herself, bestows on Sītā a heavenly garland, beautiful garments, jewellery and a precious salve. With that ointment applied to her body, she states, Sītā will adorn Rāma to the same degree that Śrī adorns Viṣṇu. The next morning, Rāma, Sītā and Lakṣmaṇa enter the vast forest (ch. 111).

Image: Anusūyā is depicted offering Sītā the precious salve. Atri stands behind her. He has an ascetic rod and holds the sacred scriptures.

Aranyakāṇḍa: 'Section of the Forest'

30. १विनाधनाउसव् नामवद्धव् यूद्ध जूल॥ १लक्ष्मण॥ १सीता॥
Virādharākṣasava Rāmacandrava yuddha jula. Lakṣmaṇa. Sītā.
A fight between the demon Virādha and Rāma occurs. Lakṣmaṇa. Sītā.

VR: In the Daṇḍaka Forest, Rāma, Lakṣmaṇa and Sītā behold the demon Virādha, clad in a tiger skin and covered with blood (ch. 2). He holds an iron pike on which three lions, four tigers, two wolves, ten dappled antelopes and the head of an elephant are impaled. Virādha, in reality a celestial musician (sa. *gandharva*) but cursed by Vaiśravaṇa, takes Sītā by force. Rāma strikes him with his arrows but since Brahmā granted him the boon that no weapon on earth could ever kill him, Virādha does not die (ch. 3).
Image: Virādha is already struck by an arrow. The vertical projecting hair reveals him to be a demon. Other demonic features described in the text (ch. 2), his huge size, sunken eyes, huge mouth and the deformed belly, are not depicted. In contrast to the text, Virādha is further depicted wearing a chain armour.

31. १विनाधनाउस वध॥
Virādharākṣasa vadha.
Death of the demon Virādha.

VR: Rāma and Lakṣmaṇa put an end to Virādha as Lakṣmaṇa breaks his left arm and Rāma the right one (ch. 3). The southern Recension and later southern renderings alike, add that Rāma resolves to bury Virādha in a great pit thereafter, in order to ensure his death.[189]
Image: The image again differs from what is described in the Vālmīki Rāmāyaṇa. It appears as if Virādha was killed by Rāma's arrows. One has been driven into his hips, another one into his chest.
Other sources: In the Ānanda Rāmāyaṇa[190] as well as in the Kṛttivāsi Rāmāyaṇa,[191] Rāma kills Virādha with his arrows. The event as related in the Rāmacaritamānasa leaves ample room for interpretation. It reads as follows: "On the way, he [Rāma] met with a demon named Virādha who was thundering aloud in anger at the sight of Rāma. Immediately on his arrival there, Śrī Rāma killed Virādha."[192]

32. १लक्ष्मणन् सूर्प्यनखाया ह्नास (धढ॥ १सूर्प्यनखा सुन्दरीरूपन् रामचंद्रयाक वव॥ १सीता॥ १लक्ष्मण॥
Lakṣmaṇana Sūrppanakhāyā hnāsa dheṅa. Sūrppanakhā sundarīrūpana Rāmacandrayāke vava. Sītā. Lakṣmaṇa.

a) The beautifully disguised Śūrpanakhā comes to Rāma. Sītā. Lakṣmaṇa.
b) Lakṣmaṇa chops off Śūrpanakhā's nose.

VR: Rāma, Sītā and Lakṣmaṇa set forth for Pañcavaṭī, a woodland of flowering trees in the Daṇḍaka Forest (ch. 12). On their way they meet the vulture Jaṭāyu, a nephew of Garuḍa and long time friend of king Daśaratha. He offers to join them and keep watch over Sītā whenever Rāma and Lakṣmaṇa are away (ch. 13). Having reached Pañcavaṭī, Lakṣmaṇa builds a hermitage where they settle down to a happy life (ch. 14). One day, Śūrpaṇakhā, the sister of the demon king Rāvaṇa, chances to pass by and immediately falls in love with Rāma (ch. 16). As she rushes to devour Sītā, Lakṣmaṇa cuts off her ears and nose (ch. 17).
Image: Śūrpaṇakhā approaches Rāma in a beautiful guise. According to the Vālmīki Rāmāyaṇa by contrast, Śūrpaṇakhā approaches Rāma in her true repelling nature, old and haggard, misshapen and potbellied, with copper hair and beady eyes (ch. 16). On the left side of the image, Lakṣmaṇa cuts off Śūrpaṇakhā's nose. According to the text, he acts in a rage, using a sword (ch. 17). The image, however, shows Śūrpaṇakhā kneeling before him as he carefully cuts off her nose with a knife-like weapon.
Other sources: Śūrpaṇakhā assumes a beautiful guise in numerous northern and southern renderings alike. She assumes a beautiful form already in the Kamba Rāmāyaṇa[193] and likewise takes to a charming form in the Ānanda Rāmāyaṇa.[194] In the Kṛtti-

189 Goldman 1991: III, note to 3.3.16 and Nagar 2008 I, p. 269.
190 Nagar 2006 I, p. 74.
191 Nagar and Nagar 1997 I, pp. 154f.

192 Nagar 2014 II, p. 1082.
193 Nagar 2008 I, p. 289.
194 Nagar 2006 I, p. 76.

/ 33 / 32 / 31 / 30 /

vāsi Rāmāyaṇa she takes to the beautiful form of Rati, Kāma's spouse,[195] and she assumes a beautiful form, too, in the Rāmacaritamānasa[196] and in the Bhāvārtha Rāmāyaṇa.[197] Only as Śūrpaṇakhā rushes at the exiled, the demoness reveals her true horrible form. The weapon Lakṣmaṇa uses to disfigure Śūrpaṇakhā varies in the individual texts. The representation matches with the version from the Kamba Rāmāyaṇa where Lakṣmaṇa pulls Śūrpaṇakhā by the hair, throws her over the ground and then cuts off her nose and ears with his dagger.[198] According to the Kṛttibāsi Rāmāyaṇa, Lakṣmaṇa shoots off Śūrpaṇakhā's nose and ears with an arrow.[199] He likewise uses an arrow to cut off her nose and ears (as well as her lips and breasts) in the Ānanda Rāmāyaṇa.[200] The weapon is not specified in the Rāmacaritamānasa.[201]

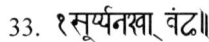

detail of scene32

33. १सूर्प्यनखा_वंढ॥

Sūrppanakhā vaṃṅa.
Sūrpanakhā departs.

VR: Śūrpaṇakhā utters a terrible cry and, mutilated and blood-spattered, she leaves (ch. 17).
Image: Śūrpaṇakhā covers her mutilated face with her hand as she walks away.

195 Nagar and Nagar 1997 I, p. 160.
196 Nagar 2014 II, p. 1104.
197 Sathe and Vaishampayana 2016, p. 376.
198 Nagar 2008 I, p. 296.
199 Nagar and Nagar 1997 I, p. 162.
200 Nagar 2006 I, p. 77.
201 Nagar 2014 II, p. 1106.f

/ 35 / 34 /

34. १त्रिशिरा॥ १दूषण॥ १खर॥ १युद्ध॥ १रामचन्द्र॥ १लक्ष्मण॥ १सीता॥
Triśirā. Dūṣaṇa. Khara. yuddha. Rāmacandra. Lakṣmaṇa. Sītā.
Triśiras. Dūṣaṇa. Khara. Fight. Rāma. Lakṣmaṇa. Sītā.

VR: Śūrpaṇakhā complains to her brothers Khara and Dūṣaṇa, famed for their martial qualities (ch. 17). Khara sends fourteen powerful demons to kill Rāma and Lakṣmaṇa but Rāma slays them all (chs. 18f.). Śūrpaṇakhā then urges Khara to fight himself (ch. 20). Khara attacks with Dūṣaṇa and 14,000 dreadful demons (ch. 21).
Image: Depicted are Khara, Dūṣaṇa and the general Triśiras. As the name indicates, Triśiras is a three-headed demon, but he is depicted with only one head. Still, all three of them have the vertical projecting hair and demoniac facial traits. Lakṣmaṇa is depicted fighting along with Rāma although according to the text, he withdrew with Sītā to an inaccessible mountain cave prior to the attack (ch. 23).
Other sources: The Bhāvārtha Rāmāyaṇa is the only text according to which Sītā and Lakṣmaṇa are present during Khara's attack.[202] Eknāth even states that it is generally believed that both of them withdrew to a cave but that his version differs in that Rāma is not afraid of the demons and, being certain of victory, has no reason to hide Sītā. Anyway, according to the Bhāvārtha Rāmāyaṇa too, Rāma slays the demons alone.

202 Sathe and Vaishampayana 2016, p. 384.

Western face of the temple (scenes 35 to 62):

35. १त्रिशिरा् वध॥ १दूषण् वध॥ १खर् वध॥
Triśirā vadha. Dūṣaṇa vadha. Khara vadha.
Death of Triśiras. Death of Dūṣaṇa. Death of Khara.

VR: According to the Vālmīki Rāmāyaṇa, Rāma first slays Dūṣaṇa (ch. 25). As Rāma cuts off both his arms, Dūṣaṇa sinks to the earth and succumbs to his injuries. Thereafter Rāma destroys the entire demon host. Only Khara and Triśiras survive. As Triśiras engages Rāma in combat, Rāma cuts off his three heads with his shafts (ch. 26). Lastly Khara rushes on Rāma (ch. 27). Rāma takes up a fiery arrow, strikes Khara in the chest and the demon is consumed by the flames (ch. 29).
Image: The image shows them either all die simoultaneously or in a different order. From left to right first Khara is depicted lying dead on the ground, then Dūṣaṇa and lastly Triśiras.
Other sources: The three of them die simultaneously according to the Ānanda Rāmāyaṇa[203] and the Rāmacaritamānasa.[204] In both texts, Rāma uses the power of illusion. According to the Ānanda Rāmāyaṇa, he appears before the demons with 14,000 bodies and fights with each of them. According to the Rāmacaritamānasa, Rā-

203 Nagar 2006 I, pp. 77f.
204 Nagar 2014 II, p. 1116.

/ 37 / 36 /

ma turns all 14,000 demons, including Khara, Dūṣaṇa and Triśiras, into his own form. In consequence, the demons rush at each other.

36. १सूर्प्यनखान् ह्नास (धढ धक् नावणयाकं ह्लाक॥ १मन्धायनी॥
Sūrppanakhāna hnāsa dhena dhaka Rāvaṇayāke hlāka. Mandodarī.
Śūrpaṇakhā talks to Rāvaṇa, saying her nose was chopped off. Mandodarī.

VR: Śūrpaṇakhā now approaches her eldest brother, Rāvaṇa, the ten-headed king of Laṅkā (ch. 30). She tells him about her mutilation and about the slaying of Khara and Dūṣaṇa. As she further tells him about the beautiful Sītā, Rāvaṇa decides to slay Rāma and Lakṣmaṇa and to take Sītā as his wife (chs. 32f.).
Image: Rāvaṇa and Śūrpaṇakhā are depicted in conversation. Rāvaṇa is sitting on his canopied throne and looks towards his sister who still covers her mutilated face with her hand. On the right side, Mandodarī, Rāvaṇa's favourite queen, is depicted, together with a fly-whisk bearer. It is the first time here that Rāvaṇa is pictured. His appearance differs significantly from those of the other demons. In accordance with the text, he is depicted with ten heads and twenty arms but surprisingly, he has only nine human heads whilst his tenth and uppermost head is that of a horse or a donkey. The way of representing Rāvaṇa remains unaltered for the further course of the pictorial representation of the epic. With his hands Rāvaṇa holds various attributes, mostly weapons, the most prominent one being his sword.

detail of scene 37: Rāvaṇa with horse head

Other sources: Although it is in general nothing unusual that demons have animal heads, no Indian version of the epic is known according to which Rāvaṇa has the head of a horse or a donkey. Rāvaṇa's horse head is, however, well known in the Tibetan versions of the Rāmāyaṇa.[205] The oldest known version was found at Dunhuang and was either written there during the Tibetan occupation from 787 to 848 CE or brought there from central Tibet during this occupation. Rāvaṇa's horse head is even of special importance for the Tibetan story. At the beginning, Rāvaṇa obtains from Śiva the boon of immortality, as long as his horse head is not cut off. In the end, Rāvaṇa consequently dies as Rāma slices it off. De Jong mentions other Tibetan versions of the story, dating from the 13th to 16th century CE which are similar to the Dunhuang version and include the same details about Rāvaṇa's tenth head.

205 De Jong 1983, pp. 163ff.

37. (previous page) [१]नावणया सखाय॥ १नावणव् मानीचदैत्यव् संवाद॥
Rāvaṇayā sakhāya. Rāvaṇava Mārīcadaityava saṃbāda.
A companion of Rāvaṇa. Conversation of Rāvaṇa and the demon Mārīca.

VR: Ever since Mārīca was defeated by Rāma, out of fear of Rāma, he lives the life of an ascetic (chs. 36f.). Rāvaṇa now seeks his help (ch. 34). He calls on Mārīca to assume the form of a golden deer in order to entice Rāma and Lakṣmaṇa away from Sītā. He states that then, he could easily carry Sītā off. Also, it would be possible to kill Rāma when he suffers on account of the seperation from his beloved wife. Mārīca tries to dissuade Rāvaṇa from his plans repeatedly, but in vain.
Image: Rāvaṇa is accompanied by a demoniac attendant. Mārīca has the typical vertical projecting hair, too, but at the same time his ascetic nature is emphasised. In his outstretched hand he holds a rosary of *rudrākṣa* seeds (sa. *akṣamālā*) and he wears an additional chain of *rudrākṣa* seeds around his neck. Mārīca sits on a stone platform admidst trees. They have a variety of blossoms and birds are squatting on their branches. By this means, the quaint landscape is beautifully pictured.

38. १मानीच् लूँचला जूयाव् नामया भन वव॥ १सीतान् लूँचना केंढा॥ १लक्ष्मण॥
Mārīca lũcalā juyāva Rāmayā bhana vava.[206] Sītāna lũcarā keṅā. Lakṣmaṇa.
Mārīca turns into a golden deer and goes to Rāma. Sītā is pointing out the golden deer. Lakṣmaṇa.

VR: Mārīca assumes the form of a deer of exceeding beauty (ch. 40). It has a golden fur dappled with silver spots, gemmed horns and several of its body parts are gleaming with the colours of precious stones and flowers. In his disguise he seeks to capture Sītā's glances. As she beholds the magnificent deer, she begs Rāma to capture it for her (ch. 41).
Image: Rāma, Sītā and Lakṣmaṇa are sitting on a stone platform, surrounded by trees. Sītā points the deer out to Rāma.

206 According to Jørgensen (1941, p. 89) the postposition for *going to s.b.* is *-yā bhin vayāva* but in all cases of the Kṛṣṇa temple's inscriptions it is *-yā bhana vane*. The formulation clearly derives from the Sanskrit *bhāna* (n.) - *perception*, so that literally translated the formulation means *going into the perception of s.b.*

39. १लूँचला् वसे वं॥ १नामचन्द्रन् लूँचला लिक॥
lũcalā bese vaṃ. Rāmacandrana lũcalā lika.
The golden deer flees. Rāmacandra pursues the golden deer.

VR: As Lakṣmaṇa states that the golden deer is certainly none other than Mārīca, Rāma resolves to slay him (ch. 41). He instructs Lakṣmaṇa to keep watch over Sītā and sets off. The deer appears suddenly here and suddenly there and entices Rāma far away from the hermitage (ch. 42). Finally, Rāma pierces Mārīca's heart with a flaming arrow. On the point of death, Mārīca cries for help in Rāma's own voice in order to additionally entice Lakṣmaṇa away from the hermitage.
Image: Rāma has already struck the deer with two arrows. Depicted might be the moment before Mārīca utters the cry for help.

40. १लक्ष्मण् नामया भन वं॥ १सीता् लक्ष्मणन् पयाव चोढ॥
Lakṣmaṇa Rāmayā bhana vaṃ. Sītā Lakṣmaṇana peyāva coṅa.
a) Sītā is kept safe by Lakṣmaṇa.
b) Lakṣmaṇa goes to Rāma.

VR: As Sītā hears Rāma's voice, she urges Lakṣmaṇa to go to Rāma's assistance (ch. 43). At first, Lakṣmaṇa refuses to leave but being entreated repeatedly by Sītā, he finally gives in. Unwillingly, he sets forth towards Rāma.
Image: Sītā is placed in a twofold ring instead of the leaf hut. Lakṣmaṇa is depicted twice. On the right side he is keeping watch over Sītā. On the left side, he walks away, looking back at her, as described in the text (VR 3.43.37).
Other sources: It is evident that the twofold ring around Sītā symbolises the protection provided by Lakṣmaṇa. Various versions of the epic, southern and northern ones alike, attest to the persistence of this protection after Lakṣmaṇa has left. In the Telugu Raṅganātha Rāmāyaṇa, Lakṣmaṇa draws seven protective lines not to be crossed by Sītā before he leaves.[207] In several other Telugu versions and in the Kannada Aṣṭottara Rāmāyaṇa as well, Lakṣmaṇa draws seven lines around Sītā, too.[208] The motive reappears in the Ānanda Rāmāyaṇa, where Lakṣmaṇa uses his bow to

207 Sarma 1973, p. 90.
208 Rao 1984, pp. 68ff.

/ 40 / 39 / 38 /

draw one line around Sītā and one line around Pañcavaṭī.[209] In the Kṛttivāsi Rāmāyaṇa[210] and in the Bhāvārtha Rāmāyaṇa alike,[211] he draws one line around the cottage. According to the Rāmacaritamānasa by contrast, Lakṣmaṇa entrusts the care of Sītā to the gods of the forest and the directions.[212]

41. [...] १लॅूचलारूप तोरताव् मारीच वध॥ १रामचंद्र॥

[...]. lũcalārūpa toratāva Mārīca vadha. Rāmacaṃndra.

a) Abandoning the form of the golden deer Mārīca dies. Rāma.

b) [...]

VR: As Rāma pierces Mārīca's heart with the flaming arrow, Mārīca gives up his illusory form and again takes on his true demoniac shape (ch. 42). Meanwhile, Lakṣmaṇa proceeds towards Rāma and Rāvaṇa approaches Sītā in the guise of a wandering mendicant (ch. 44). Sītā welcomes him and honours him with the acts of hospitality but as he asks her to become his wife, she rejects him (chs. 45f.). Rāvaṇa thereupon reveals his true form (ch. 47).

Image: On the right side of the image, Mārīca is depicted, having reassumed his true form. He lies on the ground, his chest pierced with an arrow. The left part of this image is badly damaged and the related inscription no longer extant. Still, the content

/ 41 /

is clear. Rāvaṇa is seen approaching Sītā in the guise of a mendicant, with matted hair, carrying a waterpot (sa. *kamaṇḍalu*). As already in the previous scene, Sītā is placed inside a protective magical ring. She faces away from Rāvaṇa as he breaks the circle by grabbing her hand.

Other sources: Sarma and Rao give no details on how Rāvaṇa breaks the circle or else overcomes the obstacle in the southern versions. They only state that he abducts her as she falls unconscious, having seen his real form.[213] According to the Ānanda Rāmayāṇa,[214] the Kṛttivāsa Rāmāyaṇa[215] and the Bhāvārtha Rāmāyaṇa,[216] Rāvaṇa lures Sītā out of the circle with a trick. As she brings alms for the mendicant, Rāvaṇa forcibly takes her hand.

209 Nagar 2006 I, p. 80.
210 Nagar and Nagar 1997 I, p. 172.
211 Sathe and Vaishampayana 2016, p. 411.
212 Nagar 2014 II, pp. 1130f.

213 Sarma 1973, p. 90 and Rao 1984, pp. 68ff.
214 Nagar 2006 I, p. 81.
215 Nagar and Nagar 1997 I, p. 173.
216 Sathe and Vaishampayana 2016, p. 418.

42. १नावधन् सीगा् हनध याद्वाव् यंद॥

Rāvaṇana Sītā haraṇa yāṅāva yaṃṅa.

Rāvaṇa abducts Sītā and takes her away.

VR: Rāvaṇa seizes Sītā by her hair and by her thighs (ch. 47). Instantly, Rāvaṇa's unearthly chariot appears, fashioned by magic, with wheels of gold and harnessed with donkeys. Rāvaṇa presses Sītā to his chest, ascends with her and takes her away.
Image: Rāvaṇa is depicted on his chariot, in his true demoniac form. As described in the text, he clasps the overpowered Sītā to his chest. The donkeys and the chariot wheels are not depicted. As the heavenly chariot takes off, clouds of dust whirl up.

43. १नामचंद्रव् लक्ष्मधव् नाप लाक्

Rāmacandrava Lakṣmaṇava nāpa lāka

Rāma and Lakṣmaṇa meet.

VR: After Rāma has slain Mārīca, Rāma quickly starts back (ch. 55). On the way he sees terrible portents. Then, Rāma catches sight of Lakṣmaṇa. As the two of them meet, Rāma rebukes Lakṣmaṇa for having left Sītā alone.
Image: Depicted is the moment Rāma and Lakṣmaṇa meet. Rāma approaches from one side, Lakṣmaṇa from the other one.

44. १ऊटायू् मूर्छा ज़ूव॥ १ऊटायूमंगलव् नावधव् यूद्ध॥

Jaṭāyu mūrchā juva. Jaṭāyujhaṅgalava Rāvaṇava yuddha.

a) Fight between the bird Jaṭāyu and Rāvaṇa.

b) Jaṭāyu faints.

VR: From deep in sleep, Jaṭāyu hears Sītā's cry (ch. 48). She tells him to inform Rāma and Lakṣmaṇa but Jaṭāyu decides to fight himself (ch. 49). He destroys Rāvaṇa's chariot and weapons. Then, he hurls himself violently upon Rāvaṇa's back wounding him severely. In rage, Rāvaṇa casts Sītā aside. With his sword he cuts off Jaṭāyu's wings, feet and flanks and the vulture falls to the earth, at the point of death. Rāvaṇa again lays hold of Sītā and rapidly flies with her to Laṅkā, the capital of his kingdom (chs. 50ff.).

Image: Rāvaṇa is again depicted on his heavenly chariot. Jaṭāyu is represented twice. Above, Rāvaṇa is about to cut off his wings as he attacks from the air. Below, he is lying on the ground, seriously injured. Srikingly, Jaṭāyu retains his wings and feet in the image.

45. १नामया् लक्ष्मधया् वैनाग्य॥

Rāmayā Lakṣmaṇayā vairāgya.

Rāma and Lakṣmaṇa's apathy.

VR: Rāma and Lakṣmaṇa find the hermitage deserted (ch. 58). Rāma searches Sītā everywhere without success. Overcome by anxiety and anguish he falls into despair (ch. 59).
Image: The image shows Rāma and Lakṣmaṇa. Both of them are sunk in an abyss of grief. They lean onto their bows, not knowing what to do further.

46. १ऊटायूसिक् नामन् लंष [गा]नका॥

and above the image: १लक्ष्मध॥

Jaṭāyusika Rāmana laṃṣa tonakā.

Rāma has water offered to Jaṭāyu's dead body (lit. 'causes to drink').

above: Lakṣmaṇa

VR: Inspired with courage by Lakṣmaṇa, Rāma attempts another search for Sītā (ch. 59). Suddenly he beholds Jaṭāyu, lying on the earth and covered with blood (ch. 63). Jaṭāyu tells him of Sītā's abduction by Rāvaṇa and passes away (ch. 64). Rāma and Lakṣmaṇa construct a pyre for Jaṭāyu and perform the funeral rites. Among others, they go down to the Godāvarī river and pour the funeral libation (sa. *udaka*, presentation of water to the deceased).
Image: Jaṭāyu is depicted on the funeral pyre, erected by Rāma and Lakṣmaṇa. In accordance with the text, Rāma offers water to him.

/ 48 / 47 / 46 / 45 / 44 / 43 / 42 /

47. [१]कवंधव् नामचंद्रव् यूद्ध॥ १लक्ष्म[ण]॥
Kabandhava Rāmacandrava yuddha. Lakṣmaṇa.
Fight between Kabandha and Rāma. Lakṣmaṇa.

VR: Rāma and Lakṣmaṇa continue to search the forest in quest of Sītā (ch. 65). They come upon the demon Kabandha, a headless titan with his face set in his belly. He has massive arms, each one of them a league in length. Kabandha lives on everything that his long arms can seize hold of. After having fallen into Kabandha's arms, Rāma and Lakṣmaṇa cut them off with their swords (ch. 66).
Image: Again, the representation of the demon is not in accordance with the characteristics given in the text. However, his figure is somehow individualised. The forms and proportions of Kabandha's body parts are improper and the whole figure seems a bit odd. He is pot-bellied but the face is not shown. Kabandha is depicted without the typical demonic vertical projecting hair. On the other hand, the far too small head gives him a colossal appearance. Rāma and Lakṣmaṇa are fighting with bow and arrow though according to the text, it does not come to that.

48. १कवन्ध् वध॥
Kabandha vadha.
Death of Kabandha.

VR: Kabandha succumbs to his wounds. Once, he was endowed with a beautiful form but having incurred the wrath of a great seer, he was cursed to retain the ferocious form described before (ch. 67). In consequence of his encounter with Rāma, Kabandha is released. As he raises up from the funeral pyre to attain heaven, he advises Rāma to enter into alliance with Sugrīva (ch. 68).
Image: In contrast to the text, Kabandha is depicted lying on the ground, struck by an arrow.
Other sources: The whole Kabandha episode rather points to a retelling like Tulsīdās' Rāmacaritamānasa, wherein neither physical abnormities nor the killing method are specified.[217]

217 Nagar 2014 II, pp. 1145f.

/ 51 / 50 / 49 /

49. १शवरीव् रामचंद्रव् संवाद॥ १लक्ष्मण॥
Śabarīva Rāmacandrava saṃbāda. Lakṣmaṇa.
Conversation between Śabarī and Rāma. Lakṣmaṇa.

VR: On their way Rāma and Lakṣmaṇa behold the hermitage of Śabarī, an aged female ascetic (ch. 70). Having met Rāma, she acquires perfection. She immolates herself in fire and ascends to the highest imperishable worlds.
Image: Rāma and Śabarī are greeting each other. At the same time, Rāma looks back at Lakṣmaṇa who, as according to the text (VR 3.70.25), makes a gesture to support Rāma in giving Śabarī leave to go.

Kiṣkindhākāṇḍa: 'Section of Kiṣkindhā'

50. १ऋष्यमूकपर्ब्बत॥ १ऋष्यमूकपर्ब्बतस् हनूमन्तव् राम् लक्ष्मणव् नाप लाक॥
Ṛṣyamūkaparbbata. Ṛṣyamūkaparbbatasa Hanumantava Rāma Lakṣmaṇava nāpa lāka.
a) At the mountain Ṛṣyamūka Hanumān meets with Rāma and Lakṣmaṇa.
b) The mountain Ṛṣyamūka.

VR: Kiṣkindhā is ruled by the monkey king Vālin. His younger brother, Sugrīva, once crowned himself king on the assumption that Vālin had been killed by the demon Māyāvin. As Vālin later returned victoriously, he banished Sugrīva who thereupon withdrew to the Ṛṣyamūka mountain. As Rāma and Lakṣmaṇa draw closer to Ṛṣyamūka, Sugrīva beholds them (chs. 1f.). He fears that they could be sent by Vālin but Hanumān reasons with him. He approaches Rāma and Lakṣmaṇa in the guise of a mendicant (ch. 3). After Lakṣmaṇa has related their story, Hanumān leads them to Sugrīva (ch. 4).
Image: Rāma, Lakṣmaṇa and Hanumān are depicted on the slopes of the mountain. All three show the gesture of fearlessness (sa. *abhayamudrā*). In contrast to the text, Hanumān is represented in his own shape. The mountain is pictured with geometric patterns in the foreground, while its peaks in the background frame the depicted figures. Attached to this scene is another beautiful representation of the Ṛṣyamūka mountain with trees and with wild animals living on it.

51. १लक्ष्मण॥ १रामचन्द्रव् सुग्रीवव् हनूमन्तन् त्वाय चिनका॥
Lakṣmaṇa. Rāmacandrava Sugrīvava Hanumantana tvāya cinakā.
Lakṣmaṇa. Hanumān ritually forms the friendship between Rāma and Sugrīva.

VR: Sugrīva is freed from anxiety and feels honoured to be asked for friendship (ch. 5). Rāma receives Sugrīva's hand and Hanumān places a fire between the two of them. By reverently circling the fire, Rāma and Sugrīva enter into alliance. Sugrīva promises that he would help Rāma bring back Sītā and Rāma in turn promises to slay Vālin (chs. 6ff.).
Image: Hanumān forms the friendship between Rāma and Sugrīva by bringing together their hands. The fire is not depicted. Once again, Rāma and Lakṣmaṇa are

/ 54 / 53 / 52 /

depicted with bare torsos and, presumably on account of the sanctity of the act, Rāma is not wearing any weapons. Anyway, the exiled princes retain their crowns and jewellery and from scene 56 onwards they also regain their armours.

52. १वारिव् सुग्रीवव् युद्ध॥ १रामचन्द्रन् वारि चिनालपे म फयाव् वला जुको दोयाव् चो[ङ॥]
and above the image: १लक्ष्मण॥

Vāriva Sugrīvava yuddha. Rāmacandrana Vāri cinālape ma phayāva valā juko doyāva coṅa.
Fight between Vālin and Sugrīva. Rāma is not able to recognise Vālin and the arrow only rests on the bow.
above: Lakṣmaṇa.

VR: Rāma, Lakṣmaṇa and Sugrīva start out for Kiṣkindhā (ch. 12). From a dense wood close to the city Sugrīva challenges his brother by uttering a deep roar. As Vālin hears this clamour he rushes out and a tumultuous battle ensues. Since Rāma is not able to distinguish Vālin from Sugrīva, he does not dare to discharge his deadly arrow. Sugrīva is overcome by Vālin and again takes refuge at Ṛṣyamūka.
Image: In accordance with the text, Vālin and Sugrīva strike each other with their fists and palms only (VR 4.12.18). The monkeys are wearing loincloths with long sashes, platelegs and chest harnesses. Rāma watches them from a distance. He holds his bow stretched without loosing the shaft.

53. १पुनर्व्वार् वारिव् सुग्रीवव् युद्ध॥ १रामचन्द्रन् वारि् वलान ह्ङ्याक॥ १लक्ष्मण॥
punarvvāra Vāriva Sugrīvava yuddha. Rāmacandrana Vāri valāna hṅyāka. Lakṣmaṇa.
Again, fight between Vālin and Sugrīva. Rāma hits Vālin with an arrow. Lakṣmaṇa.

VR: Rāma asks Sugrīva to challenge his brother again (ch. 12). Lakṣmaṇa places a garland of *gaja* flowers around Sugrīva's neck that would help Rāma to recognise Sugrīva whilst engaged in combat. Then, Sugrīva again utters a dreadful roar (ch. 14). Almost, Vālin overcomes Sugrīva again but then Rāma looses his arrow at Vālin's chest (ch. 16).
Image: Vālin and Sugrīva are again depicted in single combat but this time Sugrīva wears the flower garland. From a distance Rāma shoots his deadly arrow. The arrow is depicted twice. Firstly, on Rāma's arrow and secondly, having hit Vālin's chest.

54. १ताराया् वैराग्य॥ १वारि् वध॥
Tārāyā vairāgya. Vāri vadha.
Tārā's apathy. Death of Vālin.

VR: Mortally wounded, Vālin reproaches Rāma (ch. 17). Later however, he relents (ch. 18). He asks Rāma and Sugrīva to look after his son, Aṅgada, and gives up his life (ch. 22).
Image: Vālin is depicted lying on the ground, struck down by Rāma's arrow. Vālin's chief queen, Tārā, is represented close by, wiping off her tears.

/ 58 / 57 / 56 / 55 /

55. १किस्किं धास् सुग्रीव राजा जुव॥ १तारा॥
Kiskindhāsa Sugrīva rājā juva. Tārā.
In Kiṣkindhā Sugrīva becomes king. Tārā.

VR: After Vālin's death Sugrīva regains the kingdom and his consort, Rumā (ch. 25). In accordance with the tradition, pure, auspicious water is poured over Sugrīva in the course of the coronation ceremony. Aṅgada is installed as heir apparent and the widowed Tārā becomes a queen to Sugrīva, too. Image: Sugrīva and Tārā are sitting under the royal canopy. Represented is not the coronation ceremony itself but an associated rendering of homage. However, the goblet used for the consecration with water is placed next to Sugrīva. On the left side of the image, an attendant carrying a hand fan is depicted, while the two attendants on the right side hold the precious parasol and the chowrie (sa. cāmara) mentioned in the text (VR 4.25.21). This image is one of the rare examples in which the artist made an attempt to create depth, for the attendant further back is represented considerably smaller. In addition to this, as a rare feature seen here for the first time, small hairs are engraved on the undersides of Sugrīva's arms and, even more clearly, on the undersides of the arms and tail of his attendant (see detail).

56. १लक्ष्मणन् वोध याक॥ १राम् वैराग्यन चोंठ॥
Lakṣmaṇana vodha yāka. Rāma vairāgyana coṅa.
a) Rāma dwells in apathy. b) Lakṣmaṇa encourages (him).

VR: After Sugrīva's coronation, Rāma and Lakṣmaṇa retire to Mount Prasravaṇa, not far from Kiṣkindhā (ch. 26). Rāma, incessantly thinking of Sītā, gives himself up to grief again. As Lakṣmaṇa states that he will not be able to slay Rāvaṇa with an agitated mind, he receives Lakṣmaṇa's counsel and regains his courage. The brothers spend the rainy season in a large cave on the peak of Prasravaṇa, awaiting the autumn when Sugrīva would make good on his promise to help them free Sītā (ch. 27). Image: Rāma is depicted on the right side, with his head resting on the back of his hand. Lakṣmaṇa sits close by. Whereas Rāma looks downwards, Lakṣmaṇa directs his gaze upwards. The gesture he makes further points to his supportive role.

57. १लक्ष्मणन् सुग्रीवयाक् वंठ॥
Lakṣmaṇa Sugrīvayāke vaṃṅa.
Lakṣmaṇa goes to Sugrīva.

VR: With his goals achieved and his suffering ended, Sugrīva dedicates his time to worldly pleasures and forgets about his obligation (ch. 28). Rāma, in distress, sends Lakṣmaṇa to Kiṣkindhā in order to urge Sugrīva to keep his promise (chs. 29f.). Image: The image shows Lakṣmaṇa on his way to Kiṣkindhā.

/ 60 / 59 /

58. १हनूमन॥ १लक्ष्मणन् सूग्रीव् वाना वव॥ १अङ्गद॥
Hanumanta. Lakṣmaṇana Sugrīva vonā vava. Aṅgada.
Hanumān. Lakṣmaṇa comes along with Sugrīva. Aṅgada.

VR: Enraged, Lakṣmaṇa reaches Kiṣkindhā (ch. 30). Aṅgada announces him to Sugrīva. Admidst the monkey counselors, Hanumān advises Sugrīva to stand by his agreement (ch. 31) and Tārā manages to pacify Lakṣmaṇa (ch. 34). As a sign of loyalty, Sugrīva, freed from intoxication, puts aside his wonderful garland (ch. 35).
Image: Lakṣmaṇa is standing in front of Sugrīva. He points at the bow and arrow he holds, indicating that the time for battle has come. Sugrīva is placed under the royal canopy, in a thoughtful pose. The two of them are flanked by Hanumān and Aṅgada who, in a salutatory and pacifying manner, both show the gesture of fearlessness (sa. *abhayamudrā*).

59. १नामचन्द्रया त्तन् लक्ष्मणन् सूग्रीव् वाढाव हव॥ १जाम्बवान॥ १हनूमन॥ १अङ्गद॥ १नल॥ १नील॥
Rāmacandrayā bhana Lakṣmaṇana Sugrīva voṅāva hava. Jāmbavāna. Hanumanta. Aṅgada. Nala. Nīla.
Lakṣmaṇa brings Sugrīva to Rāma. Jāmbavān. Hanumān. Aṅgada. Nala. Nīla.

VR: Lakṣmaṇa asks Sugrīva to come with him and to console Rāma (ch. 35). Immediately, Sugrīva summons his troops (ch. 36). Accompanied by his chief monkeys he meets with Rāma (ch. 37). Next, all the troop leaders appear, together with their armies of millions of monkeys (ch. 38). At Rāma's command, Sugrīva inaugurates the search for Sītā. He sends out monkeys in all four cardinal directions (chs. 39ff.).
Image: Rāma is sitting on a low stool with a blanket. His head rests on the back of his hand as if he was reflecting about what should be done next. Apart from Lakṣmaṇa and Sugrīva, Jāmbavān, Hanumān, Aṅgada, Nala and Nīla are depicted. They all form part of the search party which Sugrīva sends to the southern region (ch. 40).
Other sources: In several later Rāmāyaṇa versions, Jāmbavān is the king of the bears. This is the case for example in the Kṛttivāsa Rāmāyaṇa[218] and the the Rāmacaritamānasa.[219] It is however clear that he was originally viewed as a monkey[220] and the artist has also rightly depicted him as one.

60. १नामचन्द्रन् हनूमन् अंगुलि वियाव् छ्वाक॥ १लक्ष्मण॥ १सूग्रीव॥ १अंगद॥ १जाम्बवान॥
Rāmacandrana Hanumanta aṅguli viyāva choka. Lakṣmaṇa. Sugrīva. Aṅgada. Jāmbavāna.
Rāma gives Hanumān the finger (ring) and sends (him) away. Lakṣmaṇa. Sugrīva. Aṅgada. Jāmbavān.

218 Nagar and Nagar 1997 I, p. 216.
219 Nagar 2014 II, p. 1224.
220 He is repeatedly called monkey in the VR, see Kiṣkindhākāṇḍa, 40.2-5, 58.2, 64.18,20 and 66.26. See also the critical notes to the mentioned veres and p. 38f. in the introduction to the Kiṣkindhākāṇḍa.

VR (scene 60): Since Rāma believes that Hanumān will be the one to find Sītā, he gives him his ring as a token (ch. 43). He states that it would help Sītā to recognise Hanumān as his friend.
Image: Rāma and Lakṣmaṇa are sitting on a bench covered with a folded layer. Rāma is about to give his ring to Hanumān who receives it on his knees. On the right side, Sugrīva, Aṅgada and Jāmbavān are depicted. Sugrīva and Aṅgada, king and heir apparent, are placed under the canopy-like tasselled cloths.

61. १हनूमन्त् अंगुलि आढाव् वं॥
Hanumanta aṅguli joṅāva vaṃ.
Hanumān takes up the finger (ring) and departs.

VR: Hanumān receives Rāma's ring, touches it to his head, offers obeisance to Rāma's feet and departs (ch. 43).
Image: Perfectly matching with the text, the image shows Hanumān placing the ring to his forehead and heading off.

62. १संयागिमंगलव् हनूमन्तव् संवाद॥
Sampātijhaṅgalava Hanumantava saṃvāda.
Conversation of the bird Sampāti and Hanumān.

VR: Not being able to find Sītā, the monkeys exploring the southern regions give way to disappointment on a foothill of the Vindhya mountain (ch. 52). By chance, they meet the vulture Sampāti, Jaṭāyu's brother (ch. 55). The monkeys inform him about his brother's death and Sampāti reports on Sītā's abduction. He says that Rāvaṇa has carried her off to the city of Laṅkā, located on an island in the sea (ch. 57). As he speaks to the monkeys, his wings, which had been burnt by the sun earlier, reappear (ch. 62). Finally, the monkeys resolve that Hanumān should leap over the ocean to trace Sītā (chs. 64f.).
Image: The beautiful depiction of the Vindhya mountain reminds of the former representation of Ṛṣyamūka. Hanumān is perching on its slopes, representing the entire search party. The giant vulture Sampāti turns back his head to look at him. His wings have already grown again.

Northern face of the temple (scenes 63 to 87):

Sundarakāṇḍa: 'Beautiful Section'

63. १हनूमन्तन् समूद्र गाव॥
Hanumantana samudra gāva.
Hanumān leaps over the ocean.

VR: Hanumān assumes gigantic dimensions and crosses the mighty sea with one single impetuous leap (ch. 1). In a rapid flight he negotiates one hundred leagues (VR 4.75.20). While leaping over the ocean, Hanumān overcomes the goddess Surasā who puts him to a test in the guise of a female demon and he also overcomes the demoness Siṃhikā. Having reached the further shore, Hanumān again reduces his body. From the top of Mount Lamba, Hanumān then beholds the city of Laṅkā.
Image: The ocean is beautifully pictured, wavy and alive with fish, sea monsters (sa. *makaras*) and other aquatic animals. Hanumān leaps over it, at full power. His arms are stretched out and his hands clenched to fists, which gives him an energetic appearance. Surasā and Siṃhikā are not depicted.

64. १नावण् काथास् यट चाट॥ १मंदायनी॥ १हनूमन्तन् लंकास् सीता माल् आव॥
Rāvaṇa kothāsa deṅa coṅa. Mandodarī. Hanumantana Laṅkāsa Sītā mola jova.
a) Hanumān searches Sītā in Laṅkā.
b) Rāvaṇa lays asleep inside the room. Mandodarī.

VR: At night, Hanumān enters the city (ch. 3). He penetrates into the centre and finds the palace of Laṅkā encircled by a shining wall and guarded by terrible demons (ch. 5). As he enters Rāvaṇa's abode, he beholds the heavenly flying palace Puṣpāka and a thousand lovely women who have fallen asleep under the influence of wine. In their midst, he beholds Rāvaṇa, asleep on a magnificent bed (chs. 7f.). Rāvaṇa's wives lay asleep at his feet, except for Mandodarī, his favourite queen, who lies fast asleep on a marvellous bed set apart. Hanumān searches Sītā in every room but his efforts are without success (ch. 10).
Image: This is the only image of both the friezes in which an open, multistoreyed

/ 65 / 64 / 63 / 62 / 61 /

building is depicted. Insight is provided into five chambers of Rāvaṇa's palace. Hanumān is about to climb the roof of the palace. In the central compartment, Rāvaṇa himself is depicted. He lies asleep on a bed with a flowery layer. In contrast to the text, Mandodarī is depicted clinging to his feet. In both the lower compartments women with goblets are depicted while the upper compartments comprise additional representations of the incessantly searching Hanumān.

65. १अशोकवनिकास् रावणन् सीता वोध याक् हनुमन्तन् ङेङाव चोङ॥

Aśokavanikāsa Rāvaṇana Sītā vodha yāka; Hanumantana ṅeṅāva coṅa.

As Rāvaṇa (tries to) persuade Sītā in the Aśoka grove, Hanumān sits listening.

VR: Next, Hanumān resolves to search Sītā in the Aśoka grove attached to the palace (ch. 11). From upon a *śiṃśapā* tree he finally beholds her (ch. 13). Sītā is consumed with grief and surrounded by female demons. At daybreak, Rāvaṇa shows up and again begs her to become his wife (chs. 16ff.). Sītā, however, rejects all his advances (ch. 19).

Image: Rāvaṇa is depicted in his demoniac form. It is clear that Sītā rejects him for she is facing away from him. Hanumān is shown twice. On the upper branch of the tree he searches for Sītā in the Aśoka grove, while on a lower branch, having finally found her, he listens to her conversation with Rāvaṇa.

scene 63 enlarged

/ 69 / 68 / 67 / 66 /

66. १सीता्पयाव चाढ नाऊसीपनि॥ १हनूमन्तन्‌ नामया अंगुलि्‌ सीता बिव॥
Sītā peyāva coṅa rākṣasīpani. Hanumantana Rāmayā aṅguli Sītā biva.
Demonesses guarding Sītā. Hanumān gives Sītā Rāma's finger (ring).

VR: Rāvaṇa returns to his palace (ch. 29). Thereupon, Hanumān speaks to Sītā from atop the tree. Glancing from side to side and up and down, she finally espies him. Hanumān makes himself known to her and tells her about Rāma's plan (chs. 32ff.). In order to reassure Sītā about his good intentions, he hands over Rāma's ring (ch. 34). Image: The image depicts this very moment. Still perching on the branch of the *śiṃśapā* tree, Hanumām hands over Rāma's ring to the desolate Sītā. The demonesses guarding Sītā are depicted at some distance, with vertical projecting hair.

67. १हनूमन्तन्‌ नावणया वन्‌ भंग याक॥
Hanumantana Rāvaṇayā vana bhaṅga yāka.
Hanumān destroys Rāvaṇa's forest.

VR: Hanumān takes leave of Sītā (ch. 39). In order to be able to accurately determinate the strength of Rāvaṇa's forces, he evokes Rāvaṇa's wrath by destroying the Aśoka grove. He roots up trees and creepers, causing the crests of the hills to break away until finally, all that was fair lays waste.
Image: Hanumān is depicted vigorously plucking leaves and branches from the trees.

68. १नाऊस वध॥ १नाऊस वध॥ १नाऊस वध॥ १हनूमन्तन्‌ अ्ऊयकुमान्‌ वध याक॥
rākṣasa vadha. rākṣasa vadha. rākṣasa vadha. Hanumantana Akṣayakumāra vadha yāka
Death of a demon. Death of a demon. Death of a demon. Hanumān kills the prince Akṣaya.

VR: Rāvaṇa sends numerous demons to seize Hanumān (chs. 40ff.). Hanumān however slays them all. Among the ones Rāvaṇa sends is also his son, the prince Akṣa (ch. 45). He attacks from atop a chariot equipped with all sorts of weapons. After Hanumān has deprived him of his chariot and horses, Akṣa leaps high into the air. Hanumān seizes hold of his legs, spins him around thousands of times and finally, throws him violently on the ground.
Image: On the left side of the image, three demons are depicted lying dead on the ground. They represent the many demons slain by Hanumān already. Semi-detached, by a tree in the background, Hanumān is depicted overpowering Akṣa. Interestingly, Akṣa is neither wearing a crown, nor conspicuous clothing and not even an armour. He is thus indiscernible from the other demons.
Other sources: Akṣa is Akṣaya in later versions, southern and northern ones alike. Examples are the Kambā Rāmāyaṇa,[221] the Kṛttivāsi Rāmāyaṇa[222] and the Rāmacaritamānasa.[223]

221 Nagar 2008 II, p. 83.
222 Nagar and Nagar 1997 I, p. 277.
223 Nagar 2014 III, p. 1259.

/ 73 / 72 / 71 / 70 /

69. १ॐ इन्द्रजितव् हनूमन्तव् युद्ध॥
Indrajitava Hanumantava yuddha.
Fight between Indrajit and Hanumān.

VR: As Rāvaṇa hears about his son's death, he is mad with anger (ch. 46). He consequently sends his eldest son to battle, Indrajit, whom he considers invincible in combat.
Image: The image shows Hanumān in battle with Indrajit. According to the text, Indrajit discharges his arrows from upon his chariot. In the image by contrast, he fights on the ground with a sword. In contrast to Akṣa, Indrajit is depicted with armour and with a crown behind of which his demonic hair stands on end.
Other sources: Again, the weapons used are not specified in later versions like for example the Ānanda Rāmāyaṇa[224] or the Rāmacaritamānasa.[225]

70. १ॐ इन्द्रजितन् हनूमन्त चयाव यंङ॥
Indrajitana Hanumanta ceyāva yaṃṅa.
Indrajit fetters Hanumān and leads him away.

VR: Indrajit strikes Hanumān with the divine Brahmā Weapon in order to render him immobile (ch. 46). Hanumān realises that he would still be able to free himself but since he wants to come face to face with Rāvaṇa, he willingly lets Indrajit take him captive. Hanumān is bound with ropes of hemp and dragged before Rāvaṇa.
Image: Indrajit is dragging Hanumān by the ropes constricted around his wrists.

71. १हनूमन्तया ह्निपोतस मि् च्याचको॥ १ॐ इन्द्रजितन् हनूमन्त चयाव् रावणया् सभास् हव॥
Hanumantayā hnipotasa mi cyācako. Indrajitana Hanumanta ceyāva Rāvaṇayā sabhāsa hava.
a) After tying him, Indrajit brings Hanumān to Rāvaṇa's palace.
b) On Hanumān's tail a fire is kindled.

VR: Rāvaṇa commands his counselor Prahasta to question Hanumān concerning the purpose of his coming (ch. 48). At Hanumān's answer, Rāvaṇa orders him to be put to death (ch. 50). Yet, Rāvaṇa's younger brother, Vibhīṣaṇa, firm in justice and committet to proper conduct, deems it contrary to justice to take the life of a messenger. He advises Rāvaṇa to spare Hanumān's life and to inflict some punishment other than death upon him (ch. 51). Considering the tail to be the most cherished possession of a monkey, Rāvaṇa gives order to set Hanumān's tail on fire.
Image: Rāvaṇa is sitting inside his palace which is beautifully depicted, with latticed windows (sa. *jālis*) and an opened curtain. On the right side, an attendant with a fly-whisk is depicted. On the left side, Hanumān is dragged before Rāvaṇa and still further left, a servant is about to ignite Hanumān's tail.

224 Nagar 2006 I, p. 108.
225 Nagar 2014 III, p. 1260.

72. (previous page) १हनूमन्तन् लंका् मि च्वाक॥
Hanumantana Laṅkā mi coka.
Hanumān sets Laṅkā on fire.

VR: Bound and with his tail ablaze, Hanumān is led through the city (ch. 51). He slips free from his bonds as he first assumes a mountainous appearance and then again reduces his size. Looking about him, he spies a beam attached to a gate, adorned with black iron. Hanumān uses it to slay the guards and afterwards sets the city on fire (ch. 52).
Image: The image depicts the moment when Hanumān seizes the beam from the gate. The gate is a double roofed building with latticed windows and closed latticed doors. Surprisingly, no flames are depicted on Hanumān's tail. The inscription however implies that it is still burning.

73. १रामचन्द्रव् हनूमन्तव् नाप राक् लिसल कंढ॥
Rāmacandrava Hanumantava nāpa rāka lisala kaṃṅa.
As Rāma and Hanumān meet, (Sītā's) answer is told.

VR: As the city is consumed by the flames, Hanumān leaps back across the sea (ch. 55). Having reached the northern shore, he reports to Aṅgada (ch. 56). Thereafter, having accomplished the mission, the search party returns to Rāma. Rāma asks about Sītā's situation and Hanumān answers in great detail (chs. 63ff.).
Image: Hanumān supports his report with gestures. For the first time, a mandorla is depicted around Rāma's head. This mandorla reappears in the next scene, around Rāma's head as well as around Lakṣmaṇa's. It is again omitted for the rest of the cycle.

scene 73 enlarged

Yuddhakāṇḍa: 'Section of the Combat'

74. १रामचन्द्र् हतार [वं]॥ १लक्ष्मण॥ १सूग्रीव॥ १जामवन्त॥ १हनूमन्त॥ १अङ्गद॥ १नल॥ १नील॥
Rāmacandra hatāra vaṃ. Lakṣmaṇa. Sugrīva. Jāmavanta. Hanumanta.. Nala. Nīla.
Rāma goes to battle. Lakṣmaṇa. Sugrīva. Jāmbavān. Hanumān. Aṅgada. Nala. Nīla.

VR: In order to bring back Sītā, Rāma and Lakṣmaṇa set forth towards the south, together with a vast monkey army (ch. 4). Rāma is placed at the centre of the troops, mounted on Hanumān, while Lakṣmaṇa is mounted on Aṅgada.
Image: In contrast to the text, the image shows Rāma and Lakṣmaṇa on foot, leading the troops. That they are not depicted on the shoulders of Hanumān and Aṅgada might be due to the limited height of the frieze. The sculptor again intends to create depth for the figures of Aṅgada and Nala are depicted somewhat smaller. The impression that Aṅgada, Nala and Nīla march side by side is strengthened by the fact that the figures of Aṅgada and Nala overlap slightly.

75. १माकरतोसेन् समूद्र पंढ॥ १माकलपनिसेन् समूद्र पने यात् पर्ब्बत हव॥
mākaratosena samudra paṃṅa. mākalapanisena samudra pane yāta parbbata hava.
a) The monkey troop brings mountains in order to stop the ocean.
b) The monkey troop stops the ocean.

VR: Rāma and his troops reach the shores of the sea (ch. 4). Nala, the son Viśvakarman, the architect of the gods, constructs a bridge over the ocean (ch. 15). All the others assist him. They dig up stones as big as elephants and myriads of trees, drag them to the sea and fling them into it until an immense causeway runs through the middle of the ocean.
Image: The image shows two monkeys bringing huge boulders. A third monkey is handing over a boulder to the ones building the bridge. His foot rests on the already partly constructed causeway. Between elements serving as supports, the turbulent sea shows up, with a sea monster (sa. *makara*) in the first field and a fish in the second one. In marked contrast to this, no aquatic creatures at all are depicted in the open waters. This perfectly matches with the text, according to which the personi-

/ 75 / 74 /

fied sea (sa. *sāgara*) assists the monkeys in their undertaking by holding back its sea monsters, crocodiles and sharks.

76. १विभीषणन् सीता तोरतेव धायाव् रावणन् लकामन् न्याङाव् विभीषण पितिं छोक॥
Vibhīṣaṇana Sītā torateva dhāyāva Rāvaṇana lakāmana nyāṅāva Vibhīṣaṇa pitiṃ choka.
Vibhīṣaṇa suggests to release Sītā but Rāvaṇa kicks[226] Vibhīṣaṇa with his shoe and banishes him.

VR: Vibhīṣaṇa, fixed in the knowledge of what is just, advises Rāvaṇa to send back Sītā (chs. 9f.). Rāvaṇa erupts in anger and speaks harsh words to his younger brother. Affronted by Rāvaṇa, Vibhīṣaṇa takes his departure. He flies over the sea, intending to take refuge with Rāma (ch. 11).
Image: Rāvaṇa is depicted inside his palace. In an attached chamber his favourite queen, Mandodarī, is sitting. Vibhīṣaṇa sits on the ground, on the left side of the image, with his mace in hand. He wears an elaborate crown and, as seen in the following image, his armour is also more elaborate that that of all others. Rāvaṇa kicks Vibhīṣaṇa with his foot, which is not mentioned in the Vālmīki Rāmāyaṇa.

226 Kölver und Shresthacarya 1994, p. 191: nyāye, i.a. to kick.

/ 76 /

Other sources: Rāvaṇa kicks Vibhīṣaṇa in several medieval recensions, southern and northern ones alike. The incident is included for example in the Telugu Rāmāyaṇas of Raṅganātha and Molla.[227] According to the Rāmacaritamānasa, Vibhīṣaṇa holds Rāvaṇa's feet while begging for Sītā's release, which tempts Rāvaṇa to kick him.[228] The representation matches perfectly with this version. According to the Kṛttivāsi Rāmāyaṇa by contrast, Rāvaṇa first rushes at Vibhīṣaṇa and brings him down with a kick, and then kicks him again as he lies on the ground.[229]

227 Sarma 1973, p. 103 and Rao 1984, p. 100.
228 Nagar 2014 III, pp. 1295f.
229 Nagar 1997 I, p. 293.

77. १सुग्रीव॥ १लक्ष्मण॥ १नामयाक् विरीषण् वव॥

Sugrīva. Lakṣmaṇa. Rāmayāke Vibhīṣaṇa vava.

Sugrīva. Lakṣmaṇa. Vibhīṣaṇa comes to Rāma.

VR: Vibhīṣaṇa seeks refuge in Rāma (ch. 11). Sugrīva and others are leery but, following the advice of Hanumān, Rāma accepts him as his ally (ch. 12). Vibhīṣaṇa promises to assist Rāma in battle with all his strength and thereat, in the midst of the monkey leaders, Rāma has him anointed as the king of the demons (ch. 13).
Image: Vibhīṣaṇa approaches from the right. He is received by Rāma, Lakṣmaṇa and a scared looking Sugrīva. Again, the order of the events was changed. According to the text, Rāma receives Vibhīṣaṇa prior to the building of the causeway.

78. १अंगदन् दूत वढाव् नावणया् मटूक कायाव यंढ॥

Aṅgadana dūta vaṅāva Rāvaṇayā maṭuka kāyāva yaṃṅa.

Aṅgada goes as messenger and takes away Rāvaṇa's crown.

VR: As the troops arrive at the gates of Laṅkā, Rāma sends Aṅgada to Rāvaṇa to find out if his purpose could also be accomplished without using force (ch. 31). As Rāvaṇa orders Aṅgada to be put to death, Aṅgada leaps to the top of Rāvaṇa's palace and smashes its pinnacle.
Image: Aṅgada is depicted snatching one of Rāvaṇa's crowns while Rāvaṇa tumbles inside his palace. It is not mentioned in the text of the Critical Edition that Rāvaṇa's crown is stolen but some of the manuscripts forming the southern recension of the Vālmīki Rāmāyaṇa tell of a similar humiliation of Rāvaṇa by Sugrīva in an additional chapter before chapter 31. In the course of an impulsive and unauthorised attack on Rāvaṇa, Sugrīva tears off his splendid crown and casts it down.[230]
Other sources: The Kamba Rāmāyaṇa further states that Sugrīva picks the crown up and carries it to Rāma.[231] The same is narrated in the Ānanda Rāmāyaṇa after Aṅgada has returned.[232] The event of Aṅgada snatching away Rāvaṇa's crown by contrast, is reported in several medieval northern renderings like the Kṛttivāsi Rāmāyaṇa,[233] the Rāmacaritamānasa[234] and the Bhāvārtha Rāmāyaṇa.[235] According to the Rāmacaritamānasa for example, Aṅgada, in anger, throws his hands over the ground, causing the earth to shake, and all the crowns fall from Rāvaṇa's heads. Rāvaṇa is able to place some back over his heads but four of the crowns are thrown by Aṅgada towards Rāma. Aṅgada further puts Rāvaṇa to disgrace as he challenges his companions to lift up his foot.[236] In the Ānanda Rāmāyaṇa[237] as well as in the Kṛttivāsi Rāmāyaṇa[238], Aṅgada offends Rāvaṇa's pride as he sits on his tail, higher than Rāvaṇa and in the Ānanda Rāmāyaṇa it is further said that Aṅgada binds Rāvaṇa's hands and feet with his tail and severely slaps his faces before he returns to Rāma.[239] Rāvaṇa is thus humiliated in various ways in the individual texts.

79. १लक्ष्मण॥ १नामचन्द्र॥ १अंगदन् मटूक् विव॥

Lakṣmaṇa. Rāmacandra. Aṅgadana maṭuka biva.

Lakṣmaṇa. Rāma. Aṅgada presents the crown.

VR: Since it is not reported in the Vālmiki Rāmāyaṇa that Aṅgada took Rāvaṇa's crown, of course it is not stated that he hands it over to Rāma.
Image: The image shows Aṅgada presenting Rāvaṇa's crown to Rāma.
Other sources: The version from the Rāmacaritamānasa no longer matches with the representation. Firstly, Aṅgada snatches several crowns according to this text and secondly, having been thrown by Aṅgada, it is Hanumān who collects them and places them before Rāma.[240] The plot as represented here, corresponds very well to the version from the Kṛttivāsi Rāmāyaṇa. Here, Aṅgada catches hold of only one of Rāvaṇa's crowns. Additionally, he returns immediately, without further challenging Rāvaṇa, and he places the crown before Rāma himself.[241] It is also Aṅgada who

230 Goldman 2009: VI, translated at note to 6.30.26.
231 Nagar 2008 II, p. 192.
232 Nagar 2006 I, p. 139.
233 Nagar and Nagar 1997 II, p. 27.
234 Nagar 2014 III, p. 1382.
235 Sathe and Vaishampayana 2016, p. 811.
236 Nagar 2014 III, pp. 1386ff.
237 Nagar 2006 I, p. 137.
238 Nagar and Nagar 1997 II, pp. 18f.
239 Nagar 2006 I, p. 138.
240 Nagar 2014 III, p. 1383.
241 Nagar and Nagar 1997 II, p. 27.

hands over the crown in the Bhāvārtha Rāmāyaṇa but according to this version, Aṅgada also carries with him Rāvaṇa's assembly hall,[242] borrowing from the Ānanda Rāmāyaṇa where Aṅgada inadvertently brings the entire palace.[243]

/ 78 / 77 /

80. १सूकव_सानणव_माकननूपन_नामवद्धया_सैय सान_वव॥ °नामवद्धन_सढवंध यान याक॥
१सूग्रीव॥ १जाम्बवान॥ १हनूमन्त॥ १अंगद॥ १नल॥ १नील॥

and above the image: [१लक्ष्मण॥ १विभीषण॥]

Sukava Sāraṇava mākararūpana Rāmacandrayā sainya sora vava. Rāmacandrana setuvandha pāra yāka. Sugrīva. Jāmbavāna. Hanumanta. Aṅgada. Nala. Nīla.

a) Rāma crosses the bridge. Sugrīva. Jāmbavān. Hanumān. Aṅgada. Nala. Nīla.

above: [Lakṣmaṇa. Vibhīṣaṇa.]

b) Śuka and Sāraṇa, in the guise of monkeys, come to see Rāma's troop.

VR: Again, the order of the events is changed. The crossing of the ocean is described in chapter 15 of the Vālmiki Rāmāyaṇa. Afterwards, Rāvaṇa orders his counsellors Śuka and Sāraṇa to take on the form of monkeys and to spy on Rāma's army (ch. 16). In the further course, all the events depicted up to scene 85 actually precede Rāma's sending of Aṅgada.

Image (scene 80): Rāma crosses the ocean, followed by Lakṣmaṇa, Vibhīṣaṇa and the monkey host. The causeway constructed by Nala is not depicted. The troop appears to be supported by the waves instead. Śuka and Sāraṇa are waiting at the shore of the ocean, in the guise of monkeys. The inscription above the image is only scarcely traceable.

/ 80 / 79 /

242 Sathe and Vaishampayana 2016, p. 811.
243 Nagar 2006 I, p. 138.

81. १विभीषणन् सुक् सारण् सेयाव् चेयाव हव् रामचन्द्रन् तोरताव् छोव धाव॥
and above the image: १लक्ष्मण॥
Vibhīṣaṇana Suka Sāraṇa seyāva ceyāva hava Rāmacandrana toratāva chova dhāva.
As Vibhīṣaṇa, after recognising Śuka and Sāraṇa, brings them fettered, Rāma suggests to release them and send them (as messengers).
above: Lakṣmaṇa.

VR: Vibhīṣaṇa recognises Śuka and Sāraṇa under their disguise (ch. 16). He seizes them and denounces them to Rāma. Rāma however spares their lives and sends them as messengers to Rāvaṇa in order to announce his attack for the next day.
Image: Vibhīṣaṇa leads Śuka and Sāraṇa to Rāma. The disguised demons have their hands tied behind their back. Vibhīṣaṇa drives them forth with his raised mace. Rāma, devoted to the welfare of all beings, shows the gesture of fearlessness (sa. *abhayamudrā*).

82. १सुक् सारण् नेह्म[सेनं रामचंद्र]या् सत्यया महिमा [रावण] कं॥
Suka Sāraṇa, nehmasenaṃ Rāmacandrayā satyayā mahimā Rāvaṇa kaṃ.
Both,[244] Śuka and Sāraṇa, tell Rāvaṇa about the true greatness of Rāma.

VR: Śuka and Sāraṇa tell Rāvaṇa about Rāma's good nature and thereafter give a report on his troops (chs. 16ff.). They appeal to Rāvaṇa to make peace with Rāma and to return Sītā but Rāvaṇa refuses to give in.
Image: Rāvaṇa is sitting inside the palace, a beautiful two-storeyed building, richly ornamented (compare with scene 78) and with composite creatures as supports. Śuka and Sāraṇa approach him with their heads bowed and their hands raised, either salutatory or pacificatory. In between, an attendant whith a fly-whisk is depicted. His small size suggests that he stands further back.

244 Jørgensen 1941 (grammar), p. 45: nehmasenam - both.

83. १विद्युज्जिह्वान् रामचन्द्रया् [मायामो]र् सीता केङ॥
and above the image: [... सरमान बोध] याक॥
a) Vidyujjihvāna Rāmacandrayā māyāmora Sītā keṅa.
Vidyujjihva shows Sītā an illusory head of Rāma.
above: b) [...] Saramāna bodha yāka.
Saramā encourages [Sītā].

VR: On account of the report on Rāma's troops, Rāvaṇa becomes agitated and makes another attempt to win over Sītā (ch. 22). He instructs Vidyujjihva, a powerful and skilled magician, to create, through the power of illusion, a head resembling the one of Rāma. Then, Rāvaṇa approaches Sītā. He makes up a story how Rāma was slain and Vidyujjihva presents the false head. Rāvaṇa again asks Sītā to submit herself to his desire but she refuses, stating that she would prefer to be united with Rāma in death (ch. 23). After Rāvaṇa has left, Saramā, a friendly demoness, tells Sītā that she has been tricked by magic (ch. 24). Saramā serves as a female counterpart to Vibhīṣaṇa and she is even identified as Vibhīṣaṇa's wife, already in a number of commentaries to the Vālmīki Rāmāyaṇa.[245] Furthermore, Vidyujjihva is identified as Śūrpaṇakhā's husband in the Uttarakāṇḍa (VR 7.12.2).
Image: Vidyujjihva holds Rāma's false head by the hair as he presents it to Sītā. Sītā supports her head with the back of her hand and she sorrowfully faces down while Saramā is calming her down.
Other sources: The episode is included in some later versions, as for example the Kṛttivāsi Rāmāyaṇa[246] while others, like the Rāmacaritamānasa, omit it. Kambar comes up with an interesting alteration. Here, Rāvaṇa orders Mahodara to create an illusory Janaka.[247] As Sītā refuses to accept Rāvaṇa, this Janaka appears and tries to get her to relent. Sītā however denounces her father and the demoness Trijaṭā, identified by Kambar as Vibhīṣaṇa's daughter,[248] later informs her about the illusion.

245 Goldman 2009: VI, p. 87 and note to 6.24.1.
246 Nagar and Nagar 1997 I, p. 295.
247 Nagar 2008 II, pp. 251ff.
248 ibid., p. 57.

/ 84 / 83 / 82 / 81 /

84. १माकलपनिसन् लंका भेन थुं॥ १नामचंद्र॥ १लक्ष्मण॥ १विभीषण॥
mākalapanisena Laṅkā bhera thuṃ. Rāmacandra. Lakṣmaṇa. Vibhīṣaṇa.
The monkey troop surrounds Laṅkā. Rāma. Lakṣmaṇa. Vibhīṣaṇa.

VR: Rāma gives order for the leading monkeys to force an entry through the city gates and to oppose the demons stationed there (ch. 28). Rāma himself directs towards the northern gate, where Rāvaṇa is stationed.
Image: Numerous monkeys are depicted, climbing onto a city gate and attempting to tear it down. Like the gate depicted in scene 72, it has a multi-tiered roof, latticed doors and a raised base. This scene marks the beginning of the big fight, for Rāma and Lakṣmaṇa have already released their arrows from the bow string. They are accompanied by Vibhīṣaṇa although the text states that he was to take up his position at the central encampment together with Sugrīva and Jāmbavān (VR 6.28.31).

85. above the image: १इन्द्रजितन् आकासन वयाव् नाम लक्ष्मण् नागपासन् ह्यां[क]॥
below: १गरुडन् नाम लक्ष्मणया् नागपास फेंट॥
above: a) Indrajitana ākāsana vayāva Rāma Lakṣmaṇa nāgapāsana hṅyāka.
Indrajit appears suddenly from the sky and hits Rāma and Lakṣmaṇa with a (magical) snake noose.
below: b) Garuḍana Rāma Lakṣmaṇayā nāgapāsa pheṅa.
Garuḍa tears asunder Rāma and Lakṣmaṇa's snake noose.

/ 85 /

VR: The battle continues until after sunset (ch. 34). Aṅgada destroys Indrajit's chariot whereupon Indrajit conceals himself and looses arrows in the form of great serpents at Rāma and Lakṣmaṇa. The countless arrows strike down Rāma and Lakṣmaṇa and they consequently swoon away (ch. 35). While Rāvaṇa proclaims victory, Rāma regains consciousness (ch. 39). Still, he is unable to escape the net of arrows until suddenly Garuḍa appears (ch. 40). As the serpents behold Garuḍa, they flee in all directions. Then, Garuḍa heals Rāma's and Lakṣmaṇa's wounds by stroking their faces with both his hands.
Image: Rāma is depicted battling with Indrajit who is concealed behind clouds. From his raised position Indrajit looses his arrows on the brothers. Rāma and Lakṣ-

maṇa are already tightly bound in the bonds of Indrajit's arrows and Lakṣmaṇa is no longer fighting. The arrows wind as snakes around the two of them with their heads at face level of Rāma and Lakṣmaṇa. In contrast to the text, Garuḍa comes in direct contact with the snakes as he pulls on the end of the snake constricting Rāma.
Other sources: Although no direct contact is described in the Kṛttivāsi Rāmāyaṇa either, Garuḍa at least touches the snakes with his breath to break their hold on the brothers.[249]

86. १कुम्लकर्ण्ल् थंढा॥
Kumbhakarṇṇa thaṃṅā.
Kumbhakarṇa has been aroused.

VR: In an ensuing battle Rāma overcomes Rāvaṇa but, recognising that Rāvaṇa is exhausted, Rāma spares his life (ch. 47). Thereupon, Rāvaṇa resolves that his brother Kumbhakarṇa must be awakened (ch. 48). Kumbhakarṇa, who sleeps up to nine months at a time, is overwhelmed by sleep. In order to wake him up the demons roar loudly in their thousands, they blow conches and beat drums, they beat him violently and let horses, camels, donkeys and elephants trample upon him until suddenly, he emerges from sleep.
Image: Kumbhakarṇa is depicted six-armed. In his hands he holds an elephant goad (sa. *aṅkuśa*), an arrow (sa. *bāṇa*), a sword (sa. *khaḍga*), a shield (sa. *kavaca*), a bow (sa. *dhanu*) and a noose (sa. *pāśa*). He is wearing armour and his body is provided with several fierce looking faces. He wears round earrings, a moustache and a crown resembling Vibhīṣaṇa's. As the only demon apart from Rāvaṇa, Kumbhakarṇa possesses a second head: an animal head resembling a deer (here) or maybe a lizard (next scene). The colossus is lying on a large, canopied bed. On both sides minor demons blow trumpets and play cymbals in order to wake him up.
Other sources: There is no text known to me to mention Kumbhakarṇa's animal head.

249 Nagar and Nagar 1997 II, p. 38.

87. १कुम्लकर्ण्ल् हथान वं॥ १नावधया तन् कुम्लकर्ण्ल् वव॥
Kumbhakarṇṇa hathāra vaṃ. Rāvaṇayā bhana Kumbhakarṇṇa vava.
a) Kumbhakarṇa comes to Rāvaṇa.
b) Kumbhakarṇa goes to battle.

VR: Kumbhakarṇa inquires of Rāvaṇa why he has been awakened (ch. 50). Rāvaṇa tells him that, all other resources being exhausted, he has to slay the enemy. As many before, Kumbhakarṇa tries to lead Rāvaṇa in the paths of righteousness. He finally relents out of respect for his elder brother (ch. 51).
Image: On the right side of the image, Kumbhakarṇa is kneeling in front of Rāvaṇa. The latter is depicted here with a moustache, too. Kumbhakarṇa is shown again on the left side of the image, leaving for battle.

Again, eastern face of the temple (scenes 88 to 99):

88. १कुम्लकर्ण्लव् नामवद्भव् युद्ध॥ १लक्ष्मध॥
Kumbhakarṇṇava Rāmacandrava yuddha. Lakṣmaṇa.
Fight between Kumbhakarṇa and Rāma. Lakṣmaṇa.

VR: Kumbhakarṇa slays and even devours the monkeys in great numbers (chs. 54f.). As Sugrīva attacks, Kumbhakarṇa seizes him and carries him off but Sugrīva rends his ears and nose and manages to escape. Afterwards, Lakṣmaṇa enters the fight but Kumbhakarṇa bypasses him and instead rushes at Rāma.
Image: Rāma and Lakṣmaṇa are about to loose their arrows at Kumbhakarṇa while the latter sinks to the ground, struck by an arrow at his chest.

89. १कुम्लकर्ण्ल् वध॥
Kumbhakarṇṇa vadha.
Death of Kumbhakarṇa.

VR: Rāma shoots off Kumbhakarṇa's arms and legs, fills his huge mouth with arrows and finally also uses his arrows to shoot off the demon's head.
Image: Kumbhakarṇa is lying on the ground. In contrast to the text, he retains his weapons and body parts.

/ 89 / 88 / 87 / 86 /

90. १हनूमनन् पर्ब्वग हव॥ १नामया् वैनाग्य १लक्ष्मण मूर्छा जुव॥ १ऌ्द्रजिगन् लक्ष्मण् शक्तिन कयका॥

Hanumantana parbbata hava. Rāmayā vairāgya. Lakṣmaṇa mūrchā juva. Indrajitana Lakṣmaṇa śaktina kayako.

a) Indrajit hits Lakṣmaṇa with the *śakti* (-javelin). b) Lakṣmaṇa faints.

c) Rāma's apathy. d) Hanumān brings the mountain.

/ 90 /

VR: Indrajit asks permission of Rāvaṇa to take action against Rāma (ch. 60). He offers oblations to Agni at the shrine of Nikumbhilā. Then, he sets out for the battlefield, his form no longer perceptible. Invisible, he plunges in among the monkey ranks and puts Sugrīva's army out of action. Finally, he cuts down Rāma and Lakṣmaṇa with his arrows. As they lie without consciousness, Indrajit returns to his father's palace. On Jāmbavān's instruction, Hanumān leaps up and swiftly flies to the Himālayas in order to bring the healing herbs (ch. 61). He reaches the mountain of medicinal herbs but is not able to find the herbs required. Hanumān therefore decides to bring the entire summit. As Rāma and Lakṣmaṇa inhale the scent of the powerful herbs, they are instantly healed of their wounds.

Image: In the image, Indrajit attacks not with bow and arrow, but with a javelin. Moreover, according to the Vālmiki Rāmāyaṇa, Rāma and Lakṣmaṇa both fall senseless. Here on the contrary, only Lakṣmaṇa lies on the ground whereas Rāma is depicted in deep mourning. On the left side of the image, Hanumān brings the summit of the mountain of medicinal herbs. The details were apparently confused with the second time that Hanumān brings the summit of this mountain, after Rāvaṇa has almost killed Lakṣmaṇa in battle (chs. 88 f.). In this context, Rāma sits beside his mortally wounded brother, in deep mourning, while Hanumān is addressed to return to the mountain of medicinal herbs. The depicted weapon also points to the later event for the weapon Rāvaṇa hurls at Lakṣmaṇa is a special javelin, namely the *śakti*.[250] It is the same javelin that Maya, the architect of the demons, had given to Rāvaṇa on the occasion of the latter's marriage to his daughter, Mandodarī (VR 7.12.19). The inscription also explicitly states that the javelin depicted is the *śakti*.

250 Goldman 2009: VI, note to VR 6.88.22.

/ 91 /

91. १ꣳद्रजित वध १हनूमं[त]न् निकं[त]नायज्ञ् विध्वंस याक॥ १ꣳद्रजितव् लक्ष्मणव् यूद्ध॥ १हनूमन्त॥ १विभीषण॥

Indrajita vadha. Hanumantana Nikambhirāyajña vidhvaṃsa yāka. Indrajitava Lakṣmaṇava yuddha. Hanumanta. Vibhīṣaṇa.

a) Fight between Indrajit and Lakṣmaṇa. Hanumān. Vibhīṣaṇa.

b) Hanumān destroys the Nikumbhilā sacrifice.

c) Death of Indrajit.

VR: Rāvaṇa again orders Indrajit into battle (ch. 67). After slaying an illusory Sītā, Indrajit retires to the Nikumbhilā shrine in order to perform a sacrifice that would render him unassailable in battle (chs. 68f.). Rāma, himself still immersed in grief on account of the illusion, sends Lakṣmaṇa, Vibhīṣaṇa and the monkey leaders to interrupt the sacrifice (chs. 71f.). Hanumān wreaks great slaughter among the demon host, whereupon Indrajit rises up, his sacrifice still incomplete (ch. 73). Then, Lakṣmaṇa challenges him to a duel (ch. 74). Bereft of his charioteer and horses, Indrajit continues to fight on foot (ch. 77). Indrajit falls in battle as Lakṣmaṇa cuts off his head with an arrow (ch. 78).

Image: Indrajit and Lakṣmaṇa are fighting with bow and arrow. Indrajit draws back his arrow while Lakṣmaṇa has already hit Indrajit's chest with his one. Next to them fighting, Hanumān destroys Indrajit's sacrifice. Whereas the text informs us that Hanumān disturbs the sacrifice rather indirectly, he here brings the sacrifice directly to an end by pulling down the pot with the oblations. On the left side of the image, Indrajit's death is depicted. He is lying on the ground, his chest pierced with an arrow.

Other sources: The representation reminds of the version from the Kṛttivāsi Rāmāyaṇa, according to which the sacrifice is not only disturbed but indeed destroyed. With a single kick Hanumān extinguishes the fire and afterwards throws away the offerings.[251] Other versions, southern and northern ones alike, like the Kamba Rāmāyaṇa[252] or the Rāmacaritamānasa,[253] also state that Lakṣmaṇa and the monkeys destroy Indrajit's sacrifice but in doing so no special role is attributed to Hanumān. On the other hand, the way that Indrajit's death is depicted, is in accordance with the version from the Rāmacaritamānasa.[254] Here, Lakṣmaṇa pierces his heart with an arrow, while in most other versions the shooting off of Indrajit's head is retained.

On the whole, the destruction of Indrajit's sacrifice reminds of the destruction of Dakṣa's sacrifice in the later versions of the Dakṣa story. The destruction of the sacrifice together with the devastation of the sacrificial site and the beheading of Dakṣa is described for example in the Liṅga Purāna.[255] The text reads as follows: [...] the leading *gaṇa* burnt the sacrificial chamber. The infuriated leaders of the *gaṇas* uprooted the sacrificial posts and hurled them about along with the *hotṛ* (sa., sacrificing priest) and *prastotṛ* (sa., assisting priest). They burned everything. [...] As it (the sacrifice) fled towards the sky in the guise of a deer, Vīrabhadra seized and beheaded it. Thereafter [...] he cut off Dakṣa's head and burned it in the fire. (LP 100.13-37). It is at least possible that the later accounts of Indrajit's sacrifice were influenced by the later versions of the Dakṣa sacrifice.

251 Nagar and Nagar 1997 II, p. 130.
252 Nagar 2008 II, pp. 367f.
253 Nagar 2014 III, p. 1460.
254 ibid., p. 1462.
255 Shastri 2009 (1973) II, pp. 555ff.

/ 93 / 92 /

92. १नावणया्सखाय॥ १नावणया सखाय॥ १नावणव्नामचन्द्रव युद्ध॥ १लक्ष्मण॥ १विभीषण॥
[१]माकलसैन्य॥
Rāvaṇayā sakhāya. Rāvaṇayā sakhāya. Rāvaṇava Rāmacandrava yuddha. Lakṣmaṇa. Vibhīṣaṇa. mākalasainya.

A companion of Rāvaṇa. A companion of Rāvaṇa. Fight between Rāvaṇa and Rāma. Lakṣmaṇa. Vibhīṣaṇa. The monkey troop.

VR: Since all his great warriors have been slain in battle, Rāvaṇa now rushes at Rāma himself (ch. 87). Indra, in order to make the combat a fair one, instructs Mātali to act as Rāma's charioteer (ch. 90). Rāma severely wounds Rāvaṇa with hails of arrows and the monkeys assist him by throwing masses of stones (ch. 92). On account of Rāvaṇa's bad condition, his charioteer then drives the chariot from the field. Rāvaṇa rebukes his charioteer for acting on his own understanding and he urges him to set out to the battlefield again (ch. 93). A hundred times Rāma strikes off one of Rāvaṇa's heads but every time a new head, equal to the former, emerges from Rāvaṇa (ch. 96).
Image: In the centre of the image, Rāma and Rāvaṇa are fighting with bow and arrow. An arrow already struck Rāvaṇa's horse head. In accordance with the text, Rāma and Rāvaṇa are both depicted on chariots, beautifully carved with large blossoms adorning the wheels. On Rāma's side, Lakṣmaṇa, Vibhīṣaṇa and the monkeys are fighting. The latter march on the ground, jump on trees and even range through space like birds. On Rāvaṇa's side, two of his companions are depicted, representing the host of the demons.
Other versions: The fact that an arrow is depicted having hit Rāvaṇa's horse head immediately reminds the viewer of the Tibetan versions of the Rāmāyaṇa, mentioned in course of the discussion of scene 36. Anyway, the horse head is not really sliced off here.

93. १नावणया सखाय्वध॥ १नावण वध॥
Rāvaṇayā sakhāya vadha. Rāvaṇa vadha.
Death of Rāvaṇa's companion. Death of Rāvaṇa.

VR: Rāvaṇa is slain as Rāma discharges the Brahmā Weapon against him (ch. 97).
Image: Ultimately overcome, the lord of the demons falls to the ground. One of his companions, representative for the entire host, falls dead to the ground, too. In the background, a monkey pulls on Rāvaṇa's horse head.
Other sources: The monkey figure either symbolically points to the monkeys' contribution to Rāvaṇa's death or else accounts for a direct participation of the monkeys in the final battle. The latter is not attested in the Vālmīki Rāmāyaṇa but described in great length in the Rāmacaritamānasa.[256] According to this version, in the course of the final battle Rāma pushes aside Vibhīṣaṇa, faces Rāvaṇa's *śakti* and

256 Nagar 2014 III, pp. 1500ff.

faints. Until he regains consciousness, the monkeys (and bears) throw themselves upon Rāvaṇa repeatedly. In addition to the multiple attacks of crores of monkeys, single combats are mentioned between Hanumān and Rāvaṇa, Aṅgada and Rāvaṇa, between Nala, Nīla and Rāvaṇa and between Jāmbavān and Rāvaṇa.

94. १मन्दोदरीया विलाप॥
Mandodarīyā vilāpa.
Mandodarī's lamentations.

VR: On account of Rāvaṇa's death, his wives are overwhelmed with grief (ch. 98). They enter the battlefield and find him lying dead on the ground. Mandodarī, his favourite queen, especially gives way to lamentation (ch. 99).
Image: The image shows Mandodarī weeping for her deceased lord.

95. १हनूमन्तन सीता वोनाव हव॥ १लंकास विभीषण राजा साले॥ १मंदोरी॥
Hanumantana Sītā vonāva hava. Laṅkāsa Vibhīṣaṇa rājā sāle. Mandorī.
a) In Laṅkā Vibhīṣaṇa is proclaimed king. Mandodarī.
b) Hanumān goes for Sītā and brings her.

VR: Vibhīṣaṇa is crowned king of Laṅkā as a reward for his loyalty to Rāma (ch. 100). Afterwards, Rāma sends Hanumān to Sītā in order to inform her about his victory. As Hanumān returns he informs Rāma that Sītā desires to see him and Vibhīṣaṇa is finally sent to bring her (ch. 102).
Image: Like in case of Sugrīva's coronation (scene 55), an act of rendering homage is depicted instead of the ceremony itself. On the left side of the image, an attendant waves a fly-whisk, while the attendant on the right side holds a hand fan. Vibhīṣaṇa is accompanied by Mandodarī. The text does not say that Vibhīṣaṇa takes over Rāvaṇa's widowed queen(s) but since Vālin took over Sugrīva's queen(s) and later Sugrīva took over Vālin's, there is evidence to suggest that Vibhīṣaṇa takes over Rāvaṇa's widowed queen(s), too. On the left side of the image, Hanumān is depicted bringing Sītā although according to the text, Hanumān only conveys Rāma's message and Vibhīṣaṇa later brings her.

Other sources: Several later versions narrate that Mandodarī becomes a *satī* after Rāvaṇa's death. The Sanskrit term denotes a *good and faithful wife* and refers to a practice by which a woman is burnt together with the corpse of her deceased husband. The events as given in the Kṛttivāsi Rāmāyaṇa however contradict this.[257] Kṛttivāsi creates a story according to which Rāma mistakes Mandodarī to be Sītā, grants her the boon that she will always remain with a husband and consequently indeed hands her over to Vibhīṣaṇa.

96. १सीता मेस दु ब्वाक॥
Sītā mesa du bvāka.
Sītā leaps into the fire.

VR: Because Sītā spent much time in the presence of another man, her virtue is in doubt and Rāma feels constrained to repudiate her (ch. 103). Rejected by her husband in public, Sītā undergoes a trial by fire in order to prove her purity (chs. 104ff.) She asks Agni to protect her and enters the flames.
Image: The raging fire surrounds Sītā like a halo. With her left hand she shows the gesture of fearlessness (sa. *abhayamudrā*).

97. १लक्ष्मण॥ १रामचन्द्र॥ १ब्रह्मा विष्णु इन्द्र दशरथ थ्वतिस्यनं सीताया सत्य धक रामचंद्रयाके ह्लाक॥
Lakṣmaṇa. Rāmacandra. Brahmā Viṣṇu Indra Daśaratha thvatisyanaṃ Sītāyā satya dhaka Rāmacandrayāke hlāka.

Lakṣmaṇa. Rāma. Brahmā, Viṣṇu, Indra and Daśaratha tell Rāma that the fortunate Sītā speaks the truth.

VR: Vaiśravaṇa, Yama, Indra, Varuṇa, Śiva and Brahmā all appear and reproach Rāma for letting Sītā undergo this ordeal (ch. 105). Agni affirms that Sītā has committed no sin and gives her back to Rāma (ch. 106). Then Daśaratha appears to Rāma (ch. 107). As Rāma is safe after all, he is freed from his sorrow and attains to the world of Indra.

257 Nagar and Nagar 1997 II, pp. 201ff.

/ 97 / 96 / 95 / 94 /

Image: According to the inscription, one of the deities that appear before Rāma is Viṣṇu. Gail therefore assumes that here, Rāma's identification with Viṣṇu is negated.[258] In my opinion, Viṣṇu's appearance before Rāma would not necessarily have any effects on Rāma's identification with the god. In fact, Rāma's divine nature is even attested in another context: Rāma is part of the *daśāvatāra* series on the first floor of the temple, where he is even depicted four-armed, holding the conch (sa. *śaṅkha*), one of Viṣṇu's main attributes.[259]

Besides, it is obvious that the figure in this scene was initially not intended to be Viṣṇu. The four-armed deity is in fact Śiva. With his upper hands he holds a rosary of *rudrākṣa* seeds (sa. *akṣamālā*) and the trident (sa. *triśūla*).

At this point it is interesting to, once again, point out different hands that were involved in the artistic designs of the temple. Among the manifold representations of the trident that appear, some are kept as simple as possible while others are elaborately designed. The first category includes among others the tridents held by the male dancers accompanying Gaṇeśa in the opening scenes of both the cycles, the Rāmāyaṇa and the Mahābhārata, as well as the one held by Bṛhaspati (Pl. 05). The trident held by Śiva in this scene belongs to the second category, like also the one held by Īśāna in the closing scene of the Mahābhārata cycle (sc. 165) and those held by Rāhu and Maṅgala (Pl. 05). Taking account of the Maṅgala representation it is not possible to mistake the trident depicted in this scene for Viṣṇu's club, for Maṅgala holds both, a similar-looking trident and the club.

detail of scene 97

detail of scene 165, Mbh: Īśāna

258 Gail 1988, p. 37.
259 V. supra, pp. 25ff..

/ 98 /

98. १तनगन् नामचंद्र नाप लाक॥ १नामचद्र सीगा ञ्याध्या लिहा वं॥ १लक्ष्मग॥ १विलीषग॥ १सुग्रीव॥ १हनूमन्त॥
Bharatana Rāmacandra nāpa lāka. Rāmacandra Sītā Ayodhyā lihā vaṃ. Lakṣmaṇa. Vibhīṣaṇa. Sugrīva. Hanumanta.

a) Rāma and Sītā return to Ayodhyā. Lakṣmaṇa. Vibhīṣaṇa. Sugrīva. Hanumān.
b) Bharata meets with Rāma.

VR: Rāma, Sītā and Lakṣmaṇa return to Ayodhyā on the flying palace Puṣpaka (chs. 110f.). They are accompanied by Vibhīṣaṇa and the foremost of monkeys. Hanumān swiftly informs Bharata and the latter immediately sets out to meet Rāma (chs. 113ff.). As Bharata beholds him standing atop the celestial palace, he cups his hands in reverance (ch. 115). Then Bharata takes Rāma's sandals, places them back on his feet and by this means returns the kingdom to Rāma.
Image: Rāma and Sītā are depicted atop the flying palace Puṣpāka. Lakṣmaṇa, Vibhīṣaṇa, Sugrīva and Hanumān follow on foot although according to the text, they all mounted the flying palace, too (VR 6.110.21). On the left side of the image, Bharata approaches Rāma with joined palms (sa. *añjalimudrā*). That the palace is actually flying is evident since whirly clouds replace the vehicle's wheels. The flying palace has a standard with a double-pennant flag.

99. १नील॥ १नल॥ १अङ्गय॥ १हनूमन्त॥ १जांववान॥ १सुग्रीव॥ १लक्ष्मग॥ १नामचद्र् सीगा ञ्याध्यास् सता दयकाव चाट॥ १तनग॥ १शत्रुघ्न॥ १विलीषग॥
Nīla. Nala. Aṅgada. Hanumanta. Jāṃbavāna. Sugrīva. Lakṣmaṇa. Rāmacandra Sītā Ayodhyāsa sabhā dayakāva[260] coṅa. Bharata. Śatrughna. Vibhīṣaṇa.

Nīla. Nala. Aṅgada. Hanumān. Jāmbavān. Sugrīva. Lakṣmaṇa. In Ayodhyā, Rāma and Sītā are constantly holding court. Bharata. Śatrughna. Vibhīṣaṇa.

VR: In preparation for the coronation, Rāma's matted locks are shorn, he is bathed, clothed in costly robes and covered with multicoloured garlands (ch. 116). The monkeys bring the water for the consecration ceremony, officiated by Vaśiṣṭha. After the ceremony, Sugrīva returns to Kiṣkindhā, Vibhīṣaṇa occupies the throne of Laṅkā and Rāma, in supreme felicity, rules over the kingdom of Kośala for a period of ten thousand carefree years.
Image: Rāma and Sītā are sitting on a canopied throne, with a pair of lions as supports. Both show the gesture of fearlessness (sa. *abhayamudrā*). Rāma is still wearing his armour but is additionally adorned with a large garland of flowers. Depicted is again a courtly act of rendering homage instead of the coronation ceremony itself. Yet, a vessel for the consecration is placed on the throne. On the left an attendant with a hand fan is depicted, on the right an attendant with a fly-whisk. On the left side, Lakṣmaṇa and the most important representatives of the monkey host show Rāma respect. It is interesting to note that Jāmbavān is here distinguishable from the other monkeys. Being old and wise, he is depicted with a beard and holding the scriptures. On the right side Bharata, Śatrughna and Vibhīṣaṇa are sitting on low pieces of furniture. These items, as well as the many canopies hung over the entire assemblage, are all differently designed. In this final scene, one last time, the artists' passion for detail finds expression.

260 Jørgensen (1936) translates *sabhā dayakë* only as "to sit in judgement" (p. 162) but it is clear that *sabhā* in the connection given here denotes the court of the king, not the court of justice.

/ 99 /

The Rāmāyaṇa cycle at the Kṛṣṇa Temple ends here. No attention has been paid to the seventh and last section, the Uttarakāṇḍa. According to the Vālmīki Rāmāyaṇa, the rumours about Sītā and Rāvaṇa persist (ch. 42) and Rāma again repudiates Sītā (chs. 44ff.). She goes to the hermitage of Vālmīki (ch. 48) where she gives birth to the twins Lava and Kuśa (ch. 58). As Rāma performs a horse sacrifice (sa. *aśvamedha*) in order to consolidate the sovereignty of his power, Vālmīki commands the twins to recite the Rāmāyaṇa before Rāma (ch. 84). Rāma recognises Lava and Kuśa as his sons. He realises that he wronged Sītā and sends for her (ch. 87). Sītā however doesn't take him back. Instead, she calls upon the Earth Goddess and descends back into the earth from which she once sprung (ch. 88).

The Vālmīki Rāmāyaṇa's Uttarakāṇḍa provides a rather uncompassionate ending for the otherwise so heroic tale. Later Rāmāyaṇa poets dealt with that in different ways. Kambar and Eknāth for example omit the story altogether. Tulsīdās by contrast concludes his work with an Uttarakāṇḍa that differs significantly from the Vālmīki Rāmāyaṇa's Uttarakāṇḍa. He tells about the births of Lava and Kuśa[261] but he says nothing about Sītā's second exile. It seems thus that it was more appreciated to conclude the story with Rāma and Sītā reunited, enthroned in Ayodhyā, than to conclude it with their final seperation. Rāma's decision to banish Sītā might have been considered morally doubtful and this ending probably did not appeal to devotional viṣṇuite cults, with whom also the construction of the Kṛṣṇa Temple is linked.

The final scene with Rāma and Sītā enthroned in Ayodhyā is given special prominence at the Kṛṣṇa Temple. The frieze begins slightly offset about the temple's main entrance and thus, underlining the significance of the heroic ending, it is this final scene that is depicted directly above the entrance.

261 Nagar 2014 III, p. 1616.

3.3. The Mahābhārata Frieze

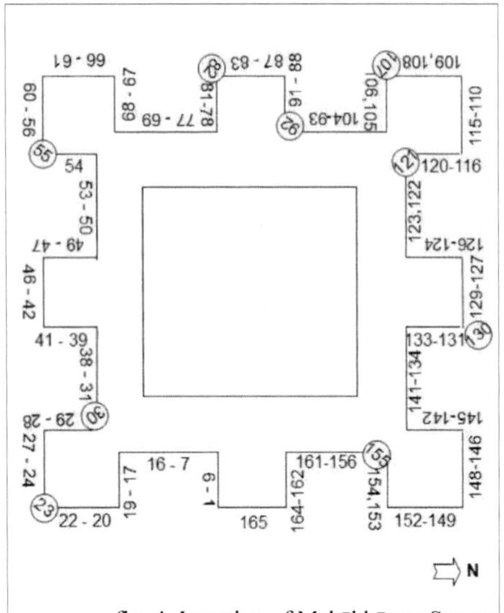

fig. 4: Location of Mahābhārata Scenes

The pictorial representation of the Mahābhārata begins slightly offset above the temple's main entrance, too. The cycle runs clockwise around the structure, on the lintels meandering around the arcade aisle and the small pavilions. Figure 4 shows these lintels in cross section with the location of the individual scenes. The numbers are placed according to reading direction. Whenever a number is placed inside a ring (nos 23, 30, etc.), the corresponding scene runs around the corner.

The Mahābhārata frieze consists of 165 scenes and is thus notably longer than the Rāmāyaṇa frieze. As apparent from the adjacent table, the cycle of the Kṛṣṇa Temple covers all 18 books (sa. *parvas*), with a preference for the events from the first *parvas*. Most of the *parvas* thereafter have not been given weight to but every *parva* is represented with at least one scene. More significance has again be given to the closing *parvas*.

Book	Number of Scenes	
(introductive invocation)	1	(1)
1: Ādiparva	37	(2-38)
2: Sabhāparva	15	(39-53)
3: Vanaparva	38	(54-91)
4: Virāṭaparva	20	(92-111)
5: Udyogaparva	10	(112-121)
6: Bhīṣmaparva	3	(122-124)
7: Droṇaparva	4	(125-128)
8: Karṇaparva	2	(129-130)
9: Śalyaparva	5	(131-135)
10: Sauptikaparva	5	(136-140)
11: Strīparva	1	(141)
12: Śāntiparva	1	(142)
13: Anuśāsanaparva	2	(143-144)
14: Aśvamedhikaparva	1	(145)
15: Āśramavāsikaparva	1	(146)
16: Mausalaparva	8	(147-154)
17: Mahāprasthānikaparva	5	(155-159)
18: Svargārohaṇaparva	6	(160-165)

In what follows, again, every scene will be discussed separately, with its inscription in Nepālākṣara, transcription and English translation. The Mahābhārata tells of the great battle between the Pāṇḍavas (acknowledged sons of Pāṇḍu) and their cousins, Dhṛtarāṣṭra's sons, referred to as Kauravas. Though the Pāṇḍavas are descendants of Kuru, too, only Dhṛtarāṣṭra's sons are commonly referred to as Kauravas for his line forms the older line of descent from the ancient king. As in case of the Rāmāyaṇa frieze, each image will first be compared with the events as given in the Critical Edition. I therefore use the first complete English translation of the Mahābhārata's Critical Edition by Bibek Debroy.[262] In case of the Mahābhārata, the comparison with other versions is difficult for there are simply no translations available so far. Anyway, the subsequent discussion about comparable narrative representations will hopefully provide useful informations on region-specific characteristics.

262 Debroy 2015 (2010-2014), 10 Vols. set.

The Mahābhārata cycle also opens with a representation of Gaṇeśa.

/ 1 /

1. The first image has no inscription. It is certainly also for the same luck gaining purpose that the giver of success is represented here but it might be noted that according to common belief, Gaṇeśa is attributed a special role in the context of the Mahhābhārata. Vyāsa, to whom the authorship of the Mahābhārata is attributed, is said to have dictated the text to Gaṇeśa, who wrote it down with his tusk. This popular belief was, however, excluded from the Critical Edition's text.[263]

   Image: The image resembles very much the representation of the god at the beginning of the Rāmāyaṇa cycle. He is again depicted dancing on two rats, accompanied by the same attendants and he also holds the same objects. As the only addition he now holds a bowl with sweets (sa. *modakapātra*), too, and he is grasping some with his trunk.

263 Debroy 2015 Vol. I (2010), p. xxii.

Ādiparva: 'The Book of the Beginning'

The Ādiparva gives an account of the genealogy of the Bhāratas (descendants of Bhārata). It also covers the early life of the Pāṇḍavas and the Kauravas and deals with the incurrence of the enmity between the cousins. Figure 5 shows the genealogical relationships between the main characters.

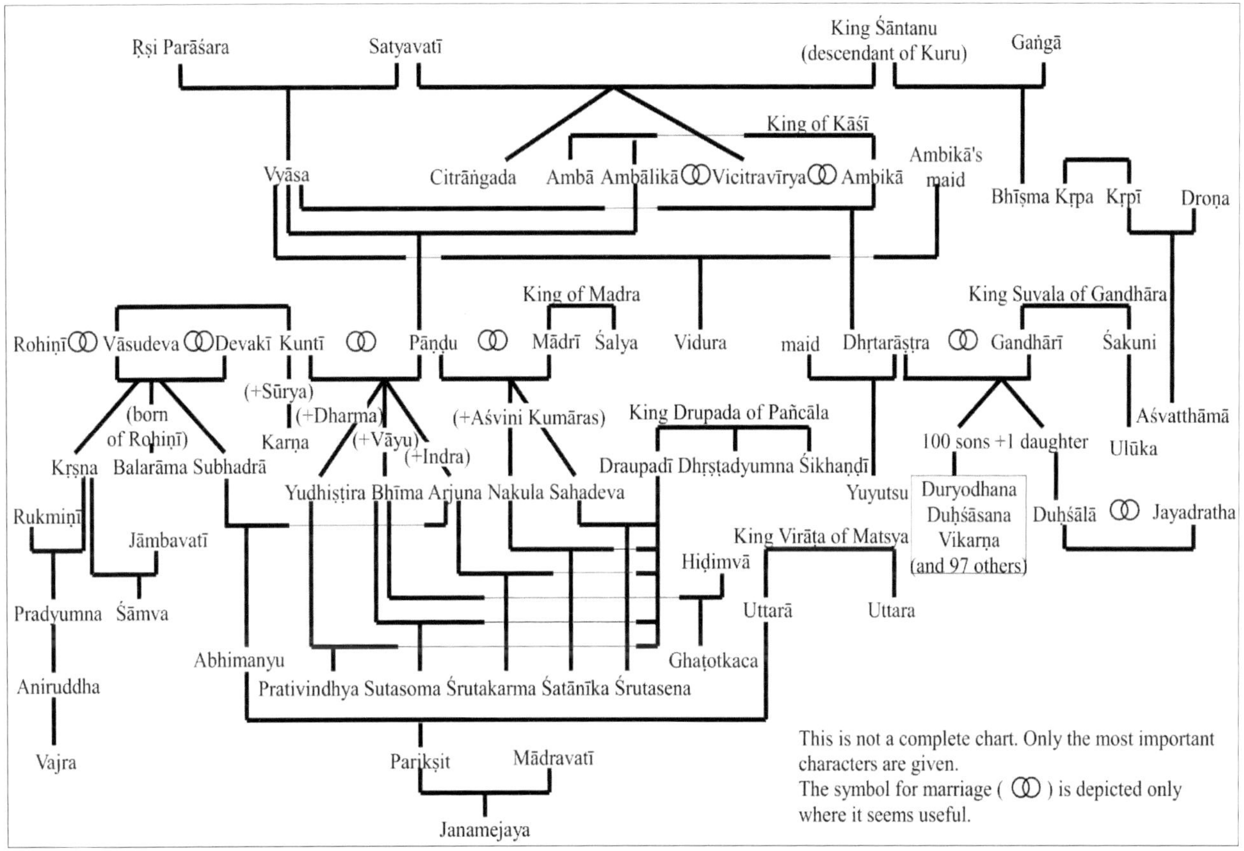

fig. 5: Genealogy of the Mahābhārata

The chart starts with Ṛṣi Parāśara. According to the text, he falls in love with a beautiful girl, Satyavatī, and she bears him a son, Kṛṣṇa Dvaipāyana Vyāsa (ch. 57). Vyāsa is said to have devided the Vedas and he is also the considered author of the Mahābhārata. After marrying king Śāntanu, Satyavatī has two more sons, Citrāṅgada and Vicitravīrya, but they both die childless (chs. 95f.). Bhīṣma, Śāntanu's son with Gaṅgā, had earlier vowed lifelong celibacy and is therefore without children, too (ch. 94). For the continuation of the lineage, Satyavatī asks Vyāsa to beget children upon Vicitravīrya's widowed wives, Ambikā and Ambālikā (ch. 99). Dvaipāyana is so unsightly that Ambikā closes her eyes while the sage unites with her and she brings forth a blind son, Dhṛtarāṣṭra (ch. 100). Ambālikā for her part turns pale as she beholds Dvaipāyana and she brings forth a son who is pale in complexion, Pāṇḍu (sa., pale, white). Finally, Dvaipāyana begets a third son upon Ambikā's maid. He becomes known by the name of Vidura. Since his older brother is blind, Pāṇḍu becomes king (ch. 102). Dhṛtarāṣṭra marries Gāndhārī with whom he has 100 sons and one daughter (chs. 103, 107). Pāṇḍu marries Kuntī and Mādrī (chs. 104f.). On account of a curse he is not able to beget children himself but he has five sons through his wives, born from the gods (chs. 109ff.). After Pāṇḍu's death, Dhṛtarāṣṭra becomes king and all the children are brought up at court, together (ch. 119). The struggle among the princes about superiority begins at this early stage.

The first scene from the Mahābhārata shows Pāṇḍu's hunt as the source for the curse put on him.

2. १ऋषि् नेह्मतिपुर् चरारूपन् प्रसंग याक् पाण्डुराजान् अहल वनेन कयको॥
ṛṣi nemhatipura carārūpana prasaṅga yāka Pāṇḍurājāna ahala vanena kayako.
King Pāṇḍu [who has] gone hunting, strikes the Sage and his wife[264] who are mating in the form of deer.

Text: While roaming in the woods, Pāṇḍu beholds a large stag coupling with a doe (ch. 109). King Pāṇḍu shoots his arrows at them. As the deer falls down on the ground, he utters lamentations in a human voice. He reveals himself to be sage Kindama, who had taken the form of a deer in order to unite with his wife.
Image: The image shows Pāṇḍu on a horse, his bow bent. The deer couple is visually separated from him by a tree. The arrow already hit its target and the deer turns his head back towards his assailant. No space is left empty. The leaves of the trees fill the space above the figures while dustclouds and small plants are depicted between the hoofs of the animals and underneath the horse's raised front hoof. A nice detail is the horse's tail knot.

3. १चरारूपन् चोङ् ऋषि् वध्
carārūpana coṅa ṛṣi vadha.
Retaining the form of the gazelle, the sage dies.

Text: The dying sage curses Pāṇḍu to suffer the same fate (ch. 109). If he ever unites with one of his wives again, he would die and the respective wife would follow him into death.
Image: The deer is depicted supine, dying or almost deceased, on a bed of stone. The arrow has hit him in the chest.

264 Jørgensen 1995 (1936), p. 103: *nehmatipuli*, man and wife.

/ 4 / 3 / 2 /

4. १माद्री॥ १कुंती॥ १ऋषिया् सरापन् पाण्डुराजाया् वैराग्य॥
Mādrī. Kuntī. Ṛṣiyā sarāpana Pāṇḍurājāyā vairāgya.
Mādrī. Kuntī. King Pāṇḍu's apathy in consequence of the sage's curse.

Text: Pāṇḍu and his wives are overcome by deep sorrow on account of the curse (ch. 110). In order to attain salvation, Pāṇḍu decides to renounce the kingdom and to live the life of an ascetic instead. Together with Mādrī and Kuntī he leaves for the woods.
Image: Pāṇḍu is depicted sad-looking. He sits on his lion-throne as Mādrī and Kuntī approach with joined palms to attain permission to accompany him.

5. १धर्म्मराजव् कुंतिव प्रसंग॥
Dharmmarājava Kuntiva prasaṅga.
Sexual union of king Dharma and Kuntī.

Text: On account of the curse, Pāṇḍu cannot beget children but still, he longs for a son (ch. 111). Kuntī tells him of a boon she once obtained from sage Durvāsā (ch. 113). According to this, the recitation of a special formula (sa. *mantra*) would enable her to summon any of the gods in order to obtain offspring. After consultation with Pāṇḍu she summons the god Dharma for conception (ch. 114).
Image: Dharma and Kuntī are turned towards each other. The seating furniture very much resembles the one in the previous image. Dharma has laid his arm around Kuntī's neck and they both show the gesture of fearlessness (sa. *abhayamudrā*).

/ 12 / 11 / 10 / 9 / 8 / 7 / 6 / 5 /

6. १युधिष्ठिन् जम्म जुव॥
Yudhiṣṭhira janma juva.
Yudhiṣṭhira is born.

Text: As Kuntī gives birth to the son conceived by the god of justice and virtue (sa. *dharma*), an invisible voice declares that he will be known by the name of Yudhiṣṭhira, that he will be a famous king and supreme among those who uphold *dharma* (ch. 114).
Image: The image shows Kuntī inside the palace, holding the newborn child in her arms.

7. १वायुव् कुंतिव् प्रसंग॥
Vāyuva Kuntiva prasaṅga.
Sexual union of Vāyu and Kuntī.

Text: Having obtained this virtuous son, king Pāṇḍu asks for a second son who has great strength (ch. 114). In order to conceive a child with such qualities, Kuntī invokes Vāyu, the mighty god of the wind.
Image: Kuntī and Vāyu are depicted in the same way as were Kuntī and Dharma before.

8. १भीम् जम्म जुव॥
Bhīma janma juva.
Bhīma is born.

Text: From Kuntī's union with Vāyu results a child endowed with terrifying strength (ch. 114). He is given the name Bhīma and it is noted that his cousin Duryodhana, the eldest son of Dhṛtarāṣṭra and Gāndhārī, is born the same day.
Image: Kuntī is again shown inside the palace, with her second son on her lap.

9. १इन्द्रव् कुंतिव् प्रसंग॥
Indrava Kuntiva prasaṅga.
Sexual union of Indra and Kuntī.

Text: Pāṇḍu wishes to obtain another son, one who would attain worldwide renown (ch. 114). In order to please Indra, the lord of the thirty gods, Pāṇḍu performs severe austerities for one year. Then Indra appears and agrees to give him a son who would be famous in the three worlds, one who would ensure the welfare of gods, brahmins and relatives alike.
Image: Kuntī is now depicted together with Indra. The lord of the gods is recognisable by his conical crown, in distinction from the three pointed crowns seen before.

10. (previous page) १अर्ज्जुन् जन्म जुव॥
Arjjuna janma juva.
Arjuna is born.

Text: The child begotten by Indra is given the name Arjuna (ch. 114). The invisible voice again appears and declares that this one will acquire all kinds of divine weapons and by this means will become invincible in battle.
Image: Kuntī is again depicted inside the palace with her infant son on her lap. Though the palace has in general always the same structure, the representations differ in detail. This concerns the design of the layers, pillars, brackets, superstructures of the roofings as also the bottom section with lion's feet in this case or semicircular flowery motifs before.

11. (previous page) १अश्विनीकुमारनेह्मव् माद्रीव् प्रसंग॥
Aśvinīkumāranehmava Mādrīva prasaṅga.
Sexual union of both the Aśvinī Kumāras and Mādrī.

Text: Pāṇḍu is greedy for more sons but since Kuntī is apprehensive of being called promiscuous, she refuses to invoke another god (ch. 114). At Pāṇḍu's request however, Kuntī allows Mādrī to use the secret formula (ch. 115). In order to double the fruits, Mādrī summons two gods, the Aśvinī twins.
Image: Mādrī is sitting between the two gods. One of them has placed his arm around her waist, the other one puts his around her shoulder. Mādrī's headdress differs from Kuntī's in the previous picture but it is not possible to reliably tell one from the other on this basis. Mādrī might also be represented without the top knot (scs. 4, 13) and Kuntī might likewise be represented with (sc. 7).

12. (previous page) १नकुल् सहदेव् जन्म जुव॥
Nakula Sahadeva janma juva.
Nakula and Sahadeva are born.

Text: Because she had summoned two gods, Mādrī gives birth to twins (ch. 115). They possess a beauty unmatched on earth and they are named Nakula und Sahadeva. Pāṇḍu later again requests Kuntī on behalf of Mādrī but Kuntī feels deceived since Mādrī had managed to obtain two sons with only once using the formula. Kuntī now fears to be surpassed by Mādrī in the number of her children and she does not allow her to use the formula again.
Image: Mādrī is depicted inside the palace with one of her infant sons in each of her arms.

13. १कुन्ती॥ १पाण्डुराजाव् माद्रिव् प्रसंग॥
Kuntī. Pāṇḍurājāva Mādriva prasaṅga.
Kuntī. Sexual union of king Pāṇḍu and Mādrī.

Text: The Pāṇḍavas grow up in a great forest on the Himālaya Mountains. One day in the season of spring, as Pāṇḍu roams through the forest with Mādrī, he becomes overpowered by desire (ch. 116). Mādrī tries to stop him but he forcibly takes her. As Pāṇḍu lies dead on the ground Kuntī appears, alerted by Mādrī's lamentations.
Image: In contrast to the text, Pāṇḍu is represented with both his wives. However, he seeks only Mādrī's embrace while Kuntī is uninvolved in their loveplay. Another deviation from the text is that they are depicted inside, though the scene actually takes place in the open.

14. १माद्री सती वं॥ १पाण्डुराजा [मृ]त्यु जुल् अग्निसंस्कार[॥]
Mādrī satī vaṃ. Pāṇḍurājā mṛtyu jula agnisaṃskāra.
a) King Pāṇḍu's death occurs; fire ceremony.
b) Mādrī becomes a *satī*.

Text: Since Pāṇḍu died because of the desire for Mādrī, Mādrī resolves to follow him into death (ch. 116). She asks Kuntī to bring up her sons, too, ascends the funeral pyre and is burnt together with Pāṇḍu's corpse. This practice, known as *satī* (sa., good, faithful wife) was long popular in India.
Image: Pāṇḍu's dead corpse is depicted on the funeral pyre. Mādrī is kneeling at his feet. The flames above enclose them both.

/ 16 / 15 / 14 / 13 /

15. १[धृतरा]ष्ट्र॥ १ऋषिन् कुंती युधिष्ठिन् भीम् अर्ज्जुन् नकुल् सहदेव् धृतराष्ट्र लव ह्लाक॥
Dhṛtarāṣṭra. ṛṣina Kuntī Yudhiṣṭhira Bhīmā Arjjuna Nakula Sahadeva Dhṛtarāṣṭra lava hlāka.

Dhṛtarāṣṭra. The sage commits Kuntī, Yudhiṣṭhira, Bhīma, Arjuna, Nakula and Sahadeva to (the care of) Dhṛtarāṣṭra.

Text: After Pāṇḍu's death, the sages living in the woods resolve that it would be best to give Pāṇḍu's infant sons and Kuntī to Bhīṣma and Dhṛtarāṣṭra who had taken on regnal tasks since Pāṇḍu's departure for the woods (ch. 117). Thousands of sages and singers (sa. *cāraṇas*) leave with them for Hastināpura. On their arrival, the eldest sage informs Dhṛtarāṣṭra about everything that has happened.
Image: Dhṛtarāṣṭra is represented on the left side. He makes a reverential gesture (sa. *añjalimudrā*) as the sage approaches with Kuntī and the sons of Pāṇḍu. The sage is depicted just like the sages from the Rāmāyaṇa frieze. He has his matted hair tied up in a knot, wears simple clothes, a *rudrākṣa* chain and he holds the scriptures. Pāṇḍu's sons, represented on a twofold lotus pedestal, are likewise wearing simple clothes and have long matted hair. This is probably rather to indicate their young age than to point to the ascetic life they were so far leading with their parents. The Pāṇḍavas are arranged according to birth. This is retained for the entire cycle.

16. १कुंती युधिष्ठिन् भीम् अर्ज्जुन् नकुल् सहदेव् वारनावत वंढ॥
Kuntī Yudhiṣṭhira Bhīmā Arjjuna Nakula Sahadeva Vāraṇāvata vaṃṅa.
Kuntī, Yudhiṣṭhira, Bhīma, Arjuna, Nakula and Sahadeva have gone to Vāraṇāvata.

Text: From now on, the Pāṇḍavas grow up in princely style (ch. 119). Whenever engaged in play with Dhṛtarāṣṭra's sons, the Pāṇḍavas excel over them. Bhīma especially demonstrates his strength and humbles the Kauravas repeatedly wherefore Duryodhana repeatedly tries to bring about his death. As the princes grow naughty, Bhīṣma decides to make Droṇa their preceptor (ch. 122). Within a short time, the Kauravas and the Pāṇḍavas alike all become proficient in the use of arms. Arjuna becomes the most skilled one among them (ch. 123). Voices are then heard in the city that Yudhiṣṭhira, the eldest, should be installed as king soon (ch. 129). Duryodhana feels overlooked and entreats Dhṛtarāṣṭra to banish the Pāṇḍavas (chs. 129f.). Dhṛtarāṣṭra sends them to the town of Vāraṇāvata to attend the Paśupati festival (ch. 131).
Image: The artists chose not to depict the events at the court of Hastināpura. Thus the arising enmity between Pāṇḍavas and Kauravas, the reason for the upcoming war, is not payed attention to. We come directly to the Pāṇḍavas' sojourn at Vāraṇāvata. The five brothers together with Kuntī are depicted inside their abode. It is a building with three compartments, supported by columns and crowned with a tapered roofing and a good many small superstructures.

17. १कुंती॥ युधिष्ठिर् अर्ज्जुन् नकुल् सहदेव् वनस बेसे वं॥ १भीमन् छे मि तयाव वं॥ १पुरोचन् दाह जुव॥

Kuntī Yudhiṣṭhira Arjjuna Nakula Sahadeva vanasa bese vaṃ. Bhīmana che mi tayāva vaṃ. Purocana dāha juva.

a) Bhīma sets the house on fire and leaves. Purocana is burnt.

b) Kuntī, Yudhiṣṭhira, Arjuna, Nakula and Sahadeva escape into the woods.

Text: After Dhṛtarāṣṭra has sent the Pāṇḍavas to Vāraṇāvata, Duryodhana instructs his counsellor, Purocana, to swiftly go there, too (ch. 132). At Duryodhana's command, Purocana builds an inflammable mansion. He invites the Pāṇḍavas and Kuntī to stay there with the intention to burn everything down while they are asleep. Vidura, however, foresees the danger and warns Yudhiṣṭhira (ch. 133). The Pāṇḍavas secretly dig a tunnel in the ground and after one year they kindle a fire themselves (chs. 135f.). Bhīma sets the house on fire and while Purocana burns to death, the sons of Pāṇḍu together with Kuntī escape through the tunnel. The citizens later find the burnt bodies of a hunter woman (sa. *niṣāda*) and her five sons among the ashes whom they take to be Kuntī and her sons (ch. 137). Thus the news spread that the Pāṇḍavas have been burnt to death.

Image: Bhīma sets the house of lac on fire, with Purocana sleeping inside. The mansion is a typical Nepalese one, with a raised floor and a tapered, multi-tiered roof enriched with small superstructures. As the inscription ascertains, the figure of Bhīma also pertains to the fleeing group. The tunnel is not represented. Pictorically, this scene marks the outbreak of the hostilities. The Pāṇḍavas are from now on depicted wearing an armour and their distinctive attributes. Yudhiṣṭhira holds the sacred scriptures, Arjuna holds bow (sa. *dhanu*) and arrow (sa. *bāṇa*), Nakula a spear (sa. *kunta*) and Sahadeva a sword (sa. *khaḍga*). Bhīma's attribute is the club (sa. *gadā*). It is not depicted here for he holds the torch instead, and it is neither depicted in the next scene where he carries his brothers, but Bhīma's club is depicted from scene 19 onwards. This assignment of weapons is retained for the entire cycle and it is therefore possible to identify each of the five brothers even without the inscription. In addition to that, the Pāṇḍavas from now on also wear a crown. In this scene, Arjuna, Nakula and Sahadeva have a three pointed crown, Yudhiṣṭhira, the one supposed to be king, wears a rounded crown and Bhīma wears a jagged crown with a layer behind.

18. १भीमन् सकल्यं बुयाव यं॥

Bhīmana sakalyaṃ buyāva yaṃ.

Bhīma carries them all away.

Text: As a result of fear and lack of sleep, the brothers can not proceed quickly (ch. 136). The mighty Bhīma however manages to lift all his brothers and his mother and he then carries them as he proceeds in great haste. According to the text, he carries his mother on his shoulder, the twins on his hips and the others on his arms.

Image: The image agrees perfectly with the text. Kuntī is mounted on Bhīma's shoulder, Yudhiṣṭhira and presumably Arjuna are depicted on Bhīma's arms and the others he holds with his hands on his hips. That Bhīma proceeds with great haste is evident from the big step he takes foreward and from the many fluttering cloths.

19. १हिडिंवराक्षस् तमन् वव॥ १हिडिंवाव् भीमव् संभाषण॥ १कुंती॥ युधिष्ठिर् अर्ज्जुन् नकुल सहदेव् नेलाव् देङ चों॥

Hiḍiṃvarākṣasa tamana vava. Hiḍiṃvāva Bhīmava sambhāṣaṇa. Kuntī Yudhiṣṭhira Arjjuna Nakula Sahadeva nelāva deṅa coṃ.

a) Kuntī, Yudhiṣṭhira, Arjuna, Nakula and Sahadeva have become tired and are sleeping.

b) Conversation of Hiḍimvā and Bhīma.

c) The demon Hiḍimva comes in wrath.

Text: The Pāṇḍavas proceed in a southern direction to a dense forest (chs. 137f.). Tired, thirsty and overcome with sleep they rest under a beautiful *nyagrodha* (sa., fig or banyan tree). Bhīma leaves in order to bring water but as he returns the others have all fallen asleep. Bhīma stays awake and keeps watch over them. As the demon Hiḍimva beholds the sleeping ones, he directs his sister Hiḍimvā to slay them so they could eat their flesh together (ch. 139). Yet, as Hiḍimvā beholds Bhīma, she immediately falls in love with him. Assuming a beautiful form, she approaches him and asks him to become her husband. Since his sister takes too long, Hiḍimva him-

/ 19 / 18 / 17 /

self proceeds to where the Pāṇḍavas are sleeping (ch. 140). As he beholds Hiḍimvā in that charming human form, he becomes furious and rushes at her.
Image: The brothers and Kuntī are not represented sleeping on the ground but on a large pedestal covered with multiple layers. Additionally they have pillows made of carefully tied grasses or something alike. Even while sleeping they hold their distinctive attributes. The shade-providing tree is depicted above them with fruits upon which a large bird and a nature spirit (sa. *yakṣa*) are feeding. Bhīma holds his club as he speaks with the beautifully disguised Hiḍimvā. Her brother rushes at her, his hands raised in wrath. Since Bhīma is keeping watch over the others, he is represented between them and the demons.

20. १हिडिंव् वध॥ १हिडिंवनाऊसव् भीमव् यूद्ध॥
Hiḍiṃva vadha. Hiḍiṃvarākṣasava Bhīmava yuddha.
a) Fight between the demon Hiḍimva and Bhīma.
b) The killing of Hiḍimva.

Text: Bhīma reproaches Hiḍimva and challenges him to fight it out with him instead (ch. 141). Hiḍimva stretches out his arms and rushes at Bhīma but Bhīma seizes his arms, dashes him on the ground and drags him away. They clasp and drag each other again and again until finally Bhīma whirls Hiḍimva in the air a hundred times and violently crushes him on the ground (ch. 142). Finally, Bhīma tears the dead body into two.

Image: In accordance with the text, Hiḍimva rushes at Bhīma with his arm outstretched while Bhīma is about to catch hold of him. A large tree in the background subdivides the image. On the left side, Hiḍimva lies flung down on the ground, at the point of death.

21. १घटोत्कच् उत्पत्ति॥ १भीमव् हिडिंवाव् क्रीडा॥
Ghaṭotkaca utpatti. Bhīmava Hiḍiṃvāva krīḍā.
a) Bhīma and Hiḍimvā's amorous play.
b) Arising of Ghaṭotkaca.

Text (scene 21): As the Pāṇḍavas proceed, they are followed by Hiḍimvā (ch. 142). She further expresses her feelings for Bhīma who agrees to stay with her until she obtains a son (ch. 143). Hiḍimvā speeds with him through the sky to the most beautiful regions. In time, she conceives and the very same day brings forth a son, Ghaṭotkaca. Immediately, the child grows a youth. Ghaṭotkaca departs after promising unto his father that he would reappear immediately whenever he would wish to see him.
Image: Bhīma and Hiḍimvā are depicted in intimate embrace. Their newly born son sits next to them, already grown up. As, according to the text, he has nothing human in him, he is represented with the typical demonic hair. He holds his hands in reverential gesture (sa. *añjalimudrā*), saluting his parents.

--23 / 22 / 21 / 20 /

/ 25 / 24 / 23--------------------------

22. १व्यासव युधिष्ठिनव नाप लाक॥ १कुन्ती॥ १भीम॥ १अर्ज्जुन॥ १नकुल॥ १सहदेव॥
Vyāsava Yudhiṣṭhirava nāpa lāka. Kuntī. Bhīma. Arjjuna. Nakula. Sahadeva.
Vyāsa and Yudhiṣṭhira meet. Kuntī. Bhīma. Arjuna. Nakula. Sahadeva.

Text: In the garb of ascetics, the Pāṇḍavas and Kuntī wander from forest to forest (ch. 144). One day they meet Vyāsa. He tells them not to grieve since all that has happened was for their own good.
Image: Vyāsa and Yudhiṣṭhira are conversing. The sage makes a gesture as if to calm his grandson down. The others are represented behind Yudhiṣṭhira, arranged according to birth as always. Like in case of the Rāmāyaṇa cycle, the princes retain their crowns and jewellery, weapons and armour though, according to the text, they put on robes of bark and deerskin. The part around Vyāsa and Yudhiṣṭhira seems to be unfinished. Several lines roughly defining the forms remain and it is questionable whether the halo around Vyāsa's head was actually meant to be one.

Scene 23 is already partly depicted on the southern face of the temple. We remain on the southern face up to scene 60.

23. १ब्राह्मणी॥ १एकचक्रानगरस ब्राह्मणयाक् युधिष्ठिन वं॥ १कुन्ती॥ १भीम॥ [१अ]र्ज्जुन॥ १नकुल॥ १सहदेव॥
brāhmaṇī. Ekacahrānagarasa brāhmaṇayāke Yudhiṣṭhira vaṃ. Kuntī. Bhīma. Arjjuna. Nakula. Sahadeva.
Brahmin (f.). In the city Ekacakra Yudhiṣṭhira goes to a brahmin (m.). Kuntī. Bhīma. Arjuna. Nakula. Sahadeva.

Text: Vyāsa leads the brothers to a safe place, the house of a brahmin at the city Ekacakra, and tells them to wait for his return (ch. 144).
Image: Yudhiṣṭhira is represented inside the house of the brahmin on the part of the image on the south side of the temple. The building is indicated only through pillars with brackets and the tasseled cloths hanging from the ceiling. The brahmin offers him hospitality with his wife in attendance. Kuntī, Bhīma, Arjuna, Nakula and Sahadeva are waiting outside, represented on the east side.

24. १वकनाञसव् तीमव् यूद्ध॥
Vakarākṣasava Bhīmava yuddha.
Fight between the demon Vaka and Bhīma.

Text: Kuntī comes to know that the brahmin's family is threatened by the demon Vaka (chs. 145ff.). Vaka protects the country but expects from the citizens to offer him food in regular intervals, consisting of rice, two buffaloes and the human being who takes these to him. Now, the turn to send him his food has come to the brahmin's family. Kuntī resolves that Bhīma should deliver the food for the demon would not be able to kill him (ch. 149). The following day, Bhīma sets out to where Vaka lives (ch. 151). As Vaka beholds Bhīma eating the food intended for him, he becomes filled with wrath. He uproots many trees and dashes them at Bhīma but Bhīma ignores this and slowly finishes eating. Only then he likewise attacks Vaka with trees until the demon is overcome by great fatigue.
Image: Vaka is represented with vertical projecting hair and demonic facial traits. He grasps the branch of a tree while his opponent grasps his arm and holds the club upraised.

25. १वकनाञस् वध॥
Vakarākṣasa vadha.
The killing of the demon Vaka.

Text: In order to bring about Vaka's end, Bhīma presses him down on the ground, pushes his back down with his knee and by tugging at his neck with one hand and at his loincloth with the other hand, he tears Vaka into two (ch. 151).
Image: Vaka is represented dashed on the ground but he has not (yet) been torn into two.

26. १कून्ती् यूधिष्ठिन् तीम् [ज्]ज्ञून् नकू[ल् सहदेव ... नग]नस् वंढ॥
Kuntī Yudhiṣṭhira Bhīma Arjjuna Nakula Sahadeva [...] nagarasa vaṃṅa.
Kuntī, Yudhiṣṭhira, Bhīma, Arjuna, Nakula and Sahadeva go to the city [Kāmpila].

Text: A while later Vyāsa returns (ch. 157). He tells the Pāṇḍavas about king Drupada of Pañcāla and his daughter Draupadī. According to Vyāsa she is destined to be

/ 26 /

their common wife because she had asked five times for a husband in a previous life. On his advice, the Pāṇḍavas and Kuntī start out for the city of Pañcāla, Kāmpila (ch. 158). On the banks of the Gaṅgā they meet the king of celestial musicians (sa. *gandharvas*), named Aṅgāraparṇa. After defeating him, he advises them to appoint Dhaumya as their priest (ch. 174).
Image: The image shows Kuntī and her five sons on their way to Kāmpila. Strikingly, Kuntī is depicted going first and what is even more surprising is that she comes upon a dog. She stretches out her hand towards him and Yudhiṣṭhira and Bhīma are greeting him, too. The scene recalls an event that took place earlier, when the Pāṇḍavas still lived in Vāraṇāvata. After Droṇa had become their preceptor, they went on a hunt with a dog (ch. 123). The dog wandered off and came upon Ekalavya. As the dog barked at him, Ekalavya silenced him by shooting seven arrows into his mouth and the dog dashed back to the Pāṇḍavas, its mouth full of arrows. The image does not really match with the text for firstly, the described event occured earlier, secondly, no arrows are seen in the dog's mouth and thirdly, Kuntī certainly didn't accompany the Pāṇḍavas on their hunt. The image therefore either depicts an altered version of this story or it refers to another event. This would then point to a later transcreation for there is no other such dog-story found in the Ādiparva of the Critical Edition.

27. १द्रौपदीन् स्वानमाल् जोङाव् चोङ॥ १द्रुपदराजा् स्वयंवरया थायस् चोङ॥

Draupadīna svānamāla joṅāva coṅa. Drupadarājā svayaṃvarayā thāyasa coṅa.

a) King Drupada sits at the place of *svayaṃvara*.[265]

b) Draupadī is holding the garland of flowers.

Text: Accompanied by Dhaumya the Pāṇḍavas go to Draupadī's *svayamvara* (ch. 176). They take up their quarters in a potter's house where they stay in the guise of brahmins, unrecognised by the people. King Drupada causes a very hard bow to be made and an artificial machine to be erected in the sky with a golden target attached to it. As all are assembled, Draupadī enters the showplace, richly attired, adorned with every ornament and holding in her hand a golden prize for the winner. Dhṛṣṭa-dyumna, Drupada's son, declares that his sister would be given in marriage to whomsoever succeeds in shooting the mark above the machine, through the hole in its centre.

Image: Drupada sits on his throne, surrounded by two attendants with a hand fand and a fly-whisk. Draupadī faces away from the king towards Arjuna shooting the target, represented in the next scene. In her hands she already holds the garland of flowers which she is later reported to give to Arjuna.

28. १सहदेव॥ १नकुल॥ १भीम॥ १युधिष्ठिन॥ १द्रौपदीया स्वयम्वनस् अर्ज्जुनन् ङा् कयको॥

Sahadeva Nakula Bhīma Yudhiṣṭhira. Draupadīyā svayamvarasa Arjjunana ṅā kayako

Sahadeva. Nakula. Bhīma. Yudhiṣṭhira. At Draupadī's *svayaṃvara* Arjuna hits the fish

Text: Many illustrious kings and princes have come for Draupadī's hand, including Dhṛtarāṣṭra's sons and Karṇa, the illegitimate son of Kuntī and Sūrya (ch. 177). After they have all failed to string the bow, Arjuna advances towards it (ch. 178). The people wonder how a brahmin, unpractised in arms, can assume to succeed in that act but Arjuna strings the bow within the twinkling of an eye and shoots the target down (ch. 179). Draupadī then presents him with a white garland of flowers.

265 *svayamvara* means *self-choice* and stands for the election of a husband by a princess at a public assembly of suitors, frequently by means of a competition. Arjuna wins Draupadī like Rāma had won Sītā. Thus, being the price the winner obtains, one can not really agree that the lady chooses her husband.

/ 30 /

Image: Arjuna strings the bow. His brothers are depicted next to him. In contrast to the text, the Pāṇḍavas are not dressed like brahmins. Except for Yudhiṣṭhira, they even regain their armours. The machinery described in the text is not depicted. Instead, Arjuna, while looking downwards, looses his arrow at one of five fish attached to a tree. The fish he hits is depicted thrice, as it falls down on the ground.[266] The image contrasts the text in many ways. There is no literary version to describe this event the way it is depicted here but similar representations are found throughout India, from the early 12th century CE onwards. These pictorial parallels will be discussed later in detail.

29. १सहदेव॥ १नकुल॥ १अर्ज्जुन॥ १भीम॥ १युधिष्ठिन॥ १द्रुपदराजान् द्रौपदी कन्यादान बिव॥

Sahadeva. Nakula. Arjjuna. Bhīma. Yudhiṣṭhira. Drupadarājāna Draupadī kanyādāna biva.

Sahadeva. Nakula. Arjuna. Bhīma. Yudhiṣṭhira. King Drupada gives Draupadī (to them) as (their) wife.

Text: The invited monarchs feel betrayed and a struggle ensues (ch. 180). Kṛṣṇa, the son of the Yādava chief Vāsudeva and Kuntī's nephew, recognises the Pāṇḍavas and puts the fight to an end (chs. 180f.). Afterwards Dhṛṣṭadyumna follows Bhīma and

266 One could likewise give the number of the fish depicted as seven. This would mean that Arjuna hits several fish which would be yet another deviation from the text as well as from all other known images.

/ 29 / 28 / 27 /

Arjuna to the potter's house (ch. 184). He hides near the house. At night he overhears the Pāṇḍavas' conversation and in the morning reveals their identity to Drupada (chs. 184f.). Thereupon the king is filled with delight. He vows to restore Yudhiṣṭhira on his paternal throne and at Yudhiṣṭhira's request, Draupadī becomes the common wife of all the five Pāṇḍavas (chs. 187ff.).
Image: As described in the text, Draupadī is first given in marriage to Yudhiṣṭhira, then in succession to Bhīma, Arjuna, Nakula and finally to Sahadeva.

30. १कूंगी॒ यूधिष्ठिन्॒ गीम्॒ अर्ज्जुन्॒ नकूल्॒ सहदव्॒ द्रौपदी॒ हस्तिनापून् वंढ॥
Kuntī Yudhiṣṭhira Bhīma Arjjuna Nakula Sahadeva Draupadī Hastināpura vaṃṅa.
Kuntī, Yudhiṣṭhira, Bhīma, Arjuna, Nakula, Sahadeva and Draupadī go to Hastināpura.

Text: As Dhṛtarāṣṭra gains knowledge of the Pāṇḍavas' marriage, he sends Vidura to ask them to return to Hastināpura (chs. 192ff.). At Bhīṣma's and Droṇa's advice, Dhṛtarāṣṭra gives them half of the kingdom (chs. 195ff.). The Kauravas stay in Hastināpura and the Pāṇḍavas are sent to Indraprastha (Khāṇḍavaprastha), in order to prevent the ongoing of the strife (ch. 199).
Image: The scene again runs around a corner. Kuntī, the five sons of Pāṇḍu and their common wife are depicted on their way to Hastināpura, after Dhṛtarāṣṭra had sent for them.

detail of scene 28

/ 36 / 35 / 34 / 33 / 32 / 31 /

31. १युधिष्ठिनव् द्रौपदीव चाट् अर्ज्जुनन् लिया काल वं॥
Yudhiṣṭhirava Draupadīva cone Arjjunana lipā kāla vaṃ.
As Yudhiṣthira and Draupadī stay (together), Arjuna comes to take the bow.

Text: At Nārada's advice the five brothers bind themselves with a rule in regard to their common wife (ch. 204). When Draupadī is lying with any of them, she should be unseen by the others. Else, the one interrupting has to go to the forest for twelve years and live the life of a *brahmacārin*, a student following the path of a brahmin. Some time later, thieves rob the cattle of a brahmin (ch. 205). Even though the weapons are kept in the room where Yudhiṣṭhira and Draupadī are together that moment, Arjuna fetches his bow because his duty obliges him to protect the brahmin.
Image: Yudhiṣṭhira and Draupadī are sitting together inside the chamber where the weapons are kept. The bow is represented next to Yudhiṣṭhira. Arjuna, knowing that he should actually not enter, only quickly grabs hold of his bow.

32. १अर्ज्जुन वनवास वं॥
Arjjuna vanavāsa vaṃ.
Arjuna goes to (take up) residence in the forest.

Text: Arjuna recovers the cattle and returns to the city (ch. 205). Then, because he has violated the rule, he departs in order to live in the forest for twelve years.
Image: Arjuna is represented leaving for the woods, in his characteristic attire.

33. १अर्ज्जुनन् कृष्ण नाल लाक॥
Arjjunana Kṛṣṇa nāpa lāka.
Arjuna meets Kṛṣṇa.

Text: Arjuna completes his pilgrimage at Prabhāsa, where he meets Kṛṣṇa (ch. 210). He tells him all that has happened and thereafter, they both set off for Dvārakā, Kṛṣṇa's place.
Image: The image shows Arjuna paying homage to Kṛṣṇa as he comes upon him at Prabhāsa. Kṛṣṇa is clearly identified with Viṣṇu for he is represented four-armed, holding the discus (sa. *cakra*), the lotus (sa. *padma*), the club (sa. *gadā*) and the conch (sa. *śaṇkha*). This iconography is retained for the entire cycle (see details).

34. १अर्ज्जुनन् सुभ[द्रा] हनध या[त॥]
Arjjunana Subhadrā haraṇa yāta.
Arjuna abducts Subhadrā.

Text: As Arjuna behold Kṛṣṇa's sister, Subhadrā, his mind is agitated by desire (ch. 211). At the advice of Kṛṣṇa, and with the consent of Yudhiṣṭhira, Arjuna forcibly carries her away for marriage (chs. 211f.).
Image: Arjuna is depicted forcing Subhadrā onto his chariot, as described in the text.

35. [१कृ]ष्णव् अर्ज्जुनव् चोङ॥

Kṛṣṇava Arjjunava coṅa.

Kṛṣṇa and Arjuna are staying.

Text: Kṛṣṇa manages to pacify the incensed citizen by telling them that he approved Arjuna's conduct (chs. 212f.). Arjuna returns and marries Subhadrā. Afterwards, he stays at Dvārakā for a whole year.

Image: Kṛṣṇa and Arjuna are sitting together. They are not depicted conversing, so the artist probably only intended to illustrate that they stayed together. This scene could likewise refer to Kṛṣṇa staying with Arjuna, described in the text a while later. Accordingly, Arjuna returns to Indraprastha with Subhadrā as the twelve years of exile are over (ch. 213). Kṛṣṇa then follows and stays with them at Indraprastha. However, since Arjuna is turned towards Kṛṣṇa, rather Kṛṣṇa to Arjuna, the first interpretation is preferred.

detail of scene33

detail of scene 41

36. १अग्निन अर्ज्जुनयात् गाण्डिवलिपा बिव॥

Agnina Arjjunayāta Gāṇḍivalipā biva.

Agni gives Arjuna the bow Gāṇḍiva.

Text: Subhadrā gives birth to Abhimanyu and at intervals of one year Draupadī obtains five sons through her five husbands: Prativindhya is born from Yudhiṣṭhira, Sutasoma from Bhīma, Śrutakarma from Arjuna, Śatānīka from Nakula and Śrutasena from Sahadeva (ch. 213). One day, as Arjuna and Kṛṣṇa spend their time on the banks of the Yamunā, Agni arrives in the guise of a brahmin (ch. 214). He tells them that he desires to burn down the dreadful Khāṇḍava Forest and asks them for help, for the forest is protected by Indra (ch. 215). Varuṇa bestows upon Arjuna the bow Gāṇḍiva to support the undertaking (ch. 216). Additionally, Arjuna obtains two inexhaustible quivers and a chariot with divine horses, a monkey on the banner and many weapons on it. Kṛṣṇa obtains the discus and the mace.

Image: The birth of the sons is not depicted. We come straightaway to Agni presenting Arjuna with the bow Gāṇḍiva. For Arjuna obtains the weapon through him, he is shown in place of Varuṇa. Agni is depicted with a beard but besides this, he has no distinctive iconographic features. It would thus be difficult to identify him without the inscription.

detail of scene 47

detail of scene 112: Even while sleeping he keeps his attributes.

/ 41 / 40 / 39 /

37. १खाण्डवन दाह॥ १कृष्ण सारथि याङाव अर्ज्जुनन खाण्डवन दाह याक॥
Khāṇḍavavana dāha. Kṛṣṇa sārathi yāṅāva Arjjunana Khāṇḍavavana dāha yāka.
a) Kṛṣṇa acts as charioteer and Arjuna sets the Khāṇḍava Forest on fire.
b) Burning of the Khāṇḍava Forest.

Text: Having obtained their weapons, Arjuna and Kṛṣṇa consider themselves capable of helping (ch. 216). Agni encircles the forest and begins to consume it from all sides. Arjuna and Kṛṣṇa for their part station themselves on their chariots on both sides of the forest in order to prevent the flight of the creatures living within (ch. 217). As the creatures are burning in their thousands, Indra covers the sky with clouds and begins to pour down rain. With the help of Indra, Aśvasena, the son of the *nāga* king Takṣaka, manages to escape (ch. 218). Arjuna and Kṛṣṇa repulse the celestials who try to intervene. Then the celestials again leave the place and the forest is burnt to the ground (ch. 219).
Image: The entire ground of the forest is covered with flames. The animals living within, deer, birds and a snake, are depicted in the attempt to escape. The snake may or may not refer to Aśvasena. On the right side of the image, Arjuna is mounted on his chariot, his bow bent. The inscription states that he sets the forest on fire and admittedly, he helps Agni with his fire-tipped arrows according to the text. Anyway, the text gives no explanation for Kṛṣṇa acting as Arjuna's charioteer for therein, Kṛṣṇa is mounted on his own chariot and in equal measure adds to the burning of the forest.

38. [१मयदैत्य॥ १कृ]ष्ण॥ १अर्ज्जुन॥
Mayadaitya. Kṛṣṇa. Arjjuna.
The demon Maya. Kṛṣṇa. Arjuna.

Text: As everything is burning, the demon Maya seeks refuge with Arjuna and his life is spared (ch. 219). With the help of Arjuna and Kṛṣṇa, Agni consumes the whole Khāṇḍava Forest. In the end, Indra, gratified with the great feat, grants Arjuna and Kṛṣṇa a boon (ch. 225). Arjuna asks Indra for all his celestial weapons and Indra assures that he will bestow them to him at some later stage. Kṛṣṇa for his part asks that his friendship with Arjuna might be eternal.
Image: Arjuna's chariot is still lead by Kṛṣṇa. Maya is depicted on his knees. With joined palms he seeks refuge with Arjuna.

Sabhāparva: 'The Book of the Assembly Hall'

39. [१सहदेव॥] १नकूल॥ १भीम॥ १युधिष्ठिरव कृष्णव नाप नाक। १[अ]र्ज्जुन॥ १[मयदै]त्य॥
Sahadeva. Nakula. Bhīma. Yudhiṣṭhirava Kṛṣṇava nāpa rāka. Arjjuna. Mayadaitya.
Sahadeva. Nakula. Bhīma. Yudhiṣṭhira and Kṛṣṇa meet. Arjuna. The demon Maya.

Text: Since Arjuna has saved his life, Maya desires to do him a favour (ch. 1). Kṛṣṇa suggests that Maya, the architect of the demons, may build an assembly hall (sa. *sabhā*) for Yudhiṣṭhira in which the designs of the gods, of demons and humans alike

/ 38 / 37 /

can be seen. Maya thereupon draws up a design for the hall in the shape of a celestial chariot (sa. *vimāna*). Kṛṣṇa and Arjuna introduce Maya to Yudhiṣṭhira and explain what has happened.
Image: Kṛṣṇa and Arjuna approach Yudhiṣṭhira and the others, in company with Maya.

40. [१अर्ज्जुन]॥ १भीम॥ १युधिष्ठिरव् नारदव् म[णिमय सभास चोङ॥] १नकुल॥ १सहदेव॥ १मयदैत्यन् मणिमय सभा् ज्याङाव बिव॥
Arjjuna. Bhīma. Yudhiṣṭhirava Nāradava maṇimaya sabhāsa coṅa. Nakula. Sahadeva. Mayadaityana maṇimaya sabhā jyāṅāva biva.

a) For the benefit of the others, the demon Maya builds an assembly hall made of jewels.
b) Arjuna. Bhīma. Yudhiṣṭhira and Nārada are sitting (together) in the assembly hall of jewels. Nakula. Sahadeva.

Text: Maya begins the construction of the assembly hall and Kṛṣṇa returns to Dvārakā (chs. 1f.). Maya goes to the north of the Kailāśa, to the abode of Vṛṣaparva, the king of the demons, where he has kept lots of jewels and treasure (ch. 3). He brings these back and within fourteen months he builds a matchless assembly hall encrusted with jewels. As the first assembly is held in the newly built hall, the celestial sage Nārada appears and advises Yudhiṣṭhira to perform a great royal sacrifice (sa. *rājasūyayajña*), so that he might shine eternally (chs. 5ff.).
Image: On the right side of the image, Maya is depicted constructing the assembly hall for Yudhiṣṭhira. In keeping with the text, this hall has the design of a celestial chariot (sa. *vimāna*). The left part of the image shows the Pāṇḍavas sitting inside the assembly hall together with Nārada. The hall has now an ordinary design but the image could likewise only show one of its many chambers.

41. [१]कृष्ण् भीम् अर्ज्जुन् जरासंधयाक् वंङ॥
Kṛṣṇa Bhīma Arjjuna Jarāsandhayāke vaṃṅa.
Kṛṣṇa, Bhīma and Arjuna go to Jarāsandha.

Text: Yudhiṣṭhira sends for Kṛṣṇa and asks his advice on the performance of the sacrifice (ch. 12). Kṛṣṇa tells him that Jarāsandha, the king of Magadha, has conquered and imprisoned 86 great kings with the intention of sacrificing them to Śiva when their tally becomes 100 (chs. 13f.). This is also the reason why the Yādavas have abandoned Mathurā and fled to Dvārakā. In Kṛṣṇa's view, Yudhiṣṭhira's sacrifice can only be successful if first the imprisoned kings are set free and Jarāsandha is slain. In the guise of brahmins Kṛṣṇa, Bhīma and Arjuna set out for Magadha (ch. 18).
Image: The image depicts the three of them on their way to Magadha in their usual characteristic attire.

detail of scene 37

/ 46 / 45 / 44 / 43 / 42 /

42. १अर्ज्जु[न॥ १]भीम॥ १कृष्णव् जरासंधव नाप लाक॥
Arjjuna. Bhīma. Kṛṣṇava Jarāsandhava nāpa lāka.
Arjuna. Bhīma. Kṛṣṇa and Jarāsandha meet.

Text: Jarāsandha welcomes Kṛṣṇa, Bhīma and Arjuna at his court (ch. 19). Kṛṣṇa reveals their identity to the king and challenges him either to release the imprisoned kings or to fight (ch. 20). Not willing to refrain from his intended sacrifice, Jarāsandha chooses to do battle.
Image: The image depicts the arrival of Kṛṣṇa, Bhīma and Arjuna at Jarāsandha's court. They are all greeting each other friendly.

43. १जरासंधव् भीमव् गदायुद्ध॥
Jarāsandhava Bhīmava gadāyuddha.
Fight with clubs between Jarāsandha and Bhīma.

Text: When asked with whom of the three he wants to do battle, Jarāsandha chooses Bhīma (ch. 21). With bare arms as their only weapons they start a wrestling match. They drag and push each other, exchange blows and violently throw each other to the ground. On the night of the fourteenth day of battle, Kṛṣṇa notices that Jarāsandha weakens.
Image: In contrast to the text, Bhīma and Jarāsandha are not fighting with their bare arms alone but with clubs.

44. १भीमन् जरासंध् वध याक॥
Bhīmana Jarāsandha vadha yāka.
Bhīma kills Jarāsandha.

Text: In the end, Bhīma whirls Jarāsandha around one hundred times, throws him down on his knee and breaks his back into two (ch. 22).
Image: Bhīma has Jarāsandha thrown down on his knee and tears him in two by pulling apart his legs.

45. १कृष्णु भीम् अर्ज्जुन् लिहा वं॥
Kṛṣṇa Bhīma Arjjuna lihā vaṃ.
Kṛṣṇa, Bhīma and Arjuna return.

Text: Kṛṣṇa, Bhīma and Arjuna set the kings free and return to Indraprastha (ch. 22).
Image: The image depicts them on their way back.

46. १शिशुपाल् कृष्णयातन् न्वाक॥ १राजसूययज्ञस युधि[ष्ठि]रन ह्नपा कृ[ष्णया] पुजा याक॥ १भीम॥ १अर्ज्जुन॥ १नकुल॥ १सहदेव॥
Śiśupāla Kṛṣṇayātana[267] nvāka. rājasūyayajñasa Yudhiṣṭhirana hṅapā Kṛṣṇayā pujā yāka. Bhīma. Arjjuna. Nakula. Sahadeva.

267 Verbs like *nvāya* - to blame, to revile take the dative, the case ending of which is usually *-yāta* (sg.). The suffix *-yātana* occurs only rarely.

/ 49 / 48 / 47 /

a) At the *rājasūya* sacrifice Yudhiṣṭhira honours first Kṛṣṇa. Bhīma. Arjuna. Nakula. Sahadeva.

b) Śiśupāla reviles Kṛṣṇa.

Text: Kings arrive from all the regions in order to attend Yudhiṣṭhira's sacrifice (chs. 30ff.). At the end of the royal sacrifice (sa. *rājasūya*) Yudhiṣṭhira has to make offerings to the attendants, according to what they deserve (ch. 33). The first part has to be given to the one who is the most deserving among them. On Bhīṣma's advice, Yudhiṣṭhira honours first Kṛṣṇa. Śiśupāla, the king of Cedi, feels insulted on account of this. He censures Bhīṣma and Yudhiṣṭhira and challenges Kṛṣṇa to battle (chs. 34ff.).
Image: In the centre Yudhiṣṭhira is depicted presenting the first offering (sa. *arghya*) to Kṛṣṇa. His brothers are depicted on the right side. On the left side of the image, Śiśupāla reproaches Kṛṣṇa, the left hand resting on his hip, the right one raised up. Kṛṣṇa for the moment keeps his temper (beginning of ch. 33). He points to his foot as if to say that Śiśupāla should bow down to him. At the far right, Sahadeva turns away from the others, one hand resting on his hip, his leg stretched sideways. According to the text (ch. 33), Sahadeva displayes his foot and adresses the assembled kings stating that he would place it on the head of those who won't accept that Kṛṣṇa is the one deserving the homage. The kings remain silent and a shower of flowers rains down on Sahadeva.

47. १शिशुपाल वध॥ १कृष्णन् चक्रन् कयका॥
Śiśupāla vadha. Kṛṣṇana cakrana kayako.
a) Kṛṣṇa strikes with the discus.
b) Death of Śiśupāla.

Text: As Śiśupāla insults Kṛṣṇa in front of the assembled kings, Kṛṣṇa angrily takes up his discus (sa. *cakra*) and cuts off his head (*ch.* 42).
Image: Śiśupāla's head has just been sliced off. Kṛṣṇa still holds his discus high in the air. He is adorned with a large garland of flowers or pearls.

48. १(धौम्य॥ १युधिष्ठिनया् राजसूययज्ञ॥ १युधिष्ठिन॥ १भीम॥ १अर्ज्जुन॥ १नकुल॥ १सहदेव॥ १द्रौपदी॥
Dhaumya. Yudhiṣṭhirayā rājasūyayajña. Yudhiṣṭhira. Bhīma. Arjjuna. Nakula. Sahadeva. Draupadī.
Dhaumya. Yudhiṣṭhira's royal sacrifice. Yudhiṣṭhira. Bhīma. Arjuna. Nakula. Sahadeva. Draupadī.

Text: Yudhiṣṭhira completes the royal sacrifice (ch. 42). Thereafter the kings return to their own kingdoms and Kṛṣṇa returns to Dvārakā. Only Duryodhana and Śakuni, the Kauravas' maternal uncle, remain in Yudhiṣṭhira's celestial hall.
Image: The image depicts Dhaumya as officiating priest. He holds a ladle and the scriptures. On the opposite side, the Pāṇḍavas and Draupadī are represented with folded hands.

49. (previous page) १दुर्य्योधनन लाषमदले लंङ थसोव॥ १युधिष्ठिर भीम अर्ज्जुन नकुल सहदेव मणिमय सभास चोङ॥

Duryyodhanana lāṣamadale laṃṅa thasova. Yudhiṣṭhira Bhīma Arjjuna Nakula Sahadeva maṇimaya sabhāsa coṅa.

a) Yudhiṣṭhira, Bhīma, Arjuna, Nakula and Sahadeva are sitting inside the assembly hall consisting of jewels.

b) At an open space with no water, Duryodhana pulls up his garment.

Text: Duryodhana is confused by the many celestial designs of the assembly hall and repeatedly attracts the Pāṇḍavas' mockery for acting strangely (ch. 43). Mistaking a crystal surface for a pool of water, he draws up his clothes. Then again, mistaking a lake of crystal water for land, he falls into the water with all his clothes on. Image: The five brothers are watching Duryodhana as he draws up his garment in order to cross the non-existing pool of water. All of them are holding their distinctive attributes. The assembly hall is not depicted. Not for the first time, the interior of the building is incicated only by seating furnitures and tasseled cloths but this is slightly confusing here because the Pāṇḍavas were represented the same way in the previous scene, which probably plays outside.

50. १पुतिहाव लुखास ताहाव धक कोमछोङा दुहा याव दुर्य्योधनया कपाल हाक॥ १ताहाव लुखास पुतिहाव धक कोछोङाव दुर्य्योधन दुहा वंङ॥

putihāva lukhāsa tāhāva dhaka komachoṅā duhā yāva Duryyodhanayā kapāla hāka. tāhāva lukhāsa putihāva dhaka kochoṅāva Duryyodhana duhā vaṃṅa.

a) Taking the tall door to be short, Duryodhana goes inside, bending down.

b) Taking the short door to be tall, Duryodhana tries to go inside without bending down and hits his head.

Text: On another occation Duryodhana mistakes a closed door (possibly made of crystal too) to be open and as he tries to walk through, he hurts his forehead against it (ch. 43). Another door he mistakes to be closed and steps away from the doorway. The Pāṇḍavas burst out in laughter every time he commits an error. Insulted and miserable Duryodhana goes back to Hastināpura.

Image: The image recalls the version translated by Roy, according to which Duryodhana hits his head on a closed door mistaking it to be open and afterwards tumbles through another one as he attempts to open an already open door.[268] Moreover, the inscription tells of another misfortune which is likewise represented. Duryodhana thus hits his head on a short and closed door, taking it to be tall and open and he tumbles through the tall and open door, taking it to be short and closed.

51. १भीष्मन गंङ॥ १धृतराष्ड्रन गंङ॥ १विदुरन गंङ॥ १पतासेया दो॥ १दुःशासनन द्रौपदीया पतास [लु]क॥ १कर्ण्ण॥ १दुःशासन॥ १दुर्य्योधन॥ १शकुनिव युधिष्ठिरव जुल ल्वाक द्रौपदी जुरस पाक॥ १भीम॥ १अर्ज्जुन॥ १नकुल॥ १सहदेव॥

Bhīṣmana gaṃṅa. Dhṛtarāṣdrana gaṃṅa. Vidurana gaṃṅa. patāseyā do. Duḥśāsanana Draupadīyā patāse luka. Karṇṇa. Duḥśāsana. Duryyodhana. Śakuniva Yudhiṣṭhirava jula lvāka Draupadī jurasa pāka. Bhīma. Arjjuna. Nakula. Sahadeva.

a) Karṇa. Duḥśāsana. Duryodhana. Śakuni and Yudhiṣṭhira gamble (and) Draupadī is bet at play. Bhīma. Arjuna. Nakula. Sahadeva.

b) Duḥśāsana tugs at Draupadī's lower garment.

c) Heap of lower garments.

d) Bhīṣma stops (him). Dhṛtarāṣṭra stops (him). Vidura stops (him).

Text: As Duryodhana expresses his intention to subjugate the Pāṇḍavas, his uncle Śakuni recommends him to win the wealth of Yudhiṣṭhira through dice (ch. 44). Śakuni, himself skilled in dice, plays for Duryodhana. Yudhiṣṭhira on the other hand does not know how to play but as Śakuni challenges him he does not want to ignore the summons either (ch. 52). In the company of the others he goes to Hastināpura. Yudhiṣṭhira gambles away his wealth, his realm, his brothers, himself and finally Draupadī (chs. 53f., 58). As Duryodhana sends for Draupadī, Vidura warns him. Still, Duḥśāsana takes Draupadī before the assembly, dragging her forcibly by the hair and disregarding the fact that she is, because in her menses, only scantily dressed (chs. 59f.). Draupadī raises the question if Yudhiṣṭhira was actually allowed to stake her after having first gambled away himself but Bhīṣma states that he is unable to decide the point Draupadī had put. Then Duḥśāsana seizes Draupadī's attire and drags it off (ch. 61). However, every time Duḥśāsana tugs away Draupadī's

268 Roy 2012 (1884) II, p. 104 (ch. 47).

/ 51 / 50 /

garment, another similar garment appears instantly. As still nobody wants to decide on the question put, Dhṛtarāṣṭra, out of compassion for Draupadī, grants her two boons (ch. 63). She first asks him to free Yudhiṣṭhira and then her other husbands. Dhṛtarāṣṭra sends Yudhiṣṭhira back to Indraprastha, together with his brothers and Draupadī and with all his wealth, to rule his kingdom further on (ch. 63).
Image: The type of dice game is not specified in the text. What is depicted is a *chausar* field. Variations of the closely related Pachisi (hi. *paccīs* - twenty-five) are played all over the world, as for example the English variant *Ludo* or the German variant *Mensch ärgere dich nicht*. In order to determine the player's move, four-sided long dice (sa. *pāśakas*) are used which have however not been depicted.[269] Śakuni and Yudhiṣṭhira both seem to make their move on the field. Yudhiṣṭhira plays with Draupadī as a stake. She sits on Yudhiṣṭhira's lap and he has placed his arm around her. His brothers, who have already been won by Śakuni, sit behind him. In Śakuni's company Duryodhana, Duḥśāsana and Karṇa are represented. The image is devided into several areas by the many pillars of the hall (sa. *sabhā*). The hall is extended in like manner and covers also the immediately consecutive events. To the left Draupadī pleads Duḥśāsana to stop as he tugs at her half-garment. The next compartment contains the mass of garments piled up in the middle of the hall (Mbh 2.61). Vidura. Dhṛtarāṣṭra and Bhīṣma are represented right beside. According to the inscription they all prevent Duḥśāsana from going on whereas according to the text, Vidura presses for an answer to Draupadī's question, Bhīṣma repeatedly states that he is incapable of answering it and only Dhṛtarāṣṭra finally ends the humiliation.

269 They are depicted in scene 110 of the same frieze.

52. (next page) १पूनर्व्वार् युधिष्ठिरव् शकुनिव् जुल ल्वाक॥
punarvvāra Yudhiṣṭhirava Śakuniva jula lvāka.
Yudhiṣṭhira and Śakuni gamble again.

Text: Out of fear of a retaliatory attack and in order to bring the Pāṇḍavas under their sway, Duryodhana asks his father to give permission for a second game of dice with the single stake of exile (ch. 66). As suggested by Duryodhana, whoever loses, either Pāṇḍavas or Kauravas, will have to retire to the woods for twelve years. A thirteenth year has to be spent unrecognised in an inhabitant place. Albeit, if re-cognised another twelve years of exile follow. Since Yudhiṣṭhira cannot disobey Dhṛtarāṣṭra's command, he agrees and with only one throw of the dice he is defeated (ch. 67).

Image: This time only Śakuni and Yudhiṣṭhira are depicted. The former shows the dice score to the latter as to prove that he has won.

detail of scene 51

/ 55

/ 54---

53. १शामलन पुयाव युधिष्ठिर वनवास वंङ॥ १वाहा सोयाव भीम वनवास वंङ॥ १फिचोन हायकाव अर्ज्जुन वनवास वं॥ १ह्मस लेपन याङाव नकुल वन वं॥ १ष्वाल् वोयाव सहदेव वन वं॥ १स् फहन तयाव् द्रौपदी् वन वं॥ १कुश जोङाव वेद पडपाव धौम्य वन वं॥

śāmalana puyāva Yudhiṣṭhira vanavāsa vaṃṅa. bāhā soyāva Bhīma vanavāsa vaṃṅa. phicona hāyakāva Arjjuna vanavāsa vaṃ. hmasa lepana yāṅāva Nakula vana vaṃ. ṣvāla boyāva Sahadeva vana vaṃ. sa phahana tayāva Draupadī vana vaṃ. kuśa joṅāva veda paḍapāva Dhaumya vana vaṃ.

a) Covering with a shawl-like cloth, Yudhiṣṭhira goes to a dwelling in the forest.
b) Looking at his arms, Bhīma goes to a dwelling in the forest.
c) Scattering sand-dust, Arjuna goes to a dwelling in the forest.
d) Besmearing his body, Nakula goes to the forest.
e) Rubbing his face, Sahadeva goes to the forest.
f) Her hair torn, Draupadī goes to the forest.
g) Having seized *kuśa* grass and reciting the veda, Dhaumya goes to the forest.

Text: The Pāṇḍavas cast off their royal robes and put on deerskins (ch. 68). Then they leave Hastināpura (ch. 69). As Yudhiṣṭhira leaves for the woods, he covers his face with his garment so that his angry eyes will not burn down the citizens (ch. 71). Bhīma spreads his mighty arms as he goes, thinking about everything they could do to the enemy. Arjuna scatters sand as a symbol for the many arrows he would shower in battle. Sahadeva besmears his face so that no-one might recognise him and Nakula stains his entire body with dust in order to prevent the women looking at him from loosing their hearts. Draupadī, still in her menses, wears a single garment smeared with blood and she has not braided her hair. As she goes she thinks about how the wives of her enemies would find their relatives dead in the fourteenth year and how their bodies would be covered with the blood of their beloved ones. Dhaumya also follows them to the woods. He holds *kuśa* grass and chants terrible hymns (sa. *mantras*) of the *Sama Veda*, which he believes the Pāṇḍavas will also chant after having finally killed their enemies.

Image: In keeping with the text, Yudhiṣṭhira is about to cover himself up with his shawl, Bhīma spreads his mighty arm, Arjuna scatters sand, Nakula stains his body with dust and Sahadeva besmears his face. Draupadī is depicted with only a half-garment and with open hair. Regardless of whether she simply wears her hair untied as depicted or she has not braided it as according to the text or she actually tears her hair as according to the inscription it all comes to the same, that her hair is dishevelled since Duḥśāsana dragged her before the assembly (cf. Mbh. 3.12). Dhaumya is holding the *kuśa* grass and the scriptures and the inscription further states that he is reciting the veda.

---54 / 53 / 52 /

Vanaparva: 'The Book of the Forest'

54. १तीमन् किम्मीननाउस् वध याक॥ १किम्मीननाउसव् तीमव् यूद्ध॥ १यूधिष्ठिन॥ १अर्ज्जुन॥
१नकूल॥ १सहदेव॥ १द्रौपदी॥ १(धौम्य॥
Bhīmana Kirmmīrarākṣasa vadha yāka. Kirmmīrarākṣasava Bhīmava yuddha.
Yudhiṣṭhira. Arjjuna. Nakula. Sahadeva. Draupadī. Dhaumya.
a) Fight between the demon Kirmīra and Bhīma. Yudhiṣṭhira. Arjuna. Nakula. Sahadeva. Draupadī. Dhaumya.
b) Bhīma kills the demon Kirmīra.

Text: The Pāṇḍavas go from forest to forest until they reach the Kāmyaka woods on the banks of the Sarasvatī (ch. 6). Suddenly the demon Kirmīra obstructs their way. Vaka was his brother, Hiḍimva a friend of his and Kirmīra now wants to wreak vengeance on Bhīma for having slain them. Bhīma and Kirmīra beat each other with uprooted trees, grasp each other's arms and drag each other until Bhīma throws his adversary down. The battle comes to an end as Bhīma whirls Kirmīra in the air to the point of unconsciousness. He places his knee on Kirmīra's hips, his hands on his throat and finally chokes him to death.
Image: The killing of Kirmīra is represented exactly as described in the text. In the first part of the image, Bhīma holds an uprooted tree and Kirmīra likewise grasps the branch of a tree in order to use it in battle. At the same time they also grasp each other's arms. The left part of the image shows Kirmīra flung down on the ground and in keeping with the text, Bhīma presses him down with his knee as he chokes him to death.

55. १उद्धव॥ १कृष्णव् यूधिष्ठिनव नाप नाक॥ १तीम॥ १अर्ज्जुन॥ १नकूल॥ १सहदेव॥ १द्रौपदी॥ १(धौम्य॥
Uddhava. Kṛṣṇava Yudhiṣṭhirava nāpa rāka. Bhīma. Arjjuna. Nakula. Sahadeva. Draupadī. Dhaumya.
Uddhava. Kṛṣṇa and Yudhiṣṭhira meet. Bhīma. Arjuna. Nakula. Sahadeva. Draupadī. Dhaumya.

Text: As Kṛṣṇa comes to know that the Pāṇḍavas have been exiled, he swiftly goes to them, followed by a large retinue (ch. 13). They exchange about the recent events. Kṛṣṇa states that had he been present at Hastināpura, he could have prevented the gambling (ch. 14). In answer to the question of why he was absent he states that he was engaged in battle with Śālva (ch. 15). The king of Mārttikāvata had attacked Dvārakā, impelled by wrath for the destruction of Śiśupāla at Yudhiṣṭhira's royal sacrifice. Śālva was defeated by Pradyumna, Kṛṣṇa's son, and had left the place when Kṛṣṇa returned (ch. 20). Kṛṣṇa however decided to follow after him and he finally cut Śālva into two with his discus (chs. 21ff.). Having completed his narration, Kṛṣṇa again leaves for Dvārakā (ch. 23).
Image: Kṛṣṇa and Uddhava are approaching from one side, Yudhiṣṭhira, his brothers, Draupadī and Dhaumya from the other side. Uddhava is Kṛṣṇa's councellor. He is not explicitly mentioned in the text but represents the large retinue accompanying Kṛṣṇa.

/ 60 / 59 / 58 / 57 / 56 /

56. १स्रा कयकल धक्‌ अर्ज्जुनव्‌ किनाट्‌ गम चाव॥ १अर्ज्जुनन्‌ स्रा्‌ कयका॥
phā kayakala dhaka Arjjunava kirāṭa tam cāva. Arjjunana phā kayako.

a) Arjuna strikes the boar.

b) Arjuna says he struck the boar and the *kirāṭa* becomes angry.

Text: The Pāṇḍavas proceed to the sacred lake of the Dvaita woods (ch. 25). Vyāsa appears and states that the time has come for Arjuna to obtain Indra's celestial weapons (cf. sc. 38) as also those from Śiva and the Lokapālas, the *Protectors of the World* (ch. 37). Arjuna crosses the Himālayas and arrives at Indrakila (ch. 38). Indra then says he will give Arjuna the weapons when the latter beholds Śiva. Thus, in order to please Śiva, Arjuna practises severe asceticism (ch. 39). After a lapse of four months, Śiva takes to the form of a *kirāṭa* (sa., indegenous people of the mountainous regions) and descends the Himavat (ch. 40). As the demon Mūka seeks to slay Arjuna in the form of a boar, Arjuna and the *kirāṭa* both strike him with their shafts. Mūka again assumes the terrible form of a demon (sa. *rākṣasa*) and gives up his life. The dispute about who struck him first leads to a fight between Arjuna and the *kirāṭa*.

Image: Arjuna and the *kirāṭa* have both lost their arrows at Mūka. The demon is depicted in between, in the guise of a boar, pierced by the two arrows that simultaneously struck him.

57. १किनाटव्‌ अर्ज्जुनव्‌ यूद्ध॥
kirāṭava Arjjunava yuddha.

Fight between the *kirāṭa* and Arjuna.

Text: Arjuna and the *kirāta* attack each other with arrows (ch. 40). Then Arjuna additionally strikes the *kirāṭa* with his bow, his sword, with trees and rocks but all the weapons prove futile. Then both of them exchange blows. As the *kirāṭa* finally presses Arjuna with his full might, he falls to the ground, out of breath.

Image: Depicted is the fight with arrows. Why the *kirāṭa* is represented with a crown is not clear. He is depicted with a turban in the previous as well as in the following scene.

58. १अर्ज्जुनन्‌ महादवयाक्‌ छाया्‌ स्वानमाल्‌ किनाटया मोलस चाव वंढ॥
Arjjunana Mahādevayāke chāyā svānamāla Kirāṭayā molasa cova vaṃṅa.

The garland of flowers, offered by Arjuna to Śiva, ascends to the *kirāṭa*'s head.

Text: Pleased with Arjuna, Śiva reveals himself (ch. 40).

Image: On the left side of the image, Arjuna honours a Śiva *liṅga* with a large garland of flowers. That same garland is again depicted on the right side, atop the *kirāṭa*'s head. He shows the gesture of fearlessness (sa. *abhayamudrā*) which might refer to the point of him not being angry with Arjuna for having fought with him.

Other sources: The image depicts an event that was excluded from the Critical Edition of the Mahābhārata. Still, the story is a popular one and is among others included in Roy's translation.[270] In his text, Arjuna forms a clay image of Śiva and worships it with offerings of floral garlands. As the garland which Arjuna had offered to the clay image, decks the crown of the *kirāṭa* instead, Arjuna recognises Śiva.

59. [१अर्ज्जुनन महा]देव सयाव [नम]स्कान याक॥
Arjjunana Mahādeva seyāva namaskāra yāka.
Arjuna recognises Śiva and pays homage.

Text: After Śiva has revealed himself, Arjuna worships him and asks for forgiveness (ch. 40).
Image: Arjuna bows his head and worships Śiva with joined palms. Śiva might be still depicted in his disguise as a *kirāṭa* for in contrast to the next image, he still wears the crown. Anyway, in other instances Śiva is depicted with a crown, too, and the image is worn out too much to ascertain any assumption.

60. [...]
Text: Śiva bestows upon Arjuna the Paśupati weapon. Like all the celestian weapons, it is based on secret formulas (sa. *mantras*) and can be released through the bow as well as through thought, eyes or words (ch. 41).
Image: The image is badly damaged and the inscription no longer extant but the plot is clear. The revealed Śiva is represented in his true form with a crown of matted hair (sa. *jaṭāmukuṭa*), the third eye and prolonged earlobes with no jewellery. He hands over to Arjuna his divine weapon, which is again depicted as an arrow (cf. R.sc. 8).

Western face of the temple (scenes 61 to 109):

61. १कुवेनन अस्त्र विव॥ १वनुणन अस्त्र विल॥ १यमन अस्त्र विल॥ १इन्द्रन अर्ज्जुनयात अस्त्र [विल॥]
Kuberana astra biva. Varuṇana astra bila. Yamana astra bila. Indrana Arjjunayāta astra bila.

270 Roy 2012 (1884) III, p. 89 (ch. 39).

/ 61 /

a) Indra gives Arjuna (his) weapon. b) Yama gives (his) weapon.
b) Varuṇa gives (his) weapon. d) Kubera gives (his) weapon.

Text: Śiva disappears and the Lokapālas arrive (ch. 42). At first Varuṇa, the lord of the waters and guardian of the western regions, appears. Then Kubera, the lord of riches and guardian of the northern regions, arrives. Next Yama, the lord of death and guardian of the southern regions, appears and finally Indra, the chief of the celestials and guardian of the eastern regions. Yama bestows upon Arjuna his staff (sa. *daṇḍa*) together with the required formulas (sa. *mantras*). Varuṇa gives Arjuna his noose (sa. *pāśa*) and Kubera his celestial weapon known as Antardhāna (sa., invisibility, disappearance), which can put the enemy to sleep. Indra announces that he will send his chariot to take Arjuna to heaven where Indra would finally bestow his celestial weapons upon him, too.
Image: The gods are recognisable by means of their mounts (sa. *vāhanas*). Indra is seated on the back of his celestial elephant, Airāvata. Yama's mount is a buffalo, Varuṇa's mount a *makara*, an aquatic composite being, and Kubera is riding on a horse. Indra and Varuṇa additionally wear distinctive crowns. According to the text, in this context the divine weapons consist of the formulas and specific objects. However, they are again all depicted as arrows. It also has to be noted that, according to the text, Indra does not yet bestow any weapon to Arjuna whereas in the image he also holds an arrow out to Arjuna.

/ 66 / 65 / 64 / 63 / 62 /

62. १ꣳइन्द्रन् अर्ज्जुनयात् रथ विसे हव॥
Indrana Arjjunayāta ratha vise hava.
Indra leaves his chariot at Arjuna's share.

Text: The gods return to whence they had come and immediately afterwards Mātali, Indra's charioteer, appears with Indra's celestial vehicle (ch. 43).
Image: The inscription states that Indra leaves his chariot at Arjuna's share but the figure represented is clearly not Indra (note the crown). It therefore rather means that Indra has sent his chariot, not that he himself presents it to Arjuna. The chariot itself is, according to the text, drawn by ten thousand tawny horses. These are not depicted. Instead, a sea-monster (sa. *makara*) appears.

63. १अर्ज्जुन स्वर्ग्ग वं॥
Arjjuna svargga vaṃ.
Arjuna goes to heaven.

Text: Arjuna ascends with Mātali to the regions of the celestials, seen from the earth in the form of stars (ch. 43). Then he beholds Amarāvatī, the city of Indra.
Image: Arjuna has mounted the chariot which is directed by Mātali towards Indra's realm. In place of the sea-monster (sa. *makara*) from scene 62 a snake appears (cf. scene 84). Two flagstaffs with double-pennants are attached to the vehicle.

64. १उर्व्वशी॥ १ꣳइन्द्रव अर्ज्जुनव सभास चोङ॥
Urvvaśī. Indrava Arjjunava sabhāsa coṅa.
Urvaśī. Indra and Arjuna sit inside the assembly hall.

Text: Arjuna enters the city, alights from the chariot and approaches his father (ch. 44). Indra makes him sit on his throne and even takes him upon his lap. Arjuna stays for five years in Indra's palace. He learns about all the celestial weapons, together with the means of withdrawing them (ch. 45).
Image: Inside Indra's assembly hall (sa. *sabhā*), Arjuna sits with his father on his sacred throne, exactly as the text reads: "Seated on the same seat, they made the assembly hall shine [...]."[271] On the right side an attendant waves a fly-whisk, on the left side a female figure is represented, according to the inscription Urvaśī. The Critical Edition states that she was among the *apsaras* (sa., female spirits of unearthly beauty) who engaged in supreme dancing after Arjuna's arrival (ch. 44).
Other sources: The image marks the start of a popular story, which was however again excluded from the Critical Edition. Urvaśī's desire for Arjuna is the subject matter of the following two scenes. Again, the context will be given as according to Roy's translation.[272]

---

271 Debroy 2015 (2010), Vol. II, p. 400, l. 22.
272 Roy 2012 (1884) III, pp. 101ff. (chs. 45-47).

/ 68 / 67 /

65. १अर्ज्जुनयाके उर्व्वशी वव॥

Arjjunayāke Urvvaśī vava.

Urvaśī comes to Arjuna.

Image: Arjuna sits on the throne. In his hands he holds the bow and, instead of the arrow usually depicted, a dart. It might refer to the celestial weapons he was tought. Urvaśī is cautiously leaning against his seat.

Other sources: According to Roy, Urvaśī falls in love with Arjuna after being told about his virtues. She repairs to Arjuna's abode and pleads him to accept her.

66. १उर्व्वशी लिहा वं॥

Urvvaśī lihā vaṃ.

Urvaśī returns.

Image: Urvaśī is leaving again. A bird atop the tree enlivens the scene.

Other sources: According to Roy, Arjuna worships Urvaśī but rejects her because of her being his primordial mother. In anger, Urvaśī curses Arjuna that he will live as a dancer among females, bereft of his manhood. Indra however reduces the curse to a duration of one year only.

67. १निवातकवचदैत्यपनि वध॥ १निवातकवचदैत्यव् अर्ज्जुनव युद्ध॥ १इन्द्र॥

Nivātakavacadaityapani vadha. Nivātakavacadaityava Arjjunava yuddha. Indra.

a) Fight between the Nivātakavaca demons and Arjuna. Indra.

b) Death of the many Nivātakavaca demons.

Text: After Arjuna has perfectly learned the use of all weapons, Indra, in return for his tuition, asks him to slay the Nivātakavacas, thirty million demons identical in form, strength and radiance (ch. 165). Arjuna agrees, ascends Indra's chariot and sets out to the abode of the Nivātakavacas. The demons try to defeat Arjuna with all kind of weapons as also by the help of illusion (chs. 166ff.). Arjuna wards off the attacks of the Nivātakavacas with his numerous weapons and destroys the demon hosts (ch. 169). Afterwards he returns together with Mātali. In the Critical Edition, Arjuna gives an account of these events only after he has returned from the heavens.

Image: Three demons, representing the many Nivātakavacas, are depicted fighting with Arjuna. They are mounted on chariots and armed with bow and arrow, dart, sword and shield. They are again represented on the left side of the image, where they lie on the ground, pierced by Arjuna's shafts. Arjuna himself is depicted on Indra's chariot with Mātali as his charioteer. In contrast to the text, Indra also does battle with the Nivātakavacas, mounted on his elephant Airāvata.

/ 73 / 72 / 71 / 70 / 69 /

68. (previous page) १अर्ज्जुनन वनयात इन्द्रयाके आज्ञा फोङ॥
Arjjunana vaneyāta Indrayāke ājñā phoṅa.
Arjuna asks permission of Indra to leave.

Text: After Mātali has reported on the events, Indra states that the time has come for Arjuna to return to his brothers (chs. 170f.).
Image: Arjuna approaches his father with joined palms. Indra is seated on his throne and shows the gesture of fearlessness (sa. *abhayamudrā*). The inscription states that Arjuna asks permission to depart, whereas according to the text, it is on Indra's behalf that Arjuna leaves.

69. १अर्ज्जुन लिहा वव॥
Arjjuna lihā vava.
Arjuna returns.

Text: Arjuna returns and meets with his brothers on the mountain Gandhamādana (ch. 171).
Image: Whereas, according to the text, Arjuna returns with Mātali on Indra's chariot, he arrives on foot in the image.

70. १युधिष्ठिन भीम् नकुल् सहदेव् द्रौपदी् धौम्य् गन्धमादनपर्व्वत वं॥
Yudhiṣṭhira Bhīma Nakula Sahadeva Draupadī Dhaumya Gandhamādanaparvvata vaṃ.
Yudhiṣṭhira, Bhīma, Nakula, Sahadeva, Draupadī and Dhaumya go up Mount Gandhamādana.

Text: While Arjuna spends his time in Indraloka, the others visit sacred *tīrthas*, places of pilgrimage (chs. 91ff.). Among others, they go up the mountain Gandhamādana (also Mandāra), towards Kubera's abode (ch. 140). At the foot of the mountain, the brothers, Draupadī and the many sages accompanying them are caught in a violent storm (ch. 143).
Image: The mountain is again represented by means of geometrical patterns. That the group has just entered the mountain is clear from its gentle gradient. The brothers are holding their distinctive attributes. Dhaumya carries a staff (sa. *daṇḍa*) and a water-pot (sa. *kamaṇḍalu*).

71. १सहदेव॥ १नकुल॥ १भीम॥ १द्रौपदी मूर्छा जुव् युधिष्ठिनन वोध याक॥
Sahadeva. Nakula. Bhīma. Draupadī murchā juva Yudhiṣṭhirana vodha yāka.
Sahadeva. Nakula. Bhīma. As Draupadī faints, Yudhiṣṭhira instructs.

Text: They weather out the storm and proceed but soon Draupadī, worn out with the

/ 75 / 74 /

fatigues of the journey and additionally exhausted from the storm, becomes faint and falls down (ch. 144). Yudhiṣṭhira takes her on his lap, while Dhaumya and the other sages perform rites and recite formulas (sa. *mantras*) to keep the demons away. Slowly, Draupadī regains consciousness.
Image: In keeping with the text, Draupadī is depicted on Yudhiṣṭhira's lap. A sage, possibly Dhaumya, waves a fly-whisk over them. This could refer to the cool breeze which helps Draupadī to recover according to the text. Bhīma, Nakula and Sahadeva are sitting to the left, their heads supported by the hand, awaiting Draupadī's recovery.

72. १घटोत्कचन भीम नाप लाक वव॥
Ghaṭotkacana Bhīma nāpa lāka vava.
Ghaṭotkaca comes to meet Bhīma.

Text: Yudhiṣṭhira fears that Draupadī will not be able to withstand the further exertions of their journey (ch. 144). Bhīma suggests that Ghaṭotkaca, his son with Hiḍimvā, could carry her. Ghaṭotkaca appears immediately, as he had promised before (cf. sc. 21).
Image: Ghaṭotkaca approaches his father with joined palms (sa. *añjalimudrā*). He has a large belly, demonic hair and demonic facial traits.

73. १घटोत्कचन् द्रौपदी बुयकाव् युधिष्ठिन् भीम् नकुल् सहदेव् धौम्य वं॥
Ghaṭotkacana Draupadī buyakāva Yudhiṣṭhira Bhīma Nakula Sahadeva Dhaumya vaṃ.
Ghaṭotkaca carries Draupadī while Yudhiṣṭhira, Bhīma, Nakula, Sahadeva and Dhaumya walk.

Text: Ghaṭotkaca carries Draupadī, while other demons (who presumably had arrived with him) carry the brothers, Dhaumya and all the sages in their company (ch. 145). They reach the hermitage of Nara and Nārāyaṇa where they stay in expectation of again beholding Arjuna (ch. 146).
Image: The image shows them on their way to the hermitage. Ghaṭotkaca carries Draupadī on his shoulders. In contrast to the text, the others proceed on foot. This is additionally stressed in the inscription.

74. १द्रौपदीन् पलेस्वान् थुव॥
Draupadīna palesvāna thuva.
Draupadī detects a lotus-flower.

Text: After six days Draupadī detects a celestial lotus which the wind had brought (ch. 146).
Image: The image shows her picking it up.

75. १द्रौपदीन पलेस्वान् युधिष्ठिनपनि केङ् हयकाव् विव धाव॥
Draupadīna palesvāna Yudhiṣṭhirapani keṅa hayakāva dhāva.
Draupadī shows the lotus-flower to Yudhiṣṭhira and the others, asking (them) to bring for her (more).

Text: Draupadī asks Bhīma to bring for her more flowers of the same kind, stating that she wants to take them to their hermitage in the Kāmyaka woods (ch. 146). Afterwards Draupadī presents the unearthly lotus to Yudhiṣṭhira.
Image: Draupadī shows the lotus-flower to Yudhiṣṭhira and his brothers. While it is not clear from the inscription who, in particular, she asks to bring more, the gesture Bhīma makes indicates that he will take on the task.

/ 81 / 80 / 79 / 78 / 77 / 76 /

76. १रीमन पलस्वान काल वं॥
Bhīmana palesvāna kāla vaṃ.
Bhīma goes in order to take the lotus-flowers.

Text: In order to fulfil Draupadī's wish, Bhīma goes further up the Gandhamādana in the direction from which the celestial lotus was brought (ch. 146).
Image: The image depicts him leaving.

77. १रीमन् हनूमनया् ह्निपाग ह्लंद॥
Bhīmana Hanumantayā hnipota hlaṃṅa.
Bhīma (tries to) lift Hanumān's tail.

Text: Hanumān and Bhīma are both Vāyu's sons and thus considered as brothers. Hanumān warns his younger brother not to continue on his path for it would be too dangerous. In order to protect Bhīma, he obstructs the way with his huge body (ch. 146). He tells Bhīma that if he wants to move on he would have to move aside his long tail (ch. 147). Having not yet recognised the monkey to be Hanumān, the immensely strong Bhīma tries to lift the tail repeatedly but fails.
Image: Bhīma is represented tugging at Hanumān's tail with both his hands but the tail remains unmoved. In the background the peaks of the mountain are represented, those to which Hanumān obstructs the way.

78. १रीमन् हनूमन नमस्कान याक॥
Bhīmana Hanumanta namaskāra yāka.
Bhīma pays homage to Hanumān.

Text: Since Bhīma is not able to lift the tail, he joins his hands in salutation and asks the monkey to reveals his identity (ch. 147). At the repeated request of Bhīma, Hanumān assumes the gigantic form that he had adopted when he leapt over the ocean (ch. 149). The overwhelmed Bhīma again joins his hands and praises Hanumān. Hanumān tells Bhīma that incorrect behaviour in Kubera's grove has consequences. Especially, he advises him not to pluck any flowers himself. Afterwards, Hanumān lets Bhīma pass (ch. 150).
Image: Hanumān has assumed his gigantic form. According to the text, this form of his is immensely terrible, with copper-coloured eyes, sharp teeth and eyes marked by frowns (ch. 149). The sharp teeth and the frowns are depicted as well as pointed ears and vertical projecting hair. Bhīma has his hands joined in reverence (sa. *añjalimudrā*).

79. १कुबेनया् वन नञा याक नाञसपनि् रीमव् यूद्ध याढाव् वस वं॥
Kuberayā vana rakṣā yāka rākṣasapani Bhīmava yuddha yāṅāva vese vaṃ.
Having fought a battle with Bhīma, the demons guarding Kubera's forest take flight.

Text: Bhīma reaches Kubera's pond, filled with celestial lotuses (ch. 151). Disregar-

/ 82 /

ding Hanumān's advice, he plunges into the water to pluck the blossoms without first taking Kubera's permission. The demons (sa. *rākṣasas*) guarding the lake rush at him in wrath (ch. 152). Bhīma however defeats them. He slays hundreds and the remaining ones flee in terror.
Image: On the right side of the image, Bhīma does battle with one of the demons guarding the pond. On the left side of the image, two others are leaving the place, looking back at the mighty Bhīma.

80. १तीमन् कुवनया् वनस पलस्वान काव॥
Bhīmana Kuberayā vanasa palesvāna kāva.
Bhīma takes lotus-flowers in Kubera's forest.

Text: After having defeated the demons, Bhīma gathers lotuses in abundance (ch. 152). Meanwhile, the surviving demons approach Kubera who, with a laugh, gives his approval. The demons thereupon renounce their anger.
Image: The pond from which Bhīma plucks the lotus(es) is depicted wavy and alive with fish. According to the text, Bhīma plunges into the waters before gathering the flowers whereas, in the image, he stands on the lakeshore.

81. १[तीम]न् द्रौपदीयाग पलस्वान विव॥
Bhīmana Draupadīyāta palesvāna biva.
Bhīma gives Draupadī the lotus-flower(s).

Text: As they behold terrible omens, Yudhiṣṭhira and the others set out for that lake, too (ch. 153). They find Bhīma admidst the bodies of the demons he slew. With Kubera's permission, they all stay in his realm.
Image: Bhīma hands over a celestial lotus to Draupadī. The text does not explicitly say that he gives her the lotuses but since Bhīma had come only for that reason, it is implied that he does so.

82. १अर्ज्जुनव युधिष्ठिनव नाप नाक॥ १तीम॥ १नकुल॥ १सहदव १द्रौपदी॥ १धौम्य॥
Arjjunava Yudhiṣṭhirava nāpa rāka. Bhīma. Nakula. Sahadeva. Draupadī. Dhaumya.
Arjuna and Yudhiṣṭhira meet. Bhīma. Nakula. Sahadeva. Draupadī. Dhaumya.

Text: As mentioned before, the events from scene 70 onwards take place during Arjuna's sojourn in heaven. This scene now depicts the reunion of the Pāṇḍavas atop Mount Gandhamādana. Yudhiṣṭhira and the others spend an entire month in Kubera's realm until they at last behold Indra's chariot (ch. 161). Arjuna is joyfully welcomed and in response to Yudhiṣṭhira's questions, Arjuna relates all that has happened since his departure (chs. 163ff.). On this occasion also, his battle with the Nivātakavacas is described.
Image: Arjuna approaches from one side, Yudhiṣṭhira and the others from the other one. They are all greeting each other, glad that they are reunited after all.

83. १युधिष्ठिन [...]
Yudhiṣṭhira [...]

Text: The Pāṇḍavas spend four years in Kubera's realm before they continue their journey (ch. 173). They spend the twelfth year of exile in the Viśākhayūpa forest, named after a sacrificial post (sa. *yūpa*) therein (ch. 174). In a cavern, Bhīma comes across a snake of colossal proportions (ch. 175). The hungry snake violently seizes Bhīma and binds him with its body. Because of a boon the snake had received, Bhīma's mind becomes deluded and he is unable to free himself. As Yudhiṣṭhira finds Bhīma caught in the coils of the snake, he enquires of that being by which means he could procure his brother's release (ch. 177). The snake reveals itself to be the royal sage Nahuṣa who was reduced to live in the form of a serpent because he

/ 87 / 86 / 85 / 84 / 83 /

had insulted the brahmins. Nahuṣa further states that only if Yudhiṣṭhira answers accurately to his questions, he would himself be freed from the curse and could release Bhīma. Yudhiṣṭhira and Nahuṣa among others discourse about the attributes of brahmins and the relation subsisting between the self (sa. *ātman*) and the ultimate reality (sa. *brahman*) (chs. 177f.).

Image: The inscription is badly damaged but the content of the image is clear. Bhīma is bound in the coils of the snake. Only his head and his mace are visible. The snake turns its head towards Yudhiṣṭhira who stands aside, presumably answering Nahuṣa's questions.

84. १नघूषनाजा् उद्धान जूयाव् स्वर्ग्ग वं॥

Naghuṣarājā uddhāra juyāva svargga vaṃ.

King Nahuṣa is released and goes to heaven.

Text: Since Yudhiṣṭhira has accurately answered all the questions put, Nahuṣa is released from his curse (ch. 178). He discards his serpentine form, assumes his celestial shape and returns to the world of the gods. Together, Yudhiṣṭhira and Bhīma return to their hermitage.

Image: Bhīma has been released. The snake is depicted in the foreground, while in the background the released Nahuṣa ascends on his celestial chariot. For he is a royal sage, he is represented with a crown in preference to the tied up, matted hair. With one hand, he shows the gesture of fearlessness (sa. *abhayamudrā*), with the other one the boon-granting gesture (sa. *varadamudrā*).

85. [१... दु] र्य्योधनव् यूद्ध॥

[...] Duryyodhanava yuddha.

Fight between [...] and Duryodhana.

Text: The Pāṇḍavas repair to the lake of the Dvaita woods (chs. 174, 225). Fearing their forthcoming vengeance, Duryodhana, in order to taunt and outface his foes and in order to increase their grief, shows up with his entire retinue (chs. 226ff.). Dhṛtarāṣṭra gave his permission because Duryodhana had told him he would go there to inspect the herds of his cows (chs. 227f.). As the Kauravas arrive at the lakeside, they are restrained by celestial musicians (sa. *gandharvas*) on command of their king, Citrasena (ch. 229). As the Kauravas forcibly enter the forest, the *gandharvas* attack (ch. 230). Duryodhana, Duḥśāsana and others are captured while again others seek refuge with Yudhiṣṭhira (chs. 230f.).

Image: The image depicts Duryodhana in battle with Citrasena, the king of the *gandharvas*, who then captures him. Only the busts of the charioteers are depicted.

86. [१ही]म् अर्ज्जु[न...] गंधर्व्व [...]
Bhīma Arjjuna [...] gandharvva [...]
Bhīma and Arjuna [...] *gandharvas* [...]

Text: For the sake of their lineage, Yudhiṣṭhira orders his brothers to liberate Duryodhana (ch. 232). At first only a mild battle is fought but as all attempts at conciliation fail, Arjuna engages in a terrible second battle (ch. 233).
Image: The captured Duryodhana is represented bound on a chariot. It is apparently directed by a demon (sa. *rākṣasa*). Arjuna engages in battle while Bhīma who only fought with him in the mild first battle, stands aside.

87. १अर्ज्जुनन् दुर्य्योधं तोर तयकाव यं[॥]
Arjjunana Duryyodhaṃ tora tayakāva yaṃ.
Arjuna releases Duryodhana (lit. causes him to leave).

Text: The Pāṇḍavas slay hundreds until finally Citrasena intervenes (ch. 234). As Arjuna recognises the one who had become his friend at Indraloka, he lays down his weapons. At Arjuna's request, Citrasena sets Duryodhana free and, overwhelmed with shame, Duryodhana returns to Hastināpura.
Image: Arjuna leads his released cousin away.

88. १जयद्रथव [द्रौपदी]व् संभाषन॥ १८धौम्यन् द्रौपदी पयाव चोढ॥
Jayadrathava Draupadīva sambhāṣana. Dhaumyana Draupadī peyāva coṇa.
Conversation between Jayadratha and Draupadī. Dhaumya keeping Draupadī save.

Text: The Pāṇḍavas again repair to the Kāmyaka woods (ch. 244). One day, all five brothers go hunting together (ch. 248). With the permission of Dhaumya, they leave Draupadī in the hermitage. Jayadratha, the king of Sindhu and Duryodhana's brother in law, comes to pass the hermitage. As he beholds Draupadī he desires her. Jayadratha asks her to leave her husbands and to become his wife instead but Draupadī spurns him (ch. 251).

/ 89 / 88 /

Image: According to the text, Draupadī is holding onto the lowered branch of a tree as Jayadratha arrives (ch. 249) and she likewise holds onto the branch in the image. Dhaumya who had given permission to the Pāṇḍavas to leave Draupadī alone is represented next to her.

89. १जयद्रथन द्रौपदी हनलपाव यं भीमन लाक॥
Jayadrathana Draupadī haralapāva yaṃ Bhīmana lāka.
Jayadratha abducts Draupadī (and) Bhīma catches (him).

Text: Jayadratha forces Draupadī to ascend his chariot and carries her away (ch. 252). Dhaumya follows them on foot in the midst of Jayadratha's infantry. As the Pāṇḍavas come to know what has happened, they go after Jayadratha (ch. 253). Dhaumya asks Bhīma to attack and a battle ensues in the end of which Jayadratha sets Draupadī free and flees (ch. 255). While Yudhiṣṭhira returns with Draupadī and the others, Arjuna and Bhīma rush after Jayadratha. Bhīma grasps him by the hair and crushes him on the ground but for the sake of Duḥśalā, he spares his life (chs. 255f.).
Image: Jayadratha has forced Draupadī on his chariot. On the left side of the image, Dhaumya points at Jayadratha, asking Bhīma to attack. Bhīma is depicted on the left side of the image. In accordance with the text, he grasps Jayadratha by the hair.

/ 91 / 90 /

90. १तीमन द्रौपदी लषलपाव रुव् जयद्रथ युधिष्ठिन लव लाक॥
Bhīmana Draupadī laṣalapīva phava Jayadratha Yudhiṣṭhira lava lāka.
Bhīma is able to protect Draupadī (and) Jayadratha is handed over to Yudhiṣṭhira.

Text: The brothers refrain from killing Jayadratha but Bhīma shaves his head and makes him their slave (ch. 256). Afterwards, he brings him bound before Yudhiṣṭhira. Yudhiṣṭhira rebukes Jayadratha for his behaviour but orders Bhīma to set him free. Draupadī also repeats this request.
Image: Bhīma has bound Jayadratha with ropes. He leads him before Yudhiṣṭhira who welcomes them with the gesture of fearlessness (sa. *abhayamudrā*). Draupadī additionally shows the boon-granting gesture (sa. *varadamudrā*) as she supports Yudhiṣṭhira's appeal to set Jayadratha free.

91. १जयद्रथ गालगाव छ्वाक
Jayadratha tolatāva choka
Jayadratha is released and sent away

Text: Jayadratha leaves (ch. 256). He seeks refuge with Śiva and obtains the boon that he will be able to restrain in battle the Pāṇḍavas, all except for Arjuna. The Pāṇḍavas for their part return to the Dvaita woods, where they abide until the end of the twelvth year of their exile (ch. 295).
Image: The image depicts Jayadratha on his way to Gaṅgādvāra, the *door of the Gaṅgā* in the Himālayas, where he performs austerities in order to please Śiva.

Virāṭaparva: 'The Book of Virāṭa'

92. १युधिष्ठिन् [भी]म् अर्ज्जुन् नकुल् सहदेव् द्रौपदी विनाटनाजायाक गुफवास वं॥ [...]
Yudhiṣṭhira Bhīma Arjjuna Nakula Sahadeva Draupadī Virāṭarājāyāke guptavāsa vaṃ
Yudhiṣṭhira, Bhīma, Arjuna, Nakula, Sahadeva and Draupadī go to the remote state of king Virāṭa. [...]

Text: As agreed, the Pāṇḍavas have to spend their last year of exile unrecognised in an inhabitated place. They decide to go to Virāṭa, the king of the Matsyas, and to enter his service (ch. 1). Dhaumya takes leave and repairs to Drupada's abode while the Pāṇḍavas proceed to Virāṭa's kingdom (ch. 2). Before they enter the city, they deposit their weapons on a mighty *śamī* tree, a white thorn tree, in the midst of an out-of-the way forest and they disguise themselves as hunters (ch. 5).
Image: In this case the tree on the left side not only serves as a scene divider but is itself part of the image. It is the mighty tree on the outskirts of the capital on which the Pāṇḍavas hide their weapons. Among others Arjuna's bow and Sahadeva's sword are depicted. There appears to have been a short inscription below the tree, too, but it is no longer legible. To the right, the Pāṇḍavas and Draupadī enter the city of Virāṭa. As usual, they retain their armours and crowns in the image even though, according to the text, they entered Matsya attired as hunters (ch. 5).

93. १युधिष्ठिन कंकनाम ब्राह्मण धक विनाटनाजायाक ववा॥
Yudhiṣṭhira Kaṅkanāma brāhmaṇa dhaka Virāṭarājāyāke vava.
Yudhiṣṭhira goes to king Virāṭa, saying he was a brahmin named Kaṅka.

Text: The Pāṇḍavas and Draupadī arrive at Virāṭa's court in different disguises. Yudhiṣṭhira is the first to approach Virāṭa (ch. 6). He introduces himself as a brahmin named Kaṅka, skilled in dice and friends with Yudhiṣṭhira. The king receives him with the utmost respect.
Image: Yudhiṣṭhira approaches Virāṭa to offer his service. Instaed of a crown, he now wears matted locks tied up in a knot. Virāṭa's palace (or its assembly hall) is indicated by two pillars and a simple roofing. The same chamber is depicted repeatedly under a single roof for the immediate consecutive events up to scene 98.

/ 98 / 97 / 96 / 95 / 94 / 93 / 92 /

94. १भीम् वल्लवनाम् सूवार धक विराटराजायाके ववा॥
Bhīma Vallavanāma suvāra dhaka Virāṭarājāyāke vava.
Bhīma goes to king Virāṭa as a cook named Ballava.

Text: Bhīma approaches Virāṭa in the guise of a cook, with a spoon and a ladle in his hands (ch. 7). He sais his name is Ballava, that he is skilled at cooking and wrestling and that he formerly served Yudhiṣṭhira. Virāṭa instates him as the superintendent of his kitchen.
Image: Bhīma holds a large spoon indicative of his adopted profession. Like Yudhiṣṭhira, he now wears matted locks tied up in a knot instead of his crown. The same is true for Sahadeva and Nakula in scenes 96 and 98. Virāṭa is depicted on his throne as he receives Ballava (Bhīma).

95. १द्रौपदी् सैरंध्री धक् उदेष्णायाके ववा॥
Draupadī sairandhrī dhaka Udeṣṇāyāke vava
Draupadī goes as a *sairandhrī* to Sudeṣṇā.

Text: Draupadī dresses herself as a *sairandhrī*, an independent maidservant (ch. 8). As Sudeṣṇā,Virāṭa's queen, beholds her wandering around the city, she summons her. Draupadī states that she is the wife of five celestial musicians (sa. *gandharvas*), the sons of a *gandharva* king of exceeding power. She further states that she is adept at dressing the hair, that she knows to make beautiful garlands and that she earlier had served Kṛṣṇa's favourite queen, Satyabhāmā, as well as Draupadī. Thereupon Sudeṣṇā offers her residence. For Draupadī mentions no name she is simply adressed *sairandhrī* in the following.
Image: Draupadī is shown in conversation with Sudeṣṇā.

96. १सहदेव् तन्त्रीपालनाम् सालहिक ध[क] विराटराजायाके ववा॥
Sahadeva Tantrīpālanāma sālahika dhaka Virāṭarājāyāke vava.
Sahadeva goes to king Virāṭa as a cow-rearer named Tantrīpāla.

Text: Sahadeva introduces himself to Virāṭa as a cowherd named Ariṣṭanemi (ch. 9). He states that he formerly numbered the cows of Yudhiṣṭhira and that he was known by the name of Tantrīpāla. He further says that under his hand, cows would multiply swiftly and never suffer from disease. Virāṭa is pleased and places all his herds and the herdsmen in Sahadeva's charge.
Image: In order to indicate the profession Sahadeva adopts, he is represented holding a stick to drive the cattle. Virāṭa receives him at court.

97. १अर्ज्जुन् वृ[ह]न्नलानाम् नपूंसक धक ववा॥
Arjjuna Vṛhannalānāma napuṃsaka dhaka vava.
Arjuna goes as one of the neuter gender named Vṛhannalā.

Text (scene 97): [Due to Urvaśī's curse,] Arjuna appears at the court as one of the neuter gender, decked in the ornaments of women (ch. 10). He states that his name is Vṛhannalā, that he is proficient in dance and skilled in singing and playing musicial instrumets. He is hired by the king as the dancing-master for his daughter Uttarā, her friends and attendants.
Image: Arjuna is represented in the attire of women. He wears a long cloth to cover his loose hair and large earrings. Like his brothers before, he is also received by Virāṭa.

98. (previous page) १नकुल ग्रन्थिकनाम असवार धक् वव॥
Nakula Granthikanāma asavāra (read: *aśvavāla*) dhaka vava.
Nakula goes as a horse-keeper named Granthika.

Text: Nakula introduces himself as a trainer of horses (ch. 11). He states that he was formerly employed as the tender of Yudhiṣṭhira's horses and that people used to call him Granthika. He says he would perfectly know how to break the temper of steeds and that no horse in his hands would ever become vicious or ill. Virāṭa instates him as his charioteer. He consigns all his horses and mounts to his care and subordinates his other charioteers and horse-keepers to him.
Image: Given the profession Nakula adopts, the object he holds might be a whip. Again, Virāṭa welcomes his new employee.

99. १कीचकन् सुदेष्णाया ह्नवन् सैरंध्री कलात काय ह्लात॥
Kīcakana Sudeṣṇāyā hṅavane sairandhrī kalāta kāya hlāta.
In front of Sudeṣṇā, Kīcaka tells Sairandhrī to become his wife.

Text: The Pāṇḍavas and Draupadī live at Virāṭa's court in disguise, unrecognised by the people. After ten months, Kīcaka, Virāṭa's general and Sudeṣṇā's brother, chances to behold Draupadī (Sairandhrī) in Sudeṣṇā's abode (ch. 13). Kīcaka immediately desires her. He states that he would give up his other wives and even subordinate himself to her but Draupadī turns him down with reference to her character's *gandharva* husbands.

Image: Kīcaka asks Sudeṣṇā about her maidservant. Draupadī sits close by. She supports her head with her hand, unfortunate in this situation. Underneath the furniture on which Sudeṣṇā and Draupadī are seated small vessels are depicted.

100. १सैरन्ध्रीन वल्लवयाके दुःख् खं ह्लाल वव॥
sairandhrīna Vallavayāke duḥkha kaṃ hlāla vava.
Sairandhrī comes to tell Ballava of (her) trouble.

Text: After collusion with Kīcaka, Sudeṣṇā sends Draupadī (Sairandhrī) to his residence to fetch some liquor for her (ch. 14). Kīcaka forcibly tries to get hold of her but she manages to get away with the help of an invisible demon (sa. *rākṣasa*) whom Sūrya had sent to protect her (chs. 14f.). At night, Draupadī goes to the quarters of Bhīma (Ballava), tells him of her misfortune and begs for vengeance (chs. 16ff.). Bhīma thereupon promises to slay Kīcaka (ch. 21).
Text: The miserable Draupadī again supports her head as she tells of the trouble that has befallen her. Bhīma, in his disguise as Ballava, with top-knot and ladle, raises his hand as he swears to exact vengeance on Kīcaka.

101. १वल्लव् सैरन्ध्री धक् संकेतस्थानस चोङ कीचकन् जोन॥
Vallava sairandhrī dhaka saṅketasthānasa coṅa Kīcakana jona.
Kīcaka catches Ballava who is in the meeting place, pretending to be Sairandhrī.

Text: Bhīma (Ballava) tells Draupadī (Sairandhrī) that she should arrange a meeting with Kīcaka (ch. 21). She invites him to the dancing hall for the next evening. Instead of Draupadī, Bhīma then awaits Kīcaka there. As Kīcaka enters, he sees someone reclining on a divan. The figure is obscured by the darkness and Kīcaka consequently approaches, assuming this would be Sairandhrī.
Image: Kīcaka has entered the dancing hall. An apparently female figure reclines on a couch and the inscription states that it is Bhīma (Ballava) pretending to be Draupadī (Sairandhrī). In the text it is not mentioned that he dresses as a woman, only that he hides in the dark. With an inappropriate touch Kīcaka draws attention to himself.

/ 104 / 103 / 102 / 101 / 100 / 99 /

102. १कीवकव् वल्लवव् युद्ध॥

Kīcakava Vallavava yuddha.

Fight between Kīcaka and Ballava.

Text: As Kīcaka comes closer, Bhīma (Ballava) leaps up and the two of them start a wrestling match (ch. 21).

Image: In accordance with the text, Bhīma and Kīcaka are fighting with bare arms. Bhīma is again represented in his character's attire.

detail of scene 101

103. १वल्लवन् कीवक् वध॥

Vallavana Kīcaka vadha.

Ballava kills Kīcaka.

Text: As Kīcaka weakens, Bhīma (Ballava) presses his chest until he loses consciousness (ch. 21). In rage he then thrusts Kīcaka's arms, legs and his neck into his body.

Image: Bhīma is depicted forcing Kīcaka's arm into his trunk.

104. १कीवकया् सीकह्म॥

Kīcakayā sīkahma.

Kīcaka's dead body.

Text: In the end only a mound of flesh remains (ch. 21).

Image: The slain Kīcaka is depicted exactly as described. Only his trunk is shown with his head, hands and feet while his arms, legs and neck have been forced into his body.

/ 109 / 108 / 107--

105. १समसानस् सिमा जाढाव् वल्लव चाढ॥ १कीचकया बान्धवपनिसन् सैरन्ध्री मि बिचके यं॥

samasānasa simā joṅāva Vallava coṅa. Kīcakayā bāndhavapanisena sairandhrī mi bicake yaṃ.

a) A troop of Kīcaka's kinsmen leads Sairandhrī away to make her pay[273] with (death by) fire. b) After seizing a tree, Ballava is at the cremation ground.

Text: Draupadī (Sairandhrī) tells the guards that Kīcaka was slain by her *gandharva* husbands (ch. 21). Then Kīcaka's relatives arrive at the place (ch. 22). Since it was on her account that he was murdered, they decide that Draupadī has to be killed, too. In order to do what would have brought pleasure to Kīcaka, they decide to burn her together with him. As Kīcaka's kinsmen forcibly carry Draupadī in the direction of the cremation ground, she wails aloud for protection. Hearing her lamentations, Bhīma (Ballava) rushes towards the cremation ground. He extends his body so that no-one might recognise him and in his rush, he uproots a large tree. Beholding him approach in that way, Kīcaka's kinsmen take him to be one of the five *gandharvas*. Panic-struck, they release Draupadī and flee towards the city.

Image: Kīcaka's kinsmen have seized Draupadī by the arms. The inscription explains why. As they are about to drag her away, Bhīma dashes at them with the uprooted tree in his hand.

273 *bicake*: causative of *'biya - i. a. to pay (a dept)'*, given by Jørgensen as *biyake*: Jørgensen 1995 (1936), p. 128. The end of the verb's base may, however, vary before the causative.

106. १वल्लवन् कीचकया बान्धवपनि् वध याढाव् सैरन्ध्री लिछ्राक॥

Vallavana Kīcakayā bāndhavapani vadha yāṅāva sairandhrī lichoka.

Ballava kills Kīcaka's kinsmen and sends back Sairandhrī.

Text: Bhīma (Ballava) slays 105 of the fleeing Kīcakas and sends Draupadī (Sairandhrī) back to the city (ch. 22). He himself then takes another route back to Virāṭa's kitchen.

Image: Bhīma uses uprooted trees to slay Kīcaka's relatives while Draupadī stands by.

107. १सूशर्म्माया् सहाय[॥] १सूशर्म्माव यूद्ध॥ १वल्लव॥ १तन्त्रीपाल॥ १ग्रन्थिक॥ १कंक॥ १विराटराजा् दक्षिण गोग्रहस ग्वाहाल् वं॥

Suśarmmāyā sahāya. Suśarmmāva yuddha. Vallava. Tantrīpāla. Granthika. Kaṅka. Virāṭarājā dakṣiṇa gograhasa gvāhāḷ vaṃ.

Suśarmā's companion. Fight with Suśarmā. Ballava. Tantrīpāla. Granthika. Kaṅka. In order to help, king Virāṭa goes to the (place of) cattle seizure in the south.

Text: Suśarmā, the king of the Trigartas, had earlier been repeatedly defeated by the Matsyas, under Kīcaka's command (ch. 29). With Kīcaka's death, Virāṭa is weakened and Suśarmā suggests to Duryodhana to invade the Matsya kingdom with the united forces of the Kauravas and Trigartas. The Trigartas set out first, in a south-eastern direction. As Virāṭa's herdsmen report that their kine is being seized by thousands, Virāṭa sets out with his forces (ch. 30). Since he is convinced that Kaṅka (Yudhiṣ-

---107 / 106 / 105 /

ṭhira), Ballava (Bhīma), Tantrīpāla (Sahadeva) and Granthika (Nakula) are skilled in fight, he orders chariots to be brought for them, too. In the evening the Matsyas encounter the Trigartas and the combatants rush against each other (ch. 31). At night, Suśarmā takes Virāṭa captive (ch. 32). The four Pāṇḍavas however slay the Trigartas by thousands and Bhīma finally overpowers the fleeing Suśarmā, too. Virāṭa is freed and the Pāṇḍavas retrieve the cattle.
Image: Virāṭa sets out for battle together with four of the Pāṇḍavas, Yudhiṣṭhira, Bhīma, Nakula and Sahadeva. Bhīma is at the same time depicted in single combat with Suśarmā, in reference to the Pāṇḍavas' victory. The Pāṇḍavas are, only for once, depicted in apparently arbitrary order.

108. १वृहन्नला सानथि याढाव् उत्तनकुमान् उत्तन गोग्रहस् ग्वाहाC वं॥
Vṛhannalā sārathi yāṅāva Uttarakumāra uttara gograhasa gvāhāḷ vaṃ.
Vṛhannalā becomes charioteer and, in order to help, prince Uttara goes to the (place of) cattle seizure in the north.

Text: After Virāṭa has set out southwards in pursuit of the Trigartas, the Kauravas invade his realm (ch. 33). It becomes clear later, that this second raid was conducted in the north of Virāṭa's realm (ch. 41). As the chief of these cowherds enters the city, he finds it empty. Virāṭa had left his son Uttara in charge, who is requested for help. Draupadī (Sairandhrī) recommends Arjuna (Vṛhannalā) as charioteer, for he would formerly have driven Arjuna's steeds (ch. 34). Uttara accepts and Arjuna drives the chariot towards the Kauravas (ch. 35).
Image: Arjuna is depicted as Uttara's charioteer, in his disguise as one of the third gender, with long braided hair.
It becomes most clear from here on that crowns do not serve as reconition feature. Whereas Uttara has a crown with a flowery design in this scene, it is Arjuna who wears that same crown in the next scene, while Uttara receives the typical tripod one (109). Again in the following scene, Virāṭa has the flowery crown (110) and thereafter Yudhiṣṭhira while Arjuna is again depicted with the tripod crown (111). Moreover, the crowns of Nakula and Sahadeva in scene 111, as well as those of Arjuna and Duryodhana in scene 112 deserve to be mentioned too, for their design is quite unique.

109. [१द्]र्य्योधन् सा [ञा]ढाव ब्व[स...] वं॥ १अश्वत्था[म]ा॥ १कृपाचार्य्य॥ १कर्ण्ण॥
१द्रोणाचार्य्य॥ १भीष्म॥ १उत्तनकुमान सानथि याढाव अर्ज्जुनन प्रकटनं युद्ध याक॥
Duryyodhana sā joṅāva bvasainya vaṃ. Aśvatthāmā. Kṛpācāryya. Karṇṇa. Droṇācāryya. Bhīṣma. Uttarakumāra sārathi yāṅāva Arjjunana prakaṭanaṃ yuddha yāka.

a) Aśvatthāmā. The spiritual teacher Kṛpa. Karṇa. The spiritual teacher Droṇa. Bhīṣma. Prince Uttara becomes the charioteer and Arjuna, revealed, fights.
b) Duryodhana seizes the cows and leaves with a part (of the army).

Text (scene 109): As Uttara beholds the Kauravas' mighty host he loses courage. He jumps down from his chariot and flees afoot (ch. 36). Arjuna (Vṛhannalā) drags him back, tells him to control the horses and states that he himself would fight in Uttara's stead. After fetching the hidden weapons from the *śamī* tree, he reveals himself to the prince (chs. 38f.). Meanwhile, Bhīṣma comes to the conclusion that the time of the Pāṇḍavas' exile has expired (ch. 47). He sends Duryodhana back to Hastināpura with the kine and half of the army, arraying the remaining soldiers for battle. Arjuna ignores the assembled chariots, hastens after Duryodhana and recovers the kine (ch. 48). Only thereafter Arjuna and Uttara vanquish the Kauravas in battle (chs. 49ff.). The herdsmen are send ahead to proclaim Uttara's victory (ch. 62).
Image: Uttara is now depicted as Arjuna's charioteer. For Arjuna revealed himself, he is no longer represented in disguise. On the left side of the image, Duryodhana is seen in his attempt to escape with the kine, while Aśvatthāmā, Kṛpa, Karṇa, Droṇa and Bhīṣma are stationed for battle. According to the text, Arjuna challenges them one after the other, after having regained the cattle. Bhīṣma's charioteer is also depicted. A horse is yoked to Kṛpa's chariot, a composite aquatic being (sa. *makara*) to Aśvatthāmā's while the other chariots and the driven cattle as well whirl up clouds of dust.

Northern face of the temple (scenes 110 to 148):

110. १विराटराजान् कंक् त्वाकन ष्याक सैरंध्रीन हि फव॥
Virāṭarājāna Kaṅka tvākana ṣyāka sairandhrīna hi phava.
King Virāṭa hurts Kaṅka with a block of wood (and) Sairandhrī collects[274] the blood.

Text: As the messengers proclaim Uttara's victory, Virāṭa is delighted and wishes to cast dice with Yudhisthira alias Kaṅka (ch. 63). He tells Draupadī (Sairandhrī) to bring the dice. However, before the gambling commences, Yudhiṣṭhira insists that Arjuna (Vṛhannalā) is accountable for Uttara's triumph. Virāṭa becomes enraged and strikes Yudhiṣṭhira on the face with the dice. Draupadī gathers the blood flowing from Yudhiṣṭhira's nose in a golden vessel so that Arjuna will not see it when he enters. It is explained that Arjuna had sworn an oath to slay anyone who causes Yudhiṣṭhira's blood to fall, be it not in an act of battle.
Image: Virāṭa strikes Yudhiṣṭhira on the face with the dice. Yudhiṣṭhira is not yet revealed and therefore still represented in his disguise as a brahmin. Draupadī holds back his hair with one hand and in the other hand she holds the vessel to gather the blood. It is surprising that, although the scene takes place inside, there is nothing to indicate this. In contrast to scene 51, the game field is not depicted here but of course, this time the dice are. Virāṭa strikes Yudhiṣṭhira with one of them and Yudhiṣṭhira holds two more in his hand. The dice can be no others than the depicted *pāśakas*, four-sided long blocks. Cowrie shells are also used as dice and according to Lüders, Vibhītaka nuts, too,[275] but neither of these would have caused any pain. According to the inscription, Virāṭa's *pāśakas* are made of wood, as it is most frequently the case. Even so, other materials are used too. According to the text, Yudhiṣṭhira's dice are made of lapis lazuli and gold (ch. 6), I have seen *pāśakas* made of bone and metal and Lüders knows also of ivory *pāśakas*.[276]

111. १विराटराजान् उत्तरकुमा[रन] युधिष्ठिरयाके स्तुति॥ १युधिष्ठिर् भीम् अर्ज्जुन् नकुल् सहदेव द्रौपदी् प्रकाश जुव॥
Virāṭarājāna Uttarakumārana Yudhiṣṭhirayāke stuti. Yudhiṣṭhira Bhīma Arjjuna Nakula Sahadeva Draupadī prakāśa juva.
a) Yudhiṣṭhira, Bhīma, Arjuna, Nakula, Sahadeva and Draupadī become revealed.
b) King Virāṭa and prince Uttara honour Yudhiṣṭhira .

Text: Uttara enters and states that it was the son of a god who has won back the cattle and vanquished the Kauravas (ch. 64). Some days later, the time of exile has expired. The Pāṇḍavas enter the assembly hall and seat themselves on thrones (ch. 65). As Virāṭa enters, they reveal themselves to the king (chs. 65f.). Virāṭa propitiates them and they take up their abode in Upaplavya, a city in Virāṭa's kingdom (ch. 67). Virāṭa's daughter Uttarā is married to Abhimanyu, Arjuna's son with Subhadrā.

274 Kölver und Shresthacarya 1994, p. 219: *phaye*, i.a. to collect.

275 Lüders 1907, pp. 17ff.
276 ibid, p. 16.

/ 112 / 111 / 110 /

Image: Virāṭa's palace is indicated by framing pillars and a decorated cei-ling with a variety of pendants. The Pāṇḍavas are revealed and again depicted with crowns, armours and their distinctive weapons. Draupadī wears costly garments, jewellery and has her hair plaited into a thick braid. On the left side, Uttara and Virāṭa are honouring Yudhiṣṭhira and the others. In accordance with the text, the brothers and Draupadī are sitting on thrones while Virāṭa and Uttara are kneeling before them on the ground.

detail of scene110

Udyogaparva 'The Book of Effort'

112. १अर्ज्जुन् Cकोस चों॥ १कृष्णु दढाव विज्याक् १दुर्य्योधन् ठुसस् चोढ॥

Arjjuna ḷkosa coṃ. Kṛṣṇa deṅāva vijyāka. Duryyodhana phusasa coṅa.

Arjuna sits at the foot of the bed. Kṛṣṇa is sleeping. Duryodhana sits at the head of the bed.[277]

Text: On account of the impending war between Pāṇḍavas and Kauravas, Duryodha-na and Arjuna both set out for Dvārakā to seek Kṛṣṇa's help (ch. 7). As they arrive, Kṛṣṇa lies asleep. Duryodhana enters the room first and sits down at the head of the bed. Then Arjuna positions himself at the back of the bed.

Image: Pictorially, Kṛṣṇa's abode merges with Virāṭa's palace from the previous scene. The figures are depicted in three compartments. The central one has Kṛṣṇa lying asleep on his bed. The artist has chosen not to depict a layer and instead offers a view under the bed where different vessels are placed. Though asleep, Kṛṣṇa holds his four attributes. Arjuna and Duryodhana are identifiable only by the inscription for they are depicted without any attibutes. For the first time, a building is depicted with a back wall – one with a latticed pattern (sa. *jāli*) from top to bottom.

277 Kölver und Shresthacarya 1994, p. 289: *likva*, foot of a bed and p. 223: *phusa*, head of a bed.

113. १दूर्य्योधन् अक्षोहिणीसेना जोङाव वं॥
Duryyodhana akṣohiṇīsenā joṅāva vaṃ.
Duryodhana takes the *akṣauhiṇī* troop and departs.

Text: As Kṛṣṇa wakes from sleep he asks Arjuna and Duryodhana the reason for their arrival (ch. 7). Kṛṣṇa bears the same relationship to both of them and promises to lend them both his assistance. He leaves it up to Arjuna, the younger of them, to choose first the type of support. He offers either the support of the Nārāyaṇas, a great army of unassailable warriors, or his own support, stating ,however, that he himself won't fight on the field. Arjuna chooses Kṛṣṇa and Duryodhana departs with the Nārāyaṇa army consisting of one *akṣauhiṇī* (21.870 chariots, 21,870 elephants, 65,610 horses and 109,350 foot soldiers).
Image: Duryodhana is depicted leaving the place. The vast army is not represented but is mentioned in the inscription.

114. १अर्ज्जुन् कृष्ण वोणाव यं्
Arjjuna Kṛṣṇa voṇāva yaṃ
Arjuna leads Kṛṣṇa away.

Text: After Duryodhana has left, Kṛṣṇa asks Arjuna the reason for choosing him (ch. 7). Arjuna states that he desires Kṛṣṇa's help as his charioteer and Kṛṣṇa agrees. Accompanied by Kṛṣṇa, Arjuna returns.
Image: Kṛṣṇa and Arjuna are leaving the place together. They are both holding their distinctive attributes.

115. १अर्ज्जुनन् कृष्णव् युधिष्ठिरव् नाप लाचका॥
Arjjunana Kṛṣṇava Yudhiṣṭhirava nāpa lācako.
Arjuna causes Kṛṣṇa and Yudhiṣṭhira to meet.

Text: The text does not expand on the reunion of Kṛṣṇa and Yudhiṣṭhira. It is mentioned in only one sentence that, after Kṛṣṇa has assured to act as Arjuna's charioteer, Arjuna, accompanied by Kṛṣṇa returns to Yudhiṣṭhira (ch. 7).
Image: Arjuna and Kṛṣṇa are facing Yudhiṣṭhira, who welcomes them with the gesture of fearlessness (sa. *abhayamudrā*). The three of them are somehow framed by the architectural components of the Pāṇḍavas' abode at Upaplavya.

116. १धृतराष्ट्रव् विदुरव् चाचछिं् ख् समधाल॥
Dhṛtarāṣṭrava Vidurava cācachiṃ kha samadhāla.
Dhṛtarāṣṭra and Vidura's consultation lasts the whole night.

Text: The Kauravas and the Pāṇḍavas send for their allies (chs. 8ff.). Dhṛtarāṣṭra's messenger, Sañjaya, asks the Pāṇḍavas to desist from battle (ch. 25). Yudhiṣṭhira sends back Sañjaya to tell Dhṛtarāṣṭra that he leaves it up to the Kauravas, either to restore Indraprastha to him or to embark on the fight (chs. 26ff.). Before Sañjaya returns and gives Yudhiṣṭhira's response, Dhṛtarāṣṭra suffers from sleeplessness and summons Vidura (ch. 33). The entire night they consult about what should be done (chs. 33ff.). Vidura repeatedly advises Dhṛtarāṣṭra to reconcile with the Pāṇḍavas.
Image: Dhṛtarāṣṭra and Vidura are represented in conversation.

117. १कृ[ष्णन दूर्य्योधनयाके] दूत वं॥
Kṛṣṇana Duryyodhanayāke dūta vaṃ.
Kṛṣṇa goes as a messenger to Duryodhana.

Text: After Sañjaya has announced Yudhiṣṭhira's reply, Dhṛtarāṣṭra repeatedly advises Duryodhana to make peace with the Pāṇḍavas, but Duryodhana refuses (chs. 46ff.). Then, Kṛṣṇa decides to go to the Kauravas himself and to attempt to establish peace (ch. 70).
Image: Kṛṣṇa is depicted on his chariot, on his way to Hastināpura.

118. १कृष्णव् दूर्य्योधनव् ख ह्लाक॥
Kṛṣṇava Duryyodhanava kha hlāka.
Kṛṣṇa and Duryodhana talk.

Text: Kṛṣṇa enters the assembly hall (ch. 93). For the welfare of both the sides, Kṛṣṇa advises Dhṛtarāṣṭra and Duryodhana to make peace and to restore to the Pāṇḍavas their share of the kingdom (chs. 93ff.). Paraśurāma, the sages Kaṇva and

/ 119 / 118 / 117 / 116 / 115 / 114 / 113 /

Nārada, Bhīṣma, Droṇa, Vidura and Dhṛtarāstra all entreat Duryodhana to act accordingly but Duryodhana still refuses (chs. 94ff.).
Image: Instead of a large assembly, only Kṛṣṇa and Duryodhana are represented inside the assembly hall, with a courtly attendant on Duryodhana's side. Again, the building seems to merge with its repeated depiction in the following scene but at least the ceiling's design changes.

119. १कृष्ण॥ १कृष्ण॥ १दूर्याधनन् सकल्यं कृष्णमूर्त्ति खं॥ १कृष्ण॥ १कृष्ण॥
Kṛṣṇa. Kṛṣṇa. Duryyodhanana sakalyaṃ Kṛṣṇamūrtti khaṃ. Kṛṣṇa. Kṛṣṇa.
Kṛṣṇa. Kṛṣṇa. Duryodhana sees all over figures of Kṛṣṇa. Kṛṣṇa. Kṛṣṇa.

Text: As Duryodhana, Duḥśāsana, Karṇa and Śakuni wish to take Kṛṣṇa captive, Kṛṣṇa reveals his divine form (chs. 128f.). From his body emerge the thirty gods, as radiant as the fire but as small as a thumb. Nature-spirits (sa. *yakṣas*) appear, too, as well as celestial musicians (sa. *gandharvas*), demons (sa. *rākṣasas*), the five sons of Pāṇḍu, the Andhakās and Vṛṣṇis (Yādava clans). Rays emerge from the pores of Kṛṣṇa's body and terrible flames from his ears and nose. Then Kṛṣṇa again withdraws his divine form and leaves the court.
Image: Duryodhana is surrounded by four figures of Kṛṣṇa. In contrast to the text, no myriads of divine beings are emerging from his body. Instead, he multiplies himself.

120. (next page) १कृष्णु लिहा वंढ॥
Kṛṣṇa lihā vaṃṅa.
Kṛṣṇa returns.

Text: After all attempts of securing peace have failed, Kṛṣṇa returns to Upaplavya (ch. 135).
Image: Kṛṣṇa is again depicted on his chariot, drawn by a pair of winged horses. In contrast to preceding scenes, the charioteer, Dāruka, is depicted atop the chariot, too, holding the reins.

121. (next page) १कृष्णन् युधिष्ठिन् लिसल कंढ॥ १भीम॥ १अर्ज्जुन॥ १नकुल॥ १सहदेव॥
Kṛṣṇana Yudhiṣṭhira lisala kaṃṅa. Bhīma. Arjjuna. Nakula. Sahadeva.
Kṛṣṇa gives Yudhiṣṭhira answer. Bhīma. Arjuna. Nakula. Sahadeva.

Text: Kṛṣṇa reports to Yudhiṣṭhira that his attempts have failed and that war is inevitable (chs. 145ff.). Thereupon, the troops of both sides march out to the field of battle (chs. 149ff.). Dhṛṣṭadyumna is consecrated as the overall general of Yudhiṣṭhira's forces while Bhīṣma is installed as the commander-in-chief on the Kaurava side.
Image: Kṛṣṇa reports to Yudhiṣṭhira and his brothers. Dharma's son is depicted with a pointed chin beard and a chain of *rudrākṣas*. Not for the first time the scene runs across the corner but there is an unusual discontinuity here in the form of presentation. Nakula and Sahadeva, depicted on the first segment, are sitting inside their

/ 123 / 122--

abode at Upaplavya, indicated by framing pillars and cloths hanging from the ceiling. The figures depicted on the next segment are by contrast framed by two battle standards, indicating the imminent war and establishing a relation to the next scene.

Bhīṣmaparva: 'The Book of Bhīṣma'

122. १दुःशासन॥ १अश्वत्थामा॥ १कृपाचार्य्य॥ १द्रोणाचार्य्य॥ १भीष्म॥ १दुर्य्योधन हथार ववा॥
१कृष्णन् अर्ज्जु[नयात] विश्वरूप कं[ण॥] १अर्ज्जुन॥ १कृष्ण सारथि याङाव् अर्ज्जुन हथार वं॥
१युधिष्ठिर॥ १भीम॥ १नकुल॥ १सहदेव॥ १धृष्टद्युम्न॥

Duryyodhana hathāra vava. Bhīṣma. Droṇācāryya. Kṛpācāryya. Aśvatthāmā. Duḥśāsana. Kṛṣṇana Arjjunayāta viśvarupa keṃṅa. Arjjuna. Kṛṣṇa sārathi yāṅāva Arjjuna hathāra vaṃ. Yudhiṣṭhira. Bhīma. Nakula. Sahadeva. Dhṛṣṭadyumna.

a) Kṛṣṇa becomes charioteer and Arjuna goes to battle. Yudhiṣṭhira. Bhīma. Nakula. Sahadeva. Dhṛṣṭadyumna.
b) Kṛṣṇa displays his universal form to Arjuna. Arjuna.
c) Duryodhana goes to battle. Bhīṣma. The spiritual teacher Droṇa. The spiritual teacher Kṛpa. Aśvatthāmā. Duḥśāsana.

Text: The troops array for battle (ch. 1). The Pāṇḍavas station their seven *akṣauhiṇī* troops on the western part of Kurukṣetra (sa., the field of the Kurus) while the Kauravas station eleven *akṣauhiṇī* troops in the east (chs. 1, 20). Then Kṛṣṇa drives Arjuna's chariot in between the two armies (ch. 23). As Arjuna beholds his relatives and friends arrayed for battle on both the sides, he wishes to abstain from battle. Kṛṣṇa, however, explains that he has to fulfil his duty. He reveals himself as the indestructible origin of all beings who in his unmanifest form pervades the entire universe (chs. 29ff.). Then, he gives Arjuna divine sight and displays his divine form (ch. 33). As Arjuna sees in Kṛṣṇa the entire universe in one place, his doubts are dispelled.

Image: In the centre, Kṛṣṇa is depicted displaying his universal form, with many arms and heads in three rows. He is surrounded by a blazing ring of fire and accompanied by two female attendants, possibly Rukmiṇī and Satyabhāmā (also represented in the temple's central shrine). Arjuna is depicted paying homage to him. Yudhiṣṭhira's forces are depicted on one side with Dhṛṣṭadyumna as the overall general, Duryodhana's forces are seen on the other side with Bhīṣma as overall general. Coincidence or not, the troops are arrayed exacty as described in the text. Given the position of the scene on the frieze, Yudhiṣṭhira's forces are indeed represented on the western side, facing east, and Duryodhana's forces are seen on the eastern side, facing west. Arjuna and Kṛṣṇa have stationed themselves in between the two armies. All the chariots are drawn by horses, some of which are winged. On the Kaurava's side they wield up dust. Most of the charioteers are depic-ted atop the chariots, with the exeption of Bhīṣma's charioteer and Kṛṣṇa who plays a special role in this context. The charioteers hold the warriors' standards. Some of them have a pointed form

---122 / 121 / 120 /

while others have double pennants. They do not display specific emblems and do therefore not help to identify the characters as within Hoysaḷa representations. The form of the standards varies too. Bhīṣma, for example, has a standard with a double pennant in this scene and a pointed one in the next.

detail of scene 122: Kṛṣṇa displays his universal form to Arjuna

123. १कृ[ष्ण] अ[स्त्र] जोङाव भीष्मयाक् दु ब्वाक् भीष्मन् स्तुति याक॥ १अर्ज्जुन॥
Kṛṣṇa astra joṅāva Bhīṣmayāke du bvāka Bhīṣmana stuti yāka. Arjjuna.
As Kṛṣṇa takes the weapon and rushes at Bhīṣma, Bhīṣma praises (him). Arjuna.

Text: At Duryodhana's insistence, Bhīṣma rushes against the Pāṇḍavas on the third day of battle (chs. 54f.). On account of his respect for Bhīṣma, Arjuna counters him only with mildness. As Yudhiṣṭhira's allies flee from the field, Kṛṣṇa decides to slay Bhīṣma himself. He takes up his discus (sa. *cakra*) and rushes towards him but as Bhīṣma praises Kṛṣṇa, Arjuna prevents Kṛṣṇa from slaying him. The same happens again on the ninth day of battle, except that Kṛṣṇa now rushes at Bhīṣma with a whip in his hand (ch. 102).
Image: Arjuna shoots his arrows. Kṛṣṇa still holds the reins but he also holds his club (sa. *gadā*) raised for battle. With what weapon Kṛṣṇa attacks is apparently not important. He confronts Bhīṣma who is depicted praising him with a lowered head and his hands joined in reverence (sa. *añjalimudrā*).

/ 126 / 125 / 124 /

124. [१भीष्म शरशय्यास दन॥ १]भीष्मव् शिखण्डीव् युद्ध॥ १कृष्ण॥ १अर्जुन॥
Bhīṣma śaraśayyāsa deṅa. Bhīṣmava Śikhaṇḍīva yuddha. Kṛṣṇa. Arjjuna.
a) Fight between Bhīṣma and Śikhaṇḍī. Kṛṣṇa. Arjuna.
b) Bhīṣma rests on a bed of arrows.

Text: The night after the ninth day of battle, the Pāṇḍavas go to Bhīṣma and ask him by which means he could be vanquished (ch. 103). Bhīṣma states that he would never do battle with Śikhaṇḍī. His story is given in the Udyoga Parva (Mbh. 5.170ff.). Śikhaṇḍī was Ambā in a previous life, the oldest daughter of the king of Kāśī whom Bhīṣma had taken by force to become the wife of his half brother Vicitravīrya. Ambā was again released because she had already chosen the king of Śālva as her husband and only her sisters were married to Vicitravīrya. Śālva however abandoned her because of fear of Bhīṣma. Ambā underwent great austerities and obtained the boon that, in order to exact revenge on Bhīṣma, she would be reborn as a woman who would later become a man. Knowing that Bhīṣma would never do battle with Śikhaṇḍī because he was born a woman, the Pāṇḍavas place Śikhaṇḍī at the forefront as they again rush at Bhīṣma on the tenth day of battle (chs. 104ff.). Arjuna fights Bhīṣma behind Śikhaṇḍī. Pierced with arrows all over, Bhīṣma falls down from his chariot (ch. 114). He consequently lies on a bed of arrows, without touching the ground with his body. Anyway, he retains his life awaiting the right time for his death. In the evening, the combatants of both sides all lie down their weapons and repair to Bhīṣma (ch. 115). Arjuna supports his head with three more shafts and after the night has passed, he pierces the earth with another shaft to offer Bhīṣma water from the emerging stream (chs. 115f.).
Image: Arjuna advances Bhīṣma with Śikhaṇḍī at the forefront. Kṛṣṇa is depicted as Arjuna's charioteer. While Arjuna's and Śikhaṇḍī's chariots are drawn by horses, a mythical aquatic being (sa. *makara*) is yoked to Bhīṣma's chariot. Bhīṣma is again depicted on the left side, on a bed of arrows, with an additional arrow supporting his head.

Droṇaparva: 'The Book of Droṇa'

125. १जयद्रथव् अभिमन्युव् युद्ध॥ १अभिमन्यु वध॥
Jayadrathava Abhimanyuva yuddha. Abhimanyu vadha.
Fight between Jayadratha and Abhimanyu. Death of Abhimanyu.

Text: In consequence of Bhīṣma's fall, Droṇa becomes the supreme commander of the Kauravas' forces (ch. 5). On the thirteenth day of battle, Yudhiṣṭhira instructs Abhimanyu, Arjuna's son with Subhadrā, to penetrate Droṇa's *cakra vyūha*, a circular battle formation (ch. 34). Jayadratha, who had earlier been humiliated by the Pāṇḍavas, prevents all others from following Abhimanyu (ch. 42). With no-one to protect him, Abhimanyu has to fight the enemy alone. Abhimanyu is finally killed

by Duḥśāsana's son, in a fight with clubs (ch. 48). The next day, Arjuna takes an oath to kill Jayadratha (ch. 51).
Image: Abhimanyu is depicted in battle with Jayadratha. According to the text, it doesn't come to the depicted duel. Anyway, Jayadratha is held responsible for the killing of Abhimanyu and he is therefore depicted bringing about his death. To the right, Abhimanyu's dead body is placed on a flowery bed.

126. १जयद्रथ वध॥ १जयद्रथव् अर्ज्जुनव् युद्ध॥
Jayadratha vadha. Jayadrathava Arjjunava yuddha.
a) Fight between Jayadratha and Arjuna.
b) Death of Jayadratha.

Text: In order to protect Jayadratha, Droṇa stations him far behind, surrounded by a large force (ch. 63). Arjuna penetrates the formation towards Jayadratha. The battle lasts the whole day. As Arjuna finally reaches Jayadratha, Kṛṣṇa adresses Arjuna (ch. 121). He states that Jayadratha's father, Vṛddhakṣatra, was told long ago that someone would cut off his son's head in battle. Thereon he devoted himself to ascetic austerities and achieved a boon that the head of the person causing his son's head to fall on the earth would crack into a hundred pieces. On Kṛṣṇa's advice, Arjuna cuts off Jayadratha's head in such a way that it is thrown upon the lap of Vṛddhakṣatra himself. As Vṛddhakṣatra stands up, his son's head falls on the earth and his own head cracks into a hundred fragments.
Image: Arjuna and Jayadratha are depicted in battle. Arjuna's chariot is now equipped with a double-pennant flagstaff, in contrast to the pointed flagstaff seen in scenes 122 and 123. On the right side of the image, Jayadratha falls dead to the ground, pierced by Arjuna's shafts.

127. (next page) १कर्ण्णव् घटोत्कचव् युद्ध॥ १घटोत्कच वध॥
Karṇṇava Ghaṭotkacava yuddha. Ghaṭotkaca vadha.
Fight between Karṇa and Ghaṭotkaca. Death of Ghaṭotkaca.

Text: Though darkness already sets in, the battle goes on (ch. 126). In order to light up the darkness the soldiers light lamps (ch. 138). As Karṇa and Droṇa cause the forces of the Pāṇḍavas to flee in terror, Kṛṣṇa commands Ghaṭotkaca, Bhīma's son with Hiḍimvā, to advance against Karṇa (chs. 147f.). Ghaṭotkaca dies as Karṇa hurles Indra's invincible spear at him, which he had actually preserved for Arjuna (ch. 154). As Ghaṭotkaca crushes on the ground, he assumes gigantic dimensions and thereby again shatters thousands.
Image: Karṇa is depicted atop his chariot. In his hand he holds Indra's invincible weapon, represented as a dart. Ghaṭotkaca is armed with sword and shield. He has assumed a gigantic form, as described in the text. On the right side, he is depicted again, lying dead on a bed of stone, pierced by the dart.

128. (next page) १द्रोणाचार्य्य वध॥ १द्रोणाचार्य्यव अभिमन्युव् युद्ध॥
Droṇācāryya vadha. Droṇācāryyava Abhimanyuva yuddha.
a) Fight between the spiritual teacher Droṇa and Abhimanyu.
b) Death of the spiritual teacher Droṇa.

Text: As day dawns on the fifteenth day of battle, the troops are rearranged and the battle goes on (ch. 161). After Droṇa slays Drupada and Virāṭa, Dhṛṣṭadyumna vows to revenge them. Kṛṣṇa suggests to bring about Droṇa's end through deception (ch. 164). As Bhīma exclaims that he had killed Aśvatthāmā, Droṇa assumes that his son was slain though, in reality, Bhīma had only slain an elephant with the same name. Droṇa becomes afflicted with grief upon the supposed death of his son. As Dhṛṣṭadyumna again rushes against him, he is not able to fight as he had done before. Droṇa lays aside his weapons and devotes himself to yoga (ch. 165). As he is about to ascend to heaven, Dhṛṣṭadyumna cuts off his head with his sword. Aśvatthāmā later vows to revenge his father (ch. 166).
Image: According to the inscription, the image depicts Abhimanyu battling with Droṇa but the inscription is certainly wrong for Abhimanyu was slain already in scene 125. The archer opposing Droṇa therefore has to be Dhṛṣṭadyumna. On the left side of the image, the preceptor is again depicted, lying dead on a bed of stone. In contrast to the text, he retains his weapons and his head. His death is indicated only by an arrow that pierces his chest.

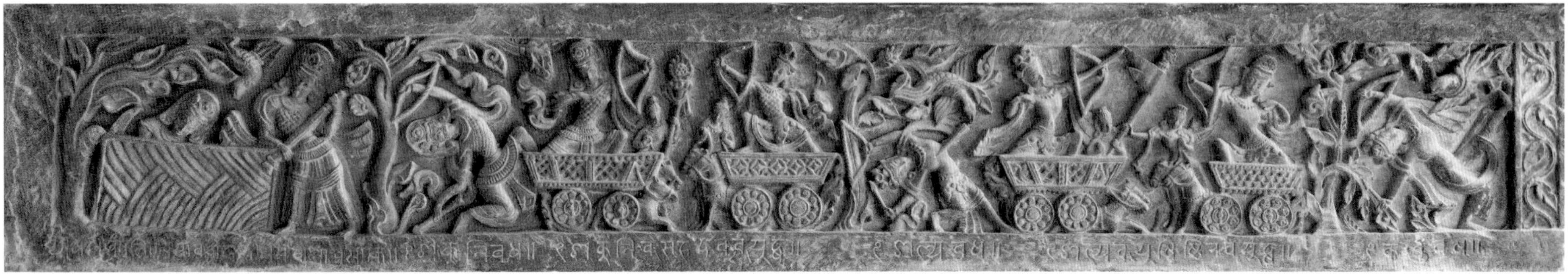

/ 133 / 132 / 131 / 130--------------------

Karṇaparva: 'The Book of Karṇa'

129. १भीमन् दुःशासन वध॥ १दुःशासनव् भीमव युद्ध॥

Bhīmana Duḥśāsana vadha. Duḥśāsanava Bhīmava yuddha.

a) Fight between Duḥśāsana and Bhīma.

b) Bhīma kills Duḥśāsana.

Text: After Droṇa's fall, Karṇa is installed in the command of the Kaurava army (ch. 6). In the morning of the seventeenth day of battle, Karṇa vows not to return from the field without having slain Arjuna (ch. 22). Mādrī's brother Śalya, who had been tricked to fight for the Kauravas (Mbh. 5.8.), becomes Karṇa's charioteer. Later that day, Arjuna promises Yudhiṣṭhira to slay Karṇa (ch. 47). However, before the two of them encounter, Bhīma and Duḥśāsana oppose each other (chs. 60f.). As Duḥśāsana rains down his arrows on Bhīma, Bhīma hurls his club. Duḥśāsana is flung far away. As he lies on the ground, Bhīma rips open his chest and drinks his blood, as he had earlier vowed to do (Mbh. 2.68).

Image: On the right side of the image, Bhīma rushes at Duḥśāsana with his club. On the left side, he tears apart Duḥśāsana's breast in order to drink his blood.

130. १कर्ण्ण वध॥ १कर्ण्णव् अ[र्ज्जु]नव् युद्ध॥

Karṇṇa vadha. Karṇṇava Arjjunava yuddha.

a) Fight between Karṇa and Arjjuna.

b) Death of Karṇa.

Text: In the evening, Arjuna and Karṇa encounter (ch. 63). Karṇa loses off from his bow the snake Aśvasena who aims to kill Arjuna because his mother died in the conflagration of Khāṇḍava (ch. 66). However, Aśvasena fails and in the end, Arjuna slays Karṇa with an *añjalikā* arrow. This one has a head as large as the hands when joined for salutation (ch. 67).

Image: Arjuna and Karṇa are depicted in battle, with Kṛṣṇa and Śalya as charioteers. That the standards clash in the image might refer to the battle of their emblems described in the text. Accordingly, as Arjuna and Karṇa challenge each other to a duel, the standards also begin to fight each other (ch. 63). The fierce monkey on Arjuna's standard flings himself on Karṇa's standard and attempts to destroy the elephant's housing which somehow fights back. Karṇa is already struck by an arrow. Karṇa is depicted again, falling dead to the ground.

---------------------------------130 / 129 / 128 / 127 /

Śalyaparva: 'The Book of Śalya'

131. शल्य वध॥ शल्यव् युधिष्ठिरव् युद्ध॥
Śalya vadha. Śalyava Yudhiṣṭhirava yuddha.

a) Fight between Śalya and Yudhiṣṭhira.

b) Death of Śalya.

Text: On the eighteenth day of battle, Śalya becomes the supreme commander of Duryodhana's forces (chs. 5f.). The Pāṇḍavas strike out at him repeatedly. Finally, Yudhiṣṭhira brings about Śalya's end with a javelin (ch. 16).
Image: Śalya and Yudhiṣṭhira are depicted in battle. Yudhiṣṭhira's charioteer is about to bring down Śalya's standard though there is no reference in the text to Yudhiṣṭhira's charioteer intervening directly in the fight. On the left side, Śalya's death is depicted.

132. शकुनि वध॥ शकुनिव् सहदेवव् युद्ध॥
Śakuni vadha. Śakuniva Sahadevava yuddha.

a) Fight between Śakuni and Sahadeva.

b) Death of Śakuni.

Text: Later that day, Sahadeva and Bhīma encounter Śakuni and his son Ulūka in battle (ch. 27). First, Sahadeva cuts off Ulūka's head with an arrow. As Śakuni rushes at Sahadeva for revenge, Sahadeva kills him the same way he had before slain his son.
Image: Sahadeva battles and kills Śakuni. The killing method is disregarded in the image.

133. [दु]र्य्योधन पुषुलिस वैयाव चोङ् भीमन ष्वालाव सोक॥
Duryyodhana puṣulisa vaiyāva coṅa Bhīmana ṣvālāva soka.
Duryodhana escapes into a pond and stays (there); Bhīma catches (him) and looks at (him).

Text: The remnants of the Kaurava army rush against the Pāṇḍavas one last time (ch. 28). For they have no protector, they are however vanquished in a moment. Only few survive on the Kaurava side, among them Duryodhana, Kṛpa, Aśvatthāmā and Kṛtavarman. Duryodhana, severely wounded and bereft of his brothers, friends and troops, flees into a lake nearby. With magical power (sa. *māyā*) he creates a passage in the water and enters the lake. Some huntsmen discover that Duryodhana is hiding in lake Dvaipāyana and report to Bhīma (ch. 29). The Pāṇḍavas proceed there and Yudhiṣṭhira tells Duryodhana to rise from the waters and to fight (ch. 30). Duryodhana agrees to fight for kingship but with one at a time, on foot and armed only with a mace (ch. 31). Kṛṣṇa states that not even for Bhīma victory would not be certain in a fair encounter. Bhīma however is confident (ch. 32).
Image: Duryodhana is depicted hiding inside the waters, with a lowered head. Bhīma stands on the lakeside and looks at him. He holds his club with both his hands, desiring to to battle. The others are not depicted.

/ 138 / 137 / 136 / 135 / 134 /

134. १दुर्य्योधनव् भीमव् गदायुद्ध॥

Duryyodhanava Bhīmava gadāyuddha.

Fight with clubs between Duryodhana and Bhīma.

Text: The duel begins (ch. 54). Bhīma is stronger, while Duryodhana is more skilful. Though it is agreed upon that one should not strike below the navel in a duel with clubs, Bhīma strikes Duryodhana at his thighs in order to bring him down (chs. 57ff.). As Duryodhana lies on the ground, struck down unfairly, Bhīma compliments Yudhiṣṭhira on regaining the sovereignty (ch. 58).
Image: The image depicts Duryodhana and Bhīma fighting the duel with clubs. In accordance with the text, Bhīma is seen striking Duryodhana unfairly at the thighs.

135. १अश्वत्थामान वोध याक॥ १दुर्य्योधन भेत वुल॥

Aśvatthāmāna vodha yāka. Duryyodhana bheta vula.

a) Duryodhana falls down.

b) Aśvatthāmā instructs.

Text: The Pāṇḍavas spare Duryodhana's life and return to their camp (ch. 61). Kṛpa, Aśvatthāmā and Kṛtavarman find Duryodhana on the field of battle, covered with blood and surrounded by terrible carnivorous beings (ch. 64). Aśvatthāmā promises Duryodhana to slay Drupada's troops, the Pañcālas. At Duryodhana's command Kṛpa then consecrates Aśvatthāmā as the final commander.
Image: Duryodhana has been brought down. He still holds the club in his hand. Aśvatthāmā sits next to him and swears his oath with his hand raised. For he is a brahmin, he is depicted with simple clothes, long hair and a pointed chin beard. In the following image, he additionally wears a *rudrākṣa* chain and holds the sacred scriptures.

Sauptikaparva: 'The Book of the Nocturnal Events'

136. १पाण्डवपनि स्याय् धक् अश्वत्थामा वं॥

Pāṇḍavapani syāya dhaka Aśvatthāmā vaṃ.

Aśvatthāmā goes in order to kill the Pāṇḍavas.

Text: Aśvatthāmā resolves to slay his foes during the night, while they are asleep (ch. 1). Against Kṛpa's advice, he sets off in the direction of the Pāṇḍavas (ch. 5).
Image: Aśvatthāmā is depicted leaving. The inscription informs about his intentions.

137. १अश्वत्थामान् चाह्नस् पाण्डवया सैन्य वध याक॥

Aśvatthāmāna cāhnasa Pāṇḍavayā sainya vadha yāka.

At night, Aśvatthāmā slays the Pāṇḍavas' army.

Text: Earlier, Aśvatthāmā had promised to revenge his father Droṇa, who was slain by Dhṛṣṭadyumna on the fifteenth day of battle (Mbh. 7.165f.). It is for this reason that he now first enters Dhṛṣṭadyumna's chamber (ch. 8). Aśvatthāmā kills him by using his hands and feet as his only weapons. Additionally, he slays the five sons of

Draupadī, Śikhaṇḍī and the remnant of Virāṭa's and Drupada's troops. The Pāṇḍavas themselves are not affected because they spent the night outside the camp, together with Kṛṣṇa.
Image: Not all the depicted figures have been provided with an inscription. Yet, it is easy to identify them. Aśvatthāmā is depicted severing Śrutakarma's head from his body. According to the text, Draupadī's son with Arjuna is slain following the slaughter of Dhṛṣṭadyumna and Draupadī's other sons. These are depicted lying dead on the ground. Dhṛṣṭadyumna wears a crown while Draupadī's youthful sons are depicted with long unadorned hair.

138. १अश्वत्थामा[न पाण्डव]या काल ढाह्म सं्माल्हव॥ १दुर्य्योधन मृत्यु जुव॥
Aśvatthāmāna Pāṇḍavayā kāya ṅāhma saṃ mola hava. Duryyodhana mṛtyu juva.
Aśvatthāmā brings the heads of the Pāṇḍavas' five sons by the hair. Duryodhana's death occurs.

Text: As dawn breaks, Aśvatthāmā issues from the deadly silent camp and repairs to the spot where Duryodhana lies, in order to report on his triumph (ch. 9). Aśvatthāmā, Kṛpa and Kṛtavarman find Duryodhana deprived of his senses but still alive. While Aśvatthāmā tells him about the slaughter, Duryodhana regains his senses. Duryodhana honours Aśvatthāmā, bids farewell and finally passes away.
Image: The image depicts Aśvatthāmā approaching Duryodhana with the heads of Draupadī's five sons. This incident is not mentioned in the Critical Edition of the Mahābhārata. Moreover, only Śrutakarma's head is said to have been severed from the body.

139. १अश्वत्थामा्वस वं्१भीम अ[र्ज्जुन] कृष्ण अश्वत्थामा लिला वं॥
Aśvatthāmā vese vaṃ. Bhīma Arjjuna Kṛsṇa Aśvatthāmā lilā vaṃ.
Aśvatthāmā flees. Bhīma, Arjuna and Kṛṣṇa follow Aśvatthāmā.

Text: Dhṛṣṭadyumna's charioteer, the only one left alife by Aśvatthāmā, reports to the Pāṇḍavas (ch. 10). Nakula brings Draupadī from Upaplavya (ch. 11). She calls on Bhīma to slay Aśvatthāmā and to brimg the natural gem from his head, so she could be assured of his death. Bhīma sets out with Nakula as charioteer. They are followed by Kṛṣṇa, Yudhiṣṭhira and Arjuna on a second chariot.
Image: Bhīma, Arjuna and Kṛṣṇa follow Aśvatthāmā. Bhīma raises his club, intending to slay Aśvatthāmā. In contrast to the text, are all depicted on foot.

140. १भीमन्अश्वत्थामाया्मोलस्मणि काव॥
Bhīmana Aśvatthāmāyā molasa maṇi kāva.
Bhīma takes the gem from Aśvatthāmā's head.

Text: On the bank of the Gaṅgā, they behold Aśvatthāmā in Vyāsa's company (ch. 13). As Aśvatthāmā and Arjuna both release the divine Brahmā Weapon, Nārada and Vyāsa station themselves between them (chs. 13f.). Aśvatthāmā is not able to withdraw that weapon and it is thrown into the wombs of the Pāṇḍava women (ch. 15). Thereby Parikṣit, Uttarā's unborn son with Abhimanyu, is killed (ch. 16). Kṛṣṇa states that he will be revived and become the king of the Kurus, whereas he curses Aśvatthāmā to live a lonely life. Severely afflicted, Aśvatthāmā gives away the gem that was born with him which the Pāṇḍavas consequently hand over to Draupadī.
Image: As also the inscription reads, the image depicts Bhīma taking the gem from Aśvatthāmā's head. Aśvatthāmā's still holds the Brahmā Weapon in his hand, whereas Arjuna's Brahmā Weapon is put aside and now leans against the tree.

/ 140 / 139 /

/ 141 /

Strīparva: 'The Book of the Women'

141. १धृगनाष्ट्रयाव् गांधानीयाव् विलाप॥ १नाणियनिस विलाप॥
Dhṛtarāṣtrayāva Gāndhārīyāva vilāpa. rāṇipanisa vilāpa.
Lamentations of Dhṛtarāṣṭra and Gāndhārī. Lamentations of the queens.

Text: Bereft of his sons and friends, Dhṛtarāṣṭra falls into despair (ch. 1). Dhṛtarāṣṭra and Gāndhārī first take action against Kṛṣṇa and the sons of Pāṇḍu but finally reconcile with them (chs. 11ff.). On the field of battle, the Kaurava women weep for their beloved ones (chs. 16ff.). Yudhiṣṭhira gives order to perform the funeral rites for all those who were killed in action (chs. 26f.).
Image: Dhṛtarāṣṭra and Gāndhārī are depicted inside their palace, tormented by grief. Further compartments contain six more weeping women, representing the many thousand.

Śāntiparva: 'The Book of Peace'

142. १सहद्यव॥ १नकुल॥ १अर्ज्जुन॥ १तीम॥ १युधिष्ठिनन् तीष्मयाक् धर्म्मकथा ङढ॥
Sahadeva. Nakula. Arjjuna. Bhīma. Yudhiṣṭhirana Bhīṣmayāke dharmmakathā ṅeṅa.
Sahadeva. Nakula. Arjuna. Bhīma. Yudhiṣṭhira listens to Bhīṣma's discourse upon *dharma*.

Text: At Hastināpura, Yudhiṣṭhira is installed as king (ch. 40). He instates Bhīma as heir apparent and appoints each of the others to a separate task, too (ch. 41). Along with his brothers and Kṛṣṇa he goes to see Bhīṣma (ch. 46). At Kṛṣṇa's behest, Bhīṣma teaches Yudhiṣṭhira about *dharma* to be followed under different circumstances, beginning with *rājadharma*, the *dharma* to be followed of kings (chs. 50ff.).
Image: Bhīṣma rests on his bed of arrows. The Pāṇḍavas are represented next to him, with Yudhiṣṭhira as the first.

Anuśāsanaparva: 'The Book of Instructions'

143. १तीष्म मृत्यु जुव॥
Bhīṣma mṛtyu juva.
Bhīṣma's death occurs.

Text: Bhīṣma completes his teachings (ch. 152). 50 days later, the time he had destined for his death has come and Yudhiṣṭhira again sets out for Hastināpura (ch. 153). Having made his farewells, Bhīṣma gives up his life (ch. 154).
Image: Bhīṣma is again depicted on his bed of arrows.

144. १तीष्म स्वर्ग्ग वं॥
Bhīṣma svargga vaṃ.
Bhīṣma goes to heaven.

Text: The funeral rites are performed (ch. 154). As water is offered to Bhīṣma's dead body, Gaṅgā appears and weeps for her son. Kṛṣṇa comforts her and states that he has now gone to heaven and has become one of the Vasus, the elemental gods.
Image: Bhīṣma ascends on an aerial chariot. Clouds of dust whirl up as the chariot takes off.

/ 145 / 144 / 143 / 142 /

Aśvamedhikaparva: 'The Book of the Horse Sacrifice'

145. १युधिष्ठिनया अश्वमधयज्ञस नवलवा वव॥ १युधिष्ठिन॥ १कृष्ण॥ १तीम॥ १अर्जुन॥ १नकुल॥ १सहदव॥

and above the image: १धौम्यऋषि॥

Yudhiṣṭhirayā aśvamedhayajñasa navalacā vava. Yudhiṣṭhira. Kṛṣṇa. Bhīma. Arjjuna. Nakula. Sahadeva.

At Yudhiṣṭhira's horse sacrifice a mongoose appears. Yudhiṣṭhira. Kṛṣṇa. Bhīma. Arjuna. Nakula. Sahadeva.

above: Dhaumyaṛṣi.

Sage Dhaumya.

Text: Vyāsa advises Yudhiṣṭhira to perform the horse sacrifice for it would purify him from the sin of having slain his kin (ch. 3). After the sacrifice, a mongoose emerges from its hole and censures the sacrifice (ch. 92). The mongoose is in reality the personified Krodha (sa., anger) but cursed to live in this form until he censures *dharma*. He is released from the curse as he speaks ill of the sacrifice since Yudhiṣṭhira is Dharma's son and Dharma's self (ch. 96).

detail of scene 145

Image: Dhaumya is represented as officiating priest albeit no special role is attributed to him in the text. He holds the scriptures and a large ladle. On the other side of the fire altar, the Pāṇḍavas together with Kṛṣṇa are depicted, mostly with their hands in reverential gesture (sa. *añjalimudrā*). Various vessels are depicted around the sacrificial fire. The mongoose emerges at Yudhiṣṭhira's feet.

/ 148 / 147 / 146 /

Āśramavāsikaparva: 'The Book of the Residents of the Hermitage'

146. १धृगनाष्द्र् गांधानी् कुन्ती् विदुन् गपावन वं॥

Dhṛtarāṣdra Gāndhārī Kuntī Vidura tapovana vaṃ.

Dhṛtarāṣṭra, Gāndhārī, Kuntī and Vidura go to a grove in which religious austerities are performed.

Text: the Pāṇḍavas rule the kingdom, placing Dhṛtarāṣṭra at their head (ch. 1). After fifteen years, the aged Dhṛtarāṣṭra asks permission to resort to the forest with Gāndhārī in order to perform austerities and to purify his sins (ch. 5). Vidura, Dhṛtarāṣṭra's chief adviser Sañjaya, and Kuntī decide to accompany them (ch. 22). Vidura, who himself is eternal *dharma* (Mhb. 1.101), merges into Yudhiṣṭhira as he dies (ch. 33). After another two years, Nārada arrives and tells the Pāṇḍavas that Dhṛtarāṣṭra, Gāndhārī and Kuntī died in a fire and that Sañjaya has repaired to the Himālaya mountains (ch. 45).

Image: Dhṛtarāṣṭra is depicted leaving for the forest, followed by Gāndhārī, Kuntī and Vidura. Vidura is represented with a crown for he belongs to the royal family. At the same time, the learned adviser wears also a chain of *rudrākṣa* seeds (sa. *akṣamālā*). Sañjaya, who survives the conflagration, is not depicted. Therefore, the artist may have implied the death of those depicted leaving.

Mausalaparva: 'The Book of the Clubs'

147. १ब्साम्ब् मिसाछायन तियाव् छो वोयिव धक दुर्व्वासायाक् ङक॥

Śāmva misāchāyana tiyāva cho voyiva dhaka Durvvāsāyāke ṅeka.

Śāmva is adorned with women's clothes and of Durvāsā is asked what will be born.

Text: In the thirty-sixth year, the sages Viśvāmitra, Kaṇva and Nārada come to Dvārakā (ch. 2). Śāmva, Kṛṣṇa's eldest son with Jāmbavatī, is dressed up as a woman and others enquire of the sages if *she* will give birth to a son or a daughter. Enraged, the sages curse Śāmva that he will give birth to an iron club to bring about the end of the Yādavas.

Image: According to the inscription, the sage depicted is none of the ones mentioned in the text but Durvāsā, the son of Atri and Anusūyā (cf. R.sc. 29). Śāmva approaches him disguised as a woman, accompanied by two others belonging to the Yādavas.

148. १ङयषुकोटि् यादववंश् १(थथ्यं युद्ध जुव॥

ṅayaṣukoṭi yādavavaṃśa; thethyaṃ yuddha juva.

Fifty crore of the Yādava clan; Among one another it comes to a fight.

Text: Already the next day, Śāmva gives birth to an iron club (ch. 2). In order to avert the curse, the club is crushed into tiny fragments which are flung into the ocean.

The Yādavas repair to Prabhāsa (ch. 4). In the course of an evening drinking bount, Sātyaki of the Vṛṣṇi clan slays Kṛtavarman for his complicity in the nightly slaughter of the Pāṇḍava's forces. The Andhakās and Bhojās rush against Sātyaki. Pradyumna comes for Sātyaki's help but both of them are slain.
Image: Since this scene depicts the beginning of the fight among the Yādavas, the two represented in a duel on the left side might be Sātyaki and Kṛtavarman. To the right, the image might show Pradyumna standing up for Sātyaki and being slain by the Andhakās and Bhojās rushing against them. The inscription however does not ascertain the identification of the individual figures.

Again, eastern face of the temple (scenes 149 to 165):

149. १ढयषूकोटि् यादववंश् १(थथ्यं ल्वाढाव संहान जूव॥

ṅayaṣukoṭi yādavavaṃśa; thathyaṃ lvāṅāva saṃhāra juva.
Fifty crore of the Yādava clan; Among one another is fought and it comes to an end.

Text: As his son lies dead on the ground, Kṛṣṇa grasps some grass. It turns into a terrible club (ch. 4). The others also pluck out the grass and again, it turnes into clubs. With these the Yādavas slay each other until only Kṛṣṇa and his charioteer, Dāruka, are left.

Image: In the centre of the image, a few are still fighting but most of the figures are depicted already overcome, falling down or lying dead on the ground.

150. १वलभद्र् समूद्रस् दूहा वं॥

Balabhadra samudrasa duhā vaṃ.
Balarāma goes into the sea.

Text: Kṛṣṇa sends Dāruka to tell Arjuna about the destruction of the Yādavas (ch. 5). Then he approaches his brother, Balarāma, who hasn't been present at Prabhāsa. Kṛṣṇa finds him immersed in *yoga* with a giant serpent emerging from his mouth. Giving up its former body, the snake immerses into the ocean. The story implies Balarāma's association with Śeṣa.
Image: Balarāma is depicted merging into the ocean, represented as an oblong block, wavy and alive with fish. In his hands he holds the plough (sa. *hala*) and a club (sa. *gadā*). A large snake figure is depicted towering behind him. According to the text, Balarāma's body is left behind and only the giant serpent merges into the ocean, where it is received by numerous other divine snakes. On the one hand, the snake figure could represent one multi-hooded or rather multi-bodied one into which Balarāma changes as he merges into the ocean, denying the fact that it actually already priorly emerged from his mouth. On the other hand, the snake figure could represent the many ones receiving Balarāma, disregarding his transformation.

/ 150 / 149 /

/ 153 / 152 / 151 /

151. १व्याधान् कृष्णया ह्मा ळ्स बलान कयका॥ १कृष्ण सिमाकास् चाट॥
vyādhāna Kṛṣṇayā hma ḷsa balāna kayako. Kṛṣṇa simākosa coṅa.
a) Kṛṣṇa rests beneath a tree.
b) A hunter strikes Kṛṣṇa's foot with an arrow.

Text: After his brother has departed, Kṛṣṇa resorts to *yoga*, too (ch. 5). As Kṛṣṇa lies down, a hunter strikes him on the sole of his foot, where he wasn't rendered invulnerable by Durvāsā's left-over *pāyasa* (cf. Mbh. 13.144).
Image: Kṛṣṇa is depicted lying down in the forest. The image is enlivened by the figure of a large monkey, squatting on a tree and feeding upon fruits. To the left, the hunter shoots his arrow, which, in accordance with the text, strikes Kṛṣṇa on the sole of his foot.

152. [...] १[कृष्णन] शरीर ता[र]ता॥
[...]. Kṛṣṇana śarīra torato.
[...]. Kṛṣṇa leaves his body.

Text: As the hunter advances, he realises that it was not a deer at what he had shot (ch. 5). Severely distressed, he touches Kṛṣṇa's feet with his head. Kṛṣṇa comforts him, rises upwards and reaches heaven.
Image: The hunter approaches Kṛṣṇa with joined palms (sa. *añjalimudrā*). A quiver with arrows is visible on his back.

153. १नारद॥ १व्रह्मा॥ १कृष्ण वैकुण्ठस विज्याक॥ १महादेव॥ १इन्द्र॥
Nārada. Vrahmā. Kṛṣṇa Vaikuṇṭhasa vijyāka. Mahādeva. Indra.
Nārada. Brahmā. Kṛṣṇa stays in Viṣṇu's celestial abode. Śiva. Indra.

Text: Kṛṣṇa is welcomed by the gods, sages and other heavenly beings before he repairs to his own region (ch. 5).
Image: In the centre, Kṛṣṇa is depicted with two attendants. Out of the many welcoming him, Nārada, Brahmā, Śiva and Indra are depicted. They are all clearly recognisable on account of their individual characteristics and attributes. Additionally, Garuḍa is depicted worshipping Kṛṣṇa.

154. १व्यासव् युधिष्ठिरव संवाद॥ १भीम॥ १अर्ज्जुन॥ १नकुल॥ १सहदेव॥ १द्रौपदी॥
Vyāsava Yudhiṣṭhirava saṃvāda. Bhīma. Arjjuna. Nakula. Sahadeva. Draupadī.
Conversation of Vyāsa and Yudhiṣṭhira. Bhīma. Arjuna. Nakula. Sahadeva. Draupadī.

Text: Arjuna arrives at Dvārakā (ch. 6). He decides to take the Yādava women to Indraprastha, knowing that Dvārakā will soon be flooded by the ocean (ch. 8). As the women are seized by robbers on their way, Arjuna is not able to protect them. Thus confronted with the loss of his powers, Arjuna seeks out Vyāsa who explains that the time for his departure (from this world) has come (ch. 9).
Image: The artist must have followed some other version. According to the text only

/ 155 / 154 /

Arjuna visits Vyāsa whereas here, Vyāsa is depicted in conversation with Yudhiṣṭhira, with the others sitting by. Additionally, they are depicted inside a palace rather than in Vyāsa's hermitage, so we can conclude that it is Vyāsa who has come to see them. Anyway, the message conveyed is probably the same.

Mahāprasthānikaparva: 'The Book of the Great Journey'

155. १युधिष्ठि[न्] भीम् अर्ज्जुन् नकुल् सहदेव् द्रौपदी् स्वर्ग्गारोहण वं॥

Yudhiṣṭhira, Bhīma Arjjuna Nakula Sahadeva Draupadī svarggārohaṇa vaṃ.
Yudhiṣṭhira, Bhīma, Arjuna, Nakula, Sahadeva and Draupadī leave for their ascent to heaven.

Text: The Pāṇḍavas decide to leave for the forest (ch. 1). Yudhiṣṭhira hands over the entire kingdom to Yuyutsu (for supervision), Parikṣit is installed at Hastināpura and Vajra, Kṛṣṇa's great-grandson, at Indraprastha. Kṛpa becomes Parikṣit's preceptor. As the Pāṇḍavas together with Draupadī set forth, they are followed by a dog. Arjuna intends to take with him the divine bow Gāṇḍīva but Agni informs him that he could only go to the forest after casting it aside. Arjuna thereupon returns it to Varuṇa by flinging it into the water.
Image: The six of them are depicted leaving for the woods, in accordance with the text, unarmed. The dog is not represented.

156. १भीमन् शरीर तोरतो॥ १अर्ज्जुनन शरीर तोरतो॥ १नकुलन शरीर तोरतो॥ १सहदेवन्
शरीर तोरतो॥ १द्रौपदीन शरीर तोरतो॥

Bhīmana śarīra torato. Arjjunana śarīra torato. Nakulana śarīra torato. Sahadevana śarīra torato. Draupadīna śarīra torato.

Draupadī gives up her body. Sahadeva gives up his body. Nakula gives up his body. Arjuna gives up his body. Bhīma gives up his body.

Text: They pass beyond the Himālayas (ch. 2). As they proceed towards Mount Meru, one after the other falls down. Draupadī is the first one who dies, followed by Sahadeva, Nakula, Arjuna and lastly Bhīma. Yudhiṣṭhira connects this with varying misconducts they had comitted in the past.
Image: Draupadī, Sahadeva, Nakula, Arjuna and Bhīma successively pass away.

/ 156 /

/ 160 / 159 / 158 / 157 /

157. [१दे]वदूतन् यूधिष्ठिनयात विमान हव् धर्म्म षिचारूपन
devadutana Yudhiṣṭhirayāta vimāna hava Dharmma ṣicārupana
The messenger of the gods brings Yudhiṣṭhira an aerial chariot. Dharma in the shape of a dog.

Text: As only Yudhiṣṭhira and the dog are left, Indra appears and asks Yudhiṣṭhira to ascend his aerial chariot (ch. 3). Yudhiṣṭhira however insists that he would not abandon the devoted dog and forsakes Indra's chariot. Thereupun the dog changes into Dharma.
Image: Yudhiṣṭhira is depicted in the company of the dog. According to the text, it is Indra who appears with his chariot but the figure represented does not wear his characteristic crown. The inscription identifies him as the god's messenger.

158. १यूधिष्ठिन[य]ात् धर्म्मन् द[र्श्शन विव॥]
Yudhiṣṭhirayāta Dharmmana darśśana biva.
Dharma gives Yudhiṣṭhira divine sight (sa. *darśana*).

Text: Pleased with his words, Dharma praises Yudhiṣṭhira (ch. 3). He states that there is no one in heaven equal to him, that therefore Yudhiṣṭhira would ascend in his own body and obtain a divine and supreme objective.
Image: Yudhiṣṭhira praises Dharma who, having taken on his own form, tells him that he has passed the test.

159. १देवदूतन् यूधि[ष्ठि]न स्वर्ग्ग यं॥
devadutana Yudhiṣṭhira svargga yaṃ.
The messenger of the gods leads Yudhiṣṭhira to heaven.

Text: The gods take Yudhiṣṭhira to the highest region but Yudhiṣṭhira instead wants to go to wherever his brothers and Draupadī have gone (ch. 3).
Image: The messenger directs the chariot which ascends with Yudhiṣṭhira.

Svargārohaṇaparva: 'The Book of the Ascent to Heaven'

160. १दूर्योधन् दूःशासन् शकूनि् इन्द्रया् सभास् चोढ॥ १यूधिष्ठिनन् इन्द्र् नमस्कान याक॥
Duryyodhana Duḥśāsana Śakuni Indrayā sabhāsa coṅa. Yudhiṣṭhirana Indra namaskāra yāka.
a) Yudhiṣṭhira pays homage to Indra.
b) Duryodhana, Duḥśāsana and Śakuni stay in Indra's palace.

Text: Having reached the abode of the gods, Yudhiṣṭhira sees Duryodhana, blazing in prosperity (ch. 1). As he asks about his brothers, Draupadī and his well-wishers, the gods order their messenger to lead him to where they abide (ch. 2).
Image: Having descended from the chariot, Yudhiṣṭhira praises Indra who sits on his throne higher than the others. An attendant with a fly-whisk stands by. For acoording

/ 162 /

161 /

to the text, Indra and Yudhiṣṭhira have encountered already before, there is no reference to Yudhiṣṭhira praising Indra on his arrival in heaven. Additionally to Duryodhana, Duḥśāsana and Śakuni are depicted residing in the abode of the gods.

161. १द्यवद्ःगन् यूधिष्ठिन् मायाननक् कंट॥
devadutana Yudhiṣṭhira māyānaraka keṅa.
The messenger of the gods shows Yudhiṣṭhira an illusory hell.

Text: Yudhiṣṭhira follows the messenger of the gods on an inauspicious and inaccessible path, frequented by mosquitoes, infested by worms and full of crows and vultures with iron beaks (ch. 2).
Image: Yudhiṣṭhira is again depicted on an aerial chariot, lead by the messenger of the gods. Both of them, Yudhiṣṭhira and the messenger, are wearing garlands of flowers. On a large tree, possibly marking the entrance to hell, squats a big cat. The inscription already informs about what is revealed only later in the text; that what follows is only an illusion.

162. १यमकिंकन॥ १ऄसिपत्रवनस हव १कोषन ङाचकाव तव॥ १सिमास ्षायाव तव॥
१धनपास् दायका॥ १ञलसिस् ह्वाङा॥ १ननककुण्डस् थुङाव तया॥
Yamakiṅkara. asipatravanasa hava. koṣana ṅācakāva tava. simāsa ṣāyāva tava. dharaposa dāyakā. jalasisa hvāṅā. narakakuṇḍasa thuṅāva tayā.

a) Placed in the hellwell.
b) Burnt in a *jalasi* (a wide-mouthed cooking pot with two ears[278]).
c) Made boile in a pot.
d) Dragged on a tree.
e) Bitten to the bones.
f) Brought to the forest of blades.
g) A servant of Yama.

Text: The path is frequented by mosquitoes, infested by worms and there are crows and vultures with iron beaks (ch. 2). Yudhiṣṭhira sees ghosts and mutilated carcasses that emit a vile scent. The whole place is surrounded by a blazing fire. There are rivers with boiling water, forests with leaves sharp like swords and iron pots with boiling oil in every direction.
Image: The tortures are depicted at great length. Most of the depicted punishments are found in the text, too: the forest with blades as leaves, the pots, the crows biting with iron beaks and the dead corpses which are here hanging from a tree. The hellwell is an addition to the text, as well as Yama's servant rushing forward with the club.

278 Kölver und Shresthacarya 1994, p. 109: *jalasi/jaḥsi.*

/ 164 / 163 /

163. १युधिष्ठिन् अकासगंगास् स्नान याक॥
Yudhiṣṭhira akāsagaṅgāsa snāna yāka.
Yudhiṣṭhira bathes in the heavenly Gaṅgā.

Text: As Yudhiṣṭhira hears the voices of his brothers and Draupadī, he decides to remain there despite all inconveniences (ch. 2). Indra, Dharma and all the others arrive and the illusion dissolves (ch. 3). Indra states that Yudhiṣṭhira had to see hell because he earlier deceived Droṇa. On Indra's advice, Yudhiṣṭhira bathes in the heavenly Gaṅgā. He is consequently purified and freed from his sins. Giving up his human body he assumes a divine form.
Image: Yudhiṣṭhira is depicted inside the turbulent waters, without the crown and clothes. His whole appearance is in keeping with his age. On both sides large lotuses rise over the water. These flowers are connected with purity on account of the self-cleaning effect of their leaves.

164. १देवदूतन् युधिष्ठिन् लि बोङाव यं॥
devadutana Yudhiṣṭhira li boṅāva yaṃ.
Thereafter the messenger of the gods leads Yudhiṣṭhira away.

Text: Having bathed in those waters, Yudhiṣṭhira is without enmity and torment (ch. 3). Surrounded by the gods, he goes to see his brothers and all the others who arrived before.
Image: Yudhiṣṭhira is again depicted atop the aerial chariot which is led away by the messenger of the gods.

165. १ईशान॥ १कुवेन॥ १वायु॥ १वरुण॥ १नैर्मृत्य॥ १यम॥ १अग्नि॥ १इन्द्र युधिष्ठिन् सभा दयकाव चोङ॥ १भीम॥ १अर्ज्जुन॥ १नकुल॥ १सहदेव॥ १दुर्य्योधन॥ १दुःशासन॥ १शकुनि॥
Īśāna. Kuvera. Vāyu. Varūṇa. Nairṛtya. Yama. Agni. Indra Yudhiṣṭhira sabhā dayakāva coṅa. Bhīma. Arjjuna. Nakula. Sahadeva. Duryyodhana. Duḥśāsana. Śakuni.

Śiva. Kubera. Vāyu. Varūṇa. Nairṛtya. Yama. Agni. Indra (and) Yudhiṣṭhira are constantly holding court. Bhīma. Arjuna. Nakula. Sahadeva. Duryodhana. Duḥśāsana. Śakuni.

Text: Yudhiṣṭhira sees Kṛṣṇa in his form as the absolute of the universe (sa. *brahman*) and he also beholds all the others who have conquered heaven before him (ch. 4). He sees his brothers together with Karṇa, Draupadī, her sons and Abhimanyu, his father, mothers and Dhṛtarāṣṭra, the preceptors and all the other kings in radiant forms. As the fruits of their deeds are extinguished, they all enter specific gods and other heavenly beings (ch. 5). Among others, Yudhiṣṭhira and Vidura enter Dharma and, on the other hand, all of Dhṛtarāṣṭra's sons become evil spirits (sa. *yātudhānas*).
Image: Purified from their sins and without enmity, the Pāṇḍavas and the Kauravas are all sitting together with the gods. In the centre, Indra and Yudhiṣṭhira are depicted, on a canopied throne, flanked by two attendants with fly-whisks. Among the mortals, the most important characters from both the sides are depicted. They are placed on the right side of the image, while the immortals are placed on the left side. The gods are all sitting on their specific mounts (sa. *vāhanas*) and hold their characteristic attributes.

/ 165 /

detail of scene 165

Again, the sculptors preferred a more solemn ending. Instead of concluding the cycle with the characters extinguishing, they chose to close with Yudhiṣṭhira's conquest of heaven. Moreover, the final scene of the Mahābhārata is also depicted above the temple's main entrance. It extends across the whole width of the cental pavilion's front face. Considering this, anyone approaching the temple beholds first of all these two final scenes, highlighting first the conquest of earth at the ground floor level, and above the conquest of heaven at the first floor level. One can also imagine that this probably appealed to Siddhinarasiṃhamalla, the god incarnate king.

3.4. Deviations from the Critical Editions of the Rāmāyaṇa and the Mahābhārata: Preli-menary Findings

This passage gives an overview of significant deviations for further considerations.

3.4.1. Deviations from the Rāmāyaṇa's Critical Edition

It appears that in general, it is not important in which way adversaries are slain or with what weapon. The brea-king of Virādha's arms by Rāma and Lakṣmaṇa is not re-ferred to and Rāma simply shoots him with an arrow instead (sc. 31). Likewise Kabandha retains his arms and again, Rāma only shoots him with his arrows (scs. 47f.). It makes no difference whether Mārīca is blown off with the Mānava Weapon or with the Vāyu Weapon (sc. 10) or if Lakṣmaṇa disfigures Śūrpanakhā with a sword or with a dagger (sc. 32b). Physical abnormaties of the demons (sa. *rākṣasas*) are also neglected. Triśiras has only one head and Kabandha admittedly looks strange but not as described in the text. All this is nothing peculiar to the representations on the Kṛṣṇa Temple. It appears that in later literary versions as well these aspects of the Rāma story were effectively meaningless. In the Ānanda Rāmā-yaṇa as well as in the Kṛttivāsi Rāmāyaṇa, Rāma kills Virādha with his arrows while the event as related in the Rāmacaritamānasa leaves ample room for interpretation. The weapon Lakṣmaṇa uses to disfigure Śūrpaṇakhā va-ries in the individual texts. In the Rāmacaritamānasa nei-ther Kabandha's physical abnormi-ties nor the method of killing him are specified and again, with what weapon Indrajit battles Hanumān is not specified for example the Ānanda Rāmāyaṇa or the Rāmacaritamānasa (sc. 69). Leaving aside these apparently insignificant changes as well as the one instance where the inscription is defini-tely wrong (sc. 97), the following deviations remain to be considered again.

In the Bālakāṇḍa, a conversation between Nārada and Daśaratha is depicted (sc. 3), a bird snatches away the heavenly *pāyasa* (sc. 5) and Ahalyā is transformed into stone (sc. 12). In the Araṇyakāṇḍa, Śūrpanakhā assumes a beautiful form (sc. 32a), Lakṣmaṇa and Sītā are present as Khara attacks (sc. 34) and Sītā is placed in a protective ring (scs. 40, 41). In the Yuddhakāṇḍa, Rāvaṇa kicks Vibhīṣana (sc. 76), Aṅgada takes away Rāvaṇa's crown (scs. 78, 79) and Hanumān destroys the Nikumbhilā sa-crifice (sc. 91). Finally, Rāvaṇa is represented with the head of a horse or a donkey throughout (scs. 36ff.) and Kumbhakarṇa also has an additional animal head (scs. 86ff.).

Some of these deviations are popular alterations in South and North India alike. That Ahalyā was transformed into stone and that Śūrpanakhā assumed a beautiful form is according to general belief and there is hardly any later adaption of the story that narrates it otherwise. Sītā is placed in a protective ring, or even in several protective rings, in southern and northern versions alike, as in the Telugu Raṅganātha Rāmāyaṇa, the Kannada Aṣṭottara Rāmāyaṇa, the Sanskrit Ānanda Rāmāyaṇa, the Bengali Kṛttivāsi Rāmāyaṇa and in the Marathi Bhāvārtha Rāmāyaṇa. Likewise, Rāvaṇa kicks Vibhīṣaṇa in several medieval recensions, southern and northern ones alike, for example in the Telugu Rāmāyaṇas of Raṅganātha and Molla, in the Avadhi Rāmacaritamānasa and the Bengali Kṛttivāsi Rāmāyaṇa. Hanumān destroys the Nikumbhilā sacrifice only according to the Bengali Kṛttivāsi Rāmā-yaṇa but other versions, southern and northern ones alike, also attest that the monkeys in general cause the destruction of the sacrifice.

There are no deviations depicted that are found only in South Indian renditions. On the other hand, some of the depicted deviations are found only in North Indian renderings. This is true for Aṅgada snatching Rāvaṇa's crown. In South Indian versions, this is attributed to Su-grīva whereas it is Aṅgada who snatches away Rāvaṇa's crown in several medieval northern renderings, like the Bengali Kṛttivāsi Rāmāyaṇa, the Avadhi Rāmacaritamā-nasa and the Marathi Bhāvārtha Rāmāyaṇa. Two of the deviations depicted on the Kṛṣṇa Temple are found ex-clusively in Eknāth's Bhāvārtha Rāmāyaṇa, namely the bird snatching away the *pāyasa* and Lakṣmaṇa and Sītā being present as Khara attacks. Additionally, there ap-pears to be no literary source at all for the scene with Nārada informing Daśaratha. Likewise, the animal heads of Rāvaṇa and Kumbhakarṇa are not traceable in literary versions of the epos.

3.4.2. Deviations from the Mahābhārata's Critical Edition

Some of the killings in the Mahābhārata cycle are very close to the text. This is true for example for the killing of Kirmīra (s. 54) or Bhīma battling and slaying Kīcaka (scs. 102-104). It has been established for the Rāmāyaṇa cycle that deviations in the representation of single combats are based on altered, often stripped-down renderings of these particular events. The accurate representation of the above mentioned fights proves, that details were given if they were known. It is not the case that the artists chose to ignore these informations or to simplify the story. They depicted the events the way in which they were transmitted. This has to apply to the representations of the Mahābhārata cycle, too. Therefore, battles that differ in their representation from the text given, like Bhīma and Jarāsandha fighting with clubs instead of with bare arms (sc. 43), are certainly also based on altered versions of the story. It is conspicuous that neither Hiḍimva nor Vaka are torn into two (scs. 20, 25), whereas Bhīma tearing Jarāsandha into two is explicitly shown in the image (sc. 44). Sometimes even negligible details are included in the representations. For example, the *vimāna*-form of the assembly hall is emphasised (sc. 40) and in keeping with the text, Draupadī holds onto the lowered branch of a tree as Jayadratha arrives (sc. 88). It is therefore even more interesting that, again other representations differ significantly from the text. In one instance the inscription is wrong, for it is certainly not Abhimanyu who brings about Droṇa's end (sc. 128). This leaves the following variations to focus attention on.

In the Ādiparva, the union of Pāṇḍu and Mādrī takes place inside, in the presence of Kuntī (sc. 13), on their way to the city of Pañcāla, Kuntī and the Pāṇḍavas encounter a dog (sc. 26), at Draupadī's *svayamvara*, Arjuna shoots a fish from a tree (sc. 28) and already in course of the conflagration of Khāṇḍavavana, Kṛṣṇa acts as Arjuna's charioteer (sc. 37). In the Sabhāparva, in the account of Duryodhana's misfortunes, the size of the door matters (sc. 50) and the game of dice is depicted as *chausar* (sc. 51). In the Vanaparva, Uddhava accompanies Kṛṣṇa as he visits the exiled Pāṇḍavas (sc. 55), the garland of flowers which Arjuna offers to the *liṅga*, ascends to the *kirāta*'s head (sc. 58), Urvaśī desires Arjuna but is rejected (scs. 64-66) and Indra participates in the battle with the Nivātakavacas (sc. 67). In the Virāṭaparva, Bhīma dresses as a woman as he awaits Kīcaka (sc. 101). In the Udyogaparva, after Arjuna has won Kṛṣṇa as charioteer, Kṛṣṇa's get-together with Yudhiṣṭhira is emphasised (sc. 115) and Kṛṣṇa multiplies as he reveals his divine form (sc. 119). In the Bhīṣmaparva, Kṛṣṇa rushes at Bhīṣma with his club (sc. 123). In the Droṇaparva, Abhimanyu is killed in a duel with Jayadratha (sc. 125). In the Sauptikaparva, Aśvatthāmā brings the heads of the Upapāṇḍavas (sc. 138) and Bhīma forcibly takes Aśvatthāmā's jewel (sc. 140). In the Mausalaparva, the sage bevor whom Śāmva is led is identified as Durvāsā (sc. 147), eventually Balarāma's transformation is disregarded (sc. 150) and Vyāsa visits the Pāṇḍavas instead of Arjuna visiting Vyāsa (sc. 154). Finally, in the Mahāprasthānikaparva, a messenger appears with Indra's chariot instead of Indra himself (sc. 157) as a consequence of which Yudhiṣṭhira praises Indra on his arrival in heaven in Svargārohaṇaparva (sc. 160).

The stories of Arjuna worshiping a *liṅga* in the course of the *kirātārjuna* episode and of Urvaśī desiring and cursing Arjuna are popular ones and they have been given in the description of the scenes. Whereas important local versions of the Rāmāyaṇa have for the most part been translated, the same is not true for local Mahābhārata versions. Especially the medieval North Indian renderings of the story would be of importance with regard to the Kṛṣṇa Temple's representations but, if any, only select passages have been translated so far. Therefore, a comparison with other narrative representations of the two great epics will hopefully provide more insights on region-specific elements in the transmission of the great Indian epics.

4. Comparable South Asian Narrative Representations

Literary sources have already been discussed as far as possible. In addition to this, other narrative representations will be discussed in this chapter. This will hopefully help to explain also the divergences pointed out for the Mahābhārata frieze and give some more insights on region-specific traditions of both the epics.

4.1. Narrative Representations of the Rāmāyaṇa

4.1.1. Other Nepalese Representations

Only two other comparable Nepalese representations are known to exist. Firstly, the essence of the Rāmāyaṇa is given in three registers on the wooden lintel above a door in the middle wall of the Bhaktapur Palace, Lal Baiṭhak, dating to 1697 CE. The story proceeds from left to right. Not an entire cycle is given for only 15 events from the Araṇya up to the Yuddhakāṇḍa are represented (Pl. 9). In addition to the 15 narrative scenes on the lintel, the battle between the monkeys and the demons is depicted elaborately but merely decorative on the projecting ends of the threshold. The monkeys are depicted biting their enemies and seizing them by the hair. That way, their triumph over the demons is indicated. The entire door with all its representations was published and discussed by Gutschow in 2011.[279] The higth of the lintel is given by Gutshow as 8,6 cm for the central register above the door opening, and 16,2 cm for the registers on the sides.

A second narrative representation of the theme is said to be found on the Basantapur Palace (also Nautale Palace) at the Kathmandu Palace Square. The Basantapur Palace was built in 1769 CE by Pṛthvī Nārāyaṇ Śāh, shortly after his conquest of the Nepal Valley, and is one of the crowning features of Lohan Cok. Whereas I had the chance to see the specific door of the Bhaktapur palace in 2017, due to extensive restoration works I had unfortunately no chance to find the narrative carvings on the Basantapur Palace. I therefore rely entirely on Banerjee's account in describing these scenes.[280] According to him, again only the essence of the story is given, now in 12 scenes, again arranged in three registers.

The chart on page 142 lists the individual scenes of both the narrative representations for comparison. Strikingly, the choice of the depicted scenes is quite similar. Both the sequences open with Rāma, Sītā and Lakṣmaṇa resting at Citrakūṭa, a scene drawn from the Araṇyakāṇḍa. The events of the Bāla and Ayodhyākāṇḍa were disregarded in both cases. For the first part, the selected scenes of both the sequences are practically identical. Thereafter, the Kathmandu sequence focuses on the events from the Kiṣkindhā and Sundarakāṇḍa, closing with Hanumān's reports to Rāma. The Bhaktapur sequence by contrast gives only the most important events from these *kāṇḍas* and thereafter deals more detailed with the events from the Yuddhakāṇḍa. As also the cycle on the Kṛṣṇa Temple, the Bhaktapur sequence ends with a depiction of Rāma and Sītā, reunited. The events from the Uttarakāṇḍa are again not depicted.

Since no images are available of the Kathmandu sequence, nothing more can be said about these depictions. In case of the Bhaktapur sequence however, some peculiarities are to be noted. These concern firstly the 7th and 8th scenes of the sequence. The 7th scene is described by Gutschow only as follows: *'A bent backward body is seen bridging a river'*. Indeed, the water body depicted resembles rather a river than the ocean and the backward movement in crossing the sea is peculiar to this image but on the basis of the identification of the 8th scene, hardly anything else can be meant than Hanumān's leap across the ocean. The 8th scene depicts according to Gutschow *'a wild demon attacking a settlement represented by a temple-like structure'*. This image is however absolutely identical to scene 72 of the Kṛṣṇa Temple's cycle which depicts, according to the inscription, Hanumān setting Laṅkā on fire. The temple-like structure is the city gate of which Hanumān seizes the iron beam and the representation thus indicates the imminent destruction of Laṅkā.

Yet other important features of the Bhaktapur sequence are the animal heads of Rāvaṇa and Kumbhakarṇa. Even though Rāvaṇa is depicted with only one human head instead of with nine, this one head is also topped by the head of a horse or a donkey. Additionally, Kumbhakarṇa's second head appears to be again rather that of a lizard than that of a horse. This proves that there is a tradion about Kumbhakarṇa's animal head as well, either an unknown literary one or maybe an exclusively oral

279 Gutschow 2011 II, pp. 292ff.

280 Banerjee 1983, p. 161.

Lal Baiṭhak, Bhaktapur

1 2 3 4 5

6 7 8 9 10

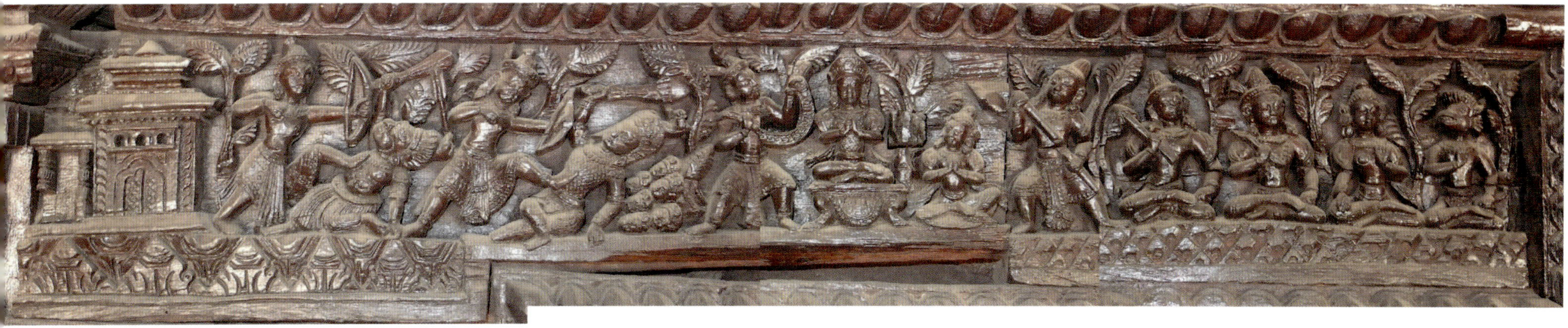

11 12 13 14 15

Plate 09

tradition. Further representations depicting Kumbhakarṇa with a lizard-like second head are however not known to me.

Apart from these narrative representations there are also some iconic ones and occasionally select events like the killing of Rāvaṇa or Rāma's coronation are depicted out of their narrative context. Two beautiful depictions of Rāma's coronation are found on the Kṛṣṇa Temple at the Bhaktapur Palace Square, on the quarter round panels framing the temple's triple portals. The temple possibly dates from the late 16th century CE.[281] In contrast to all the coronation scenes on the Kṛṣṇa Temple at Pāṭan, here the coronation itself is depicted instead of only a related act of rendering homage. On the left quarter round panel of the temple's west face, a two-armed Rāma is seated on his throne together with Sītā, flanked by Garuḍa and three attendants, two of which carry fly-whisks, the third one a parasol. The consecration is performed by two ascetic figures who pour the water over Rāma's head (sa. *abhiṣekha*). On a second quarter round panel, the left one on the temple's north face, a four-armed Rāma is seated on a lotus throne together with Sītā. The throne is supported by Garuḍa. Interestingly, the consecration ceremony is here performed by the gods. The four-headed Brahmā (only three heads are visible) and Indra (with his conical crown) pour the water over Rāma's head, while the four-armed Śiva (with the trident in his upper left hand) brings a garland of flowers. On a third quarter round panel, the right one on the west face of the same temple, the killing of Rāvaṇa is depicted. He is attacked by Vibhīṣaṇa and the monkeys in the lower register and by Rāma and Lakṣmaṇa in the upper register. Rāvaṇa is again depicted with one human head, topped by an animal head. The animal head is here very small but presumably again that of a horse. All the panels were published by Gail in 1984[282] and by Gutschow in 2016.[283]

<u>**Lal Baiṭhak, Bhaktapur (1697 CE)**</u>	<u>**Basantapur Palace, Kathmandu (1769 CE)**</u>
first register 1. Rāma, Sītā and Lakṣmaṇa at Citrakūṭa: Sītā points out the golden deer 2. The pursuit of the golden deer 3. Rāvaṇa abducts Sītā (in his true demoniac form he seizes her forcefully by the hair) 4. Fight between Rāvaṇa and Jaṭāyu (Sītā faces away as Rāvaṇa cuts off Jaṭāyu's wing) 5. Friendship between Rāma and Sugrīva (Rāma receives Sugrīva's hand. The fire is placed between them) **second register** 6. Rāma kills Vālin (second battle, Sugrīva wears the distinguishing garland) 7. Hanumān leaps over the ocean 8. Hanumān destroys Laṅkā (he seizes the beam from the gate before he sets the city on fire) 9. Hanumān reports to Rāma and Lakṣmaṇa 10. The crossing of the ocean **third register** 11. A city gate represents the arrival at Laṅkā 12. Rāma slays Kumbhakarṇa 13. Rāma slays Rāvaṇa (after cutting off his heads, six of which lie on the ground) 14. Vibhīṣana is crowned king of Laṅkā (Rāma presents him with a large garland of flowers) 15. Lakṣmaṇa, Rāma, Sītā and Hanumān (victorious and reunited)	**first register** 1. Rāma, Sītā and Lakṣmaṇa resting at Citrakūṭa 2. The pursuit of the golden deer 3. Rāvaṇa abducts Sītā (in the guise of a mendicant) 4. Jaṭāyu pursues Rāvaṇa's chariot (below Rāma and Lakṣmaṇa approach Hanumān and Sugrīva) 5. Friendship between Rāma and Sugrīva 6. Battle between Sugrīva and Vālin **second register** 7. Lament of Tārā over Vālin's dead body 8. Rāma and Lakṣmaṇa conferring with Hanumān and Sugrīva 9. Hanumān crosses the sea/arrives at Aśokavana **third register** 10. Hanumān in the presence of Rāvaṇa 11. Hanumān sets Laṅkā on fire 12. Hanumān takes leave of Sītā 13. Hanumān reports to Rāma and Lakṣmaṇa

281 Gutschow 2016, p. 120.
282 Gail 1984 (1), Pl. XLV.
283 Gutschow 2016, pp. 132ff.

4.1.2. Comparable Representations from India and Bangladesh

Single incidents from the Rāmāyaṇa, isolated from their narrative context, are frequently featured on temple walls across South Asia. Narrative representations of the Rāmāyaṇa are less common. The earliest representations within a narrative context come from North India. However, the most remarkable transmissions of Rāma's adventures in stone are found in the South Indian states of Karnataka and Tamil Nadu.

Gupta: Northern India and Bangladesh

The earliest Rāmāyaṇa representations, small panels made of terracotta, stone or scarcely stucco, date from the time of the Guptas. Only two sets of panels were found at their original location. The **Deogarh** stone panels (5th c. CE) are the best known.[284] Vats has identified eight to ten Rāmāyaṇa scenes on panels which were originally placed along the temple's plinth. The following events are represented: Rāma redeeming Ahalyā; Rāma, Sītā and Lakṣmaṇa going into exile; the three of them at the hermitage of Sage Atri; Lakṣmaṇa disfiguring Śūrpaṇakhā; Rāma and Lakṣmaṇa at archery; possibly the abduction of Sītā on a fragmentary piece; the garlanding of Sugrīva; Sugrīva having forgotten his promise; possibly Rāvaṇa and Sītā in the Aśoka grove on another fragmentary panel and finally a fragment depicting either Hanumān bringing the mountain of medicinal herbs or the second fight between Vālin and Sugrīva.[285] Additionally, Vats describes three fragments found at the site that deal with events from the Kiṣkindhākāṇḍa. One depicts the fight between Vālin and Sugrīva, another one has three monkeys carrying boulders for the construction of the bridge across the ocean.[286] Some of the panels are part of the permanent exhibition in the New Delhi National Museum.

The second set of panels found within its architectural context adorned the base of a temple at **Āpsāḍh**, Bihar, dateable to the 7th century CE.[287] A part of the temple's wall that was excavated in the 1960s has eight stucco panels with scenes from the Ayodhyākāṇḍa placed within alternating rectangular and keyhole-shaped niches. Represented is a continuous sequence with the crossing of the Gaṅgā; Rāma, Sītā and Lakṣmaṇa at the hermitage of Bhāradvāja (VR 2.48); the crossing of the Yamunā (VR 2.49); Rāma, Sītā and Lakṣmaṇa resting under a tree (also VR 2.49); possibly the three of them at the hermitage of Vālmīki[288]; Lakṣmaṇa atop a tree perceiving Bharata's army (VR 2.90); then Bharata's army and finally Bharata falling on his knees before Rāma. The entire representation is a very detailed one. On the second panel even the cow offered by Bhāradvāja to the exiles is depicted and on the fourth panel the hunted deer. It was also taken into account that the exiles cross the Gaṅgā on a boat, whereas they cross the Yamunā on a raft.

Other well known Gupta series are the terracotta panels from Nācār Kherā in Haryana and the stone panels from Nachnā in Madhya Pradesh.

From the site of **Nācār Kherā** ten Rāmāyaṇa panels have been obtained.[289] Only five of them are in a condition good enough to allow an identification of the depicted scene. These five illustrate: Rāma, Sītā and Lakṣmaṇa going to Pañchavaṭī; Triśira with two attendants; Triśira in combat; the golden deer and finally Indrajit in combat. The bricks bear inscriptions in Gupta Brāhmī characters either identifying the depicted figures or the depicted scene. The Pañchavaṭī panel even bears part of a descriptive verse from the epic.

Six sandstone panels with Rāmāyaṇa scenes have been found at **Nachnā**.[290] They are stylistically dateable to the first half of the 6th century CE and illustrate Sītā entreating Lakṣmaṇa to go and help Rāma with the golden deer; Rāvaṇa approaching Sītā in the guise of a mendicant; Rāma and Hanumān's first encounter; the first fight between Vālin and Sugrīva with Rāma and Lakṣmaṇa standing by; their second fight with Sugrīva wearing the garland and Rāma shooting his arrow and finally, Hanumān brought captive before Rāvaṇa. The panel which depicts Sītā entreating Lakṣmaṇa to go is especially interesting because Lakṣmaṇa covers his ears before he leaves. This is a free interpretation of the artist to illustrate his refusal to listen to Sītā.

284 Vats 1999 (1952), pp. 16ff. with illustrations: Pls. XV-XVII.

285 The second interpretation was suggested by Deva 1981, p. 13. As he notes the monkey wears a garland of flowers and the fragment thus resembles the representations from Nachna Kuthara, where Vālin and Sugrīva are depicted in combat with boulders raised above their heads.

286 Vats 1999 (1952), pp. 26f.

287 Sinha 1968, pp. 216ff. with illustrations: Pls. XVII-XXII.

288 According to the CE (Goldman 1986: II, note to 2.50.12) a later insertion of the Southern Recension. The event is included in Shastri's translation: 2006 (1953/62): I, p. 302.

289 Handa 2006, pp. 107ff. with illustrations: figs. 7,8 and Pls. 119,120.

290 Deva 1981 with illustrations (figs. 11-16) and Dehejia 1994, pp. 9f. Deva identifies the first scene as Śūrpaṇakhā's misadventures but Dehejia's interpretation seems more apposite.

The Bangladesh National Museum houses 53 inscribed terracotta plaques depicting scenes from the Rāmāyaṇa, dateable to the late 6th century CE.[291] Among them 17 were collected at **Saralpur** and 36 at **Palasbadi** (Bogra district). As Akmam points out, they include a number of events related only in later sources like Sītā entering a temple in the forest to pray that Rāma will become her husband, as narrated in the Rāmacaritamānasa,[292] or the preservation of Daśaratha's dead body in a boat filled with oil until Bharata returns to perform the funeral rites, as described in the Rāmacaritamānasa, too.[293] Both the events are rendered similarly in the Kṛttivāsi Rāmāyaṇa.[294]

Several later north Indian temples are decorated with Rāmāyaṇa panels, too, like for example in Rajasthan. Margabandhu mentions the twin temples of Sas and Bahu at Nagda (10th /11th c. CE), a group of temples at Kirādu (late 10th to 12th c. CE) and the Kekind Temple at Jasnagar (late 12th /early 13th c. CE).[295] Important events from the epic are depicted on miniature panels either as isolated scenes or as short sequences. A sequence on the Sas-Bahu Temple for example shows Rāma meeting Sugrīvā; Vālin and Sugrīvā in combat with Rāma aiming an arrow; Vālin's death; Sugrīvā's coronation and the monkeys setting out to search Sītā.

291 Akmam 1991, pp. 383ff.
292 Nagar 2014 I, pp. 379ff.
293 Nagar 2014 I, p. 810.
294 Nagar and Nagar 1997 I, pp. 86f. and 129.
295 Margabandhu 1983, pp. 132ff.

Of most the early northern representations, only short sequences have survived. Many longer sequences and even entire cycles are by contrast found in South Indian representations. The earliest ones date back to the 7th century CE.

Early Cāḷukya: Karnataka

The earliest narrative Rāmāyaṇa representations from South India are the sandstone carvings on the **Upper Śivālaya** on the North Fort hill at Badāmi, built in the first half of the 7th century CE.[296] Presumably 13 scenes from the Rāmāyaṇa form the southern part of the temple's basement frieze.[297] The images progress clockwise, in chronological order. Again, not an entire cycle is given but instead a sequence from the Araṇya and Kiṣkindhākāṇḍa. The representations include the Śūrpaṇakhā episode (Pl. 10a: Śūrpaṇakhā complains to Rāvaṇa), the pursuit of the golden deer (Pl. 10b), Sītā's abduction together with Jaṭāyu's death and finally, Rāma piercing the seven *śāla* trees in order to proof his strength to Sugrīva (Pl. 10d, VR 4.12).

296 Michell 2014, p. 37.
297 Identification of scenes: Loizeau 2017, pp. 182f. The affiliation to the epic of the 12th scene (Pl. 10c) is doubtful for its identification is problematic. Michell (2014, p. 68) identifies the left part as the awakening of Kumbhakarṇa. However, the placement of the awakening of Kumbhakarṇa before the *saptaśāla* episode is problematic and Michell gives no explanation for the crowning ceremony and the speared body depicted to the right.

The **Durga Temple** at Aihole, assignable to the first half of the 8th century CE,[298] has on the base of its inner porch some representations from the epic, too. On the north side six scenes from the Ayodhyākāṇḍa are included, dealing mainly with Rāma's departure to exile. The south side has a sequence from the Sundarakāṇḍa, dealing with Hanumān's exploits in Laṅkā.[299]
Several temples at Paṭṭadakal bear representations from the Rāmāyaṇa, namely the Virūpākṣa, Mallikārjuna and Pāpanātha. They are roughly contemporary. According to inscription, the first two of them were consecrated during the reign of Vikramāditya II (733-44 CE), the Mallikārjuna slightly later than the Virūpākṣa. The construction of the Pāpanātha was begun already under the reign of Vinayāditya, around 690 CE. However, the outer *maṇḍapa* was completed only during the early years of Kīrtivarman II (744-57 CE) and the Rāmāyaṇa representations on the south faces of the temple's *maṇḍapas* thus date from his reign.[300] The Rāmāyaṇa representations on the Pāpanātha are the most extensive ones among those of the Early Cāḷukyas.

The **Virūpākṣa Temple**[301] has a few representations from the Rāmāyaṇa in the niches on its south face.[302] The first one shows Rāma, accompannied by Sītā and Lakṣmaṇa. Rāma eyes the golden deer, depicted in the upper right corner of the niche. Above this, Śūrpaṇakhā approaches

298 Michell 2014, pp. 109, 127. An engraved record on the adjacent gateway mentions Vikramāditya II (733-44 CE).
299 Identification of the scenes: Loizeau 2017, p. 183.
300 Wechsler 1994, pp. 27f.
301 Plan: Michell 2014, p. 172, section and elevation: ibid. p. 196.
302 For illustrations see Wechsler 1994, pp. 32f., figs. 5-7.

Upper Śivālaya, Badāmi

a

b

c

d

Plate 10

Rāma. The second niche contains a representation of Jaṭāyu, attempting to hinder Rāvaṇa from abducting Sītā. Jaṭāyu is about to plunge his beak into Rāvaṇa's back as described in the text (VR 3.49). The violence of the combat is underlined by the representation on the small panel below. Rāvaṇa is overcome by Jaṭāyu, his arms severed and torn off. It is the moment when Jaṭāyu is almost certain of victory, that is highlighted here – the moment before Rāvaṇa's arms regrow and he on his part cuts off Jaṭāyu's wings and feet. Sītā's abduction is depicted at the upper rim of that niche. Rāvaṇa drives his chariot, having placed Sītā behind him. A third niche shows the fight between Vālin and Sugrīva. Rāma is depicted in the upper right corner. The figure is unfortunately much worn out but he bends his bow and clearly aims at Vālin. Below this, the lamentation of the deadly wounded Vālin is depicted. The scenes of the three niches are viewed in the right order if one circumbulates the temple in counterclockwise direction (sa. *apradakṣiṇa*).

Three of the Virūpākṣa's *maṇḍapa* pillars bear additional scenes from the Rāmāyaṇa on their raised cubical blocks.[303] The first pillar has representations from the Araṇyakāṇḍa arranged in four superimposed registers on one of its faces. The other faces are not sculptured. The sequence begins with Śūrpaṇakhā approaching Rāma and ends with Jaṭāyu reporting on Sītā's abduction. An inscription above the individual scenes helps to identify the figures. A second pillar is adorned with scenes from the Kiṣkindhākāṇḍa. One face reveals in two registers the story of Vālin and Māyāvin (VR 4.9). The second sculptured face shows the fight between Vālin and Sugrīva with Rāma intervening. A third pillar is sculptured on all four faces with further events from the Kiṣkindhā and Sundarakāṇḍa. The first scene, represented in the first register of the pillar's northern face, shows Rāma and Lakṣmaṇa consulting with Sugrīva and his allies on Sītā's rescue. The narration proceeds clockwise around the pillar, from top to bottom, in three registers. The third register of the fourth face is not sculptured, so that the sequence ends with Hanumān escaping from Laṅkā, represented in the third register of the pillar's southern face.

Some events from the Kiṣkindhā and Sundarakāṇḍa are also represented on one of the *maṇḍapa* pillars of the **Mallikārjuna Temple**. The pillar is sculptured on all four faces. The episodes are represented in two registers, one episode on each face.[304] The Śūrpaṇakhā episode is followed by Sītā's abduction, Jaṭāyu intervening and finally an episode in the *aśoka* grove from the Sundarakāṇḍa. The fight between Rāvaṇa and Jaṭāyu is again represented as an isolated event on the schaft of another pillar.

The latest Rāmāyaṇa representations from the reign of the Early Cāḷukyas are at the same time the most comprehensive ones. In contrast to the representations of the Virūpākṣa and Mallikārjuna, the representations of the **Pāpanātha Temple** are not located on the *maṇḍapa* pillars but instead on the temple's outer walls, where they cover niches as well as the intervening wall spaces. The niches are created from pairs of pilasters carrying pyramidal pediments. The Pāpanātha's representations form the first fully conceived cycle of the epic. The 28 images show events mainly from the Bāla, Araṇya, Kiṣkindhā and Yuddhakāṇḍa. The cycle opens with Viśvāmitra's arrival at court on the south face of the inner *maṇḍapa*, progresses counterclockwise across the south and east faces of the outer *maṇḍapa* and culminates in a panel on the southern front porch pillar.[305] The scenes bear labels in old Kannada, mainly to identify the figures. Additio-nally, the name of Baladeva is given in the scene dealing with the Śūrpaṇakhā episode. The artist is also credited with some of the Virūpākṣa's images. An inscription on the south-eastern corner of the Pāpanātha's eastern wall further connects the two temples for it mentions the sculptor who made the southern wall: Revaḍi Ovajja, disciple of the disciple of Sarvasiddhi Ācāri, author of the Virūpākṣa Temple.[306]

The final scene on the southern front porch pillar (Pl. 11a) is made up of two image parts. The lower part shows Rāma and Sītā reunited in Ayodhyā, surrounded by their entourage. Labels above read "[... A]ṅgadi [...] Sītā Rāma Aṇumā (Hanumān) (and) La(kṣmaṇa)". The upper portion of the image is clearly of subordinate significance for the depicted figures are considerably smaller in size. There are dancers and musicians and this might well represent the celebrations held in consequence of Rāma's triumph

303 Illustrations and identification of scenes: Loizeau 2017, pp. 183ff.

304 Identification of scenes: Loizeau 2017, p. 190. Illustrations of faces 2,3 and 4 on pp. 192f.

305 Identification of scenes: Wechsler 1994, p. 29 and Loizeau 2017, p. 191. Illustrations: Wechsler 1994, p. 31 & 34, Michell 2014, pp. 236f., 240ff. and Loizeau 2017, p. 194.

306 Complete inscription with discussion: Falliozat and Falliozat 2015, pp. 310f.

Paṭṭadakal & Ellora

a: Pāpanātha: southern front porch pillar

b: Virūpākṣa: detail of *maṇḍapa* pillar

c

details of c: *saptaśāla* and Hanumān before Rāvaṇa

Plate 11

as proposed by Loizeau[307] but there is clearly also another royal couple. According to Wechsler this is the monkey king Sugrīva with his queen[308] but they do not look like the monkeys depicted in the lower register and the figures next to them even seem to have demonical traits. The labels identifying the figures of the upper portion are for the most part not legible but fortunately the first one is still in a good condition, giving the name of Saramā, Vibhīṣaṇa's wife. A short verse in Sanskrit crowns the final scene. The stone is damaged and the readable part does not convey any meaning but the last line reads "jati vibhīṣaṇaḥ".[309] Conclusively, the image shows on the one hand the righteous king Vibhīṣaṇa ruling in Laṅkā and on the other hand the righteous king Rāma ruling in Ayodhyā. Sugrīva and his queen are presumably also depicted in the lower register, to the left of Rāma and Sītā.

As pointed out by Wechsler, the representations on the front porch pillars are emblems of divine kingship, conceived by the temple's royal patron to validate his own rule.[310] Interestingly, this is quite similar to the effect of the placement of the epics' final scenes on the Kṛṣṇa Temple at Pāṭan.

The Early Cāḷukya representations are in general close to Vālmīki. The only innovation is the representation of Hanumān sitting on his coiled tail before Rāvaṇa on the Virūpākṣa Temple (Pl. 11b). That he expands his tail to a large extent is found in several Telugu folk Rāmāyaṇas.[311]

307 Loizeau 2017, p. 191.
308 Wechsler 1994, p. 37.
309 Falliozat and Falliozat 2015, pp. 311f.
310 Wechsler 1994, pp. 36, 42.
311 Rao 1984, p. 88.

Rāṣṭrakūṭa: Mahārāṣṭra

On the **Kailāsanātha Temple** at Ellora, the Rāmāyaṇa and the Mahābhārata are featured as parallel friezes on the exterior walls of the front porch balustrades. The representations are dateable to the mid-8th century CE.[312] The Rāmāyaṇa is depicted on the southern balustrade, on eight superimposed rows (Pl. 11c). The first four registers are to be read in alternating direction. The fifth through eighth registers, which are probably later, in contrast all read from the left to the right.[313] The first register depicts select events from the Ayodhyākāṇḍa with a representation of the crossing of the Gaṅgā. A definite identification of the remaining scenes is problematic.[314] Important events from the Araṇyakāṇḍa, depicted in the second and third registers, include Śūrpaṇakhā's mutilation, the pursuit of the golden deer and Sītā's abduction. The fourth and half of the fifth registers are dedicated to the Kiṣkindhākāṇḍa with Rāma piercing the seven *śāla* trees, the fight between Vālin and Sugrīva and Aṅgada slaying a demon (VR 4.47). The Sundarakāṇḍa opens with Hanumān's leap across the ocean. In the sixth register he gives Rāma's ring to Sītā, destroys the *aśoka* grove, taunts Rāvaṇa by sitting higher than him on his coiled tail and sets Laṅkā on fire. The Yuddhakāṇḍa opens with the construction of the causeway in the middle of the seventh register. The last register contains several battle scenes. Most of these are not identifiable but the last scene very likely depicts Rāma beheading Kumbhakarṇa, as identified by Gail.[315] The subsequent unsculptured part of the eighth register might initially have been intended for Rāma's climactic battle with Rāvaṇa. Various theories have been expressed why the cycle remained unfinished.[316] Again, the representations are in general close to the Vālmīki Rāmāyaṇa, with the only exception of Hanumān sitting on his coiled tail higher than Rāvaṇa.

312 Loizeau 2017, p. 195.
313 Identification of scenes: Gail 1985, pp. 177ff. and Markel 2000, pp. 61ff. (with partially varying interpretations).
314 For possible interpretations see Hawley 1981, p. 78 (also n. 11), Gail 1985, p. 178 (also n. 9), Markel 2000, p. 61 and Loizeau 2017, p. 195.

Noḷamba: Tamil Nadu

The **Kāmākṣi Temple** at Dharmapuri, dateable to the late 9th century CE, provides a plinth frieze with 53 Rāmāyaṇa scenes.[317] The entire story is represented, from beginning to end, in continuous reliefs. The narration starts at the rear wall and proceeds chronologically, counterclockwise along the south side of the sanctum and around the *mahāmaṇḍapa*. The scenes represented include Daśaratha's sacrifice, the tutelage of his sons by a sage, Viśvāmitra's arrival, the death of Tāḍakā, Rāma and Sītā's wedding, Kaikeyī's intrigue, the mutilation of Śūrpaṇakhā, Rāma shooting the golden deer, Rāma piercing the seven *śāla* trees and giving his ring to Hanumān, Hanumān jumping across the ocean, the building of the bridge to Laṅkā, several battle scenes and finally the reunion of Rāma and Sītā.

315 Gail 1985, p. 180.
316 ibid. and Markel 2000, n.15.
317 Identification and location of scenes: Sanford 1974, pp. 105ff. Dating: ibid, pp. 144f.

Pāṇḍya, Cōla: Tamil Nadu

Temples of this group have miniature stone panels depicting events from the Rāmāyaṇa on their base. The earliest and at the same time most important one is the **Nāgeśvara Temple** at Kumbakōṇam. According to Sanford this temple might have been constructed under the Pāṇḍyas, in the mid-9th century CE.[318] The Nāgeśvara has two series of miniature reliefs along the base, an upper and a lower one. The upper series consists of the Rāmāyaṇa reliefs, 66 in number, the vast majority of which Sanford was able to identify.[319] The narration begins to the left of the entrance and runs clockwise along the whole structure. The first scene which is not covered by later structures depicts Daśaratha's sacrifice. The Nāgeśvara's representations are exceptional insofar as they cover important events from the Bāla- up to the Yuddhakāṇḍa, thus forming the only entire Rāmāyaṇa cycle within this group.

Additionally, the large figures in the Nāgeśvara's secondary wall niches might refer to Rāmāyaṇa characters, as suggested by Sanford.[320] They are highly individualised but not identifiable as major deities. It is clear from the miniature base panels that the Rāmāyaṇa is of particular importance for the Nāgeśvara. Sanford is able to point out correlations of the secondary niche figures, on the one hand with the content represented to their feet and on the other hand with the deities occupying the central niches, to support his thesis.

318 Sanford 1974, pp. 182f. and 1994, pp. 55ff.

319 Identification an location of scenes: Sanford 1974, pp. 78ff. and 1994, pp. 44f.

320 Sanford 1994, pp. 43ff.

The later Cōḻa temples show only select portions from the Rāmāyaṇa.

Extended sequences are found on the **Brahmapurīśvara Temple** at Puḷḷamaṅgai, dating approximately from 910 CE,[321] and on the **Śaḍaīyar Temple** at Thirucchennampūṇḍi, dating from between 915 and 920 CE.[322] The representations of the Brahmapurīśvara and the Śaḍaīyar both begin on the rear wall and run clockwise along the bases. On the Brahmapurīśvara they occur as upper series reliefs, as on the Nāgeśvara, whereas they form the lower series of reliefs on the Śaḍaīyar. Both sequences are made up of approximately 60 panels. The depictions of the Brahmapurīśvara focus on the first *kāṇḍas* of the epic, namely Bāla, Ayodhyā and Araṇyakāṇḍa. The cycle opens with the gods requesting Viṣṇu to incarnate. The last scene represented shows the fight against Kabandha.[323] The Śaḍaīyar's representations include also scenes drawn from the Kiṣkindhā- and Sundarakāṇḍa, among others the battle between Vālin and Sugrīva, Rāma and Lakṣmaṇa in council with the monkeys and Hanumān's leap across the ocean. The Yuddhakāṇḍa is omitted here, too.[324]

In addition to this, a number of temples are adorned with shorter sequences from the Rāmāyaṇa.

At least 16 panels on the plinth of the **Sāmavedīśvara Temple** at Thirumaṅgalam, dateable to (maybe the early) 10th century CE, depict events from the Rāmāyaṇa.[325] The majority of the panels on the temple's southern wall are hidden from view but if the placement and subject matter approximately parallels that on the north side, one can assume that maybe 20 of about 60 panels in total deal with events from this epic. The events are depicted in chronological order, in counterclockwise manner, interspersed with numerous blank panels, such with floral motifs, iconic and other narrative representations. Again, not the entire epic is represented. The Bālakāṇḍa as well as the beginning of the Ayodhyākāṇḍa, represented at the Brahmapurīśvara at great length, have been omitted here. The narration begins on the north side with Rāma, Lakṣmaṇa and Sītā going to exile and then crossing the Gaṅgā in Guha's boat. The last scene which is still visible shows Sugrīva's coronation.

The **Natuṇai Iśvara Temple** at Puñjai, dating from the mid-10th century CE, has some depictions from the Rāmāyaṇa on its base. Most of them (16) belong to the lower series of panels.[326] The events are represented in sections, in clockwise and counterclockwise manner, interspersed with other representations, mostly iconic ones. The largest section deals with Hanumān's exploits in Laṅkā, represented on the south side of the temple, followed by Vibhīṣaṇa changing sides and the building of the bridge. Shorter sequences show Rāma being instructed in archery and then slaying Tāḍakā, the battle between Vālin and Sugrīva followed by Vālin's death and the battle between Rāma and Rāvaṇa followed by Rāva-

321 Sanford 1974, pp. 174ff.

322 Ibid., pp. 183ff. and Sanford 1994, p. 48.

323 Identification of scenes: Sanford 1974, pp. 84ff. and Schmid 2005, pp. 151ff. with some reinterpretations.

324 Sanford 1974, pp. 91ff. for location and identification of most the panels. The rear wall, obstructed by unexcavated earth when Sanford visited the site in 1970, has meanwhile been excavated.

325 Identification of scenes: Sanford 1974, pp. 102ff. Dating on pp. 173f.

326 Identification of scenes: Sanford 1974, pp. 96ff. Dating on pp. 176ff.

ṇa's death. Other events, Virādha appearing before the exiles and Lakṣmaṇa disfiguring Śūrpaṇakhā, are depicted as individual scenes. The upper series includes a representation of Śūrpaṇakhā complaining to Khara and Dūṣaṇa and another one depicts Rāvaṇa abducting Sītā and battling with Jaṭāyu.

10 scenes from the Rāmāyaṇa are depicted along the south base of the **Varadarāja Perumāl Temple** at Thirubhuvanai. The Varadarāja Perumāl probably dates from the first half of the 11th century CE.[327] Contrary to the Natuṇai Iśvara's representations, the events are again depicted in chronological order, in clockwise manner and, though small in number, events from almost all the *kāṇḍas* are shown. Only the Sundarakāṇḍa has been omitted and, as usual, the Uttarakāṇḍa.

The latest Cōḻa temple that bears narrative representations from the Rāmāyaṇa is the **Kampahareśvara Temple** at Thirubhuvanam, build under the reign of Kullōtuṅga III (1178-1218).[328] 18 scenes from the epic are found on the southern side of the *maṇḍapa*'s base. The panels are lengthened and separated one from another by only a narrow band with floral decorations. The sequence opens with the Śūrpaṇakhā episode. Thereafter the pursuit of the golden deer is shown, Sītā's abduction together with Jaṭāyu's intervention, an episode dealing with Hanumān's exploits and his finding of Sītā in Laṅkā, the consequent battle between Rāma and Rāvaṇa and finally the reunion of Rāma and Sītā.

Within this group, only the Pāṇḍyan Nāgeśvara has an entire cycle. The Rāmāyaṇa representations set in stone under Cōḻa rule present always just select portions from the epic. From the near-ground placement of the panels and their miniature format it can be inferred that their function was merely a decorative one. Most of the Cōḻa temples bearing Rāmāyaṇa representations are śivaite. Under Cōḻa rule, the Rāmāyaṇa representations became less important over time. The trend under the Cōḻas is from greater, unified sequences to smaller sequences or a very stripped-down rendering of the story as in case of the Varadarāja Perumāl. The representations focus on different *kāṇḍas*, whereby the events from the Uttarakāṇḍa were never taken into account. Temples other than those referred to, might have select scenes from the Rāmāyaṇa, too, however depicted out of their narrative context. Such scenes are either iconic ones like Rāma and Lakṣmaṇa leaning on their bows or popular scenes like Vālin and Sugrīva wrestling. The Cōḻa representations are in general close to Vālmīki. Only one variation can be mentioned. Like also within the Kṛṣṇa Temple's cycle, Ahalyā emerges from a stone boulder on the Brahmapurīśvara (Pl. 12a). This might be the earliest representation of her transformation in South India. On the Nāgeśvara, Ahalyā stands before Rāma with folded hands, entirely human (Pl. 12b). However, her transformation might be implied on the above mentioned Gupta panel, too, where Rāma's foot rests on a stone block next to which Ahalyā is placed. The story of Ahalyā's transformation is thus considerably older than literary sources attest.

It is interesting to note that in Cōḻa representations, physical abnormities of the demons, as well as the method of killing them and the weapons used, were accurately depicted. Representations of Kabandha are found for example on the Brahmapurīśvara (Pl. 12c) and Sāmavedīśvara (Pl. 12d). He is depicted with his head set in his belly. His arms are cut off after he has seized Rāma and Lakṣmaṇa, exactly as described in the text. The Virādha episode is frequently found in Cōḻa art, within the sequences but also as an isolated event, depicted out of its narrative context. On the Nāgeśvara Temple at Kumbakōṇam, the episode is depicted in two scenes (Pl. 12e+f). On the first panel Virādha approaches. He holds a human head in one hand and a trident with a spiked animal in the other hand. This is close to the text. Sītā, whom he takes by force, is depicted behind Rāma and Lakṣmaṇa, facing away. The next, much worn out panel combines two scenes. On the right side, the demon has seized Sītā and on the left side, Rāma and Lakṣmaṇa are depicted breaking his arms. On the Brahmapurīśvara Temple at Puḷḷamaṅgai, there are two representations of Rāma and Lakṣmaṇa breaking Virādha's arms (Pl. 12g+h). The out of sequence representation includes the figure of Sītā, whom Virādha was forced to let go, as also his trident, which has fallen to the ground.

While the earliest narrative Rāmāyaṇa representations in the Kāverī delta date back to the mid-9th century CE, the latest ones are already contemporary with the early Hoysaḷa representations.

327 Identification of scenes: ibid., p. 306. Dating on p. 305.
328 Loizeau 2017, p. 202 with identification of scenes on pp. 202f.

Pāṇḍya, Cōḻa

Ahalyā

a

b

Kabandha

c

d

Virādha

e

f

g

h

a,e,f: Nāgeśvara Temple, Kumbakōṇam
b,c,g,h: Brahmapurīśvara Temple, Puḷḷamaṅgai
d: Sāmavedīśvara Temple, Thirumaṅgalam

Plate 12

(Cenna-)keśava Temple, Belūr

a

b

Plate 13

Hoysaḷa and Late Cāḷukya: Karnataka

Among the earliest of the Hoysaḷa temples, the **(Cenna-)keśava Temple** at Belūr (1117 CE) has a series of reliefs depicting events from the Rāmāyaṇa. Nine scenes from the Araṇya, Kiṣkindhā and Yuddhakāṇḍa are represented on a frieze inside the temple's central hall (sa. *navaraṅga*).[329] The events are given in chronological order but, as pointed out by Loizeau, the choice of the represented events is peculiar. The monkeys are shown setting out in search for Sītā but Rāma conferring his ring to Hanumān is not represented. Likewise the killing of Śūrpaṇakhā's son, Śambūka, is represented but the consequent mutilation of Śūrpaṇakhā is missing. Instead, the next scene shows directly the pursuit of the golden deer (Pl. 13a). The killing of Śambūka is a popular addition to the story to which more will be said later. On another panel, with Rāvaṇa fending off Jaṭāyu, Sītā is sitting with Rāma and Lakṣmaṇa in some sort of hut, for what no explanation can be found (Pl. 13b). The next scene shows Rāma and Lakṣmaṇa meeting Hanumān. Hanumān arrives not in the guise of a mendicant but assumes a small size and only after having obtained Rāma's confidence, he reveals his true form.

At Haḷebīḍ, several monuments have narrative base friezes that include Rāmāyaṇa representations.

Only a fragmented representation of the Rāmāyaṇa is included in the narrative frieze of the **Hoysaḷeśvara Temple** at Haḷebīḍ. The Hoysaḷeśvara is the earliest and at the same time largest and best known of the Haḷebīḍ group temples. The temple was built during the reigns of Viṣṇuvardhana and Narasiṃha, from 1121 to 1160 CE.[330] In total eight decorative friezes run along the temple's base, of which the narrative one is the sixth. The Rāmāyaṇa scenes, six in total, are located on the west side of the temple. Two events, the fight between Rāma and Rāvaṇa (Pl. 14a) and the *saptaśāla* episode (Pl. 14b), are represented as isolated events. The *saptaśāla* relief shows first Rāma and Lakṣmaṇa brought before Sugrīva. Thereafter, Rāma shoots his arrow through seven trees that grow on the back of a large snake. With that same arrow, he also beheads the snake and kills Vālin. Again, the representation follows a local version of the story. The remaining four scenes from the Rāmāyaṇa are grouped together as a sequence rendered in clockwise manner (Pl. 14c-e). The first scene shows the killing of Śambūka and simultaneously the arrival of Śūrpaṇakhā and the golden deer at the hermitage. The second scene shows the monkeys handing over Sītā's jewels to Rāma. The third one shows again the alliance between Sugrīva and Rāma together with the *saptaśāla* episode and in the fourth scene, Rāma gives his ring to Hanumān. The representations on the Hoysaḷeśvara tell from the Araṇya, Kiṣkindhā and Yuddhakāṇḍa, with a preference for the events from the Kiṣkindhākāṇḍa. In addition, some events from the Yuddhakāṇḍa are included in the narrative frieze of the Nandi *maṇḍapa* but they originally most likely belonged to the Nagareśvara Complex[331] described below.

A continuous depiction of events from the epic in chronological order can be seen on the **Kedāreśvara Temple** at Haḷebīḍ, constructed during the reign of Ballāḷa II (1173-1220 CE).[332] Again, the narrative frieze is the sixth of in total eight horizontal layers encircling the structure. Among other representations, it reveals 35 scenes from the Rāmāyaṇa.[333] A long sequence from the epic is located on the southern and southwestern faces of the temple, interrupted only by two representations from the Mahābhārata. The Kedāreśvara has additional representations placed out of order. Three scenes from the Rāmāyaṇa are placed on the north face of the northern sanctum and two scenes each are placed to both sides of the temple's entrance. The long sequence begins with Viśvāmitra's arrival at Daśaratha's court and ends with Rāma's coronation. The three scenes on the northern wall deal with events from the Śūrpaṇakhā episode, the scenes next to the entry tell from the battle. As Loizeau points out, the Kedāreśvara has been renovated extensively.[334] The cycle is incomplete and the placement of the out of order scenes is certainly not the original one. The scenes on the northern wall were perhaps displaced for they would perfectly add to the representations on the southern sanctum. The representations next to the entry double those from the sequence and were presumably shifted from the Nagareśvara Complex. Evans assumes that also some of the large reliefs on the outer walls of the Kedāreśvara, namely those with a creeper scroll at the pedestal, originate from the Nagareśvara Complex.[335]

329 Identification of scenes: Loizeau 2017, p. 52. Dating on p. 49.

330 Loizeau 2017, pp. 57ff.

331 Loizeau 2017, pp. 66, 68.

332 Evans 1994, p. 233, Loizeau 2017, p. 68.

333 Identification of scenes: Loizeau 2017, pp. 70ff.

334 Loizeau 2017, pp. 68ff.

335 Evans 1997, p. 223, n. 3.

Hoysaḷeśvara Temple, Haḷebīḍ.

b

a

c

Plate 14

e

d

Some Rāmāyaṇa representations are still to be seen on the ruined **Hūcheśvara Temple** and on the ruins of ne northern and southern temples of the **Nagareśvara Complex**. Since the choice of the represented scenes as also iconographic features resemble those on the Kedāreśvara, it is assumed that they date from approximately the same period.[336] Whereas the friezes of the Hūcheśvara are, as well as those of the Kedāreśvara and Hoysaḷeśvara, composed of eight layers, the temples of the Nagareśvara Complex have only six layers, the narrative one being the fourth. The events from the Rāmāyaṇa were in each case depicted on the south side. On the Hūcheśvara twelve scenes have survived, depicting events from the Kiṣkindhā, Sundara and Yuddhakāṇḍa.[337] On the southern temple of the Nagareśvara Complex 24 scenes have survived, covering events from just the same *kāṇḍas*.[338] On the northern temple only three Rāmāyaṇa scenes are still in situ,[339] on the central temple not a single Rāmāyaṇa scene is intact. Four stray panels with scenes from the epic, possibly from the Nagareśvara Complex, were published by the Mysore Archaeological Survey.[340] Additionally it has to be remembered that some of the Kedāreśvara panels as well as those on the Hoysaleśvara's Nandi *maṇḍapa* originally might have belonged to the Nagareśvara Complex.

The **Amṛteśvara Temple** at Amṛtāpura, dating from around 1200 CE,[341] has a narrative frieze along the *maṇḍapa*'s parapet. On the southern face, the Rāmāyaṇa is represented in 65 scenes on 76 panels.[342] In contrast to the narratives represented on the Amṛteśvara's north side, the Rāmāyaṇa cycle is given in counterclockwise manner. The individual events are visually separated one from the other by two pillars each with either an ornamental motif or attendant figures in between. The first scene depicts Viṣṇu on Śeṣa, followed by Daśaratha consulting with the sages on the sacrifice. The cycle ends with the reunion of Rāma and Sītā. Except for the Uttarakāṇḍa all *kāṇḍas* are represented, whereby particular attention is drawn to the events from the Yuddhakāṇḍa. As the only Hoyṣala monument the Amṛteśvara clearly emphasises Rāma's divine nature. Not only does the cycle open with a representation of Viṣṇu Anantaśāyin; On the panel depicting Rāma in battle with Rāvaṇa, Garuḍa, Viṣṇu's mount, is represented on the post of Rāma's chariot (Pl. 15a).

The **Mallikārjuna Temple** at Basrāḷ, consecrated 1234 CE,[343] has again six superimposed base-friezes. The narrative frieze is the fourth. The Rāmāyaṇa covers the entire south face with 55 scenes in a continuous cycle, rendered clockwise.[344] The cycle begins with the story of Śravana Kumara whom Daśaratha accidentally shot in his youth (VR 2.57f.). The story serves as a prologue to the actual story which starts thereafter with Daśaratha's sacrifice. The Bālakāṇḍa is represented at length with singular scenes whereas popular scenes from the Yuddhakāṇḍa, notably the defeats of Kumbhakarṇa and Indrajit, are missing. The representation of Sītā's *svayamvara* is interesting because Rāvaṇa is present (Pl. 15b). Another interesting representation is that of Sītā's abduction. It is the only Hoysaḷa representation in which Rāvaṇa's chariot is pictured. In all other representations he carries her away on foot, keeping her in a small house raised above his head. The Mallikārjuna's cycle ends with Rāma and Sītā's return to Ayodhyā. The event of Rāma piercing the seven *śāla* trees is represented twice. The scene is part of the cycle and it is again depicted on the temple's eastern side as an individual event.

The **Lakṣmīnārāyaṇa Temple** at Hosahoḷalu, dateable between 1220 and 1250 CE, has six layers of decorative friezes, too. The fourth band includes 46 scenes from the Rāmāyaṇa.[345] The cycle begins on the south face of the temple's southern sanctum and runs clockwise around the structure up to the north-western face of its main sanctum. The first scene shows Viśvāmitra's arrival at Daśaratha's court, the last one probably Rāma and Sītā enthroned in Ayodhyā. The Lakṣmīnārāyaṇa's epic cycles are almost identical with those on the Kedāreśvara.

43 scenes from the epic are included in the narrative frieze (again the fourth out of six) of the **Lakṣmīnarasiṃha Temple** at Jāvagal, consecrated at some point in the 13th century CE.[346] The Rāmāyaṇa cycle makes up a

336 Loizeau 2017, p. 76, n. 28.
337 After Loizeau 2017, pp. 76, 79 with identification of scenes. See also Evans 1997, pp. 217ff.
338 After Loizeau 2017, p. 82 with identification of scenes. See also Evans 1997, pp. 224ff.
339 Evans 1997, p. 230 and Loizeau 2017, p. 83.
340 Seshadri 1964, pp. 47f. with Pls. LVI-LVIII.
341 Evans 1997, p. 23.
342 Evans 1997, pp. 24ff. and 40ff. with detailed description and illustrations of almost all the panels. See also Loizeau 2017, pp. 87ff. with slight variations in interpretation.
343 Loizeau 2017, p. 95.
344 Identification of scenes: Loizeau 2017, pp. 96ff.
345 Identification of scenes: Loizeau 2017, pp. 108ff. Dateing on p. 103, n. 1.
346 Identification of scenes: ibid., pp. 117f. Dating on p. 113.

Other Hoysaḷa Representations

a

b

detail of a

e

d

c

Plate 15

a

b

Śambūka

c

Sītā's abduction

d

e

Plate 16

large part of the frieze as it runs clockwise from the outer wall of the southern sanctum up to the northern one. Again, the cycle begins with Viśvāmitra's arrival and ends with Rāma's enthronement and it resembles much the cycles of the Kedāreśvara and Lakṣmīnārāyaṇa.

Another Hoysaḷa temple with a narrative base frieze (the fourth out of six) is the **(Cenna-)keśava Temple** at Somnāthpur, consecrated in 1268 CE. The section encircling the southern sanctum is dedicated to the Rāmāyaṇa, rendered in 33 scenes, from a courtly scene and Daśaratha's sacrifice up to Sugrīva handing over Sītā's jewels to Rāma.[347] Thus not an entire cycle is given but a sequence from the Bālakāṇḍa up to the beginning of the Kiṣkindhākāṇḍa. Sundara, Yuddha and Uttarakāṇḍa are not includen but the (Cenna-)keśava's representations have some unique representations from the Bālakāṇḍa. Not only are the newly born princes depicted on their mothers' lap; they are additionally also shown in their cradles and afterwards crawling on all fours (Pl. 15c-e).

The same sequence with just the same exceptional representations is found on the **(Cenna-)keśava Temple** at Araḷaguppe. The temple is roughly contemporary with the (Cenna-)keśava at Somnāthpur but it is difficult to tell which one served as a model for the other. According to Loizeau the temple at Somnāthpur might be earlier on account of the higher quality of its decorative representations.[348] On the (Cenna-)keśava at Araḷaguppe the Rāmāyaṇa covers more than half the length of its narrative frieze, again the fourth out of six. It extends across the entire south face up to the north face of the sanctum. Unfortunately a large part of the south face is covered by later structures, so that a decisive part of the Rāmāyaṇa panels is not visible. Only 18 scenes remain unhidden.[349]

These two (Cenna-)keśavas are the latest Hoysaḷa temples with a narrative base-frieze and as far as known, there is no later Rāmāyaṇa sequence from the Hoysaḷas. However, there is one representation of the Rāmāyaṇa not far away from the ancient centre of the Hoysaḷa kingdom, at Bandaḷike, district Shimoga. The **Someśvara Temple** is a late Cāḷukyan monument which was consecrated in 1274 CE.[350] Twin friezes of the two great epics, the Rāmāyaṇa and the Mahābhārata, are carved on slabs to both sides of the entry, evocative of those at Ellora. The Rāmāyaṇa frieze is placed to the left side of the entry and is composed of seven superimposed registers separated from each other by ornated madaillons.[351] The narration proceeds from bottom to top. It presumably opens with Daśaratha announcing Rāma's coronation and culminates in the battle between Rāma and Rāvaṇa, depicted in the sixth register. The seventh register shows Rāvaṇa with his entourage and on the right side Rāma's abondoned wife in the *aśoka* grove. According to the text, Rāvaṇa kept Sītā captive, despite repeated appeals for him to restore her to Rāma. This scene, placed at the very top, might therefore depict his refusal to restore her as the reason for the battle seen below.

The Hoysaḷa representations of the Rāmāyaṇa can be grouped after accordances, especially concerning the choice of scenes. The cycles on the Kedāreśvara, Lakṣmīnārāyaṇa and Lakṣmīnarasiṃha are quasi-identical. All begin with Viśvāmitra's arrival at Daśaratha's court and end with Rāma and Sītā's reunion. The remainder on the Hūcheśvara as well as on the northern and southern temple of the Nagareśvara Complex resemble so much the scenes of the afornamed temples that they are also assigneable to this group. The cycles on the Amṛteśvara and Mallikārjuna show the same sequence whereby Viśvāmitra's arrival is on the Amṛteśvara preceded by a representation of Viṣṇu on Śeṣa and on the Mallikārjuna by the story of Śravana Kumara, told by Daśaratha in the Ayodhyākāṇḍa. Additionally, within both the sequences, different emphasis is placed on the individual *kāṇḍas*. The representations on the (Cenna-)keśavas at Somnāthpur and Araḷaguppe form another group for the reasons mentioned above whereas the representations on the (Cenna-)keśava at Belūr, on the Hoysaḷeśvara and Someśvara are to be viewed separately.

The Hoysaḷas especially favoured the events from the Bāla, Araṇya, Kiṣkindhā and Yuddhakāṇḍa, whereby within the distinct cycles focus is placed on different *kāṇḍas*. A comprehensive representation of the Bālakāṇḍa is included in the cycles of the Amṛteśvara and Mallikārjuna as well as in the 13th century (Cenna-)keśavas' sequences. The Someśvara opens with a scene from the Ayodhyākāṇḍa and the story of Śravana Kumara, with which the Mallikārjuna's cycle opens, is also from this *kāṇḍa*. Some more scenes from the Ayodhyākāṇḍa are

347 Identification of scenes: ibid., p. 125. Dating on p. 123.
348 Loizeau 2017, p. 131.
349 Identification of scenes: Loizeau 2017, pp. 131ff.
350 Loizeau 2017, p. 43.
351 Illustration and identification of scenes: Loizeau 2017, pp. 45ff.

included in the Mallikārjuna's cycle and in the sequences given on the two later (Cenna-)keśavas. Whether or not the Ayodhyākāṇḍa was included in the cycles on the Kedāreśvara, Hūcheśvara and the temples of the Nagareśvara Complex we do not know since these cycles are incomplete. In case of the Amṛteśvara and Lakṣmīnārāyaṇa only two scenes are dedicated to the Ayodhyākāṇḍa and it is entirely absent in the Lakṣmīnarasiṃha's cycle. Several events from the Araṇyakāṇḍa are of great importance for the Hoysaḷa representations. This is especially true for the Śūrpaṇakhā episode and the abduction of Sītā by Rāvaṇa. These events are practically never missing. Only in case of the Hoysaḷeśvara, Sītā's abduction is not represented but since the Hoysaḷeśvara possesses a fragmentary representation of the epic instead of an entire cycle this is negligible. On the Hūcheśvara and the temples of the Nagareśvara Complex these scenes are certainly only not preserved. The most important scene from the Kiṣkindhākāṇḍa, regarding the Hoysaḷa representations, depicts Rāma piercing the seven *śāla* trees in order to proof his prowess to Sugrīva. This scene is represented in several instances even more than once. Additional scenes from the Kiṣkindhākāṇḍa are found on all the monuments. Important scenes from the Sundarakāṇḍa are included where an entire cycle is represented but the events from this *kāṇḍa* never play a major role. The sequence of the (Cenna-)keśava at Belūr ends with the construction of the causeway from the very beginning of the Yuddhakāṇḍa. Among the representations on the Hoysaḷeśvara, the fight between Rāma and Rāvaṇa is depicted as an isolated event. Three of the seven registers on the slab next to the Someśvara's entrance are dedicated to the Yuddhakāṇḍa and further representations are included in the cycles of the Kedāreśvara group temples. The Yuddhakāṇḍa is depicted especially elaborate on the Amṛteśvara, whereas in case of the Mallikārjuna important events are missing. It is entirely absent on both the later (Cenna-)keśavas since their sequences end with the beginning of the Kiṣkindhākāṇḍa. The Uttarakāṇḍa has entirely been omitted in the Hosaḷa representations.

All the Hoysaḷa representations of the Rāmāyaṇa, as well as the late Cāḷukyan one, reveal an influence of a local tradition. The most interesting deviation from the Vālmīki Rāmāyaṇa might be the depiction of the killing of Śūrpaṇakhā's son, as identified by Loizeau.[352] According to Jaina Rāmāyaṇa tradition, be it early works like Vimalasūri's Prakrit Paümacariyaṃ or later works like the Kannada Pampa Rāmāyaṇa, Śūrpaṇakhā is married to Khara with whom she has two sons, Śambūka (or Śambu) and Sunda. In Nāgacandra's Rāmāyaṇa, Śambūka practises strict austerities in order to obtain a magical sword. At the same time Lakṣmaṇa roams the wood, cutting bamboo. He accidentally beheads Śambūka and thus incurs Śūrpaṇakhā's wrath. Śūrpaṇakhā consequently does not come upon Rāma by chance, but approaches the exiles with the intention of wreaking vengeance. The story is included in the Kannada Torave Rāmāyaṇa, too, and it also found its way into Telugu versions of the epic. In the Bhāskara and Raṅganātha Rāmāyaṇas, Śūrpaṇakhā's son is given the name Jambukumāra.[353] According to the Raṅganātha Rāmāyaṇa, Jambukumāra is the son of Śūrpaṇakhā and Vidyujjhiva. While Śūrpaṇakhā is still pregnant, Rāvaṇa beheads Vidyujjhiva because he feels betrayed. As Jambukumāra learns of this, he wants to wreak vengeance on Rāvaṇa. Jambukumāra practises severe asceticism, whereupon Sūrya sends him a magical sword. Lakṣmaṇa however gets it first, uses it to cut bamboo and inadvertently beheads Jambukumāra. Poems in Telugu and Kannada also tell of this story.[354] The Telugu poem *Lankā Yāgamu* has the story of Śūrpaṇakhā's son, here named Chakrabhūpāla. Lakṣmaṇa mistakes him for a bush and slays him with his sword. The killing of Śūrpaṇakhā's son by Lakṣmaṇa is further narrated in the Telugu *Lankā Sārathi* where he is accidentally beheaded as Lakṣmaṇa tests his sword by cutting bamboo. In the Kannada *Janapada Ramayana-II* Śūrpaṇakhā's son is named Sunkumāra and takes to penance in order to obtain a magical sword to kill Rāvaṇa. Again, Lakṣmaṇa gets this sword first and while testing the sharpness of this weapon (not of his own sword) he beheads Śūrpaṇakhā's son. In the Sanskrit Ānanda Rāmāyaṇa, Śūrpaṇakhā's son is known as Sāmba.[355]

The killing of Śūrpaṇakhā's son is practically never missing in the Hoysaḷa representations. Śambūka might be depicted meditating between bushes with Lakṣmaṇa raising his sword to cut the bamboo. This is the case for example on the Hoysaḷeśvara (Pl. 14c). On the Mallikārjuna, Lakṣmaṇa splits Śambūka in two (Pl. 16a), while

352 Loizeau 2017, pp. 239ff.

353 Sarma 1973, pp. 87 n. 62 (TR), 87f. (RR) and 124 (BR).
354 Rao 1984, pp. 69ff.
355 Nagar 2006, p.76.

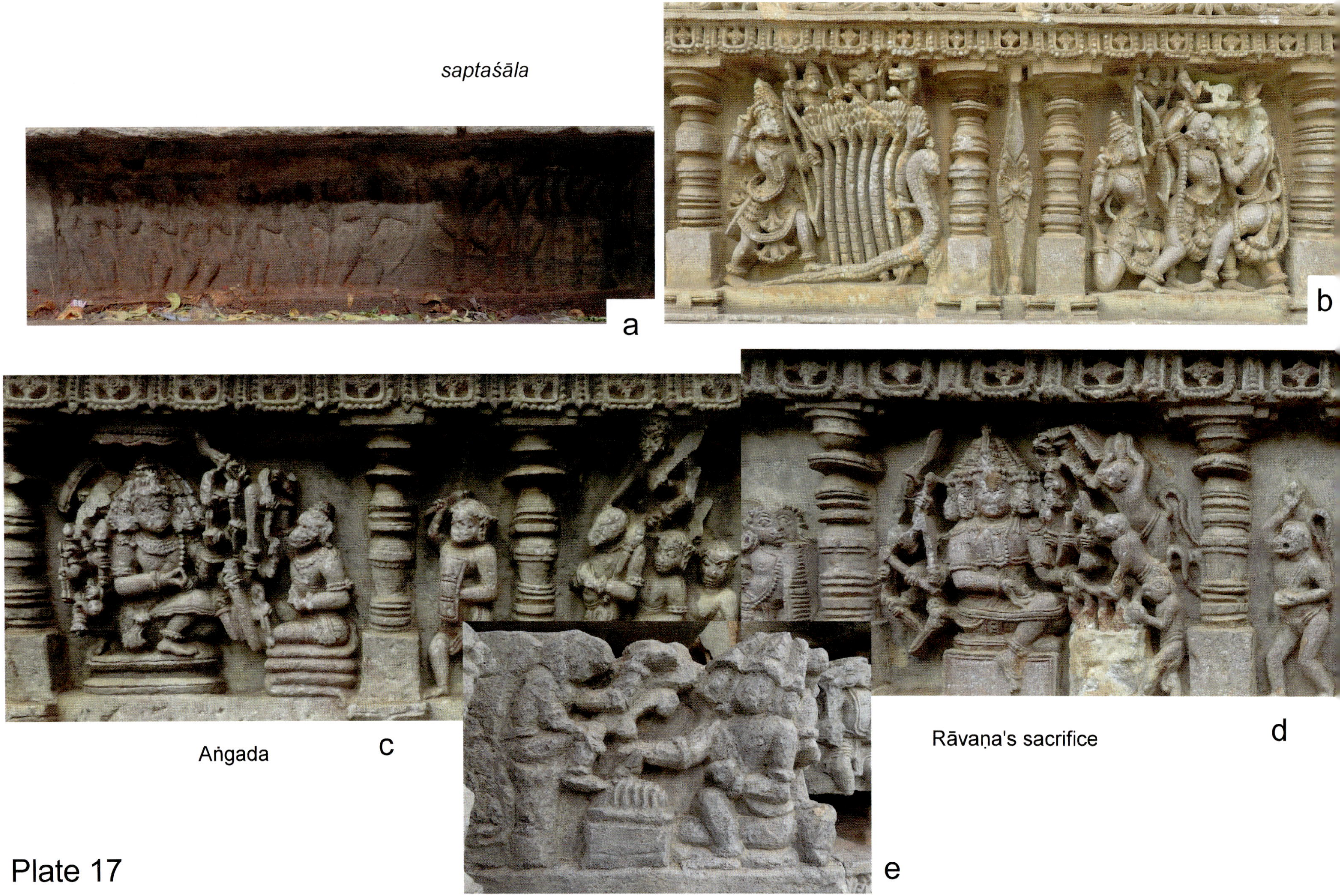

saptaśāla

a

b

Aṅgada

c

Rāvaṇa's sacrifice

d

e

Plate 17

on the Amṛteśvara his death is depicted rather symbolically. As Lakṣmaṇa cuts off Śūrpaṇakhā's nose, he simultaneously kicks at her belly and a baby Śambūka falls out (Pl. 16b). In several instances, the combat between Rāma and Khara's army precedes Śūrpaṇakhā's mutilation. This points to the versions according to which Khara is Śambūka's father. Khara's offence has then to be considered as a consequence of the killing of his son. On the (Cenna-)keśava Temple at Somnāthpur, Śūrpaṇakhā's mutilation precedes Khara's attack but still, Śambūka's death is visually connected with the attack for he is depicted next to Khara, beheaded and with blood streaming out of his neck (Pl. 16c).

Beside the killing of Śambūka, there are several other deviations from the Vālmīki Rāmāyaṇa to connect the Hoysaḷa representations with folk versions of the epic.

In almost all the Hoysaḷa representations, Rāvaṇa abducts Sītā along with a small house in which she was obviously waiting for Rāma and Lakṣmaṇa to return. According to the Tamil Irāmāvatāram, Brahmā once pronounced a curse, as a result of which Rāvaṇa could not touch the wife of another. Rāvaṇa thus has to abduct Sītā together with a block of earth.[356] This is also the case in the Telugu poems *Saṅkshepa Ramayanamu*, *Lankā Yāgamu*, *Sīta Agni Praveśamu* and *Lankā Sārathi*.[357] The block of earth is not depicted in Hoysaḷa representations. Anyway, the basic idea was probably the same. Rāvaṇa lifts Sītā in a small house, for example, on the Amṛteśvara (Pl. 16d). He might set it aside to fight with Jaṭāyu before he resumes his flight, as seen on the Kedāreśvara (Pl. 16e).

Another pecularity is the presence of a snake in the course of the *saptaśāla* event. According to Vālmīki, Rāma pierces the seven *śāla* trees in order to proof his strength to Sugrīva but it is not stated that these trees grow on the back of a snake. Earlier representations of Rāma piercing the *śāla* trees, like the one on the Upper Śivālaya at Bādāmi (Cāḷukya, Pl. 10d), that on the southern front porch wall of the Kailāsanātha at Ellora (Rāṣṭrakūṭa, Pl. 11c: detail) or on the Kāmākṣi Temple at Dharmapuri (Noḷamba, Pl. 17a) correspond to Vālmīki's version. In Hoysaḷa representa-tions by contrast, the trees grow on the back of a snake. This is in accordance with the Kambar Rāmāyaṇa.[358] The images additionally add some details. By placing his foot on the end of the snake's tail, Rāma stretches the snake and alignes the trees. The Hoysaḷas frequently also combine the *sapta-śāla* with the fight between Vālin and Sugrīva. On the Hoysaḷeśvara Temple for example, Rāma's arrow pierces first the seven trees, then the snake's neck and finally Vālin (Pl. 14b,d). On the Amṛteśvara by contrast, the *saptaśāla* event and Vālin's death are treatet individually (Pl. 17b).

In some images Ahalyā emerges out of a boulder, while in others there is no boulder depicted. On the Mallikārjuna (Pl. 15b) and on the (Cenna-)keśava at Somnāthpur, Rāvaṇa is present at Sītā's *svayamvara*. He stands aside as Rāma breaks the bow and Sītā brings the garland of flowers. Rāvaṇa is present according to the Padma Purāṇa, Ānanda Rāmāyaṇa and Torave Rāmāyaṇa. According to these versions, he tries to break the bow, too, but fails.[359] On the Amṛteśvara, Aṅgada sits on his coiled tail as described for example in the Ānanda Rāmāyaṇa (Pl. 17c). Additionally, the representations of Rāvaṇa performing a sacrifice follow a regional tradition. Rāvaṇa's sacrifice is mentioned in the Kannada Pampa Rāmāyaṇa[360] as well as in the Telugu Bhāskara and Raṅganātha Rāmāyaṇas and in the Telugu folk poems Lankā Yāgamu and Lankā Sārathi.[361] The sacrifice is interrupted by the monkeys just like in case of Indrajit's sacrifice. The destruction of Rāvaṇa's sacrifice is illustrated for example on the Amṛteśvara (Pl. 17d) and on the Kedāreśvara, in an unfinished carving (Pl. 17e).

Vijayanagara, Nāyaka: Karnataka, Andhra Pradesh and Tamil Nadu

There are also a few extensive Rāmāyaṇa representations from the Vijayanagaras. Well known are the sets of panels within the **Rāmacandra Temple** Complex at Hampi, most likely a royal foundation by Devarāya I (1406-22 CE).[362]

The first series is located on the inner face of the enclosure walls.[363] The narration begins on the inner east face of the north gateway and covers the whole area up tothe east gateway. Unfortunately, some panels are partly obscured by a later addition, the northeast columned hall (sa. *maṇḍapa*). The panels are arranged in five rows,

356 Nagar 2008 I, p. 351.
357 Rao 1984, pp. 77f.
358 Nagar 2008 I, p. 396.
359 Loizeau 2017, p. 230.
360 ibid, pp. 266f.
361 Rao 1984, pp. 91f., 102.
362 Dallapiccola et al. 1992, pp. 17ff.
363 Identification of scenes: ibid., pp. 86ff., figs. 74-114.

with an additional panel beneath the last panel of the first row. The north gateway is on the inner east face sculptured with the Śravana Kumara story in five scenes. As already on the Mallikārjuna Temple at Basrāḷ, the story serves as a prologue to the Rāmāyaṇa. Thereafter, the story reads from bottom to top and from left to right. Only the uppermost row gives the events from right to left, with the effect that the story again ends at the north gateway. The Bālakāṇḍa opens with a representation of Ṛṣyaśṛṅga and thereafter Daśaratha's sacrifice. In contrast to the Kṛṣṇa Temple's representations, the sage is depicted with his deer head and single horn. A total of 100 panels give an extensive representation of the Rāmāyaṇa, an entire cycle with scenes from all *kāṇḍas*, except for the seventh. The narration ends with a depiction of the enthroned couple of Rāma and Sītā, followed by a depiction of Viṣṇu on Śeṣa. Thus, Rāma's divine nature is emphasised.

A second series of Rāmāyaṇa panels is located on the outer faces of the principle shrine's columned hall (sa. *maṇḍapa*). The narration proceeds clockwise around the structure, in three ascending rows. 108 panels illustrate about 40 events from the epic.[364] The story opens on the north side of the shrine's west wall, in contrast to the cycle on the enclosure walls not with the Śravana Kumara story but with two conversation situations. Dallapiccola states that according to local tradition, the first panel depicts the Kannada poet Pampa together with king Devarāya. The figures of the second panel may be identified as Vaśiṣṭha and Daśaratha. Thereafter, Ṛṣyaśṛṅga, with single-horned deer head, pours the oblation into the sacrificial fire. Agni[365] emerges from the flames and hands over the heavenly *pāyasa* to Daśaratha. Six of the seven *kāṇḍas* are represented on the principle shrine's *maṇḍapa*. As Dallapiccola notes, the placement of the panels seems to follow a coordinated sculptural programme. The *kāṇḍas* begin and end at the monument's doorways and within the *kāṇḍas* relationships between the narration and the building layout can be observed.[366] Out of three circumambula-tions in total, the Bāla and Araṇyakāṇḍa each cover a ¾ circumambulation, the Kiṣkindhā and Sundarakāṇḍa each half a circumambulation, while the Ayodhyā and Yuddhakāṇḍa make up only ¼ of a round. The last Rāmāyaṇa scene on the principle shrine's *maṇḍapa* shows Rāma and Sītā enthroned in Ayodhyā, on the south side of the west wall. Still, the narration doesn't end here.

17 scenes from the Uttarakāṇḍa[367] are included in two rows of panels on the walls of the minor shrine's original structures. These structures consist of two sanctuaries (sa. *garbhagṛhas*) and a rectangular antechamber (sa. *antarāla*). On the east side, the panels are partly obscured by a later structure, the columned hall (sa. *maṇḍapa*). The first scene on the south side depicts Sītā's banishment. Lakṣmaṇa is shown escorting her to Vālmīki's hermitage. Further scenes deal with Lava and Kuśa's education, Rāma's horse sacrifice (sa. *aśvamedha*), Lava and Kuśa battling with Rāma's army, their departure for Ayodhyā and meeting with Rāma. The final scenes depict Sītā going back to earth and then Lakṣmaṇa and Rāma leaving their earthly forms. Again, the cycle closes with a representation of Viṣṇu on Śeṣa on the northern sanctuary's northwestern corner.

Apart from the narrative representations, isolated Rāmāyaṇa scenes appear on the outer walls of the principle shrine's original structures and as additional scenes beneath the minor shrine's wall panels. These representations include an image of Hanumān carrying the mountain of medicinal herbs towards the wounded Lakṣmaṇa – an event which is omitted in the cycle.

The latest extensive Rāmāyaṇa series in South India is found on the southern towered gateway (sa. *gopura*) of a temple at Hampi known as the **Old Śiva Temple**, though actually viṣṇuite. The temple is situated northeast of the Viṭhṭhala Temple and dates to the end of the 15th or beginning of the 16th century CE.[368] The events are given on 131 panels set in four rows all around the *gopura* and its entryway chambers.[369] There are no prologue scenes as in case of the Rāmacandra's series. The narration opens directly with Daśaratha's sacrifice. All *kāṇḍas* up to the Yuddhakāṇḍa have been taken into account, whereby the events of the Bāla, Kiṣkindhā and Yuddhakāṇḍa are depicted especially elaborate. This is surprising because the Yuddhakāṇḍa is dealt with only a few scenes in both the Rāmacandra's series. Another peculiarity is that the cycle closes with the battle between Rā-

364 Identification of scenes: Dallapiccola et al. 1992, pp. 93ff., figs. 117-148.

365 According to the Vālmīki Rāmāyaṇa a sacrrificial spirit (sa. *yajñapuruṣa*) emerges from the flames whereas in many of the Kannada and Telugu folk songs the fire god hands over the divine food (sa. *pāyasa*): Rao 1984, pp. 58f.

366 Dallapiccola et al. 1992, pp. 91ff.

367 Identification of scenes: ibid, pp. 97f., figs. 166-172/173.

368 Dallapiccola 1994, p. 71.

369 Identification of scenes: Dallapiccola and Verghese 1991, pp. 143ff.

Vijayanagara: Rāmacandra Temple Complex

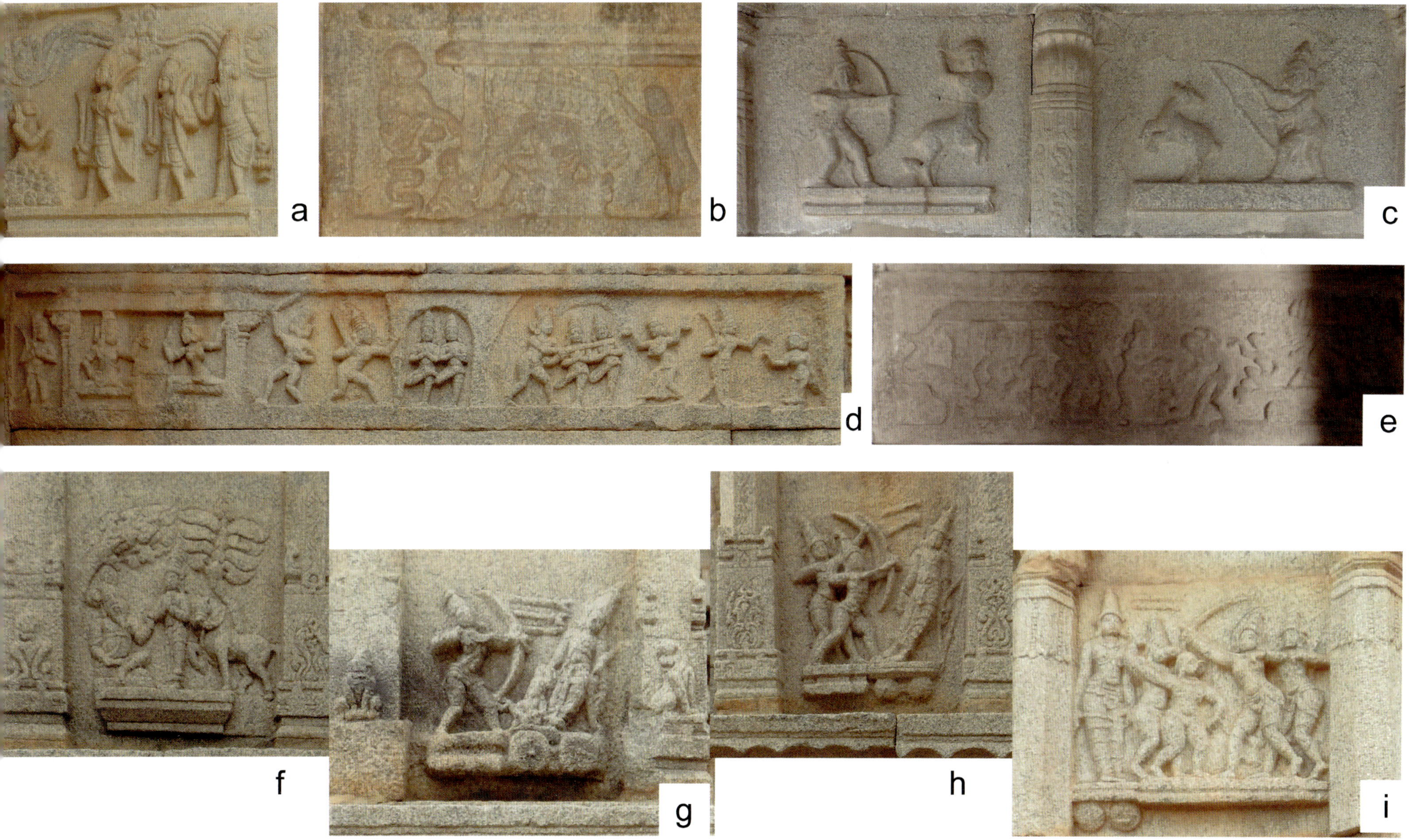

b,d,e: Cycle on the Enclosure Walls
a,c,f-i:Cycle on both Shrines

Plate 18

ma and Rāvaṇa. However, additional scenes like Rāvaṇa's death or Rāma's coronation might have been depicted on the now missing lintels and superstructure.

The Vijayanaraga representations of the Rāmāyaṇa are based upon local renditions, too. This becomes apparent in images like Ahalyā emerging from a heap of boulders on the Rāmacandra Temple's principal shrine (Pl. 18a) and the presence of the snake in the *saptaśāla* event in all three series.[370] All three cycles have also a representation of Hanumān sitting on his coiled tail before Rāvaṇa (Pl. 18b), as already seen on the Virūpākṣa Temple at Paṭṭadakal and on the Kailāsanātha Temple at Ellora. A novelty are the representations of Rāma apparently trying to capture the golden deer with his bow before he kills it (Pl. 18c). Additionally, the cycle on the Rāmacandra Temple's enclosure walls includes a representation of Lakṣmaṇa inadvertently beheading Śūrpaṇakhā's son and another ascetic (Pl. 18d) and what is most interesting with regard to the Kṛṣṇa Temple's representations, it seems that Lakṣmaṇa draws protective lines onto the earth before he leaves Sītā (Pl. 18e). Also the sequence from the Uttarakāṇḍa is clearly influenced by local renditions. Several scenes depict events which are not found in Vālmīki's Rāmāyaṇa. On the west face, lower row, the sacrificial horse is shown at Vālmīki's hermitage (Pl. 18f) and on the north face, lower row, as well as on the south face, upper row, battle scenes are included (Pl. 18g-i). These depict Lava and Kuśa fighting against Śatrughna, then Bharata and finally against Lakṣmaṇa, Hanumān and Jāmbavān. These representations are in accordance with the events as described in Telugu and Kannada poems.[371] In the Telugu poem 'Kuśalavula Yuddhamu', Lava notices a letter tied to a horse. He accepts Rāma's challenge and the battle begins. As depicted, Śatrughna gets defeated first, then Bharata and Lakṣmaṇa. Likewise, in the Kannada poem 'Sītā Vanavāsada Hādu', Lava and Kuśa capture the sacrificial horse and defeat everyone including Rāma. The battle of Lava and Kuśa is further described in the Kannada poem Lava Kuśara Kāḷaga. According to the Sampūrna Rāmāyaṇa, Lava and Kuśa defeat only Rāma and Lakṣmaṇa. The horse sacrifice is not mentioned. It comes to combat as Rāma and Lakṣmaṇa go out hunting and Lava and Kuśa tie the horse.

After the Vijayanagara period, complete Rāmāyaṇa series in stone are no longer found in South India. On the other hand, the theme grew in popularity with painters in the 17th and 18th centuries CE. Murals decorate the walls and ceilings of some of the most important temples in Tamil Nadu, Karnataka and Kerala. In North India, Rāmāyaṇa themes again gained in importance with sculptors in the course of the revival of Hindu temple architecture.

Muslim Period: West Bengal and Bangladesh

Among the medieval North Indian representations, the depictions on terracotta and scarcely stucco panels decorating the Bengali brick temples from the early 17th century CE onwards are especially charming. With the rule of Sultan Hussain Shah (1493-1519 CE) a new era began for Bengal, ushering in peace and prosperity.[372] As a result of the tolerance of the Sultan, Hinduism was revived by the vaiṣṇava preachings of Śrī Chaitanya (1487-1533 CE). The Mughal governors thereafter followed Hussain Shah's secular policy. Hindus reached high positions in civil and military administration and, reassured of a social tranquility, again began to build temples, which they embellished with terracotta decoration. Important events, such as the final battle between Rāma and Rāvaṇa, are frequently pictured, often on large scale and in a prominent place. Shorter sequences as well as extended ones are also found and in some cases even the entire story is depicted, from beginning til end. Extensive are for example the representations at the **Kantanagar Temple**, district Dinajpur of present-day Bangladesh. The temple was built in the early 18th century CE. Its third base-frieze displays about 50 scenes from the Rāmāyaṇa.[373] On the south face it covers in clockwise manner the events from Daśaratha's sacrifice and the birth of his sons up to the return of the brothers to Ayodhyā after their marriage at Mithilā. The story proceeds in counterclockwise manner on the temple's east face with the events from Mantharā's intrigue up to a

370 Only five trees are depicted in the Old Śiva's representation. Illustration: Dallapiccola and Verghese 1991, Pl. 109. On the Rāmacandra's enclosure wall the trees are placed alternately before and behind the snake instead of emerging out of its body. Illustration: Dallapiccola et al. 1992, fig. 104. Whereas the Hoysaḷas mostly combined the *saptaśāla* event with the fight between Vālin and Sugrīva, the Vijayanagaras again treat these two events individually.

371 Rao 1984, pp. 108ff.

372 Haque 2007, pp. 51ff.

373 Identification of scenes: Ahmed 1990, pp. 33ff. south face and 41ff. east face.

depiction of Rāma worshipping Durgā, followed by three out-of-sequence panels with Tārā, incensed on account of Vālin's murder and the army crossing the sea. In addition to this, the inner corridor has scenes like a monkey sitting on his coiled tail higher than Rāvaṇa, Lakṣmaṇa mortally wounded and Hanumān bringing the mountain of medicinal herbs.[374] The battle of Laṅkā is represented twice, firstly on the inner wall of the west corridor and again on the large spandrels over the arches of the temple's north face.[375]

The terracottas of Bengal require further analysis in the future. What concerns the Rāmāyaṇa depictions, some of the scenes that occur repeatedly have been illustrated by Haque.[376] These include Daśaratha's sacrifice, the marriage of Rāma and Sītā, Jaṭāyu trying to prevent Sītā's abduction, Rāvaṇa's court, Kumbhakarṇa devouring the monkeys, the battle between Rāma and Rāvaṇa, Rāvaṇa praising Rāma and finally Rāma and Sītā reunited. Many more events were however included in the representations. The clay panels of the 1758 **Rādhāśyāma Temple** at Bishnupur for example include the pursuit of the golden deer, Mārīca praising Rāma at the point of death, Rāvaṇa approaching Sītā in the guise of a mendicant, Sītā's abduction, Jaṭāyu trying to stop Rāvaṇa, Jaṭāyu reporting to Rāma and Lakṣmaṇa, the search for Sītā, Hanumān approaching Rāma and Lakṣmaṇa (or Rāma and Lakṣmaṇa brought before Sugrīva?), the fight between Vālin and Sugrīva, Vālin's death, the consultation with Sugrīva, the construction of the causeway, the battle between Rāma and Rāvaṇa as well as additional battle scenes and a few out-of-sequence scenes such as Sītā guarded by demonesses, Hanumān handing over Rāma's ring, Rāvaṇa banishing Vibhīṣaṇa and Vibhīṣaṇa changing sides.

374 Ahmed 1990, p. 54.
375 ibid., pp. 93, 98f.
376 Haque 2014, pp. 108f.

The Bengali representations also follow local renditions rather than Vālmīki. This is most apparent in the images depicting Rāvaṇa standing before Rāma with joined palms, seen for example at the Cārbāṅglā Temple at Baranagar, district Murshidabad.[377] There is no mention of Rāvaṇa praising Rāma in the Vālmīki Rāmāyaṇa but according to Kṛttivāsi, he does so.[378] As Rāvaṇa becomes aware that Rāma is Viṣṇu, he declares himself a slave at his feet and begs for forgiveness.

It was mentioned that at the Kantanagar Temple, Rāma is depicted praising Durgā. Durgā is of special importance for the Bengali tradition. According to the Kṛttivāsi Rāmāyaṇa, it is only by her grace that Rāma is able to defeat Rāvaṇa.[379] Rāma worships her for several days. Finally, he wants to please her by offering her 108 blue lotuses. As one lotus is missing, he decides to offer one of his lotus-eyes instead. Durgā intervenes and gratefully bestows on him the boon that now, he will be able to kill Rāvaṇa. Other Bengali representations refer to Durgā's role in the killing of Rāvaṇa by including a figure of Durgā Mahiṣāsuramardini in the representation of the final battle between Rāma and Rāvaṇa. This is the case for example on the 19th century Mejotaraf Temple of Hadal-Nārāyanpur, district Bankura (Pl. 19).

377 Illustration: Haque 2014, Pl. 134.
378 Nagar and Nagar 1997 II, pp. 197ff.
379 ibid., pp. 185ff.

McCutchion has drawn attention to a representation of Hanumān carrying Durgā, Rāma and Lakṣmaṇa on the Chhototaraf Temple of Hadal-Nārāyanpur (early 19th c. CE), however without providing an interpretation.[380] According to Kṛttivāsi, Rāvaṇa has a son in the netherworld, named Mahīrāvaṇa.[381] Mahīrāvaṇa is not mentioned in the Vālmīki Rāmāyaṇa. In the Kṛttivāsi Rāmāyaṇa, he kidnaps Rāma and Lakṣmaṇa as Rāvaṇa has no one else left to fight for him. Mahīrāvaṇa intends to sacrifice Rāma and Lakṣmaṇa to Durgā but Hanumān follows them to the nether-world and rescues Rāma and Lakṣmaṇa. Following the advice of Durgā, Hanumān tricks Mahīrāvaṇa and kills him. Hanumān brings back Rāma and Lakṣmaṇa and also rescues Durgā out of the nether-world. It is exactly this moment that is represented on large scale (Pl. 20). Hanumān carries the throne of Durgā with her as Mahiṣāsuramardini and two attendants. The diminutive figures of Rāma and Lakṣmaṇa rest on Hanumān's shoulders. In the lower part of the image, Hanumān is depicted again, in his killing of Mahīrāvaṇa who was asked to demonstrate how to bow down before the goddess.

Some minor observations in connection with region-specific adaptations are the following: Firstly, it was mentioned that at the Kantanagar Temple a monkey is depicted sitting on his coiled tail higher than Rāvaṇa. Contrary to Ahmed's interpretations (he takes him to be Hanumān), this has to be Aṅgada who thus offends Rāvaṇa's pride in the Ānanda Rāmāyaṇa[382] as well as in

380 McCutchion 1972 (1967), p. 28.
381 Nagar and Nagar 1997 II, pp. 159ff.
382 Nagar 2006 I, p. 137.

Mejotaraf Temple,
Hadal-Nārāyanpur

Plate 19

Chhototaraf Temple,
Hadal-Nārāyanpur

All Hadal-Nārāyanpur pictures by Manojit Pal

Plate 20

the Kṛttivāsi Rāmāyaṇa.[383] Secondly, the representation of Rāvaṇa banishing Vibhīṣaṇa at the Rādhāśyāma Temple (illustration below) is also interesting, for Rāvaṇa is depicted pushing Vibhīṣaṇa away with three of his hands. This might also follow some regional version based on the medieval recensions according to which Rāvaṇa kicks Vibhīṣaṇa with his feet. Lastly, the fact that the snake is again missing in the representation of Rāma piercing the seven trees on the Kantanagar Temple[384] is also in accordance with the event as described in medieval North Indian renditions of the story, such as the Kṛttivāsi Rāmāyaṇa.[385] Whereas this alteration is immensely popular in South India, it seems to have found no favour with North Indian poets.

It has to be mentioned that also in North India, the Indian epics became highly popular with painters from the 16th century CE onwards. Whereas in South India the events were captured in expressive murals, for the North Indian tradition of painting the epics illustrated manuscripts are of special importance. The paintings from those manuscripts are also important with regard to the Kṛṣṇa Temple's representations, for they allow for a few additional remarks on one particular region-specific characteristic, namely Rāvaṇa's horse head.

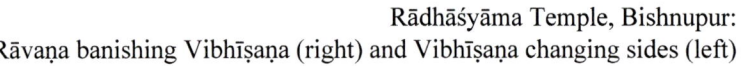

Rādhāśyāma Temple, Bishnupur:
Rāvaṇa banishing Vibhīṣaṇa (right) and Vibhīṣaṇa changing sides (left)

Excursus one: Rāvaṇa's horse head

Before going into detail, a few prelimenary remarks will be given on the manuscripts. The earliest illustrated Rāmāyaṇa manuscript was not produced for a Hindu patron but for the great Mughal emperor Akbar.[386] Akbar aimed at removing the ignorance and the antagonism between different faiths by popularising the principal texts of each religion. In 1589 CE the first Persian translation of the Rāmāyaṇa was completed by Abdul Qadir Badaoni with 120 sheets. A second imperial manuscript was completed only seven months later, in late 1589 CE, though it is suggested that its illustration was not completed for at least three years after that.[387] The manuscript is preserved today in the Maharaja Sawai Man Singh II Museum in Jaipur. The **Jaipur Rāmāyaṇa** is of immense importance for it is the earliest extant Rāmāyaṇa manuscript that is comprehensively illustrated. It consists of 365 folios with 176 miniatures rendering the principal events of the epic. While the name of the scribe is not mentioned, the names of the painters are given. As noted by Das, four of the books, the Bāla, Ayodhyā, Yuddha and Uttarakāṇḍa, have more miniatures than the other three, which suggests that court and battle scenes were particularly favoured. Only select paintings have been published but among them is one which is of particular importance for this study. It depicts Rāvaṇa tumbling inside his palace, surrounded by demons, with Hanumān snatching away his crown.[388] The painting was designed by Jagan who shows Rāvaṇa with nine human heads and

383 Nagar and Nagar 1997 II, pp. 18f.
384 Illustration: Ahmed 1990, Ph. 26.
385 Nagar and Nagar 1997 I, p. 196.

386 Das 1994, pp. 73ff.
387 Seyller 1994, p. 87.
388 Illustration: Das 1994, fig. 8.

one donkey or horse head. This is the earliest Indian painting known to me which depicts Rāvaṇa in this way. At the same time however, painters also continued to depict Rāvaṇa with ten human heads. In a painting by Kesav Kalan of the same manuscript for example, with Śuka and Sāraṇa informing Rāvaṇa, the demon king is depicted with ten human heads in a row.[389]

Soon, nobles and merchants also commissioned paintings on their own, evocative of the paintings developed in the imperial Mughal atelier. The most important of the sub-imperial Mughal manuscripts is the one commissioned by Akbar's chief commander, Abd Al-Rahim.[390] The manuscript is kept save in the Freer Gallery of Art, Washington, D.C, and therefore commonly referred to as the **Freer Rāmāyaṇa**. The Freer Rāmāyaṇa consists of 349 folios with originally 135 paintings, of which 130 are extant today. It was completed probably in 1605 CE, as the date on folio 333b suggests. The manuscript is currently not on view but fortunately all the paintings, together with Abd Al-Rahim's flyleaf inscription, can be viewed online in two volumes.[391] Although this manuscript was modelled on the imperial manuscript, there is no image in it, in which Rāvaṇa's tenth head is that of a horse or a donkey.

The finest Rāmāyaṇa manuscript produced for a Hindu ruler, is at the same time the earliest and most extensive extant of its kind. It was produced for Jagat Siṅgh I of Mewar (r. 1628-1652 CE), at the court of Udaipur. The **Mewar Rāmāyaṇa** was begun in 1649 CE. Only four books were completed during Jagat Siṅgh's reign, the Bāla, Ayodhyā, Araṇya and Yuddhakāṇḍa.[392] Jagat Siṅgh died in Oktober 1652 and his son ans successor, Rāj Siṅgh, was less interested in painting and manuscript production. The Uttarakāṇḍa was completed in May 1653 and the Kiṣkindhākāṇḍa in the month of September of the same year. As Losty writes, already the last paintings of the Uttarakāṇḍa were hastily finished while the Kiṣkindhākāṇḍa additionally bears evidence of erroneous collation, often lacks canto colophons and has unfinished paintings, too. Of the Sundarakāṇḍa only 18 paintings survive. Losty assumes that it may have been not sufficently far advanced when Jagat Siṅgh died and Rāj Siṅgh therefore simply abandoned it. The whole work consists today of 721 folios and 418 paintings, with a focus on the first and last two books of the epic. Again, it appears that court and battle scenes most attracted the painters. The number of surviving paintings of the individual books is, in correct order, 78, 68, 36, 34, 18, 90 and 94. The Mewar Rāmāyaṇa was split and today some parts are preserved in India, in the CSMVS Museum and a private collection, both in Mumbai, as well as in the Rajasthan Oriental Research Institute in Jodhpur and in the Baroda Museum, while other parts are preserved in the British Library in the UK. Fortunately, a large part of the Mewar Rāmāyaṇa was digitally reunited and can be viewed online since 2014.[393] The online version includes 377 of the surviving 418 paintings. The Araṇyakāṇḍa is missing. Interestingly, in one painting of the Sundarakāṇḍa with Hanumān perching on a tree as Rāvaṇa visits Sītā in the Aśoka grove, Rāvaṇa is again depicted with nine human heads and a donkey head on top.[394] Strikingly, of the 377 paintings that are online, this is the only painting in which Rāvaṇa is depicted this way. By contrast, in another painting of the Kiṣkindhākāṇḍa with Hanumān brought captive before Rāvaṇa, as well as in all the paintings from the Yuddhakāṇḍa, Rāvaṇa is shown with ten human heads in two rows.

Only two examples of Rāvaṇa with a horse or donkey head can be given for the mentioned works. Anyway, they mark an important turn in the way of representing Rāvaṇa. From now on, the horse/donkey head becomes a common characteristic of the demon king and countless illustrations of Rāvaṇa with a horse or donkey head are found in Northwest and Central Indian paintings. Among others, this is apparent from the numerous suchlike paintings of the National Museum in New Delhi. Several have been published. These are paintings from Uttar Pradesh, Malwa style, dateable to the mid-17th to mid-18th c. CE,[395] Rajasthani paintings, Alwar and Bikaner style, from the late 18th century CE,[396] Central Indian paintings from Bundelkhand and Raghogarh, from the late 18th to early 19th century CE,[397] Pahari paintings,

389 Illustration: Das 1994, fig. 5.
390 Seyller 1994, pp. 85ff.
391 The Ramayana (Tales of Rama; The Freer Ramayana), Volumes 1 and 2, Freer | Sackler www.freersackler.si.edu/object/F1907.271.1-172/ and www.freersackler.si.edu/object/F1907.271.173-346/

392 Losty, J.P., The Mewar Rāmāyaṇa Manuscripts, pp. 16ff. Published online: www.bl.uk/ramayana

393 www.bl.uk/ramayana
394 Illustration: www.bl.uk/ramayana (Bk 5 fol. 3r)
395 Daljeet and Mathur 2015, pp. 109, 133f., 146.
396 ibid., pp. 44, 63.
397 ibid., pp. 152f.

Guler and Kangra style, from the same span[398] and a mid-19th century Kashmiri painting.[399]

Rāvaṇa with a horse or donkey head is thus omnipresent in Northwest and Central Indian illustrations from the 17th century CE onwards. It was mentioned before that, what concerns literary tradition, Rāvaṇa's horse head is known only in Tibetan versions of the Rāmāyaṇa, where it is of special importance for the story, and that the earliest literary reference is found in the Dunhuang version (787-848 CE).[400] It was also established that in Nepal, Rāvaṇa is depicted with an additional horse head at least from the late 16th century CE onwards, whereby he is either shown with nine human heads and a horse head on top, or with only one human head topped with the horse head.[401] Now, this last form of representing Rāvaṇa is also found in a few earlier Indian representa-tions of Rāvaṇa. Several **Pratihāra** steles of Rāvaṇa shaking Mount Kailāsa show Rāvaṇa with a human head crowned with that of a horse or a donkey. One such sculpture is housed in the Allahabad Museum and was published by Sharma in his article on the theme.[402] Kala notices the horse/donkey head in another Pratihāra sculpture,[403] which was published in the Annual Report of the Seattle Art Museum, 1967.[404] Both the sculptures are dated to the 9th century CE approximately. A third Pratihāra sculpture of Rāvaṇa shaking Mount Kailāsa is housed in the National Museum, New Delhi. Again, Rāvaṇa is depicted with one human head crowned with that of a horse or a donkey.[405]

The National Museum additionally houses an image which reveals that the tradition of Rāvaṇa's horse/donkey head goes back even further. It is a fregmentary 5th century **Gupta** terracotta with Rāvaṇa, presumably approaching Sītā in the guise of a mendicant. Here, too, Rāvaṇa's human head (in this context indeed only one) is topped with that of a horse or a donkey, marking his true demonic nature.[406] The donkey head is not found in South Indian representations.

Only the Gupta terracotta predates the literary Tibetan sources but still it is clear that the idea of Rāvaṇa's horse/donkey head first evolved in North India. The Pratihāra steles date from about the same time as the earliest Tibetan references. Since the Kathmandu Valley lies across the important trade route that always linked India with Tibet, it can be assumed that the horse head was known in Nepal, too, already at that early period. However, the earliest known Nepalese representations of Rāvaṇa with a horse or donkey head have been assigned to probably the late 16th century CE and are thus contemporary with the earliest North Indian manuscript paintings. The Nepali representations were probably influenced by the growing popularity of this iconographic feature in both Tibetan and North Indian sources.

According to a note in the Critical Edition of the Rāmāyaṇa, Rāvaṇa's brother Khara is represented as a donkey in some folk Rāmāyaṇa traditions, which is probably because *khara* also means *ass*.[407] No explanation can be given for Kumbhakarṇa's additional animal head, which is found, apparently exclusively but repeatedly, in Nepalese representations.

398 Daljeet and Mathur 2015, pp. 145, 154f.
399 ibid., p. 49.
400 V. supra, p. 57.
401 V. supra, pp. 146ff.
402 Sharma 1973, fig. 6.
403 Kala 1988, p. 39.

404 Seattle Art Museum, "1967 Annual Report: 62nd Year Seattle Art Museum," *Seattle Art Museum Libraries: Digital Collections*, https://samlibraries.omeka.net/items/show/43.
405 Sivaramamurti 1974, fig. 57.
406 ibid., fig. 56.

407 Goldman 1991: Vol. III, note to 3.17.25.

4.2. Narrative Representations of the Mahābhārata

While at least two other comparable narrative representations of the Rāmāyaṇa exist in Nepal, there are no such representations of the Mahābhārata known to me. Therefore, this passage deals exclusively with representations from India and Bangladesh.

Gupta: Northern India and Bangladesh

No Gupta representations are known to me either, which would lead to believe that there were narrative representations from that time, depicting the Mahābhārata as a whole. However, series of panels depicting select episodes have been found. For example, four panels depicting the story of Sunda and Upasunda, isolated from its context, have been found at **Deogarh** (5th c. CE).[408] The story is included in the Arjunavanavāsaparva of the Ādiparva, told by Nārada as he advises the Pāṇḍavas to lay down a rule regarding their common wife (Mbh 1.16. 200ff.). Sunda and Upasunda are two demon brothers, incapable of being slain by anyone, except each other. After they have subjugated the three worlds, Brahmā sends the beautiful Tilottamā. The two brothers dispute about her and in the end strike down each other with their clubs. Both of them die. The first panel depicts Sunda and Upasunda, having established themselves in the worlds; the second scene shows them together with Tilottamā; the third one depicts them fighting with clubs; and the last panel shows both of them, lying dead on the ground.

408 Vats 1999 (1952), p. 23f. with illustrations: Pl. XX (a)-(c)

Noteworthy are also the representations on one of the *maṇḍapa* pillars found at **Rajaona** (Bihar), presently kept save in the Indian Museum, Kolkata. The architectural remains from that site are dateable to the 6th century CE. All four faces of the respective pillar were sculptured but only three faces remain intact. Illustrated is the story of Arjuna and the *kirāta*.[409] The first face shows Arjuna leaving for Indrakīla and his consequent penance. The second scene is missing but certainly dealt with Arjuna and the *kirāta* shooting simultaneously at the boar. The next scene depicts them wrestling, while in the last one, Arjuna receives the *pāśupata* weapon. There is a deviation from Vyāsa's Mahābhārata already in these early representation of the theme. According to Loizeau, it is not Śiva who hands over the weapon but a small *gaṇa*. The *kirātārjuna* story was transmitted indepen-dantly from the epos already as early as the 6th century CE, with Bhāravi's Sanskrit Kirātārjunīya.[410] In Bhāravi's version, Śiva does not hand over any tangible object to Arjuna. Instead, he transmitts to him a *mantra* embodying the knowledge and practice of the *pāśupatāstra.* The personified *mantra* thrice circumbulates Śiva with the weapon in his hands, and then enters Arjuna like the sun entering a cloud.[411] The being seen on the Rajaona pillar is thus probably rather the personified *mantra* than a *gaṇa*.

409 Loizeau 2017, pp. 424f.

410 Dating: Peterson 2016, p. ix: "The poet appears to have flourished in South India, some time after the celebrated Kalidasa (fourth-fifth centuries C.E. and earlier than the seventh century. Ravikirti, a panegyrist of the Chalukya king Pulakeshin II, named Bharavi and Kalidasa as famous poets in an inscription of 634 C.E."

411 Peterson 2016, p. 377.

Early Cāḷukya: Karnataka

In contrast to Rāmāyaṇa representations, Mahābhārata representations from the Early Cāḷukya Era are restricted to the temples at Paṭṭadakal, namely the Virūpākṣa, Mallikārjuna and Pāpanātha Temples. While the most extensive representation of the Rāmāyaṇa is found on the exterior walls of the Pāpanātha, the most extensive representation of the Mahābhārata is sculptured on the *maṇḍapa* pillars of the earliest among these temples, the Virūpākṣa.

Not the entire epic is represented, but the **Virūpākṣa Temple** (733-44 CE) features several sequences from the Mahābhārata. The *maṇḍapa* pillars have raised cubical blocks, three of which are sculptured with representations from the Mahābhārata. The first pillar has four sculptured faces with reliefs in two compartments each, the second pillar has only three sculptured faces with single compartment reliefs, while the third pillar has again four sculptured faces with reliefs in two or three compartments. Most of these compartments, 22 in total, comprise multiple consecutive events. The events depicted on the first pillar are exclusively drawn from the Kairāta and Indralokābhigamanaparva, the events depicted on the second pillar from the Abhimanyuvadhaparva. Only the events depicted on the third pillar make up more than one sequence. The events seen in the first compartment are drawn from the Kīcakavadha and Gograhaṇaparvas, the events depicted in the second compartment come from the Bhīṣmavadhaparva while the events depicted in the third compartment show the final triumph of the Pāṇḍavas with scenes from the Hradapraveśa to the Gadāyuddhaparva. Loizeau has

Virūpākṣa Temple, Paṭṭadakal

Plate 21

published illustrations of all the relevant reliefs and she also provides an identification for most the scenes.[412] The list below includes identifications for the so far unidentified scenes and it has also some reinterpretations.

Pillar 1, *apradaksina* (Plate 21, first row):

First compartment:

- east: Arjuna is adviced to repair to the Himālayas. Arjuna practices severe asceticism. Arjuna and the *kirāta* both aim at the boar.
- north: Fight between Arjuna and the *kirāta*. Śiva gives Arjuna the *pāśupata* weapon.
- west: Varuṇa, Kubera and Yama hand over their celestial weapons. Mātali appears with Indra's chariot.
- south: Arjuna is received in Indraloka by *apsaras*. Arjuna seated on Indra's lap.

Second compartment:

- east: Fight between Arjuna and the Nivātakavacas
- north: Arjuna subdues the Nivātakavacas.
- west: Arjuna returns from battle. He pays homage to Indra and reports. Arjuna again seated on his father's lap before they bid farewell.
- south: Indra stays in heaven, surrounded by apsaras. Arjuna leaves.

Pillar 2, *pradaksina* (Plate 21, second row):

- west: -/-
- north: Jayadratha prevents the Pāṇḍavas from coming to Abhimanyu's aid.
- east: Abhimanyu has to fight the Kauravas alone.
- south: Arjuna learns of Abhimanyu's death and vows vengeance. Arjuna goes to battle.

Pillar 3, *pradaksina* (Plate 21, third row):

First compartment:

- west: Bhīma awaits Kīcaka. Fight between Bhīma and Kīcaka. Kīcaka, slain amidst his kinsmen.
- north: As the Kauravas are about to seize the cattle, Arjuna attacks.
- east: Fight between Arjuna and the Kauravas in order to retake the stolen cattle.
- south: Arjuna brings back the cattle to king Virāṭa

Second compartment:

- west: Fight between Bhīṣma and Arjuna: Kṛṣṇa (who is acting as charioteer) takes up his disc and rushes against Bhīṣma himself.
- north: Bhīṣma praises Kṛṣṇa and his life is spared, still the battle goes on.
- east: Fight between Bhīṣma and Śikhaṇḍin.
- south: Bhīṣma lies on a bed of arrows.

Third compartment:

- west: -/-
- north: Final battle between the Pāṇḍavas and the Kauravas. On the Kauravas' side someone pleads for his life, in view of the Pāṇḍavas' superiority. Another figure turns away from the battlefield.
- east: The Pāṇḍavas subdue the Kauravas. Duryodhana lies on the ground, heavily wounded.
- south: The Pāṇḍavas spot Duryodhana who is hiding in a lake. Fight with clubs between Bhīma and Duryodhana.

One of the *maṇḍapa* pillars of the **Mallikārjuna Temple** (733-44 CE) is enlivened with representations from the *kirātārjuna* story and Arjuna's visit to Indra's realm. The raised cubical block is sculptured on its western face with events from the Kairātaparva, depicted in three superimposed registers. The narration proceeds clockwise around the pillar, with the events from the Indralokābhigamanaparva, depicted on the remaining three faces, with two registers each. The last scene shows Arjuna, reunited with his brothers.[413] The same sequence is depicted on the outer walls of the **Pāpanātha Temple** (744-57 CE). The representations cover niches as well as the intervening wall spaces on the northern and eastern faces of the outer *maṇḍapa*. Nine panels in total deal with the story whereby the first scene, with Arjuna and the *kirāta* shooting simultaneously at the boar, covers three of these panels: two niches and the area in between. The narration proceeds clockwise and finally culminates in a panel on the northern front porch pillar with a depiction of Arjuna defeating the Nivātakavacas.[414] The Mahābhārata representations on both the temples, the Mallikārjuna and the Pāpanātha as well, focus exclusively on two *upaparvas* of the Vanaparva, namely the Kairāta- and Indralokābhigamanaparva, and thus deal exclusively with Arjuna's encounter with the *kirāta* and his consecutive visit to Indra's realm.

412 Loizeau 2017, pp. 371ff.

413 Identification of scenes: Loizeau 2017, pp. 374, 378.

414 Identification of scenes: ibid., pp. 378f. On page 378 Loizeau illustrates two panels from the east face.
The scene on the front porch pillar is illustrated by Wechsler 1994, p. 35, fig. 9.

Ellora

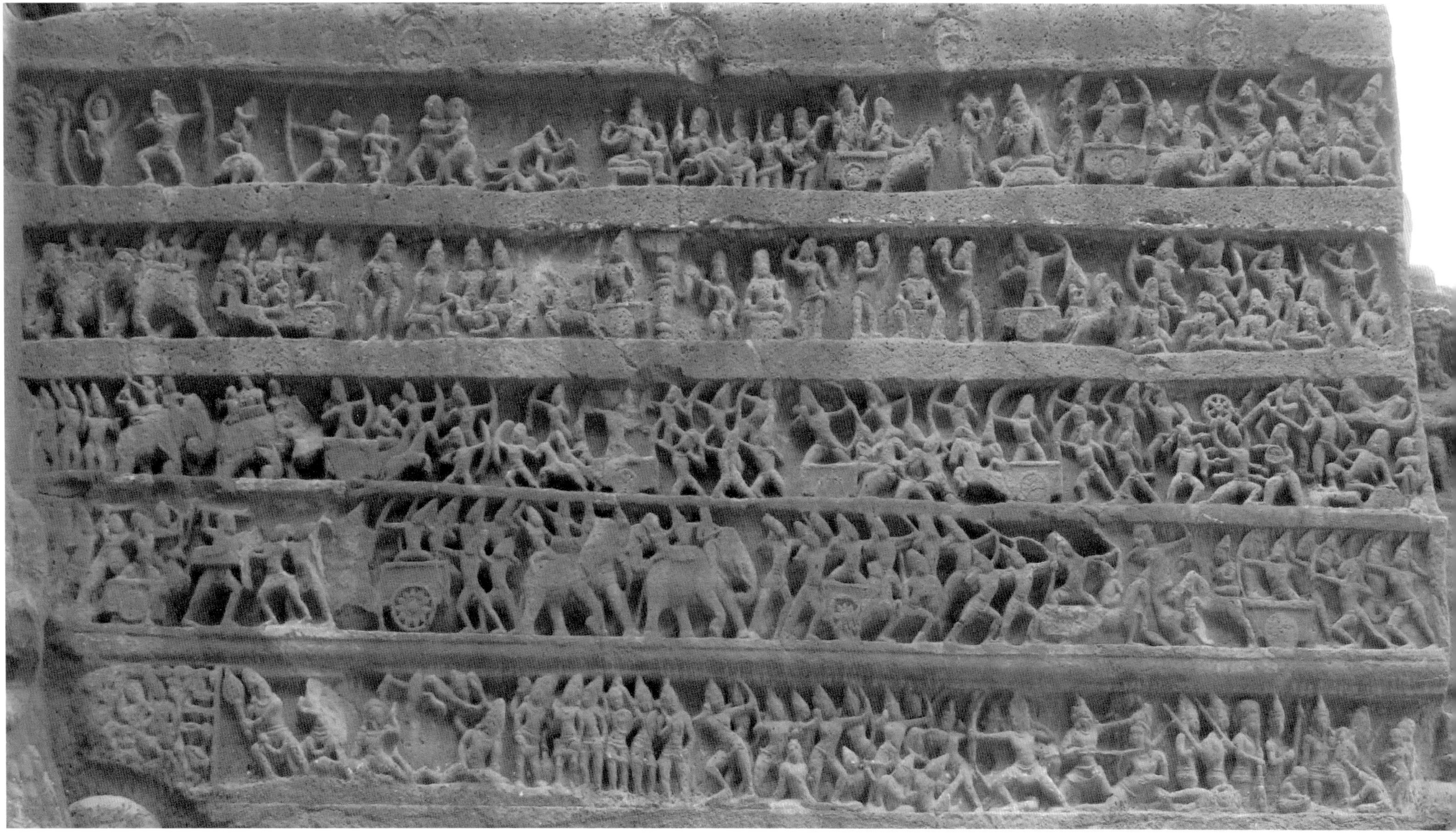

Plate 22

The Early Cāḷukyan representations, at least those dealing with the *kirātārjuna* story, again point to a local version of the story. As also according to the Critical Edition (Mbh 3.40), Pārvatī accompanies Śiva in the attire of a *kirātī* in all three representations. As an addition however, she also holds her baby boy in all three representations and one or two dogs appear on scene. According to Bhāravi, Śiva is accompanied by Skanda but the latter appears as a grown-up at the head of Śiva's army.[415] A more significant change is Arjuna's triumph over Śiva, which is likewise depicted on all three monuments. As pointed out by Loizeau, Arjuna's triumph might already be indicated in a Pallava relief on the **Kailāsanātha Temple** at Kāñcīpuram (late 7th/early 8th c. CE).[416] Here, Arjuna draws his bow, whereas Śiva has not yet pulled his arrow out of the quiver. Arjuna's triumph is attested in Kannada versions, such as the Pampa Bhārata (10th c. CE).[417] According to Vyāsa by contrast, Arjuna is oppressed by Śiva and falls down unconscious (Mbh 3.40) and in Bhāravi's version, Śiva reveals himself before the fight comes to an end.[418] In a second scene on the Kailā-sanātha, a *gaṇa* (or the personified *mantra*) hands over the *pāśupata* weapon to Arjuna. This deviation, already found on the Rajaona pillar, is completely absent in Early Cāḷukyan representations.

Loizeau mentions a Cāḷukyan relief from the site of **Alampur** (Andhra Pradesh), which bears additional details pointing to a local tradition.[419] Firstly, Pārvatī makes a gesture with the hand as Arjuna apparently overpowers Śiva. This refers to the Kannada versions according to which Arjuna is invincible in battle because of an auspicious mark on his back.[420] As Pārvatī expresses a wish to see this mark, Śiva contrives a plan. He causes the fight with Arjuna and purposely falls down. As Arjuna comes over him, Pārvatī indicates to Śiva that she has seen the auspicious mark by raising her right hand. Thereupon Śiva hands over the *pāśupata* weapon and Pārvatī additionally hands over the *añjalika* weapon, an arrow with the tip in the form of the hands when joined together for salutation (sa. *añjalimudrā*). According to Loizeau, this is depicted on the Alampur relief, too.

415 Peterson 2016, pp. 299ff.
416 Loizeau 2017, p. 425, fig. 291.
417 ibid., p. 430.
418 Peterson 2016, pp. 365ff.
419 Loizeau 2017, p. 426.
420 Peterson 2007 (1991), pp. 247f.

Rāṣṭrakūṭa: Mahārāṣṭra

The **Kailāsanātha Temple** at Ellora (late 8th c. CE), has a series of Mahābhārata representations on the outer face of its northern front porch wall (Pl. 22). Whereas the Rāmāyaṇa sequence on the southern front porch wall covers eight rows, the Mahābhārata covers only five rows. However, two additional registers below, dedicated to Kṛṣṇa's life, equalise the overall length of the two panels. The Mahābhārata proceeds in alternating direction throughout. The narration opens with the *kirātārjuna* story and Arjuna's visit to Indra's realm, depicted in the upper two rows. Again, it is most likely Arjuna who triumphs over Śiva. It is interesting to note that, like also on the Virūpākṣa Temple at Paṭṭadakal, the boar being struck turns back into the demon Mūka. On the Kailāsanātha, special focus is placed on battle scenes. Arjuna's combat against the Nivātakavacas is depicted in two scenes, with Arjuna opening the fight and then overpowering his adversaries. Registers three to five are even exclusively dedicated to battle scenes. Only few of them are identifiable though. The last scene of the third row depicts Abhimanyu's death. As described in the text (Mbh 7.47f.), he has picked up the chariot wheel as he rushes against his opponents. His limbs are however already pierced with arrows all over. The fifth row opens with a representation of Duryodhana hiding inside lake Dvaipāyana. He is subsequently struck down by Bhīma.

Pāṇḍya, Cōḷa: Tamil Nadu, Karnataka

Cōḷa representations from the Mahābhārata are again restricted to the events from individual *upaparvas*. Whereas the Rāmāyaṇa is represented frequently and in some cases at great length, representations from the Mahābhārata are practically absent. Frequently found is only the story of Arjuna and the *kirāta*. Mostly, the story is reduced to one or two scenes. If only one scene is depicted, it is in most cases the shooting of the boar. On the **Brahmapurīśvara Temple** at Puḷḷamaṅgai (~ 910 CE), only the fight between Arjuna and the *kirāta* is depicted. If the story is given on two panels, the first one usually depicts the fight between Arjuna and the *kirāta* on the first panel and, on the second one, the handing over of the Paśupati weapon. This is the case on the **Nāgeśvara Temple** at Kumbakōṇam (2nd half of the 9th c. CE), on the **Saptarṣīśvara Temple** at Lālguḍi (9th c. CE), on the **Śaḍaiyar Temple** at Thirucchennampūṇḍi (~ 915-920 CE) and on the **Karkodeśvara Temple** at Kamarasavalli (10th c. CE). The boar is always depicted at Arjuna's feet while a dog appears at the feet of the *kirāta*.

Cōḷa Representations: *kirātārjuna* (a,b) and scenes from the Natuṇai Iśvara Temple, Puñjai (c - i)

Plate 23

The *kirāta*, who is Śiva in disguise, is frequently also accompanied by Pārvatī. On the Saptarṣīśvara and possibly on the Nāgeśvara, too, it is not Śiva who hands over his weapon, but a *gaṇa* or the personified *mantra*.[421] In a few cases, as on the **Sāmavedīśvara Temple** at Thirumaṅgalam (early 10th c. CE), the representation of Arjuna and the *kirāta* shooting at the boar extends across two panels. Arjuna and the boar are represented on the first panel and the *kirāta* on the second one, accompanied by Pārvatī. The boar is already struck by an arrow, while Arjuna and the *kirāta* still hold their bows stretched.

Apart from miniature base panels, the story of Arjuna and the *kirāta* is also represented on large reliefs at some Cōḷa temples. At the entrance to the **Rājarājeśvara Temple** at Tañjāvūr (first decade of the 11th c. CE, also referred to as Bṛhadīśvara Temple) the story is given in three scenes.[422] At the bottom Arjuna's penance is depicted, followed by the fight between Arjuna and the *kirāta*. Thereover Śiva and Pārvatī are shown enthroned while a *gaṇa*, or the personified *mantra*, comes with the weapon to Arjuna. The representation of the **Bṛhadīśvara Temple** at Gaṅgalkoṇḍacōḷapuram (~1025 CE) has some additional scenes (Pl. 23a). The panels cover part of the inner wall of the vestibule to the temple's sanctum. The first scene is depicted on the right side. It shows Arjuna repairing to Indrakila. Next, Arjuna is exercising his asceticism. The boar is also depicted and on a detached panel on the left side, the *kirāta* (Śiva) approaches accompanied by a *kirātī* (Pārvatī). The panel above shows Arjuna and the *kirāta* with bow and arrow. Śiva is accompanied by Pārvatī and a group of *gaṇas*. Again below, Arjuna and the *kirāta* are exchanging blows. The panels in the upper section include the culminating point in the fight. Here, Śiva overpowers Arjuna, while some unidentified figures come running. At the very top, the worship of the Śivaliṅga is depicted. The handing over of the *pāśupata* weapon, again executed by a *gaṇa* or the personified *mantra*, is depicted in the lower section of the wall. Below, also the Lokapālas arrive. A third wall image depicting this story is found on the south face of the **Airāvateśvara Temple** at Dārāsuram (late 12th c. CE). There is again an influence of a local tradition, when Śiva is accompanied by a dog, when Pārvatī holds baby Skanda, or when an assisting being hands over of the *pāśupata* weapon, as already seen on the *maṇḍapa* pillar from the site of Rajaona and on the Kailāsanātha Temple at Kāñcīpuram. It is interesting to note that this deviation from Vyāsa, unknown in Cāḷukyan representations, is highly popular in Cōḷa art and that then again, another variation, namely Arjuna's triumph over Śiva, which is popular in Cāḷukyan art is not found in Cōḷa representations. On the contrary, on the Airāvateśvara Temple at Dārāsuram, Arjuna's inferiority is explicitly pointed out as he is depicted offering his bow to the *kirāta* (Pl. 23b).

Only very few Cōḷa temples have additional scenes from the Mahābhārata. The earliest one is the **Natuṇai Iśvara Temple** at Puñjai (mid-10th c. CE). A sequence depicts the story from the Vanaparva's Araṇeyaparva (Mbh 3.44) in seven scenes (Pl. 23c-i). The first scene depicts the *brāhmaṇa* and the deer bounding away. The *brāhmaṇa* had left the kindling (sa. *araṇi*) for his sacrifice against a tree. It struck to the antlers of a deer that rubbed itself against it and the deer is now dashing away with it. The second scene shows the distraught *brāhmaṇa* requesting the Pāṇḍavas to bring back his kindling. The pursuit of the deer is represented on two panels, the fifth scene depicts the exhausted and thirsty brothers taking a rest in the forest. Nakula climbs a tree in order to locate water, as described in the text. Nakula is then sent to bring some water from a pond but the pond turns out to be enchanted. A voice from heaven declares that Nakula would only be allowed to drink the water if he answeres a question correctly. But Nakula ignores these words. As he drinks the water he falls dead to the ground. In likewise manner Sahadeva, Arjuna and Bhīma are sent by Yudhiṣṭhira, and all die attempting to drink the water from the enchanted pond. The sixth scene shows the four brothers on the waterside. Nakula and Sahadeva have already collapsed, Arjuna is about to drink the water while Bhīma (with his mace) is approaching. The next scene shows Yudhiṣṭhira responding to the questions of the spirit (sa. *yakṣa*). The enchanted pond is depicted in the background. Yudhiṣṭhira's brothers (and others) are still depicted bereft of life. They are restored to life after Yudhiṣṭhira has answered all the questions. The spirit turns out to be Yudhiṣṭhira's father, Dharma, who stole the kindling from the *brāhmaṇa* in the form of a deer in order to test his son. Other panels on the Natuṇai Iśvara depict Bhīma combating several opponents, among them Jarāsandha, whom he tears into two halfs on another panel, and Duryodhana.

---

421 Illustrations of the Saptarṣīśvara sequence, Lāḷguḍi: Loizeau 2017, p. 382, figs. 251f.. Illustrations of the Nāgeśvara sequence, Kumbakōṇam: ibid., pp. 234f., figs. 111, 109.

422 Illustration: ibid., p. 383, fig. 253.

The **Airāvateśvara Temple** already referred to, has additional scenes dealing with Bhīma's exploits. He is depicted in combat against Hiḍimva, liberating Duryodhana, fighting against Kīcaka and racing with Puruṣamṛga. The race is a local addition, the content of which is given below. According to Loizeau, this scene is also depicted on the **Siddheśvara Temple** at Sirival in Karnataka (early 12th c. CE), together with the story of Arjuna and the *kirāta*, Arjuna in battle with Karṇa, and the combat between Bhīma and Duryodhana. On the **Kampahareśvara Temple** at Thirubhuvanam (13th c. CE) the following scenes are represented: Arjuna and the *kirāta*, Bhīma slaying Kīcaka and again, Bhīma winning the race with Puruṣamṛga.[423]

The race with Puruṣamṛga is narrated in Kumaravyāsa's Kannada Bhārata of the 15th century CE. The story has been identified in Vijayanagara reliefs by Dallapiccola and Verghese[424] and in the Nāyaka-period sculpture of Tamil Nadu by Branfoot.[425] The respecting Cōḷa images, identified by Loizeau, demonstrate that this story was known already long before Kumaravyāsa's time. However, no earlier literary version of the story is known. According to Kumaravyāsa, Bhīma is sent to invite Puruṣamṛga to Yudhiṣṭhira's coronation ceremony. On his way to Mount Kailāsa, Bhīma receives from Hanumān three hairs that would produce one million *liṅgas* each, when dropped. Puruṣamṛga agrees to follow Bhīma but states that he would kill him if he manages to catch him on the way. Bhīma starts running and every time Puruṣamṛga comes too close, he drops one of Hanumān's hairs. Puruṣamṛga, a great devotee of Śiva, has to stop in order to worship the *liṅgas* and that way, Bhīma makes it to the city. As he stumbles on the threshold of the sacrificial hall, Puruṣamṛga catches him by the waist. Kṛṣṇa however proclaims Bhīma's victory because the most important part of his body, the head, was already inside the hall. As described by Loizeau, one of the Kampahareśvara's sequences depicts Bhīma standing in front of Puruṣamṛga and then running away. On the Siddheśvara, Bhīma drops one of Hanumān's hairs and on the Rājarājeśvara Temple at Tañjāvūr, Puruṣamṛga might be depicted worshipping a *liṅga*. The Airāvateśvara's images by contrast, focus on the moment when Puruṣamṛga catches Bhīma, with Yudhiṣṭhira seated inside the sacrificial hall. In the second sequence on the Kampahareśvara, Bhīma stands in front of Yudhiṣṭhira with folded hands. Puruṣamṛga stands behind Bhīma. His victory has already been attested.[426] Thus, taken all together, the Cōḷa images tell the entire episode in a variety of scenes.

Cōḷa images always focus on isolated events from the Mahābhārata. There is never a comprehensive depiction of the epos as a whole.

Hoysaḷa and Late Cāḷukya: Karnataka

Extensive representations of the Mahābhārata in stone are found in India fonly from the Hoysaḷas.

Among the earliest of the Hoysaḷa temples, the **(Cenna-)keśava Temple** at Belūr (1117 CE), has a series of reliefs depicting events from the Mahābhārata, included on the south side into its uppermost frieze. 17 scenes are depicted on a total of 22 panels, which are separated from each other by two pillars each. At the beginning, the events are not quite represented in chronological order. The first scene depicts the game of dice from the Sabhā Parva, the following scenes depict the youthful Bhīma shaking his cousins from a tree and Duryodhana's consequent attempt to poison him, as narrated in the Ādiparva (Mbh 1.119). Thereupon the narration continues chronologically, in counterclockwise manner. It is worth noting that the events from the Vanaparva, usually highlighted in Hoysaḷa cycles, are omitted here, whereas six of the 17 scenes are dedicated to the Udyogaparva, which is absent in all other Hoysaḷa representations. The last identifiable scene shows Bhīma in combat against Bhagadatta and his elephant Supratīka, with Arjuna coming to his aid (Mbh. 6.91f.). This scene was very popular with the Hoysaḷas and is frequently also found as a large wall image, isolated from its narrative context.

The Haḷebīḍ group temples have also representations from the Mahābhārata, included in their narrative friezes. Several events from the epic are included in the narrative frieze of the **Hoysaḷeśvara Temple** (1121-1160 CE). In total 17 scenes from the epic are found on the temple's west wall. Some are depicted as isolated events while

423 Loizeau 2017, pp. 383ff.
424 Dallapiccola and Verghese 2002, pp. 73ff.
425 Branfoot 2002, pp. 77ff.
426 Loizeau 2017, pp. 385ff. with illustrations from the Airāvateśvara (fig. 257) and the Kampahareśvara (fig. 258).

others form short sequences.[427] The events within the sequences proceed most of the time clockwise, but not in all cases, and if one looks at the representations as a whole, there is no chronological order at all. Several events are represented repeatedly (among them the *kirātārjuna* episode and the battle against Bhagadatta and Supratīka) and the Mahābhārata representations are beyond that separated by other representations. Some Mahābhārata panels, originally from the Nagareśvara Complex, are included in the narrative frieze of the Nandī *maṇḍapa* in front of the temple. These include again the *kirātārjuna* episode and the game of dice. Apart from the repeated representations of the *kirātārjuna* episode, in the Hoysaḷeśvara's case special focus is placed on battle scenes.

A continuous depiction of events from the Mahābhārata, in a more or less chronological order can be seen on the **Kedāreśvara Temple** at Haḷebīḍ (bet. 1173-1220 CE). 34 scenes from the epic are incorporated in the narrative frieze of the temple.[428] A long sequence is placed along the north-western faces of the temple. The narration opens with the game of dice and ends with the fight between Duryodhana and Bhīma. Aśvatthāma finding Duryodhana is represented after a short interruption with Rāmāyaṇa scenes. Some episodes have been switched (e.g. the capture of Duryodhana by the *gandharvas* is represented prior to the *kirātārjuna* episode) but in general the events are represented chronologically, in clockwise manner. On the south-western corner of the temple's southern sanctum two more scenes from the Mahābhārata are located. These panels were certainly displaced in course of renovation. Depicted is Bhīṣma's death on the first panel and possibly Yudhiṣṭhira's sacrifice on the second one. The Kedāreśvara's representations thus deal with events from *parvas* 2 to 4, 6 to 9, 13 and possibly 14 from the Mahābhārata.

The ruins of the **Hūcheśvara Temple** and of the **Nagareśvara Complex** (late 12th/early 13th c. CE) have some Mahābhārata representations included in the northern sections of their narrative friezes. On the Hūcheśvara 12 scenes have survived. As in case of the Kedāreśvara, a number of events from the Vana- and Virāṭaparva are depicted, followed by some battle scenes from *parvas* six to eight.[429] On the southern temple of the Nagareśvara Complex 15 scenes have survived, depicting events from the Vana-, Virāṭa- and Droṇaparva.[430] The narrative frieze of the middle temple reveals two scenes from the Mahābhārata: the game of dice and Bhīma slaying Duḥśāsana.[431] Three episodes can be made out on the northern temple: the *kirātārjuna* episode, Bhīma's exploits at Virāṭa's court and the cow raid (sa. *gograhaṇa*). Battle scenes follow.[432] As also with the Rāmāyaṇa representations, the choice of scenes on all these monuments resembles much that from the Kedāreśvara. Additionally, on the Hūcheśvara and on the southern Nagareśvara, the scenes from the Vanaparva have been switched, too. Apart from the panels in situ, the panels on the Hoysaleśvara's Nandī *maṇḍapa* have to be remembered. Loizeau additionally refers to two stray Haḷebīḍ panels, possibly from the Nagareśvara Complex, which are now secured in the Bangalore Museum.[433]

The **Amṛteśvara Temple** at Amṛtāpura (~ 1200 CE), has 36 reliefs depicting events from the Mahābhārata on the north-eastern parts of the *maṇḍapa*'s parapet. Not the entire epic is represented but a sequence with episodes from the Ādi, Sabhā and Vanaparva, rendered in clockwise manner. The first scenes deal with the life at court after Pāṇḍu's death and the sequence ends with the *kirātārjuna* episode.[434] The location of the sequence on the parapet of the temple is singular. The individual scenes are framed and separated by pilasters (mostly two), with floral rhombuses, attendant figures or uncarved blocks in between.

Four more Mahābhārata sequences are found on the multi layered bases of the following temples:

22 scenes from the epic are included in the narrative frieze of the **Mallikārjuna Temple** at Basrāḷ (mid-13th c. CE). The Mahābhārata sequence forms the north-western section of the band. The first scene shows Bhīma shaking his cousins from the tree, a scene which is popular with the Hoysaḷas. Though the Mallikārjuna's sequence is made up of markedly fewer scenes than the Amṛteśvara's sequence, the representations cover events from more

427 Identification of scenes: Loizeau 2017, pp. 65f.
428 Identification of scenes: ibid., pp. 70ff.
429 Identification of scenes: Loizeau 2017, p. 79. See also Evans 1997, pp. 219f.
430 Identification of scenes: ibid., pp. 82f. Again, also Evans 1997, pp. 227ff.
431 Evans 1997, p. 229.
432 Loizeau 2017, p. 83.
433 ibid.
434 Identification of scenes: Evans 1997, pp. 27f., illustrations and detailed description: ibid., pp. 120ff. See also Loizeau 2017, p. 92.

Hoysaḷa Representations

a

b

c

d

e

f

Plate 24

parvas. The last scene from the Mallikārjuna's sequence depicts Aśvatthāmā presenting the heads of the Pāṇḍavas' sons to Duryodhana.[435]

The **Lakṣmīnārāyaṇa Temple** at Hosahoḷalu (bet. 1220 - 1250 CE) has on the northern side 36 events from the Mahābhārata included in its narrative frieze. The first scene shows again Bhīma shaking the tree and the sequence ends with Yudhiṣṭira's coronation.[436] The sequences on the Mallikārjuna and Lakṣmīnārāyaṇa are the most extensive ones. Only here, an entire cycle of the story is given.

Only a few scenes from the epic are represented on the **Lakṣmīnarasiṃha Temple** at Jāvagal (13th c. CE). The north-eastern part of the narrative frieze displays a short sequence from the Sabhā and Vanaparva. The sequence presumably opens with Yudhiṣṭira's *rājasūya*. The game of dice is represented together with Draupadī's humiliation and afterwards comes the *kirātārjuna* episode.[437]

The latest Hoysaḷa temple with narrative representations from the Mahābhārata on its base is the **(Cenna-)keśava Temple** at Somnāthpur (1268 CE). The section encircling the northern sanctum is dedicated to the Mahābhārata, rendered in 17 scenes.[438] The (Cenna-)keśava's representations deal almost exclusively with events from the Ādiparva. The first scene shows again Bhīma shaking his cousins from a tree. The representations further include the youths' training in arms, the burning of the house of lac, Bhīma's battle with Hiḍimba, the birth of his son Ghaṭotkaca, his fight agains Vaka, Draupadī's *svayamvara* and the burning of the Khāṇḍava Forest. One of the last scenes might represent Bhīma subduing Duryodhana and the sequence ends with a military procession.

The latest narrative representation of the Mahābhārata from South India is found next to the **Someśvara Temple** at Bandaḷike (Late Cāḷukyas, 1274 CE), on a slab to the right side of its entry. The slab is carved with Mahābhārata scenes, arranged in seven superimposed registers.[439] The first scene on the lowest register depicts as usual Bhīma shaking the tree. The narration proceeds to the left with the game of dice and Draupadī's humiliation. The registers above depict the recapture of the stolen cattle, Bhīma in battle with Duḥśāsana, Arjuna in battle with Karṇa, Bhīma against Bhagadatta and Supratīka and finally Bhīma against Duryodhana. The uppermost register depicts several divinities, quasi observing what happens beyond. Only Śiva and Durgā Mahiṣāsuramardinī are recognisable, though. It is noticeable that Bhīma's exploits are highlighted on the Someśvara's slab, whereas other popular motifs, like Arjuna's fight with the *kirāta*, are missing.

What concerns the Hoysaḷa representations, multiple influences of a local tradition are found. In the context of the *kirātārjuna* episode, an *apsara* tries to disturb Arjuna's penance in almost all cases. This is most likely Urvaśī, who dances in front of Arjuna according to the Pampa Bhārata.[440] Likewise, in almost all the representations, Arjuna triumphs over Śiva while Pārvatī stands behind Arjuna, raising her hand in order to indicate that she has seen the auspicious mark on his back. This reminds of the Cāḷukyan reliefs, most notably the one from the site of Alampur (Andhra Pradesh).

Other scenes also point to a local version of the story. On the Amṛteśvara, after Arjuna has brought Drupada bound as a reward for his training in archery (Mbh 1.128), Drupada clings to Droṇa's seat while Droṇa has placed his foot on the head of Drupada (Pl. 24a). According to Evans, Droṇa humiliates Drupada by using his head as a footrest in the Pampa Bhārata. He additionally kicks it afterwards.[441] Also in accordance with the Pampa Bhārata is the depiction of Brahmā intervening in the fight between Indra and Arjuna in the course of the burning of the Khāṇḍava Forest.[442] He stops the fight by revealing the latters identity to the former. Again, this is depicted most clearly on the Amṛteśvara (Pl. 24b). Yet another variation is evident in the scenes dealing with Duryodhana's liberation after the *gandharvas* have taken him captive.[443] According to the Pampa Bhārata, Duryodhana and Duḥśāsana are both captured by the *gandharvas*. In order to enable them to descend back to earth, Arjuna constructs a stairway with his arrows. It is finally Draupadī who unbinds them and again sets them free. The event is depicted exclusively on the Haḷebīḍ group temples, the Kedareśvara, Hūcheśvara and the southern temple of the Nagareśvara Complex. Though only one of the two Kaurava princes is depicted in the Hoysaḷa images, the representations clearly follow Pampa's version. On the Kedareśvara for example (Pl. 24c), the

435 Identification of scenes: Loizeau 2017, p. 100.
436 Identification of scenes: ibid., pp. 111f.
437 Identification of scenes: ibid., p. 118.
438 Identification of scenes: ibid., pp. 128f.
439 Illustration and identification of scenes: Loizeau 2017, pp. 47f.
440 Loizeau 2017, p. 430.
441 Evans 1997, pp. 124ff.
442 ibid., pp. 145f.
443 Loizeau 2017, p. 435.

stairway constructed by Arjuna is depicted. Arjuna makes a gesture with his hand as if to instruct either Duryodhana or Duḥśāsana to descend on it. Thereafter, Draupadī is depicted loosening the bonds of the Kaurava prince.

Other impacts of a local tradition are found towards the end of the story. Firstly, Draupadī dresses her hair with Duḥśāsana's blood on the Hoysaḷeśvara (Pl. 24d), Kedareśvara (Pl. 24e), Hūcheśvara, on the middle temple of the Nagareśvara Complex, on the Mallikārjuna and Lakṣmīnārāyaṇa. Her presence on the Someśvara indicates the same. The story is again told in the Pampa Bhārata. According to this version, after Duḥśāsana had brought Draupadī by the hair into the *sabhā* to disrobe her, she had vowed to leave it dishevelled until Duḥśāsana would be slain and she could dress it with his blood. Bhīma then promised to help her. Later, having slain Duḥśāsana, Bhīma soaks Draupadī's hair with Duḥśāsana's blood, uses Duḥśāsana's teeth to comb it and puts a garland of his intestines around her neck. Then, he not only drinks his blood but also eats his flesh. According to the version of Kumāra Vyāsa, Bhīma dresses Draupadī's hair with Duḥśāsana's blood, too. He additionally uses his blood to put a mark (sa. *tilaka*) on Draupadī's forehead and again decorates her with Duḥśāsana's intestines.[444]

Again according to Pampa, after Duryodhana was discovered hiding in lake Dvaipāyana, it is Balarāma who suggests that only one of the five sons of Pāṇḍu should fight with him. It is consequently also not Yudhiṣṭhira but Bhīma, having already made up his mind, who approaches Duryodhana and challenges him.[445] As noted by Loizeau, Balarāma's role in Pampa's version explains his appearance on the respective relief on the Mallikārjuna (Pl. 24f, middle). He is depicted behind Duryodhana, with the plough in his hands. Finally, as also on the Kṛṣṇa Temple at Pāṭan, Aśvatthāma is depicted bringing the five heads of the Pāṇḍavas' sons to Duryodhana on the Mallikārjuna (Pl. 24f, left) and Lakṣmīnārāyaṇa.

The most interesting deviation from the text however, is the depiction of a fish in the context of Draupadī's *svayamvara*. Representations of Arjuna shooting the fish target are found frequently also as large wall panels. These representations will be discussed later in detail.

<u>Vijayanagara, Nāyaka: Karnataka, Andhra Pradesh and Tamil Nadu</u>

Only very few representations from the Mahābhārata are found on Vijayanagara monuments but still these few reveal an impact of a local tradition. Dallapiccola has identified four narrative reliefs dealing with the Bhīma Puruṣamṛga episode at the site of Hampi, within the complexes of the great **Virūpakṣa Temple**, the **Rāmacandra Temple** and the **Prasanna Virūpakṣa Temple**.[446] The representations all date from the 15th century CE. Loizeau also found narrative reliefs of the same episode on the **Śiva Temple at Penukoṇḍa**, Andhra Pradesh (15th c. CE) and on the **Viṣṇu Temple at Gummanayakapalya**, district Chikballapur (16th c. CE).[447] Before, this episode was only found on Cōḻa monuments. It is entirely absent in the rich corpus of Hoysaḷa representations. Whereas the Cōḻa images highlight different aspects of the episode, the Vijayanagara images are practically all identical. They depict the race, with Bhīma dropping one of Hanumān's hairs. A *liṅga* appears between him and his pursuer. An additional panel on the great Virūpakṣa Temple, as well as the one on the Viṣṇu Temple at Gummanayakapalya, depict Puruṣamṛga worshipping a *liṅga*. Bhīma is absent in these representations. Branfoot has also identified Bhīma and Puruṣamṛga in the Nāyaka-period sculpture of southern Tamil Nadu.[448] He found the figures within the complexes of the **Mīnākṣī Sundareśvara Temple** at Madurai, the **Nellayappar Temple** at Tirunelveli, the **Veṇkaṭacalapati Temple** at Kṛṣṇapuram, the **Satyavāgiśvara Temple** at Kalakkad, the **Vāṉamāmalai Perumāḷ Temple** at Nanguneri, the **Nampirāyar Temple** at Tirukkurunkudi and on a reassembled *maṇḍapa* in the Philadelphia Museum of Art, probably from the **Kūṭal Aḻakat Temple** at Madurai. All these monuments date from the late 16th and 17th centuries CE. In contrast to earlier representations, Bhīma and Puruṣamṛga are here depicted on large scale. In most cases, they form a pair of lifesize figures attached to the columns or piers in the open *maṇḍapas* and corridors of the temples. In the Nāyaka-period sculpture, Bhīma and Puruṣamṛga are both depicted waving a club. Additional elements, such as the *liṅga*, are missing. The figures are either attached to the columns in such a way that they face each other, or else spread around one single column.

444 Loizeau 2017, p. 436.

445 ibid., pp. 441f.

446 Dallapiccola and Verghese 2002, pp. 73ff.

447 Loizeau 2017, pp. 386f.

448 Branfoot 2002, pp. 77ff.

Muslim Period: West Bengal and Bangladesh

The terracottas decorating Bengali brick temples also reveal only select events from the great epic. These are however often depicted on large scale in a prominent position. Above all, the battle of Kurukṣetra is depicted many times. The individual characters are usually not identifiable but sometimes particular events stand out. This is most true for representations of Bhīṣma resting on his bed of arrows with Arjuna shooting an arrow into the earth to provide water for him. In some cases, as for example on the 1694 **Madan Mohan Temple** in Bishnupur (image a), this scene is preceded by Arjuna attacking Bhīṣma with Śikhaṇḍī in front. Interestingly, on Bengali terracottas Śikhaṇḍī is invariably not depicted on his own chariot but as Arjuna's charioteer, replacing Kṛṣṇa. This probably reflects a local alteration of the story. Bhīṣma for his part, considering Śikhaṇḍī to be a woman, has put down his bow. Likewise often depicted is the battle with clubs between Bhīma and Duryodhana. In accordance with Vyāsa, the representation on the Madan Mohan shows Bhīma striking Duryodhana unfairly at the thighs (image b). As pointed out by Zulekha Haque, there are a number of panels depicting a maiden beneath a tree feeding deer. On account of the repeated portrayal of this scene she suggests that this depicts the Śakuntalā story, originally authored by Kālidāsa, which was incorporated into the Bengali version of the Mahābhārata.[449]

Among the other scenes that are to be seen occationally, there is one of particular importance. It is a representation of Arjuna shooting the fish target on the **Chototaraf Temple** of Hadal-Nārāyanpur, Bankura district (Pl. 25a). The temple dates from the early 19th century CE.[450] Arjuna is depicted in the centre of the image. He strings his bow upwards while he looks down at the reflection of the fish in a vessel filled with water. Insofar the Bengali representation of the theme closely resembles the Hoysaḷa representations. In contrast to the Hoysaḷa representations however, the vessel is not placed in front of Arjuna. He has to look back over his shoulder to see the refection. Moreover the whole image is dominated by the fish target, encircled by the other competitors. On top, they come running to point out Arjuna's arrow which has already hit the eye of the fish. Arjuna is accompanied by his four brothers. On the left side Drupada is depicted, probably together with his sons Dhṛṣṭadyumna and Śikhaṇḍī. Draupadī, the one for whom they all have assembled, is depicted at the very left, inside a small pavilion.

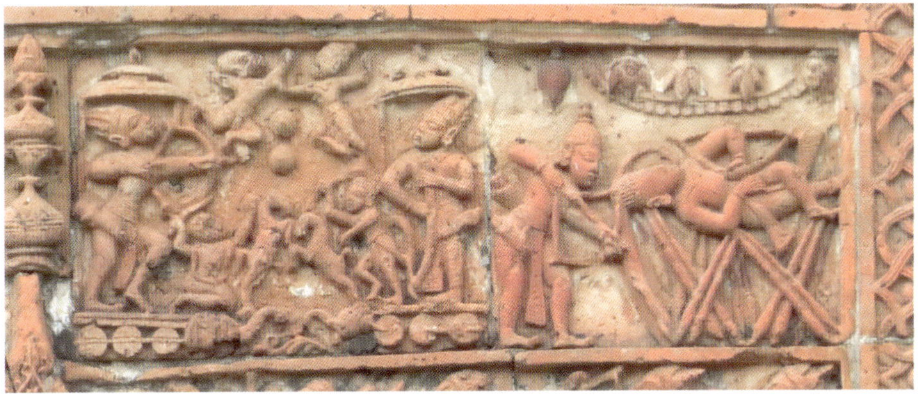

a

b

449 Haque 2014, p. 110.

450 McCutchion 1972, App. A.

Arjuna shooting the Fish Target (1)

a: Chototaraf Temple, Hadal-Nārāyanpur
Photo by Manojit Pal. See also Pl. 20.

b: Amṛteśvara Temple, Amṛtāpura

c: (Cenna-)keśava Temple, Somnāthpur

Plate 25

Excursus two: Arjuna shooting the Fish Target

In the Critical Edition of the Mahābhārata, it is nowhere mentioned that the target which has to be struck in order to win the contest and thus attain the hand of Draupadī is a fish. In fact, the original story of Draupadī's *svayamvara* differs in many ways from the representations described. According to the text (Mbh 1.176), it is still assumed that the Pāṇḍavas were burnt to death in the house of lac and they arrive disguised as brahmins, in order to remain unrecognised by the peaple. Drupada erects an artificial machine in the sky with a golden target attached to it. Additionally, a very hard bow is made which hardly anyone will be able to string. Finally, Dhṛṣṭadyumna declares that Draupadī will be given in marriage to the one who succeeds in shooting the mark above the machine, through the hole in its centre. So, according to the text, there is a very high machine, with a whole in its centre and above a golden target. Further details are not given.

It was mentioned before that in South India, more sprecifically on Hoysaḷa temples, numerous representations of the contest are found. Interestingly, there seem to be no earlier representations of the theme in the whole of South Asia. What concerns the Hoysaḷa representations, Arjuna is invaryably depicted bending his bow upwards to shoot the target, a fish, while only looking at its reflection in a waterpot placed before him. Within the narrative friezes, the shooting of the fish target is depicted twice, on the **Amṛteśvara Temple** at Amṛtāpura (~ 1200 CE, Pl. 25b) and on the **(Cenna-)keśava Temple** at Somnāthpur (1268 CE, Pl. 25c). On the **Mallikārjuna Temple** at Basrāḷ (mid-13th c. CE) only the garlanding of Arjuna is depicted. At Amṛtāpura the fish lies atop of a pole. Arjuna looks down at its reflection in a large vessel. His arrow already hit the target. A diminutive Draupadī is depicted next to him. In her hands she holds the garland of flowers. Arjuna is accompanied by his brothers. In accordance with the text, they are depicted as brahmins, whereas Arjuna himself is depicted as a warrior (sa. *kṣatriya*). In the background further spectators are depicted. A pavilion indicates the court setting. On the (Cenna-)keśava Arjuna is depicted in the same posture and again, the target is a fish placed upon a stele.

Apart from these narrative representations, the theme is portrayed on large wall panels a great many times. In these instances only Arjuna shooting the fish target is depicted. It is thus clear that already at this aerly stage, the alteration was a matter of common knowledge and did not necessarily need to be embedded in a narrative context to be understood. Of special importance are the representations of Arjuna shooting the fish on the **Cennakeśava Temple** at Belūr (1117 CE, Pl. 26a) and on the **Hoysaḷeśvara Temple** at Haḷebīḍ (1121-1160 CE, Pl. 26b) for these are the earliest known representations of the theme. Large wall panels with Arjuna shooting the fish target are also found on the **Brahmeśvara Temple** at Kikkeri (1171 CE[451]), on the **Būcēśvara Temple** at Koravaṅgala (1173 CE[452]), on the **Vīranārāyaṇa Temple** at Beḷavāḍi (~1200 CE, Pl. 26c), twice on the **Kedāreśvara Temple** at Haḷebīḍ (~1200 CE, Pl. 26d,e) with one of them (e) possibly originating from the Nagareśvara Complex (end of 12th/beginning of 13th c. CE), on the **Lakṣmīnarasiṃha Temple** at Nuggīhaḷḷi (1249 CE, Pl. 26f) and on the **Mallikārjuna Temple** at Basrāḷ (mid-13th c. CE, Pl. 26g). I was informed that the theme is also depicted on temples dating from the second half of the 13th century CE, at the sites of **Hāranahaḷḷi and Nāgalāpura**.[453] On some of the above mentioned temples, part of the narrative frieze is also dedicated to the Mahābhārata. However, on the Vīranārāyaṇa Temple at Beḷavāḍi as well as on the Lakṣmīnarasiṃha Temple at Nuggīhaḷḷi, the narrative frieze is dedicated exclusively to the life of Kṛṣṇa, the narrative friezes at the sites of Hāranahaḷḷi and Nāgalāpura are unsculpted and there is no narrative frieze at all on the Brahmeśvara and the Būcēśvara. This again points out the popularity of the theme independently from the Mahābhārata.

In most cases only Arjuna piercing the fish is depicted. The two earliest examples, those on the (Cenna-)keśava and the Hoysaḷeśvara, have also a representation of Hanumān on top of a standard to identify the hero. In later examples this appears to have not been necessary anymory. In all the 12th century representations the fish is depicted on top of a pole. The (Cenna-)keśava's representation is singular. The fish is here depicted inside an open pavilion atop the pole, giving the whole construction a more complex appearance, evocative maybe of the machinery described in the text. The pavilion is thereafter omitted and the fish only lies on top of the

451 https://www.karnataka.gov.in/Gazetteer/Publications/District Gazetteers/Mandya District/2009/Chapter-17 Mandya Dist Gaz 2009.pdf, p. 993.

452 Foekema 1996, p. 79.

453 Information provided by K. Ramesh Kumar, Head of the Photo Archives, French Institute of Pondicherry. Dating according to Loizeau 2017, pp. 44f.

Arjuna shooting the Fish Target (2)

a: Cennakeśava Temple, Belūr
b: Hoysaḷeśvara Temple, Haḷebīḍ
c: Vīranārāyaṇa Temple, Beḷavāḍi
d: Kedāreśvara Temple, Haḷebīḍ
e: Kedāreśvara Temple, Haḷebīḍ (possibly originating from the Nagareśvara Complex)
f: Lakṣmīnarasiṃha Temple, Nuggīhaḷḷi
g: Mallikārjuna Temple, Basrāḷ

a

b

c

Plate 26

d

e

f

g

pole. The Vīranārāyaṇa's representation marks a turning point in the way of representing the task. The fish is still depicted on top of the pole but it is flanked by creepers. On all later wall panels, the fish appears to be concealed by those creepers. It is depicted either embedded in creepers or above them, inside a cage or without. The representation on the Lakṣmīnarasiṃha is maybe the most admirable one. Only here and on the panel originating from the Nagareśvara, Arjuna is flanked by Hanumān and Draupadī, holding the garland of flowers. Arjuna is invaryably depicted shooting his arrow upwards while only looking down at the reflection of the fish. Interestingly, only in the earlier Hoysaḷa representations Arjuna's arrow has clearly hit the eye of the fish. This aspect becomes a regular feature in later representations.

The Vijayanagaras transferred the story of Arjuna piercing the fish target into murals. A beautiful example is included in the paintings decorating the ceiling of the large front *maṇḍapa* of the **Virūpākṣa Temple** at Hampi (15th c. CE).[454] Largely, the image corresponds to the Hoysaḷa representations. Arjuna strings his bow upwards to hit the fish target, while only looking down at its reflection in a bowl filled with water. However, the fish is neither placed on a post as in earlier Hoysaḷa representations, nor is it concealed by foliage as in later Hoysaḷa representations. Depicted is indeed some artificial machine, apparently with a whole at its centre through which Arjuna has to shoot his arrow in order to hit the target. The image thus combines perfectly the description in the text with innovative details provided by Hoysaḷa artists.

The story of Arjuna shooting the fish target spread to North India where it became a popular motive in painting. It is included in Akbar's persian rendering of the Mahābhārata, the Razmnama (Book of War). The Razmnama is a four volume work, prepared from 1582 to 1586, with 168 full-page illustrations.[455] It is now kept save intact in the Maharaja Sawai Man Singh II Museum at Jaipur and thus commonly referred to as the **Jaipur Razmnama.**[456] The respective illustration of Draupadī's *svayamvara* by Daswant and Keshav is fortunately online.[457] The fish is now dangling from a high pole. Again, Arjuna looks down at its reflection as he shoots his arrow but, as noted by Hendley, *'the task is made the more difficult as he is only allowed to see the reflection of the fish in the troubled contents of a heated cauldron'.*[458] On the right side, as well as in the background, countless spectators are depicted.
Not much later, around 1605, the **Birla Razmnama** was produced with 81 illustrations.[459] As the name indicates, it is preserved in the Birla Academy of Art and Culture at Kolkata. Although, as established by Das, the illustrations from the Birla Razmnama are clearly not based upon the ones from the Akbari manuscript, the illustration of Arjuna shooting the fish target[460] reminds of the imperial work. Again, there is a high post from which the fish was dangling. The fish has already been brought down by Arjuna and Draupadī is depicted garlanding him. On both the folios, Arjuna is correctly depicted in his disguise as a Brahmana. The water is not heated in this representation but yet another diffuculty is conceived with the fish dangling from the post in both the representations. It is assumed that the fish is spinning fast. In likewise manner, Arjuna has to hit three moving balls dangling from a post in another representation from the Birla Razmnama, dealing with the training in archery of the young Kauravas and Pāṇḍavas.[461]

Although set in stone only shortly after, the representation on the Kṛṣṇa Temple at Pāṭan again differs significantly. Here, Arjuna has to bring down one of in total five fish, hanging in a tree. The water-filled vessel is not depicted but its presence is indicated since Arjuna is depicted looking downward. The hero is again depicted as a warrior. As noted by Evans, this is based on the rules of propriety[462] and in case of the Kṛṣṇa Temple, there are many instances in which the representation of a figure transmits his character rather than to present his actual appearance at the very moment.

454 A beautiful image was published by Sivaramamurti 1985, Pl. VI. An interactive plan of all the ceiling paintings from the Virūpākṣa's *maṇḍapa* was put online by the International Institute for Art, Culture and Democracy (IIACD) at http://www.iiacd.org/murals-south-india/hampi-virupaksha-temple-ceiling-paintings-interactive-plan/index.html#/ Dating as given by Sivaramamurti, p. 29.

455 Das 2005, p. 12f.

456 The Jaipur Razmnama is not open to public. In 1884 Hendley published 148 of the Razmnama's paintings in the fourth volume of his *Memorials of the Jeypore Exhibition, 1883*. Only a few copies exist but an online version, without reproductions of the illustrations, at least contains the descriptive text. See: https://archive.org/details/MemorialsOfTheJeyporeExhibitionRazmnamah

457 https://commons.wikimedia.org/wiki/File:Arjun_hits_the_target.jpg

458 Hendley, op. cit., p. 8, n. to Plate VI.

459 Das 2005, pp. 18ff.

460 Illustration: ibid., p. 49.

461 Ibid., p. 44. With illustration on p. 45.

462 Evans 1997, p. 136.

The task is nowhere else depicted exactly the same way. The basics are always conform: Arjuna has to pierce (the eye of) a fish placed way up high, while only looking down at its reflection. Anyway, the representations vary in detail. The fish was placed on top of a post in earlier Hoysaḷa representations, concealed by foliage in later Hoysaḷa representations, attached to the artificial machine in the Vijayanagara painting, dangling from a post in North Indian illustrated manuscripts and now, there are as many as five fish hanging in a tree. In the 19th century Bengali representation, the fish is placed on a net. As far as is known, there is no literary basis for the representations of Arjuna shooting the fish target and the dissimilarities also indicate that the story was rather orally transmitted.

Surprisingly, no representations at all are kown of Draupadī's *svayamvara* dating from before the 12th century CE. Given the lack of earlier representations of the task, either as described or in a different way, it cannot be establised if the Hoysaḷas were the ones to come up with the story of Arjuna shooting the fish. If, however, it is assumed that the Hoysaḷas made up this story, it became immensely popular within only a short period. Apparently, already the earliest representations did not require a narrative context to be understood. Today, the story of Arjuna shooting the fish is one of the most popular Mahābhārata stories, despite the fact that it is not included in any of the early literary versions. It is clearly Arjuna's skill in archery that is highlighted in the narration and it is interesting to note that another such story is also developed further at about the same time. This is the story of Rāma piercing the seven *śāla* trees. As regards this story, earlier representations do exist and it was mentioned before that these correspond to Vālmīki's version of the story, whereas in Hoysaḷa representations, the trees grow on the back of a snake. In order to pierce the seven trees, Rāma has to align them by placing his foot on the snake's tail. Additionally, the same arrow which penetrates through the trees also kills the snake and finally Vālin. By attributing supernatural archery skills on the one hand to Rāma and on the other hand to Arjuna, both of them are celebrated as peerless warriors, the heroes par excellence.

That it is still Arjuna's skill in archery, the complexity of the task, that fascinates the people today, is demonstrated very well by the fact that in 1982 a stamp was released with Arjuna piercing the fish, in order to commemorate the 9th Asian Games at Delhi (image a). The event is depicted exactly as previously seen in the painted manuscripts. The representation additionally includes the reflection of the fish.

The question remains as to why the artists chose to depict a fish as the target. It is clear that they had to choose something to represent the unspecified object from the text but would not other things have been more applicable? For example, at the end of the princes' training in archery, Droṇa constructs an artificial bird and places it on top of a tree as a target (Mbh 1.123). The target is thus concealed by foliage and the princes can only hardly see it. This reminds of the later Hoysaḷa representations, in which the fish is also concealed by foliage. There is yet another parallel in both the stories. Arjuna has to ignore everything else and to focus solely on the bird's

a

head before Droṇa gives him permission to shoot. This is similar to the version in which Arjuna has to focus on the fish's eye. Given these parallels, maybe it would have been more reasonable if the artists had chosen to depict a bird as the target.

Indeed, the representation of a bridal contest at Angkor Wat (early 12th c. CE) includes a bird target, set on top of an artificial machine with a probably rotating wheel (image b). The target is again concealed by foliage as the machine reaches high above the trees, into the heavenly regions. With the bird set on top of the artificial machine the artist combines elements from Arjuna's training in archery and the display of his skill at Draupadī's *svayamvara*. Still, it is not clear if this panel really depicts the bridal contest from the Mahābhārata. As pointed out by John and Mary Brockington, in Southeast Asia, elements from the Mahābhārata were also included in the Rāmāyaṇa story.[463] The panel could therefore likewise depict Rāma at Sītā's *svayamvara*. Only three figures are depicted where one would expect to find Arjuna's four brothers. These three could however be identified as Viśvāmitra, Rāma and Lakṣmaṇa on their arrival at Janaka's court. The bow is not broken but neither is the arrow fixed to it as one would expect it within the context of Draupadī's *svayamvara*. Again, the bow is rarely broken in Southeast versions of the Rāmāyaṇa. It is enough for Rāma to lift it, or to lift and string it.[464] Regardless of whether the intended hero is Arjuna or Rāma, the artificial machine is an element drawn from the Mahābhārata and the target on top is a bird.

b: Photo by Adalbert J. Gail

In South Asia by contrast, the target is invariably a fish. The most considerable discussion as to why the fish symbol might have been chosen is given by Hiltebeitel.[465] It was mentioned before that according to South Indian tradition, Arjuna is invincible in battle because of an auspicious mark on his back. More precisely, this is described as a fish mark and Arjuna is not the only one to have it. Śiva, with whom Arjuna is repeatedly associated in the context of the Draupadī cult 207, has according to South Indian Tradition also a fish mark on his back. Hiltebeitel notes that for both of them *'to seek out or marry "fish mark"-bearing women is thus an image of the feminine completion of their masculine divine natures'*. 209,l. 1ff. Pārvatī and Kṛpī are both said to have fish marks on their thighs and these marks evoke an uncontrollable desire in Śiva. Additionally, there are the myths of Mīnākṣī, literally *'she of the fish eyes'*, whom Śiva marries repeatedly. In the second instance, she is raised by a king of fishermen. In the form of a huge fish, Nandī prompts the king to announce that the one who manages to catch the fish can marry his daughter. There is thus a contest including a fish which Śiva has to win in order to marry Mīnākṣī. This reminds of Draupadī's *svayamvara*. Whereas Arjuna shoots the fish with bow and arrow, Śiva nets it and draws it to shore. In the same way that Śiva has to see Kṛpī's fish mark as he hears about it, Pārvatī has to see Arjuna's fish mark as she hears about this one. According to South Indian tradition, this is the reason why Śiva engages in battle with Arjuna in the guise of a *kirāta*. Now, since Arjuna has himself the fish mark, it has to apply to him, too, that he has to

463 Brockington and Brockington 2010, p. 55.

464 ibid.

465 Hiltebeitel 1991, pp. 201ff.

enter a fish alliance. This is may be the best way to explain why Arjuna's union with Draupadī should involve the symbol of the fish.
However, Hiltebeitel's discussion goes way beyond this. He also takes into account the fish symbolism in the Mahābhārata which runs through the whole story from its beginnings with the fishy smelling Satyavatī and the birth of Vyāsa, up to Abhimanyu's union with Uttarā, a descendant of Satyavatī's twin brother Matsya (sa., *fish*).
Another possible interpretation of the fish contraption is based upon the fact that in Tamil the word *mīṉ* means both *fish* and *star*.[466] According to Hiltebeitel, Draupadī's elevated fish could hint at Arundhatī, Vaśiṣṭha's wife and the Tamil north star personified, with whom she is compared on account of her chastity. According to a more traditional Sanskritic cosmology, Draupadī's star, Arundhatī, forms also part of the Seven Ṛṣi constellation that revolves around Dhruva (sa., *the Fixed*), the pole star personified. Dhruva's wife is Bhramī (sa., *She who wanders*) and there is thus repeatedly a conjunction between fixity and movement, as it is also the case with the fish contraption at Draupadī's *svayamvara*. Now, Bhramī is the daughter of Śiśumāra (sa., Gangetic porpoise), yet anotheer star group of which Dhruva forms part. This is likewise interesting for, just once, Kāmpilyā is referred to as 'The City of the Śiśumāra'.

466 Hiltebeitel 1991, pp. 209f.

Clearly, the fish depicted in the context of Draupadī's *svayamvara* is not a dolphin. Also, it seems rather unlikely that the artists chose to depict a fish because of some characteristics connecting fish with stars. Why not simply depict a star? Hiltebeitel's first interpretation, based on local traditions, appears to be more suitable.

Not much can be added to Hiltebeitel's elaborate discourse on the theme but it may be, that another local tradition had also an effect on the representations. Like there is the tradition of a premarital love between Rāma and Sītā, there is also the tradition of a premarital desire between Arjuna and Draupadī.[467] The way in which the fish is depicted in early Hoysaḷa representations, as an emblem on top of a pole, reminds of the battle standards frequently found in Hoysaḷa representations, as they suit to identify the depicted characters. Now, the fish is the emblem of the god Kāma (sa., *desire*) himself, the invisible one. As pointed out by Hiltebeitel, liaisons involving fish are all connected with desire[468] and he even remarks that the five arrows provided to shoot the target are a conventional symbol of the five senses and thus of Kāma.[469] The fish could thus have been chosen to symbolise that the forthcoming union between Arjuna and Draupadī is predestined and desired.

467 ibid., pp. 198, 204.
468 ibid., p. 203.
469 ibid., p. 207, n. 33.

It was established before that the alteration according to which Arjuna is allowed only to look at the target's reflection while shooting, was made up in order to highlight his archery skills. However, in combination with the fish, there might be a connection with the practice of bowfishing. Bowfishing has a long tradition in South India. It is still practised on the west coast although nowadays, the bow is frequently replaced by a speargun. As noted by Hiltebeitel, water is not only where fish normally appear, it is also a symbol of flux, *saṃsāra* and *māyā*, and it is Arjuna's knowledge that enables him to see beyond *māyā*, even while looking into it.[470] Only thereby is he able to shoot the fish above instead of the illusory image. The affiliation of water with illusion might be based upon light distortion, on account of which bowfishing is a unique challenge. As explained by Porterfield, "Light bends at the water's surface, which distorts how underwater objects look and where they appear to be from above water. A bowfisher who aims straight at a fish is likely to miss it because of this light distortion.".[471] Thus, it is by no means surprising that the fish is not where one would expect it to be; but the illusion is developed to the maximum by placing the fish even out of the water.

470 ibid., p. 208.
471 Porterfield 2014, p. 32.

4.3. Further Information on the Deviations from the Critical Editions

It has become clear that representations from the Rāmāyaṇa and the Mahābhārata always include elements of a local tradition, to a lesser or greater extent. Artists draw upon regional literary versions and on orally transmitted alterations, incorporate other stories as include of course also their own ideas. Some of the deviations within the Kṛṣṇa Temple's narrative friezes can be traced back through a long tradition, while others bring in newly made up changes – sometimes for the first time.

4.3.1. Deviations from the Rāmāyaṇa's Critical Edition

It was established that in Pāṇḍya and Cōḻa representations, physical abnormities of the demons and the method of killing them, were accurately depicted. This is also true for early North Indian representations. For instance, Triśiras is depicted with three heads on the Gupta panels from Nācār Kherā. On the Deogarh panel Lakṣmaṇa uses a sword to forcefully cut off Śūrpaṇakhā's nose and ears, exactly as described in the text (VR 3.1721). It has also been established that medieval, predominently North Indian renderings of the Rāmāyaṇa, do not elaborate on violence and bloodshed, nor do they highlight unpleasant physical abnormities. It is thus no wonder that the representations on the Kṛṣṇa Temple are in this regard, likewise reduced to the essential. Now, this trend is already visible in Hoysaḷa and Vijayanagara representations. For example, in the few Hoysaḷa representations that deal with the Kabandha episode, instead of forcecully cutting off Kabhanda's arms, Rāma simply shoots them off with an arrow. In likewise manner, Rāma shoots off the arms of an almost cute looking Virādha on the Veṅkaṭaramaṇa Temple at Tāḍapatri (Vijayanagara).[472] In Hoysaḷa and Vijayanagara representations alike, Lakṣmaṇa is involved neither in the killing of Kabandha, nor in the killing of Virādha.

What concerns the more significant changes within the Kṛṣṇa Temple's representation of the epos, the visual narratives contribute primarily to the origin of Rāvaṇa's horse head. Apart from the many North Indian representations, in this regard also the other Nepalese representations are of importance for they likewise depict Kumbhakarṇa with an additional animal head. However, no further information can be given on this head.

Among those deviations with a long tradition are of course also Ahalyā being transformed into stone, and Śūrpanakhā assuming a beautiful shape. This is attested by literary sources as well as by pictorial ones. The findings on representations of Sītā being placed in a protective ring are also in keeping with the evidence from literary sources. This alteration, still absent in Hoysaḷa representations, appears on the enclosure walls of the Rāmacandra Temple at Hampi. That the story found its way to North India is evident not only from literary sources but from visual narratives as well. The motive of Lakṣmaṇa drawing protective lines around Sītā is until today frequently included on Bengali scrolls (sa. *paṭas*), the predominant form of Rāmāyaṇa paintings in Bengal.[473] Other North and Central Indian paintings also include the motive, as apparent from a Malwa painting with Rāvaṇa approaching Sītā (mid 17th c. CE) and a Pahari painting dealing with Sītā's abduction (late 18th c. CE), both in the possession of the National Museum, New Delhi.[474] Rāvaṇa kicking or rather pushing away Vibhīṣaṇa is represented on the Rādhāśyāma Temple at Bishnupur. It is not found in the South Indian representations but literary sources attest that the story was known in South India, too, at least since the 13th century CE.

The Kṛṣṇa Temple's representations include also some later, specifically North Indian alterations. Medieval representations of the Rāmāyaṇa on temple walls are rarely found in North India. This makes it hard to find plastic representations of these later alterations. Aṅgada snatching away Rāvaṇa's crown is however a popular motive in painting. The Metropolitan Museum of Art houses a beautiful though unfinished Pahari painting, Guler style, from the early 18th century CE, that depicts the episode in four scenes.[475] In the upper section, Aṅgada forces his way into the besieged palace. Next, he is depicted snatching away the crown from Rāvaṇa's heads. On the right side, he carries the crown to Rāma and, after Aṅgada has handed it over, Rāma places the crown over Vibhīṣaṇa's head.

What concerns the two representations based solely on Eknāth's version, namely a bird snatching away the heavenly *pāyasa* and Lakṣmaṇa and Sītā being present as Khara attacks, no comparable representations are found.

472 Illustration: Loizeau 2017, p. 246, fig. 121.

473 Bose 2017, pp. 43 and 87ff. with illustration: Āraṇya.ii.4.

474 Illustrations: Daljeet and Mathur 2015, Pls. 44f.

475 https://www.metmuseum.org/art/collection/search/37948

4.3.2. Deviations from the Mahābhārata's Critical Edition

What concerns the Mahābhārata cycle, most significantly, the visual narratives contribute to the depiction of Arjuna shooting the fish target. Again, this is a well-known variation that is not found in literary versions but pictorial renditions attest its long tradition.

Narrative representations from the Hoysaḷas also attest a long tradion for the story of Aśvatthāmā bringing the heads of Draupadī's sons to Duryodhana. The scene reappears in North Indian manuscript paintings, as for example in the Birla Razmnama.[476]

The Birla Razmnama contains some additional matches for the Kṛṣṇa Temple's representations. Pāṇḍu and Mādrī are depicted inside a cottage in intimate togetherness,[477] Kṛṣṇa is depicted as Arjuna's charioteer in course of the conflagration of the Khāṇḍava Forest[478] and the game of dice is pictured as *chausar*.[479] Also in accordance with the Kṛṣṇa Temple's representations is the fact that Jarāsandha is torn into two, but not Hiḍimva.[480] Kṛṣṇa acting as Arjuna's charioteer may be a specifically North Indian innovation for South Indian Khāṇḍavavanadāha representations never depict Kṛṣṇa as Arjuna's charioteer. By contrast, there are clearly two separate chariots in the Amṛteśvara's representation (Pl. 24b). The same applies to the depiction of *chausar* boards. The game of dice is included in most of the Hoysaḷa's Mahābhārata sequences but there appears no *chausar* board at all. In North Indian illustrations by contrast, it is frequently found.

There are representations of the battle with the Nivātakavacas, Bhīma awaiting Kīcaka, Kṛṣṇa rushing at Bhīṣma, Abhimanyu's death and Yudhiṣṭhira's ascent to heaven. However, none of the images that I am concerned with does include the peculiarities from the Kṛṣṇa Temple. Other events like Kṛṣṇa visiting the exiled Pāṇḍavas, Kṛṣṇa's get-together with Yudhiṣṭhira in the Udyogaparva or Arjuna visiting Vyāsa in the Mausalaparva, may have been considered too unimportant to include them in shorter visual renderings. It appears that in general, the events from the last *parvas* did not much attrackt sculptors.

One of the scenes for which no match was found is especially interesting. This is the scene depicting the Pāṇḍavas and Kuntī on their way to the city of Pañcāla (sc. 26) for Kuntī, Yudhiṣṭhira and Bhīma are interacting with a dog. As mentioned before, the dog reminds of the Ekalavya story but only, because there is no other such dog-story. Ekalavya makes his appearance way earlier. If this was meant to be the dog returning from Ekalavya, one would expect to see his mouth filled with arrows. Moreover, Kuntī doesn't figure in the Ekalavya story but her role is emphasised in the representation. As literary sources attest, dogs were not much admired and it can hardly be assumed that the dog is depicted only to enliven the scenery. As in case with the depiction of the bird in the context of Daśaratha distributing the heavenly *pāyasa*, there has to be a particular, largely unknown story behind this image. Maybe, it is included in one of the many medieval renderings of the Mahābhārata and maybe, if identified, this story could add to define region-specific influences.

---

476 Das 2005, pp. 134f.
477 ibid., pp. 42f.
478 ibid., pp. 50f.
479 ibid., pp. 56f.
480 ibid., pp. 52f., 58f,

5. Conclusion

The representations on the Kṛṣṇa Temple include a great number of scenes which reveal an impact of a later tradition, with regard to variations, transcreations, additions and omissions. There are no deviations depicted that are found exclusively in South Indian renditions, though quite a few trace back to South Indian sources. On the other hand, some of the depicted deviations are found exclusively in the later North Indian renderings. Regarding the Rāmāyaṇa representations, this is true for the bird snatching away the heavenly *pāyasa*, Lakṣmaṇa and Sītā being present as Khara attacks and Aṅgada snatching away Rāvaṇa's crown. As attested by pictorial sources, the animal heads of Rāvaṇa and Kumbhakarṇa are also exclusively northern characteristics.

Pictorial sources in particular, attest the same for the Mahābhārata representations. Some of the important deviations, like Arjuna shooting the fish target at Draupadī's *svayamvara* or Aśvatthāmā presenting the heads of the Upapāṇḍavas to Duryodhana, are found in both, South and North Indian representations. Other deviations by contrast, like Arjuna acting as Kṛṣṇa's charioteer already in course of the conflagration of the Khāṇḍava Forest or the game of dice being pictured as *chausar*, are found only in North Indian representations.

No versions of the epics are known to me, neither literary nor pictorially, that narrate the entire story exactly the way it is depicted on the Kṛṣṇa Temple. Eknāth compiled his work only a few decades before the Kṛṣṇa Temple was consecrated. The bird story appears to be his innovation and the alteration that Rāma sees no reason to send away Lakṣmaṇa and Sītā as Khara attacks, is even particularly stressed as a new point of view in his work. It is stated that against common believe that Rāma sent them to a cave, Rāma was not afraid of the demons and being certain of victory had no reason to hide Sītā.[481] The short time that remains between Eknāth's changes to the story and the temple's consecration leaves hardly any possibility for the compilation of another Rāmāyaṇa on which the narrative representation could entirely be based. It can therefore be taken as proven that the Kṛṣṇa Temple's narrative representation of the Rāmāyaṇa is based upon an oral transmission of the story. Or more specifically, the representation on the Kṛṣṇa Temple is based upon different medieval, in particular North Indian versions, that were brought together in oral form in the Kathmandu Valley. The same has to apply to the Mahābhārata cycle, too. While bringing together the different versions, the artists included elements which are found only in pictorial form and apparently, they also added some new elements like Nārada's conversation with Daśaratha at the beginning of the Rāmāyaṇa story.

Conclusively, the representations of both the friezes do indeed reveal an impact of region-specific charecteristics of Hindu beliefs. Moreover, the narrative representations on the Kṛṣṇa Temple are of particular importance also within the entire corpus of epic representations in South Asia. There are practically no comparable representations of the epics in Nepal. A number of Rāmāyaṇa and Mahābhārata representations in stone are found in India but still, the representations on the Kṛṣṇa Temple are outstanding in many respects. They include some scenes that are not pictured elsewhere. In case of the Rāmāyaṇa, while there are many narrative representations in stone to visualise elements from South Indian traditions, only a few such representations are found in North India. Elaborate representations of the Mahābhārata, set in stone, are found only on Hoysaḷa monuments and also within these representations, not even once the entire story is given. The cycle on the Kṛṣṇa Temple at Pāṭan is thus the only visual representation of the epos in stone to include scenes from all 18 *parvas*. A maximum of 36 scenes on Hoysaḷa monuments stands in marked contrast with the 165 scenes that are depicted on the Kṛṣṇa Temple. The Rāmāyaṇa is given in not quite as many scenes. 99 scenes deal with the story of Rāma, up to his coronation in Ayodhyā. That the Uttarakāṇḍa was omitted is by no means unusual and in case of the Kṛṣṇa Temple's representations, it was established that this is also justifed by the fact that the closing scenes serve to make perfectly clear the unquestionable character of the sovereignty of a god incarnate king like Siddhinarasiṃhamalla.

481 Sathe and Vaishampayana 2016, p. 384.

Appendix I: The Kṛṣṇa Temple's Consecration Inscription

The complete inscription was translated by Bledsoe in 2004. The text below largely follows her version, with only minor changes. The first part of the inscription consists of 35 couplets, written in Sanskrit. The second part in Newari is clearly separated from the first one, by a small gap, a second double *daṇḍa*, a remark that the language changes and ultimately by the word *svasti* (Hail!), indicating a new opening.

१ॐ नमो गोपालाय॥
Om namo Gopālāya.
Homage to Gopāla (Kṛṣṇa).

1. Creating all as Brahmā, preserving it as Hari;
taking the form of Rudra at the end of the Age - homage to you who manifest as three.

2. He who created an ocean begun by the flood of tears from the proud wives of kings opposed to him, (kings) who were destroyed/churned by the fame of him who was known for his prowess.
The king Harisiṃhadeva was born in a refined lineage of givers. He was a giver of livelihoods to good people, attaining likeness to another Pṛthu (a famed mythological king).

3. In the ocean of his lineage there arose Mahendramalla, like the great Indra, a moon above kings.
By/with whom a wish-fulfilling tree to supplicants and an ocean of virtues, the great earth became the consort of the king.

4. Scorched by the fire of his grandeur, his enemies took themselves to a mountain fastness, leaving behind their cities and abandoning the beautiful women of the inner rooms.
But the mountains too were all shaken by the echoes of his manliness, his conduct and his designs. Is there any splendour comparable to this king's mighty fame?

5. His son Śivasiṃhadeva was born, a wish-fulfilling tree in the world, a king of radiant fame.
When this Earth-Enjoyer joined the battle, his great arms destroyed many enemies at once, with ease.

6. This lord of the earth dimmed the sky with the dark of the dust clouds his infantry raised setting forth.
The Turtle, though ground down in a tender spot, somehow held up the earth; the final end came when the all-bearing earth could bear the violence no more.

7. His son was born, filled with discipline, like a Karṇa in the world.
Hariharasiṃha the king of men became a moon to the gem-bearing earth.

8. Smiting his enemies, extending his fame, steadfast, ever more illustrious as a victor on all fronts.
The image of his father and gloriously handsome, his fierce splendour circled the earth.

9. Like the Lord of the gods' beloved Indrāṇī, like Padmā dear to Viṣṇu, like the Vaidehī to the Rāghavas' finest, like the wifely Gaurī to Śiva,
the splendid wife of this king was like Bhavānī. The good queen Lālamatī had the virtues of Rati (wife of Kāma) and Bhāratī (a form of Sarasvatī) both.

10. As the sky's eastern quarter gives birth to the new-rayed sun, as Ambikā bore the elephant-faced (Gaṇeśa) in the forest's beauty,
so did this daughter of the son of kings give birth to a pure son, Siddhinarasiṃhamalla.

11. He made an ocean of tears from the long-lashed eyes of enemy wives, and held the faultless autumn moon of his splendor over [it and] all three worlds.
Victorious in childhood exploits and in his manhood now, who is as worthy in war as Siddhinarasiṃhamalla, the king?

12. In a world made pale by the floods of camphor-white glory pure as Gaṅgā water streaming from him, this earth-protecting king became the faultless lord of its night (i.e. the moon),
and did he who is its moon became the earth's servant because his mouth could pass for a lotus? May this gem of the ruling earth live long, Siddhi-the first-narasiṃha.

13. His worth is that of the wish-fulfilling tree, which actually gives lesser gifts; he pushes the bounds of the brilliant crowd; fame of astounding luster linked to his grandeur, he is

like Bhīma's younger brother when roused.
Kings who oppose him trickle away before the wrath of his two strong arms. King Śrīmān Siddhinarasiṃha stands above all.

14. He is more worthy of consecration than Yudhiṣṭhira; he is more skilful than Vasiṣṭha, his kīrti is greater than that of the full moon in Kārtika;
his speech is like that of Vyāsa; his fortune/ Lakṣmī is firm/enduring; his figure is beautiful as Rāma's. Is there anything about King Siddhinarasiṃha that is not astonishing?

15. At one point a wonderous temple was built by this exalted one, at great expense, as pleasure ground for Śrī Bālagopāla, meant to be Vaikuṇṭha's equal on earth.

16. It produces the error of wondering if it is Mount Meru, Mahendra's Himādri, the Vindhyas, or Kailāśa's stony peak.
Ah, when the gods look upon its golden spires, it makes them wonder if this is a mountain of gold.

17. In the Nepali year 757, the 10th of bright Phālguṇa, a Thursday, in an auspicious constellation of the planets,
he, the strong-armed king of Nepal, decorated the temple with 21 shiny, weighty, golden finials.

18. Precisely on this auspicious day war was begun by evil enemies, drunk with pride in conflict. [His] forts were besieged by the mercenaries of the crooked king, who were suprisingly good in battle.
Then the king, equal to Pārtha, drove off the enemies easily. He set the forts free, happy as Namuci's enemy (Viṣṇu), and got everything.

19. It was like a *rājasūya*, begun by the strong-armed king at its centre;
even the distinguished Śeṣa Nāga would not be able to describe it.

20. The officiant there was himself an ocean of worthies, together with (other) honourables;
Viśvanātha Upādhyāya was like Viśvanātha.

21. He was like the ponderous Mount Meru in his gravity; he was like the sea in his great majesty;
he was like Vyāsa in the reading of various Vaidika mantras; he was a great sage as capable as Vasiṣṭha, placed on earth.

22. How many came there, performers of frequent sacrifices, how many wise men chanting.
Approached by learned priests from many places, the ritual platform was adorned by them at this sacrifice.

23. There were able doormen at this sacrificial session, two in each door, equal to godlike sages;
the leader of them was Viśvanātha the wise, striker of those foolish enough to be his enemies, [himself] adorned/adorning.

24. In the sacrificial session of old begun by the wise/rigorous king Śibi, the punishing bearer of the Gāṇḍiva bow strew destruction in the Khāṇḍava forest, to the glory of Agni.
In this sacrificial session of king Siddhinarasiṃhamalla, the pointed one (Agni, fire) fed with endless ghee – how like a great war! – let loose tears because of the smoke.

25. It went on for forty days, the great festival of huge sacred fires;
it was performed by Śrīmat Siddhinarasiṃha, like Karṇa of the Kali age.

26. All the goods assembled for a *rājasūya* [of old]
were there at this sacrificial session, or perhaps there were even more.

27. When there were gems and gold and cows and so forth, and wealth in the form of horses and elephants, and jewelry and wonderful clothes, and slaves – male and female – and houses and pure foods of various flavours,
the lotus-face of this gem in the lineage of kings was pleased, and for forty days the one word that sprang up on every corner was "Give! Give!"

28. Mendicants who had never seen such fine clothes, bracelets and earrings before, placed them on their own bodies here, through the grace of the king.

29. Heavenly houses, heavenly fields and gems, heavenly clothes, and heavenly genuine jewelry, and heavenly gems.
Such heavenly lands and objects as were present in Nepal, that king, Siddhinarasiṃhamalla, gave them all away.

30. Things were seen here that had never been heard of,
and at this sacrificial session the Earth-Enjoyer gave them all away.

31. By him who [rules] over the three worlds, the temple, the sacred fire, and the 10,000,000 oblations were given, [and also] two hundred gold coins each day. What wealth was not given?
A mountain of rice was given by the knower of ritual precepts, a wonderful wishing-tree too. King Siddhinarasiṃhamalla is indeed an incarnation of Karṇa.

32. How many were the learned filled with good qualities, even if some of them were short on wisdom. Mendicants came by the thousands from all directions, having heard of the king's virtues.
Having fended off their poverty with rice and gold and lovely clothes and jewelry and so forth and heaps of wealth, the Indra among givers, like a god, rejoiced like king Nṛga.

33. [But] Karṇa was born of a virgin; Bali was wise but born a Daitya; a gem is [but] a stone of the gods; the tree of the gods is just a big tree;
King Nṛga too is said to have erred; the strong-armed Bhārgava [Paraśurāma] killed his mother; so who else ruling in this world can be called more blessed than King Siddhi-the first-narasiṃha?

34. There were dances and captivating songs and hearty astonishing music,
and grains and garments and ornaments of all kinds in this sacrificial session.

35. As long as the sun and moon rise, as long as the earth endures, as long as Pārvatī embraces Paśupati as her other half,
as long as Gaṅgā and Yamunā flow, may the glory-vine of King Srīmat Siddhinṛsiṃhamalla spread that long.

॥अथ नेपालभाखा लिख्यते॥

atha nepālbhākhā likhyate.

Now it is recorded in the language of Nepal (Newari).

Hail! In the year 757, on the 10th day of the bright half of month Phālguṇa, with the lunar mansion of Pūrṇavasu verging on Ārdhrā, in the Āyuṣmānyoga, a Thursday, having done the sacrifice of 10,000,000 oblations, for the deity's establishmen 21 finials were offered. For the deity's yearly income [lands] were given:
7 ro[panī] at Pobi field, 7 ro[panī] at Paiyi, 3 at Khorāgāra field, 14 ro[panī] at Tavadhara field, [and] 1 karṣa at the Thaṃthacheṃ garden. With this yearly income daily worship and pure offerings and a yearly observance at the consecration's anniversary with a sacred fire [are to be provided]. For both the procession of Buṅga[dyo][482] and the festival of Indra, lights are to be lit for three days; all of the month of Kārttika oil lamps should be lit with one *pala* of clarified butter (ghee); on Kṛṣṇāṣṭamī a ring of lamps must be lit. This is one [set of provisions].

Further: 9 ro[panī] at Yaṃpyāko field, 8 ro[panī] at Kākāpali, 12 ro[panī] beneath Gustarade, 7 ro[panī] at Khomora field [are given]. With the yearly income from these lands, at the juncture of the fullmoon day and the first day of dark Phālguṇa, the Swinging Festival (*dolayātrā*) [is to be observed]; on the fullmoon day in Jyeṣṭha, the Bathing Festival (*snānayātrā*); on the 12th of bright Āṣāḍha, the Sleeping Ceremony (*śayanapūja*); cause the god to sleep, on the 12th of bright Śrāvaṇa an annual purification ritual (*pavitrā-rohaṇa*), [and] on the 8th of dark Śrāvaṇa his Birthday Ceremony (*janmāṣṭamipūjā*); the ring of lamps must be offered; the 12th of bright Kārttika is his Awakening Ceremony (*utthānapūjā*). To the Brāhmaṇa who officiates, give 90 *pāthis* of rice each year. This is one [set of provisions].

Another 16 ro[panī] at Thyeṃ field and another 3 ro[panī] at Thyeṃ field; with the yearly income of these lands, for all the month of Kārttika, a ring of 120 lamps must be lit with 6 *kuḍa* of oil. Further, [in case what has been given] is insufficient for the pure offerings and the priestly fees *(dakṣiṇā)*, 5 ro[panī] in Jahakho field are given. This is one [set of provisions].

May it be auspicious for all.

482 Buṅgadyo is the original Newari name for Matsyendranātha, one of the most important national deities in Nepal.

Appendix II: Places mentioned in the Text: Karnataka and Tamil Nadu

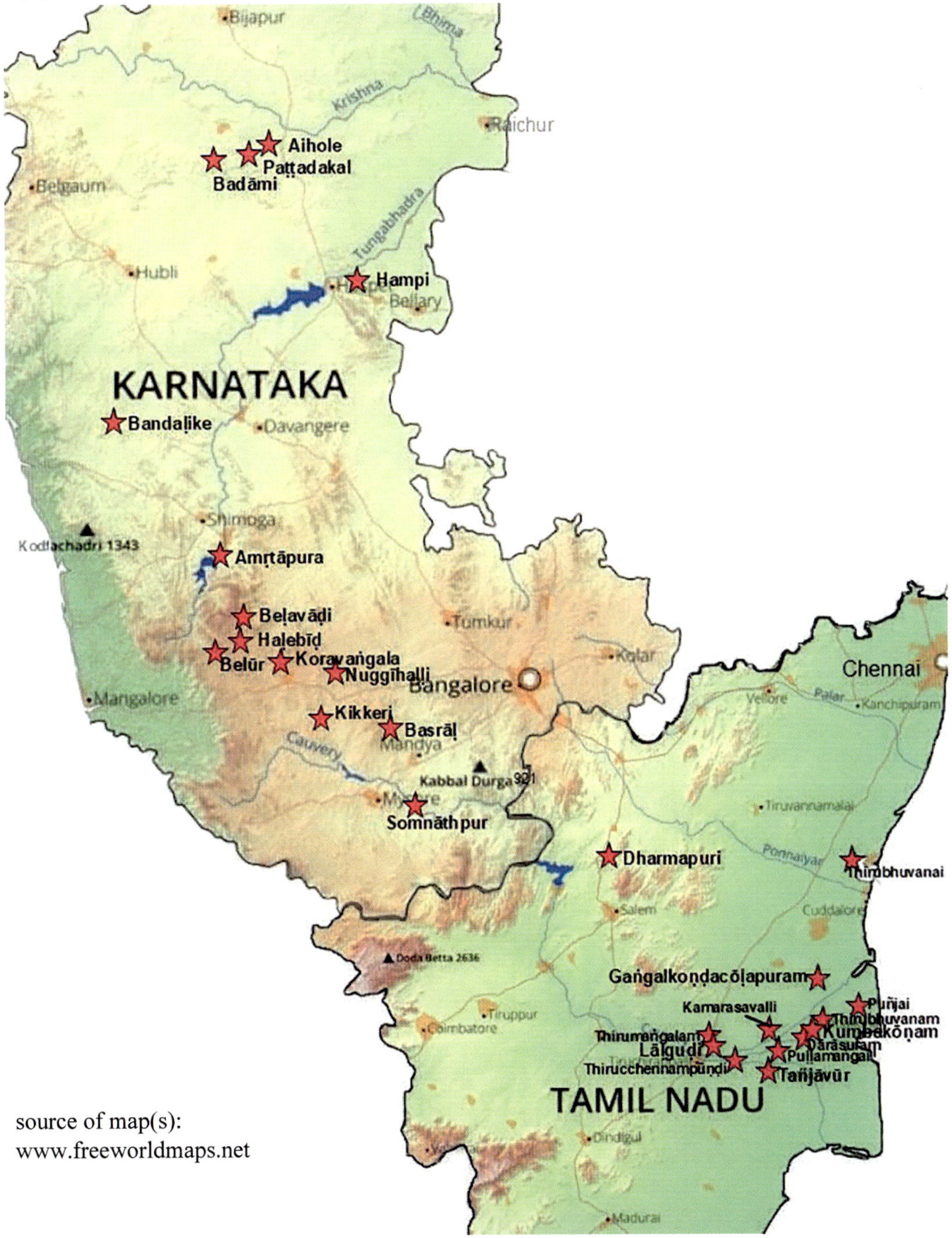

source of map(s):
www.freeworldmaps.net

Bibliography

Abbott, J.E., The Life of Eknāth: Śrī Eknāth Charita. Delhi 1983 (1927).

Ahmed, N., Epic Stories in Terracotta: Depicted on the Kantanagar Temple Bangladesh. Dhaka 1990.

Akmam, A., A Few Inscribed Terracotta Plaques depicting Scenes from the Ramayana – Recently discovered in Bangladesh, in: Studies in Archaeology: Papers presented in Memory of P.C. Dasgupta. New Delhi 1991.

Banerjee, N.R., The Ramayana Theme in Nepalese Art, in: Asian Variations in Ramayana: Papers presented at the International Seminar on 'Variations in Ramayana in Asia: Their Cultural, Social and Anthropological Significance': New Delhi, 1981. Madras 1983.

Bangdel, L.S., Nepal: Zweitausendfünfhundert Jahre nepalesische Kunst. Leipzig 1987.

– Inventory of Stone Sculptures of the Kathmandu Valley. Kathmandu 1995.

Bhatt, G.H., The Vālmīki-Rāmāyaṇa: Critical Edition Vol. I: The Bālakāṇḍa. Baroda 1960.

Bledsoe, B., Written in Stone: Inscriptions of the Kathmandu Valley's Three Kingdoms. Chicago 2004.

Boesch, H., Untersuchungen zur Morphogenese im Katmandu Valley, in: Geographica Helvetica, Vol. 29 (1974). Published online at www.geogr-helv.net.

Bose, M., Sanskrit Ramayanas, Puranas and Rama Kavyas: A Study in Evolution and Impact, in: Ramayana in Focus: Visual and Performing Arts of Asia. Singapore 2010.

– The Rāmāyaṇa in Bengali Folk Paintings. New Delhi 2017.

Branfoot, C., Bhīma and Purusamirukam in the Nayaka-period Sculpture of Tamilnadu, in: South Asian Studies, Vol. 18.1 (2002). Published online at www.tandfonline.com.

Brinkhaus, H., The Pradyumna-Prabhāvatī Legend in Nepal: A Study of the Hindu myth of the draining of the Nepal Valley. Stuttgart 1987.

Brockington, J. and Brockington, M., Rama the Perfect Man: Whatever your Faith, in: Ramayana in Focus: Visual and Performing Arts of Asia. Singapore 2010.

Chakraborty, U., Kṣemendra: The Eleventh Century Kashmiri Poet: A Study of his Life and Works. Delhi 1991.

Chandra, P., A Vāmana Temple at Maṛhiā and Some Reflections on Gupta Architecture, in: Artibus Asiae, Vol. 32.2/3. Zürich 1970.

Daljeet and Mathur, V.K., Ramayana in Indian Miniatures: From the Collection of the National Museum, New Delhi. Delhi 2015.

Dallapiccola, A.L., The City of Vijayanagara: Kishkindha, the Monkey-Kingdom, in: The Legend of Rama: Artistic Visions, editid by Vidya Dehejia. Mumbai 1994.

Dallapiccola, A.L., Fritz, J.M., Michell, G. and Rajasekhara, S., The Ramachandra Temple at Vijayanagara. New Delhi 1992.

Dallapiccola, A.L. and Verghese, A., Ramayana Panels on the Gopura of the "Old Shiva" Temple, Vitthalapura, in: Vijayanagara:Progress of Research 1987 - 88. Mysore 1991.

– Narrative Reliefs of Bhima and Purushamriga at Vijayanagara, in: South Asian Studies, Vol. 18.1 (2002). Published online at www.tandfonline.com.

Das, A.K., Akbar's Imperial Ramayana: A Mughal Persian Manuscript, in: The Legend of Rama: Artistic Visions, editid by Vidya Dehejia. Mumbai 1994.

– Paintings of the Razmnama, The Book of War. Kolkata 2011.

Debroy, B., The Mahabharata, 10 Vols. set. Haryana 2015 (2010-2014).

Dehejia, V. (ed.), The Legend of Rama: Artistic Visions. Mumbai 1994.

deJong, J.W., The Story of Rama in Tibet, in: Asian Variations in Ramayana: Papers presented at the International Seminar on 'Variations in Ramayana in Asia: Their Cultural, Social and Anthropological Significance': New Delhi, 1981. Madras 1983.

Deva, K., Gupta Rāmāyaṇa Panels from Nachnā, in: Chhavi-2: Rai Krishnadasa Felicitation Volume. Banaras 1981.

– Images of Nepal. Calcutta 1984.

Dunham, J., Manuscripts used in the Critical Edition of the Mahābhārata: A Survey and Discussion, in: Essays on the Mahābhārata. Delhi 2007 (1991).

Evans, K., Epic Narratives in the Hoysaḷa Temples: The Rāmāyaṇa, Mahābhārata and Bhāgavata Purāṇa in Haḷebīd, Belūr and Amṛtapura. Leiden [u.a.] 1997.

Foekema, G., A Complete Guide to Hoysaḷa Temples. New Delhi 1996.

Fürer-Haimendorf, C. von, Elements of Newar Social Structure, in: The Journal of the Royal Anthropological Institute of Great Britain and Ireland, Vol. 86, No. 2 (Jul. - Dec., 1956).

Gail, A.J., Rāmāyaṇa-Relief am Kailāsa in Ellora, in: Berliner Indologische Studien, Bd. 1 (1985).

– Tempel in Nepal, Vol. I: Ikonographie hinduistischer Pagoden in Pāṭan Kathmandutal and Vol. II: Ikonographische Untersuchungen zur späten Pagode und zum Śikhara-Tempel. Graz 1984/1988.

Gitomer, D.L., Rākṣasa Bhīma: Wolfbelly among Ogres and Brahmans in the Sanskrit Mahābhārata and the Veṇīsaṁhāra, in: Sharma, A. (ed.), Essays on the Mahābhārata. Delhi 2007 (1991).

Goldman, R. (ed. and transl.), The Rāmāyaṇa of Vālmīki: An Epic of Ancient India. English Translation in 7 Vols. Princeton 1984-2017.

Gutschow N., Architecture of the Newars: A History of Building Typologies and Details in Nepal, Vol. I: The Early Periods and Vol. II: The Malla Period. Chicago 2011.

– The Portals in Newar Architecture: Tiered Temples in Nepal, 13th to 19th Centuries. Kathmandu 2016.

Handa, D., Sculptures from Haryana: Iconography and Style. New Delhi 2006.

Haque, E., The Art Heritage of Bangladesh. Dhaka 2007.

Haque, Z., Terracottas of Bengal: An Analytical Study. Dhaka 2014.

Hawley, J.S., Scenes from the Childhood of Kṛṣṇa on the Kailāsanātha Temple, Ellora, in: Archives of Asian Art, Vol. 34 (1981).

Hiltebeitel, A., The Cult of Draupadī, Vol. 1: Mythologies: From Gingee to Kurukṣetra. Delhi 1991.

Indraji, P.B. and Bühler, G., Inscriptions from Nepal, in: The Indian Antequary: A Journal of Oriental Research, Vol. IX – 1880. Bombay [u.a.] 1880.

Jørgensen, H., A Dictionary of the Classical Newārī. New Delhi 1995 (1936).

– A Grammar of the Classical Newārī. Copenhagen 1941.

Kala, J., Epic Scenes in Indian Plastic Art. New Delhi 1988.

Kölver, U. and Shresthacarya, I., A Dictionary of Contemporary Newari: Newari – English. Bonn 1994.

Lienhard, S., Nepalese Manuscripts, Part I: Nevārī and Sanskrit, in: Verzeichnis der Orientalischen Handschriften in Deutschland, Band 33,1. Stuttgart 1988.

– Zur Frühgeschichte des Viṣṇuismus in Nepal, in: Nachrichten der Akademie der Wissenschaften in Göttingen aus dem Jahre 1991: Philologisch-Historische Klasse. Göttingen 1991.

– The Divine Play of Lord Krishna: A Krishnalīlā Painting from Nepal. Bonn 1995.

Loizeau, R., Traditions Narratives dans la Sculpture du Karnataka: Les représentations épiques, l'enfance de Kṛṣṇa et autres mythes puraniques dans les temples hoysaḷa (XIIe-XIIIe siècles). Paris 2017.

Lüders, H., Das Würfelspiel im alten Indien. Berlin 1907.

Margabandhu, C., Rāmāyaṇa Reliefs in Stone in Rajasthan Temples, in: Srinivasa Iyengar (ed.), Asian Variations in Ramayana: Papers presented at the International Seminar on 'Variations in Ramayana in Asia: Their Cultural, Social and Anthropological Significance': New Delhi, 1981. Madras 1983.

Markel, S., The "Rāmāyaṇa" Cycle on the Kailāsanātha Temple at Ellora, in: Ars Orientalis, Vol. 30, supplement 1 (2000).

McCutchion, D.J., Late Mediaeval Temples of Bengal: Origins and Classification. Calcutta 1972 (1967).

Michell, G., Temple Architecture and Art of the Early Chalukyas: Badami, Mahakuta, Aihole, Pattadakal. Delhi 2014.

Nagar, S.L. and Nagar, S. (trans.), Kṛttivāsa Rāmāyaṇa: by Sage Kṛttivāsa (the Divine Son of the Soil). 2 Vols. set. Delhi 1997.

Nagar, S.L. (trans.), Ānanda Rāmāyaṇa: Attributed to the Great Sage Vālmīki (Sanskrit Text with English Translation). 2 Vols. set. Delhi 2006.

– Kamba-Rāmāyaṇa (English Translation of Tamil Rāmāyaṇa of Sage Kamban). 2 Vols. set. Delhi 2008.

– Śrī Rāmacaritamānasa. 3 Vols. set. Delhi 2014.

Paniker, K.A. (ed.), Medieval Indian Literature: An Anthology. Delhi 1997.

Peterson, I.V., Arjuna's Combat with the Kirāta: Rasa and Bhakti in Bhāravi's Kirātārjunīa, in: Sharma, A. (ed.), Essays on the Mahābhārata. Delhi 2007 (1991).

– Bharavi: Arjuna and the Hunter. London 2016.

Porterfield, J., Bowfishing. New York 2014.

Pruscha, C. (ed.), Kathmandu Valley: The Preservation of Physical Environment and Cultural Heritage: A Protective Inventory. Vol. I und II. Wien 1975.

Rao, T.G.K., Folk Ramayanas in Telugu and Kannada. Nellore 1984.

Regmi, D. R., Medieval Nepal, Vol. I: Early Medieval Period 750-1530 A.D. and Vol. II: A History of the Three Kingdoms 1520 A.D. to 1768 A.D. Calcutta 1965/1966.

Roy, P. C. (transl.), The Mahabharata of Krishna-Dvaipayana Vyasa. Vol. I-IX. Calcutta 1884-96.

Sanford, D. T., Early Temples Bearing Rāmāyaṇa Relief Cycles in the Chola Area: A Comparative Study. PhD diss, University of California, 1974.

– Ramayana Portraits: The Nageshvara Temple at Kumbakonam, in: Dehejia, V. (ed.), The Legend of Rama: Artistic Visions. Bombay 1994.

Sarma, C.R., The Ramayana in Telugu and Tamil: A Comparative Study. Madras 1973.

Schmid, C., Au Seuil du Monde Divin: Reflets et Passages du Dieu d'Ālanturai à Puḷḷamaṅkai, in: Bulletin de l'Ecole Française d'Extrême Orient (BEFEO), Tome 92, 2005.

Sathe, G.N. and Vaishampayana, R., Bhavartha Ramayana (Sri Eknathi Ramayana): Marathi – Hindi. Lakhnau 2016.

Seshadri, M. (ed.), Annual Reports of the Mysore Archaeological Department for the Years 1947-1956. Mysore 1964.

Seyller, J., A Sub-Imperial Mughal Manuscript: The Ramayana of Abd Al-Rahim Khan-khanan, in: The Legend of Rama: Artistic Visions, editid by Vidya Dehejia. Mumbai 1994.

Sharma, B.N., Rāvaṇa lifting Mount Kailāsa in Indian Art, in: East and West, Vol. 23, No. 3/4 (September-December 1973).

Sharma, N., Patan Programme: Notes by Nutan Sharma after the field work in Nov. '93, Part I: The Rāmāyaṇa Inscription of Kṛṣṇa Temple of Mangal Bazar, and Part II: The Mahābhārata Inscription of Kṛṣṇa Temple of Mangal Bazar. Unpublished.

Shastri, H. P. (transl.), The Ramayana of Valmiki. Vol. I-III. London: Shanti Sadan, 2006 (1953/62, 1957, 1959).

Shastri, J.L. (ed.), The Liṅga-Purāna, in: Ancient Indian Tradition and Mythology Series. 2 Vols. set. Delhi 2009 (1973).

Sinha, B.P., Representation of Rāmāyaṇic Scenes in an old Temple at Aphsad, in: The Journal of the Bihar Research Society, Vol. LIV. Patna 1986.

Sircar, D.C., Indian Epigraphy. Delhi 1996 (1965).

Sivaramamurti, C., Birds and Animals in Indian Sculpture. New Delhi 1974.

– Vijayanagara Paintings. Calcutta 1985..

Slusser, M.S., Nepal Mandala: A Cultural Study of the Kathmandu Valley. New Jersey 1982.

Slusser, M.S. and Vajrācārya, G., Two Medieval Nepalese Buildings: An Architectural and Cultural Study, in: Artibus Asiae, Vol. 36.3. Zürich 1974.

Smith, W.W. and Bajracharya, M.B., Mythological History of the Nepal Valley from Svayambhu Purana. Kathmandu 1978.

Toffin, G., A Vaishnava Theatrical Performance in Nepal: The Kāttī-pyākhã of Lalitpur City, in: Asian Theatre Journal, Vol. 29. Honolulu 2012.

Vajrācārya, M. and Malla, K.P. (ed. and transl.), The Gopālarājavaṃśāvalī. Wiesbaden 1985.

Vats, P.M.S., The Gupta Temple at Deogarh, in: Memoirs of the Archæological Survey of India, No. 70. New Delhi 1999 (1952).

Wechsler, H.J., Royal Legitimation: Ramayana Reliefs on the Papanatha Temple at Pattadakal, in: The Legend of Rama: Artistic Visions, editid by Vidya Dehejia. Mumbai 1994.

Reports:

Government of Nepal: Department of Archaeology (DoA), Updated Report: Kathmandu Valley World Heritage Site, 01 February 2019. online: https://whc.unesco.org/document/171737

Kathmandu Valley Preservation Trust (KVPT), Nepal: Patan Darbar: Earthquake Response Campaign: Documentation of Work to Date, September 2016.

Kathmandu Valley Preservation Trust (KVPT), The Restoration of Krishna Temple at Patan Darbar Square: Work in Progress Report, April 2017.